PSYCHE
AND
SYMBOL

from

The Collected Works of C. G. Jung

VOLUMES 8, 9, 11, 13, 18

BOLLINGEN SERIES XX

PSYCHE
AND
SYMBOL

A Selection from the Writings of

C. G. JUNG

TRANSLATED BY R.F.C. HULL

Selected and Introduced by Violet S. de Laszlo

BOLLINGEN SERIES

PRINCETON UNIVERSITY PRESS

PUBLISHED BY PRINCETON UNIVERSITY PRESS

PRINCETON, NEW JERSEY 08540

Library of Congress Cataloging-in-Publication data will be found on the last page of this volume

First Princeton/Bollingen Paperback printing, 1991

Princeton University Press books are printed on acid-free paper, and meet the guidelines for permanence and durability of the Committee on Production Guidelines for Book Longevity of the Council on Library Resources

10   9   8   7   6   5   4   3   2

PRINTED IN THE UNITED STATES OF AMERICA

EDITORIAL NOTE

In the mid 1950s, the Bollingen Foundation was approached by two New York publishers, each offering the idea of an anthology of C. G. Jung's writings. General interest in Jung's work was growing, and no selection was then available which presented his entire thought, and particularly that of his later years. The Foundation enlisted a distinguished analytical psychologist and scholar of Jung, Dr. Violet de Laszlo, who undertook to organize two separate collections, each representing the Jungian corpus in a different way and of value to the general reader as well as the student. At the time, only a half dozen volumes of the Collected Works had been published, and Dr. de Laszlo drew translations from other sources or from R.F.C. Hull's translations in preparation. For the present edition, the text of the Collected Works has been substituted. Dr. de Laszlo's introduction has been retained.

Psyche and Symbol was published in 1958, one of the earliest volumes in the pioneering Doubleday Anchor paperback series. The editor's intention was to select writings "which would illustrate in convincing fashion the objects of [Jung's] symbol research and the manner of his approach, as well as a synopsis of the conclusions to which he was led." Professor Jung, who followed Dr. de Laszlo's projects with close interest, contributed a preface, written in August 1957. *The Basic Writings of C. G. Jung* was published in 1959 in the Modern Library (Random House). The editor aimed "to present as fully as possible some of the most important areas of Jung's conception of the nature and functioning of the human psyche."*

Violet Staub de Laszlo was born in Zurich in 1900 and completed her medical studies at the University of Zurich. She was a pupil of Jung's while beginning her practice in Switzerland, and during the 1930s she lived in London, playing a central role in the first organization of analytical psychologists in England. In 1940 she settled in the United States, practicing, teaching, and writing

---

* *The Basic Writings of C.G. Jung* is also published as a Bollingen/Princeton paperback.

during a twenty-five year residence. Violet de Laszlo was recognized as one of the leading exponents of the Jungian school. In 1965 she returned to Zurich, continuing an active life until her death in 1988.

*

For the paperback edition, the paragraph numbers of the Collected Works have been retained to facilitate reference.

W. McG.

TABLE OF CONTENTS

1264   Dr. de Laszlo has risked shocking the American reader by including some of my most difficult essays in her selection from my writings. In sympathy with the reader I acknowledge how tempting if not unavoidable it is to fall into the trap of appearances as the eye wanders over the pages in a vain attempt to get at the gist of the matter in the shortest possible time. I know of so many who, opening one of my books and, stumbling upon a number of Latin quotations, shut it with a bang, because Latin suggests history and therefore death and unreality. I am afraid my works demand some patience and some thinking. I know: it is very hard on the reader who expects to be fed by informative headlines. It is not the conscientious scientist's way to bluff the public with impressive résumés and bold assertions. He tries to explain, to produce the necessary evidence, and thus to create a basis for understanding. In my case, moreover, understanding is not concerned with generally known facts, but rather with those that are little known or even new. It was therefore incumbent upon me to make these facts known. In so far as such unexpected novelties demand equally unexpected means of explanation I found myself confronted with the task of explaining the very nature of my evidential material.

1265   The facts are experiences gained from a careful and painstaking analysis of certain psychic processes observed in the course of psychic treatment. As these facts could not be satisfactorily explained by themselves, it was necessary to look round for possible comparisons. When, for instance, one comes across a patient who produces symbolic mandalas in his dreams or his waking imagination and proceeds to explain these circular images in terms of certain sexual or other fantasies, this explanation carries no conviction, seeing that another patient develops wholly different motivations. Nor is it permissible to assume that a sexual fantasy is a more likely motivation than, for instance, a power drive, since we know from experience that the individual's disposition will of necessity lead him to give preference to the one or the other. Both patients, on the other hand, may have one fact in common—a state of mental and moral confusion. We would surely do better to follow up this clue and try to discover whether the circular images are connected with such a state of mind. Our third case producing mandalas is perhaps a schizophrenic in such a disturbed state that he cannot even be asked for his accompanying fantasies. This patient is obviously completely dissolved in a chaotic condition. Our fourth case is a little boy of seven who has decorated the corner of the room where his bed stands with numerous mandalas without which he cannot go to sleep. He only feels safe when they are around him. His fantasy tells him that they protect him against nameless fears assailing him in the night. What is his confusion? His parents are contemplating divorce.[1] And what shall we say of a hard-boiled scientific rationalist who produced mandalas in his dreams and in his waking fantasies? He had to consult an alienist, as he was about to lose his reason because he had suddenly become assailed by the most amazing dreams and visions. What was *his* confusion? The clash between two *equally real* worlds, one external, the other internal: a fact he could no longer deny.[2]

1266   There is no need to prolong this series since, leaving aside all theoretical prejudices, the underlying reason for producing a mandala seems to be a certain definable mental state. But have we any evidence which might explain why such a state should produce a mandala? Or is this mere chance? Consequently we must ask whether our experiences are the only ones on record and, if not, where we can find comparable occurrences. There is no difficulty in finding them; plenty of parallels exist in the Far East and the Far West, or right here in Europe, several hundred years ago. The books of reference can be found in our university libraries, but for the last two hundred years nobody has read them, and they are—oh horror!—written in Latin and some even in Greek. But are they dead? Are those books not the distant echo of life once lived, of minds and hearts quick with passions, hopes, and visions, as keen as our own? Does it matter so much whether the pages before us tell the story of a patient still alive, or dead for fifty years? Does it really matter whether their confessions, their anguish, their strivings speak the English of today or Latin or Greek? No matter

[1] [Cf. "Concerning Mandala Symbolism" (C.W., vol. 9,i), par. 687 and fig. 33.]
[2] [Cf. the dream series in *Psychology and Alchemy*, C.W., vol. 12, Part II.]

how much we are of today, there has been a yesterday, which was just as real, just as human and warm, as the moment we call Now, which—alas—in a few hours will be a yesterday as dead as the first of January anno Domini 1300. A good half of the reasons why things now are what they are lies buried in yesterday. Science in its attempt to establish causal connections has to refer to the past. We teach comparative anatomy, why not comparative psychology? The psyche is not only of today, it reaches right back to prehistoric ages. Has man really changed in ten thousand years? Have stags changed their antlers in this short lapse of time? Of course the hairy man of the Ice Ages has become unrecognizable when you try to discover him among the persons you meet on Fifth Avenue. But you will be amazed when you have talked with them for a hundred hours about their intimate life. You will then read the mouldy parchments as if they were the latest thrillers. You will find the secrets of the modern consulting room curiously expressed in abbreviated mediaeval Latin or in an intricate Byzantine hand.

1267 　 What the doctor can hear, when he listens attentively, of fantasies, dreams, and intimate experiences is not mentioned in the Encyclopaedia Britannica or in textbooks and scientific journals. These secrets are jealously guarded, anxiously concealed, and greatly feared and esteemed. They are very private possessions, never divulged and talked about, because they are feared as ridiculous and revered as revelations. They are numinous, a doubtful treasure, perhaps comical, perhaps miraculous, at all events a painfully vulnerable spot, yet presiding over all the crossroads of one's individual life. They are officially and by general consent just as unknown and despised as the old parchments with their indecipherable and unaesthetic hieroglyphics, evidence of old obscurantisms and foolishness. We are ignorant of their contents, and we are equally ignorant of what is going on in the deeper layers of our unconscious, because "those who know do not talk, those who talk do not know."[3] As inner experiences of this kind increase, the social nexus between human beings decreases. The individual becomes isolated for no apparent reason. Finally this becomes unbearable and he has to confide in someone. Much will then depend on whether he is properly understood or not. It would be fatal if he were to be misinterpreted. Fortunately, such people are instinctively careful and as a rule do not talk more than necessary.

1268 　 When one hears a confession of this kind, and the patient wants

3 [*Tao-te-ching,* ch. 56.]

to understand himself better, some comparative knowledge will be most helpful. When the hard-boiled rationalist mentioned above came to consult me for the first time, he was in such a state of panic that not only he but I myself felt the wind blowing over from the lunatic asylum! As he was telling me of his experiences in detail he mentioned a particularly impressive dream. I got up and fetched an ancient volume from my bookshelf and showed it to him, saying: "You see the date? Just about four hundred years old. Now watch!" I opened the book at the place where there was a curious woodcut, representing his dream almost literally. "You see," I said, "your dream is no secret. You are not the victim of a pathological insult and not separated from mankind by an inexplicable psychosis. You are merely ignorant of certain experiences well within the bounds of human knowledge and understanding." It was worth seeing the relief which came over him. He had seen with his own eyes the documentary evidence of his sanity.

1269   This illustrates why historical comparison is not a mere learned hobby but very practical and useful. It opens the door to life and humanity again, which had seemed inexorably closed. It is of no ultimate advantage to deny or reason away or ridicule such seemingly abnormal or out-of-the-way experiences. They should not get lost, because they contain an intrinsic individual value, the loss of which entails definite damage to one's personality. One should be aware of the high esteem which in past centuries was felt for such experiences, because it explains the extraordinary importance that we ignorant moderns are forced to attribute to them in spite of ourselves.

1270   Understanding an illness does not cure it, but it is a definite help because you can cope with a comprehensible difficulty far more easily than with an incomprehensible darkness. Even if in the end a rational explanation cannot be reached, you know at least that you are not the only one confronted by a "merely imaginary" wall, but one of the many who have vainly tried to climb it. You still share the common human lot and are not cut off from humanity by a subjective defect. Thus you have not suffered the irreparable loss of a personal value and are not forced to continue your way on the crutches of a dry and lifeless rationalism. On the contrary, you find new courage to accept and integrate the irrationality of your own life and of life in general.

1271   Instincts are the most conservative determinants of any kind of life. The mind is not born a *tabula rasa*. Like the body, it has its predetermined individual aptitudes: namely, patterns of behaviour. They become manifest in the ever-recurring patterns of psychic functioning. As the weaver-bird will infallibly build its nest in the accustomed form, so man despite his freedom and superficial changeability will function psychologically according to his original patterns—up to a certain point; that is, until for some reason he collides with his still living and ever-present instinctual roots. The instincts will then protest and engender peculiar thoughts and emotions, which will be all the more alien and incomprehensible the more man's consciousness has deviated from its original conformity to these instincts. As nowadays mankind is threatened with self-destruction through radioactivity, we are experiencing a fundamental reassertion of our instincts in various forms. I have called the psychological manifestations of instinct "archetypes."

1272　　The archetypes are by no means useless archaic survivals or relics. They are living entities which cause the preformation of numinous ideas or dominant representations. Insufficient understanding, however, accepts these prefigurations in their archaic form, because they have a numinous fascination for the underdeveloped mind. Thus Communism is an archaic, highly insidious pattern of life which characterizes primitive social groups. It implies lawless chieftainship as a vitally necessary compensation, a fact which can be overlooked only by means of a rationalistic bias, the prerogative of a barbarous mind.

1273　　It is important to remember that my concept of the archetypes has been frequently misunderstood as denoting inherited ideas or as a kind of philosophical speculation. In reality they belong to the realm of instinctual activity and in that sense they represent inherited patterns of psychic behaviour. As such they are invested with certain dynamic qualities which, psychologically speaking, are characterized as "autonomy" and "numinosity."

1274　　I do not know of any more reliable way back to the instinctual basis than through an understanding of these psychological patterns, which enable us to recognize the nature of an instinctive attitude. The instinct to survive is aroused as a reaction against the tendency to mass suicide represented by the H-bomb and the underlying political schism of the world. The latter is clearly man-made and due to rationalistic distortions. Conversely, if understood by a mature mind, the archetypal preformations can yield numinous ideas ahead of our actual intellectual level. That is just what our time is in need of. This, it seems to me, is an additional incentive to pay attention to the unconscious processes which in many persons today anticipate future developments.

1275 I must warn the reader: this book will not be an easy pastime. Once in a while he will meet with thoughts which demand the effort of concentration and careful reflection—a condition unfortunately rare in modern times. On the other hand, the situation today seems to be serious enough to cause at least uneasy dreams if nothing else.

August 1957

INTRODUCTION

The edifice of C. G. Jung's work is reminiscent of a cathedral that has been built in the course of many centuries. Those who are willing to undertake the effort of contemplating it in a spirit of genuine inquiry and with only the inevitable minimum of preconceived notions are bound to find themselves astonishingly well rewarded. They will make countless discoveries in regard to the grandeur of his original conceptions and the unanticipated richness of detail which, in the phrase of the Quakers, "speak to their condition"— the human condition of doubt and distress, of the search for meaning, of the joyful recognition of universal human sentiment and of the contemporaneous formulation of abiding truths.

Like the cathedral with its altar, its cross and its rose window, this edifice has been erected *ad majorem Dei gloriam*—to the greater glory of God—as is true of all valid creative efforts, even those which appear to be agnostically motivated. Materially speaking, its foundations rest upon the objective approach of empirical observation. Spiritually, they are informed by the omnipresent need of mankind to relate itself to that which is dimly perceived to be greater than any individual and to transcend even the total group—under whatever name the transcendent power may be invoked.

As in the case of the cathedral, the structural foundations are not discernible to the beholder or intelligible to the untrained eye, but this does not disprove their existence or their vital function. The architect's skill serves only as the carrier of the emotional, intellectual and esthetic message and achievement which in their turn culminate in the spiritual and ultimately religious experience which validates the structure as a whole. Just as the architect is influenced by and needs to take into consideration the techniques and knowledge of past generations, his conception—provided he be not a mere imitator or a juggler clever at devising striking effects—will be unique within the confines of a given style: so must C. G. Jung's work be viewed in order to arrive at a significant appraisal of it. Its numerous aspects and perspectives confront the editor with many difficult choices comparable perhaps to the dilemmas experienced by the photographer attempting to convey an adequate impression of so vast an edifice.

The chief question to be asked must concern itself with the object of Jung's interest. The answer is: the human psyche in its totality; meaning consciousness plus the unconscious. Indeed it is the latter which has received his main attention during more than half a century of passionate and painstaking research, in the course of which the concept itself grew and became transformed until it finally included the subsoil of life itself—and not the subsoil alone at the level of its instinctive sources, but also its spiritual ferment and essence. In other words, it came to comprise the totality of existence outside of consciousness, surrounding and carrying the conscious ego. The growth of the concept took place by means of observation and deduction guided by the intuitive vision characteristic of all pioneering research and creative endeavor. The elements under observation were, to begin with, the spontaneous manifestations of the unconscious which every person experiences so frequently as to take them for granted, that is, the dreams occuring during sleep, as well as various fantasy activities which take place in the waking state. From these everyday occurrences in their normal individual expression one path of observation leads in the direction of their pathological forms culminating in insanity. Another path leads towards the common denominators which can be recognized as the dominant themes in the creative phantasy activity not only on the part of individuals but of entire groups and civilizations, in the form of fairy tales, legends, myths and rituals. The deeper psyche is thus understood to express itself through its imaginative activity, either individually or collectively, and it is in this sense that Jung conceives of its symbolic language.

The psychological definition of the symbol can be said to represent the focal point of Jung's entire research. It is therefore necessary to become acquainted with this definition.[1] The living symbol expresses an essential unconscious factor. The more widely this factor operates, the more generally valid is the symbol, for in every soul it evokes a resonance. (For examples of specifically religious symbols the reader is referred to the table of contents of the present volume, viz., the symbol of the Heavenly Child, Christ as a

---

[1] Jung, *Psychological Types* (Coll. Works, vol. 6, 1971; a revision by R.F.C. Hull of the tr. by H. G. Baynes), pars. 814–829 (def. 51, "Symbol").

symbol of the Self, symbols of Transformation in the Ritual of the Mass, the Eastern symbol of the Golden Flower, the Taoist symbols from the Book of Changes, as well as the Buddhist Wheel of Life, the Tibetan Thunderbolt. For impressive reproductions see also *The World's Great Religions*, Time, Inc., N.Y., 1957.) Since the symbol is the most complete expression of that which in any given epoch is as yet unknown—and cannot be replaced by any other statement at that time—it must proceed from the most complex and subtle strata of the contemporary psychological atmosphere. Conversely, the effective, living symbol must also contain something which is shared by considerable numbers of men: it embraces that which is common to a larger group. Consequently, it must include those primitive elements, emotional and otherwise, whose omnipresence stands beyond all doubt. Only when the symbol comprehends all those and conveys them with ultimate force can it evoke a universal response. Therein resides the powerful and redeeming effect of the living social symbol.

The same holds true, says Jung, for the individual symbol. There exist individual psychic products whose manifestly symbolic character invites a symbolic approach and understanding. He is referring here to elements in dreams and phantasy sequences which are woven into the context with a clearly non-concrete, symbolic intent. For instance, the dream figure of a child who is personally known to the dreamer, while drawing his attention to his relationship with this particular child, may and does nevertheless carry a symbolical message referring to the significance of the child image as the dreamer's potential for the inner growth of his own personality. Hence also it is both rational and irrational: while the data of rationally deducible character appeal to reason, the prospective meaning and pregnant significance of the symbol speak as strongly to our feeling as to our thinking. The singularly plastic imagery of the symbol when shaped into sensuous form stimulates both our sensation and our intuition. Only the passionate yearning of a highly developed mind, for which the conventional symbol no longer expresses in one image the ultimate reconciliation of painfully conflicting elements, can create a new symbol. Yet, inasmuch as the symbol not only proceeds from man's most complex mental achievement, but has at least an equal source in the lowest and most primitive motions of his psyche, this polarity needs to stand fully revealed. Such a condition necessarily entails a violent disunion with oneself, even to the point where the conflicting elements mutually deny each other, while the ego nevertheless is forced to acknowledge their existence and its own participation in the conflict. The energy engendered by the tension of the opposites flows into the creation of the symbol, since through the activity of the unconscious a content is brought to life in which thesis and antithesis participate in equal measure—in other words, the birth of the symbol portends a reconciliation into a more fully inclusive and comprehending plane of experience, which is tantamount to the attainment of greater meaning.

This process of the integration of the personality achieved by means of the mutual participation of consciousness and the unconscious, and made manifest through the spontaneous creation of the living symbol, Jung has named the *transcendent function*. He wishes it to be understood that the word "function" in this context denotes not a simple function, but a function-complex involving every area of the psyche, while the word "transcendent" denotes not a metaphysical quality, but rather the fact that through this function a transition is created from the previous attitude to a more fully integrated one.

It is evident that this conception postulates and acknowledges the essential participation of the unconscious in the creative process. Therein is expressed a fundamental contribution on the part of Jung regarding the totality of the psyche, according to which consciousness and the unconscious are related to each other in a reciprocity where each conscious element has its unconscious counterpart of an opposite yet compensating character. Their constant interplay engenders the kaleidoscopic dynamics which in the course of any individual existence create the individual biography. In this conception the conscious ego fulfills the function of a recipient of the crude ore brought to the surface out of varying depths of the unconscious, in addition to pursuing its own goals in terms of volition, learning and judgment, and of the multiple facets of its relationships both personal and impersonal. Clearly this conception in its turn is based upon the understanding of a relative functional autonomy of the component areas of the psyche.

If the psyche is thus conceived as an organism in its own right in which no element is fortuitous, there begins to emerge the image of an inner man whose nature and functioning is the proper field of investigation of the science of psychology. Evidently psychology has yet to find and to co-ordinate a terminology designed to describe the healthy normal psyche and its experience of itself and of its environment in a language no longer borrowed from psycho-pathology. This is especially important at the level of the higher functions (e.g., those not shared by the animal) which when de-scribed in terms appropriate to the lower must needs lose their specific value and become reduced to a "nothing-but." It is one of the outstanding merits of C. G. Jung to have outlined for our era and in contemporary language a portrait of spiritual man: one is tempted to say of the anatomy and physiology of spiritual man. This is clearly illustrated in the chapters from his publication *Aion* which are included in the present volume. The chapters "The Ego," "Anima and Animus," and "The Self" represent an outline of his approach and a résumé of his far-reaching conclusions. (The meaning of "Aion" or "Aeon" is perhaps best rendered according to the Oxford Dictionary as it relates itself to Platonic philosophy as a "Power existing from eternity.") If it be true that the search for self-knowledge in the widest sense has from time immemorial been one of the most urgent passions of mankind, then it can be said that this archetypal quest itself, culminating in the manifold varieties of spiritual experience, has formed the core of Jung's re-search and observation. Instead of attempting to establish prema-ture correlations or naïve concretizations, he has for several dec-ades sought out the most meaningful representations of man's spiritual self-portraits in which by their very nature man tran-scends himself. These portraits have an intrinsic common factor: they are expressed symbolically and not conceptually. It would seem that the psyche speaks to the psyche in its own language, and that this language is no other than the symbol itself.

The pioneer work of C. G. Jung has moved far into hitherto unexplored regions. It is as yet very little understood since the general understanding of the unconscious is still in its infancy. The comparative newness and consequent alien-ness of his conceptions places great demands upon the reader, particularly upon those who are still consciously or unconsciously committed to a positivist-rationalist viewpoint. The difficulties are further increased by his dramatically intuitive approach which sweeps across the neatly es-tablished and carefully guarded confines of many disciplines. This is irksome to the specialist and admittedly dangerous. But it is not only justified but truly life-giving when rigid barriers begin to fall as the result of a logically sustained creative effort towards a wider understanding and a more complete synthesis.

In speaking of Jung's intuitive approach I have in mind the specific sense in which he himself refers to the function of intuition in his work on the *Psychological Types*.[2] It is characteristic of the introverted intuitive personality that the inner image constitutes the most convincing aspect of the totality of his life experience. This inner image, the symbol, carries for the intuitive introvert more than for any other personality type the essential meaning of existence. This is basic to an understanding of Jung's lifelong dedication to the experience of and research into symbolic expression, to which he has sacrificed to a considerable extent his clinical research in the more limited sense of the word. In a wider sense however there is manifest in his work if not exactly a clinical then definitely an empirical attitude—a fact which he has repeatedly emphasized. It would be altogether more nearly accurate to say that the wealth of his clinical observations collected during a lifetime of psychotherapeutic practice has been absorbed into the wider presentation of those common denominators of psychic existence, the archetypes. He is as yet one of the few who, like William James, have dared to assert that the features of spiritual experience can be investigated scientifically with due reverence. This is bound to be misunderstood by considerable sectors of the public, partly for reasons of superficiality and partly because the vested interests of various branches of religious and secular science prevent them from realizing that it can never be anything but the psyche itself which is the carrier of any and all experience. And it is indeed the basic types of experience—the archetypes of experience—which have formed the center of Jung's scientific preoccupation through more than half a century. The archetypes of experience can be said to extend from the instinctual-organic to the spiritual realm. The Christian antithesis of nature and the spirit becomes, in the wider view, the polarity which among all the pairs of opposites has received his most passionate attention. No doubt in obedience to his ancestral endowment, part medical and part ecclesiastical, and faithful to his own creative-spiritual caliber, he has laid a cornerstone towards the foundation of a modern understanding of the healing functions and processes in the psyche, and of the role of the healer. Psychology and religion—the cure of souls through the care of the therapist and by the grace of redemption, as well as by the self-healing and recreative faculties inherent in the psyche: these themes form the therapeutic aspect of

[2] Ibid., pars. 770–773 (def. 35, "Intuition").

Jung's research. Small wonder therefore that the experiential, symbolic and ideational content of many religions have furnished the substance for his investigations.

Small wonder also that he has been particularly attracted by the figure of Paracelsus, the sixteenth-century physician whose insights into psycho-physical relations reached far beyond his contemporaries, and who was at the same time an original expounder of alchemical theory in which he invested his unremitting thought and labor. Much of Jung's interest, like that of Paracelsus, has been devoted to the teachings of the medieval European alchemists. From the vantage point of modern psychiatric and psychological observation, the core of their endeavor has come to reveal itself as a search for the wholeness of the personality and for the indestructible essence of the soul which they expressed in countless images and symbols ranging from the elixir of life and the philosopher's stone to the image of the hermaphrodite. Even the transmutation of base metals into gold, which is commonly assumed to have been the object of their practical labors, had its transcendent counterpart, for the gold itself became a symbol of the pure indestructible essence whose sun-like color reflected the immortal quality of the psyche. The stages of transformation which the alchemist believed to have observed in the vessels of his laboratory were transposed in his imagination into the animated personification of the various elements and substances which he was trying to synthesize into a new wholeness. According to Jung's conclusions the medieval alchemical symbolism represents a powerful upsurge on the part of the unconscious in the spiritual history of Western Europe. If one were to write a history not of the conscious manifestations, but of the unconscious formative elements and forces in the Western European *Geistesgeschichte* or cultural evolution, it would probably reveal certain important parallels to the symbol content of Jung's successive phases of interest in primitive religion, in the ancient Mediterranean and the Far Eastern religions, in Gnosticism, in the profound visionary and meditational experiences of such Christian saints as Ignatius Loyola and the Swiss Nicolaus vonder Flue, and in the intermingling of their scientific-psychological-religious thinking of the alchemists and of Paracelsus, and finally in the dynamics of the symbolical message of Christianity itself.

The search for wholeness, for an integration of the personality, has been designated by Jung as the process of *individuation*. This process is twofold in that it comprises the spontaneously arising

symbol to which he refers as the *uniting* symbol,[3] and also an assimilation of its value and message into consciousness in terms of
an understanding and of a responsible participation. This in its
turn signifies the birth of a new attitude on the part of the experiencing subject towards himself and towards his life. The birth
and growth of the new attitude are discussed by Jung in reference
to the symbol of the child in his "Psychology of the Child Archetype" included in the present volume. There is a striking similarity
between Jung's concept of the principle of individuation and S. T.
Coleridge's definition of life as "the principle of Individuation, or
the power that unites a given all into a whole which is presupposed
by all its parts."

Jung defines the term "individuation" as the psychological process that makes of a human being an "individual"—a unique, indivisible unit or "whole man."[4] His frequent and extensive references to medieval alchemical literature are the result of over
twenty years of study which led him to the conclusion that the pro-
fuse and variegated symbolism contained in these texts are spontaneous products of a more or less uninterrupted imaginative activity on the part of these authors. His interpretation of the symbol
content of their treatises stems from his conviction that "consciousness grows out of an unconscious psyche which is older than it, and
which goes on functioning with it or even in spite of it."[5] In the case
of dream activity during sleep, consciousness is at its lowest ebb and
the unconscious has relatively free play. Similarly, unconscious activity can take precedence over conscious intent within the waking
state, in which case symbolic expression displaces the rational processes. In Jung's view all symbolic expression or activity has an inner purpose. This purpose is precisely that of "individuation," of the
birth and growth of the indivisible inner "whole man." This, then,
is an urge which operates with or without the cooperation of consciousness, but the degree of achievement is nevertheless dependent upon the realization and understanding of which the conscious ego is capable.

The practical incentive for his research into alchemy came to

3 "Uniting" is the expression used in the translation of the Collected Works; the
earlier translators used the word "reconciling."—Ed.

4 Jung, "Conscious, Unconscious, and Individuation" (Coll. Works, vol. 9 i, 2nd
ed., 1976), pars. 489–490. (A revision of "The Meaning of Individuation," in *The
Integration of the Personality*, tr. S. Dell, 1939.)

5 Ibid., par. 502.

Jung through certain significant series of the dreams of several patients. The images occurring in these dreams refused to fit themselves into the then known categories of interpretation and it was
only when the striking similarities with many illustrations contained in alchemical texts came to his attention that the clues presented themselves, thus leading to ever more extensive studies in
this particular field.

It was as a result of the ensuing reflections that Jung came to
speak of "symbols of individuation," thereby designating in effect
all symbols whose impact and meaning transcend the sphere of the
fleetingly secular preoccupations. The empirical material and psy-
chological-philosophical conclusions are presented in his work on
Psychology and Alchemy[6] with its careful investigation of individual
dream symbolism in relation to alchemical symbolism on the one
hand, and of religious ideas in alchemy on the other hand. Although no part of *Psychology and Alchemy* is reproduced in the present volume, it is nonetheless necessary to refer to it since all of
Jung's publications of the past two decades have been impregnated
by his contact with alchemical literature. Strange though it appears
to the twentieth-century mind this literature has served as the crys-
tallizing agent for his conception and presentation of the individuation process, the process of becoming the independent personality who is (relatively!) free from the domination of the parental
archetypes and independent of the supportive structures of the
social environment. He can therefore establish his own individual
values and relationships which are valid because they are based on
the reality of his self-knowledge and not on a system of illusions
and rationalizations. Seen in this perspective, individuation is its
own goal, its own meaning and fulfillment and is at the same time
a religious experience and, one might say, a religious way of life,
because it means to live one's own existence creatively in the awareness of its participation in the stream of an eternal becoming.

Returning once more to the subject of alchemy, some further
comment appears indicated at this point. This is in further reference to its symbol content which previous to Jung's research had
received little attention. Briefly, the writings of the leading alchemists prove that they regarded their efforts as a lifelong "opus," a
labor demanding the adept's total dedication. This opus proceeded as a series of well-defined stages in the course of which the

---

[6] Coll. Works, vol. 12 (1953; 2nd edn., 1968).

events observed in the chemist's retort were accompanied by a vast amount of theoretical and imaginative speculation and of philosophical reflection. Each of the substances entering into the process appeared to be animated by a character and a destiny of its own, frequently conceived of in terms of mythological persons (Mercury, Saturn, the King and Queen, Sol and Luna). The adept was taught in what manner these bodies were to be treated and how they were going to effect each other when brought into mutual contact. Adverse processes of disintegration were described as alternating with beneficent combinations and were interpreted as taking place in accordance with certain inner laws which it was the alchemist's endeavor to discover and interpret. The goal itself was the transformation of the crude *prima materia* into the symbolical indestructible quint-essence, the *quinta essentia* or *lapis philosophorum*, the philosopher's stone, also known under a multitude of other names each of which denotes its character of ultimate timeless value. Jung has demonstrated the psychic aspects of the alchemical work in the pursuit of which the alchemist's inner life processes, the contents of the unconscious became projected into the opus which was itself regarded as a process of redemption, of a freeing of the spirit imprisoned in matter, the successful conclusion of which therefore brought about a renewal of life. Thus it becomes clear that over and above the obvious implications of a scientific discipline the alchemical speculations expressed a religious search which in its turn culminated in a concept of the timeless inner man, the "anthropos," brought about through the integration of its constituent elements.

All this would appear to be far removed from the practice of modern depth psychology. However the contrary is true. It has become evident to the alert observer that many of the symbolic images described in alchemical writings reoccur in the dream sequences of modern men and women, inviting interpretations akin to those offered by the alchemists. This in itself would seem to justify the conclusion that the unconscious has at its disposal a language of its own. Remembering the ever-recurring themes in the religious mythologies, the motifs of initiation, of death and rebirth, of expiation and redemption and of the superhuman labors and sufferings of the redeemer-hero, one is led to the conviction that these mythologies express the ultimate concerns of the psyche in its search for spiritual fulfillment. It is C. G. Jung's specific contribution to have demonstrated the role of the transpersonal unconscious psyche as the matrix and active carrier of this search. The designation which he chose for it, the *collective unconscious*, is intended to stress its quality of omnipresence. The quest itself is thus understood as the manifestation of a primordial or archetypal urge or drive. Seen in this light all religious as well as cultural expressions become an authentic part of psychic existence and cannot be regarded as derivative. Hence the concept of sublimation becomes void. In its place we find the concept of *transformation* as evidenced by the manifold symbols which bear witness to man's deepest desire.

Indeed, Jung's first major work, published in 1912, bore the German title: *Wandlungen und Symbole der Libido* meaning "Transformations and Symbols of the Libido."[7] For Jung the concept of *libido* has a different or rather a wider meaning than it had for Freud. It comprehends the sum total of the energic life processes, of all the vital forces of which sexuality represents only one area. Jung speaks of libido as an energy value which is able to communicate itself to any field of activity whatsoever, be it power, hunger, hatred, sexuality or religion, without ever being itself a specific instinct.[8] In other words, the psychic functioning is understood as taking place within a number of relatively autonomous areas each of which is invested with a certain amount of energy. The specific energy quantum cannot be transferred from one area to another through an effort of the conscious will, but a *transformation* can take place which can be conceived of in analogy to the transformation of energy in the physical realm. The transformer itself is the symbol. The study of the symbols of transformation centers upon the basic demand which is imposed upon every individual, that is, the urge as well as the necessity to become conscious of himself, to develop that human awareness which distinguishes the mature personality from the infantile one. For Jung, the path towards this awareness is identical with the process of individuation. Inasfar as the transformation results in a new and deeper awareness, it is experienced as a rebirth, and all rebirth rituals are intended to bring this about. Specifically, the basic dynamism consists in a profound reorientation from an ego-centered subjective attitude to an objective awareness of the limitations of the ego and

[7] Revised by Jung [1952] and translated under the title *Symbols of Transformation*, subtitled "An Analysis of the Prelude to a Case of Schizophrenia" (Coll. Works, vol. 5, 1956; 2nd ed., 1967).

[8] Ibid., par. 197.

of the existence of that greater psyche which Jung designates as the *self*. Thus the transformation of the libido implies a liberation of creative forces and the possibility to put them to the service of the greater-than-personal objectives.

Jacques Maritain speaks of the poet's creative intuition as "an obscure grasping of his own self and of things in a knowledge through a union or through connaturality which is born in the spiritual unconscious, and which fructifies only in the work. . . . To attain, through the Void, an intuitive experience of the existence of the Self, of the Atman, in its pure and full actuality, is the specific aim of natural mysticism."[9] In these two passages the word *self* carries implications which are akin to the content given to it in Jung's psychological use and definition. For Jung, the *self* connotes the totality of the psyche, embracing both consciousness and the unconscious and including the individual's rootedness in the matrix of the collective unconscious. He speaks of the *soul* as the function of relationship between consciousness and the *self*,[10] and emphasizes the necessity to realize the spiritual experience not only intellectually but also fully through feeling, and finally through the imaginative activity of intuition, without which no realization is complete. "This rounds off the work into an experience of the totality of the individual. Such an experience is completely foreign to our age, although no previous age has ever needed wholeness so much. It is abundantly clear that this is the prime problem confronting the art of psychic healing in our day."[11] Since the present volume includes Jung's discussion of the *self* in Chapters IV and V of his work *Aion* under the headings of "The Self" and "Christ: A Symbol of the Self," it is hoped that despite their brevity these remarks may serve as an adequate introduction.

As is evident in the essay on the Child Archetype (see this volume), the image of the child is a symbol par excellence of the reborn psyche. In its highest incarnation, as it were, it is also a symbol of the *self*. Jung defines the *self* as the complete personality comprising the ego as the center of the conscious functioning, plus the infinitely vaster areas of the unconscious. Of these areas, the one situated closest to the ego he designates as the personal uncon-

---

[9] *Creative Intuition in Art and Poetry* (A. W. Mellon Lectures in the Fine Arts, 1; Bollingen Series XXXV:1, 1953), pp. 113, 115.

[10] "The Psychology of the Transference" (Coll. Works, vol. 16, 1954; 2nd ed., 1966), pars. 475, 489 ff.

[11] Ibid., par. 492.

scious. Beyond this, the reaches of the psyche extending into the subhuman on the one part and the supra-human on the other part are what he describes as the collective unconscious. In and through the *self*, the human personality is therefore related (paradoxical though this appears from the viewpoint of the ego) to what we might call its innermost center as well as the universe of which it forms a particle. (Compare also the attribute of the Tibetan Dalai Lama as the "Inmost One.")

What, then, are the symbols which the psyche itself has produced that it might give expression to the tremendous experience of its own potential wholeness? I can mention here only that symbol which more than any other has preoccupied Jung throughout his therapeutic and scientific endeavors, and which we find shaped into the rose window of the medieval cathedral as well as into the religious ritualistic paintings of Buddhism in the form of the *mandāla*. He has adopted the Sanskrit term *mandāla* as the general designation for all those symbolic representations of the circle motif, more specifically in its manifold combinations with the square. He regards the general pattern of these images as the "archetype of wholeness." The completeness or totality expressed in the Four-foldness of the One therefore represents the "innermost godlike essence of man," characterized by symbols which can stand for the deity as well as for the *self*, since they reflect the image of the god-head in the unfolded creation in nature and in man.[12] According to Dr. Jung, this archetypal "leitmotif" has the vital function of giving expression to the dynamics of the self-healing process through which the psyche maintains its sanity and nurtures its own growth. The reader of this volume will find in the "Commentary on *The Secret of the Golden Flower*" Dr. Jung's discussion of the nature of the *mandāla*, and in the chapter "Christ as a Symbol of the Self" from his book *Aion*, his presentation of the psychological significance of the quaternity associated with the circle. These interpretations also provide the master key to the psychological understanding of countless symbolic representations in the fields of the visual arts, architecture and the dance. Seen in this perspective, these representations, can be said to give form to the experience of the self, not only on behalf of their creators, but also through their resonance in the mind of the beholder.

---

[12] "Mandalas" (Coll. Works, vol. 9 i, 1959; 2nd ed., 1968), pars. 713–718. Originally in the Swiss monthly journal *Du*, XV:4 (April 1955).

As the editor of the present volume it has been my intention to present a selection from the writings of C. G. Jung which would illustrate in convincing fashion the objects of his symbol research and the manner of his approach, as well as a synopsis of the conclusions to which he was led by exposing himself with great courage and thoroughness to the creative manifestations of the unconscious of many epochs and cultures.

Violet Staub de Laszlo

Danbury, Connecticut
May 1957

I

FIVE CHAPTERS FROM *AION*

I

THE EGO

1   Investigation of the psychology of the unconscious confronted me with facts which required the formulation of new concepts. One of these concepts is the *self.* The entity so denoted is not meant to take the place of the one that has always been known as the *ego,* but includes it in a supraordinate concept. We understand the ego as the complex factor to which all conscious contents are related. It forms, as it were, the centre of the field of consciousness; and, in so far as this comprises the empirical personality, the ego is the subject of all personal acts of consciousness. The relation of a psychic content to the ego forms the criterion of its consciousness, for no content can be conscious unless it is represented to a subject.

2   With this definition we have described and delimited the *scope* of the subject. Theoretically, no limits can be set to the field of consciousness, since it is capable of indefinite extension. Empirically, however, it always finds its limit when it comes up against the *unknown.* This consists of everything we do not know, which, therefore, is not related to the ego as the centre of the field of consciousness. The unknown falls into two groups of objects: those which are outside and can be experienced by the senses, and those which are inside and are experienced immediately. The first group comprises the unknown in the outer world; the second the unknown in the inner world. We call this latter territory the *unconscious.*

3   The ego, as a specific content of consciousness, is not a simple or elementary factor but a complex one which, as such, cannot be described exhaustively. Experience shows that it rests on two seemingly different bases: the *somatic* and the *psychic.* The somatic basis is inferred from the totality of endosomatic perceptions, which for their part are already of a psychic nature and are associated with the ego, and are therefore conscious. They are produced by endosomatic stimuli, only some of which

3

cross the threshold of consciousness. A considerable proportion of these stimuli occur unconsciously, that is, subliminally. The fact that they are subliminal does not necessarily mean that their status is merely physiological, any more than this would be true of a psychic content. Sometimes they are capable of crossing the threshold, that is, of becoming perceptions. But there is no doubt that a large proportion of these endosomatic stimuli are simply incapable of consciousness and are so elementary that there is no reason to assign them a psychic nature—unless of course one favours the philosophical view that all life-processes are psychic anyway. The chief objection to this hardly demonstrable hypothesis is that it enlarges the concept of the psyche beyond all bounds and interprets the life-process in a way not absolutely warranted by the facts. Concepts that are too broad usually prove to be unsuitable instruments because they are too vague and nebulous. I have therefore suggested that the term "psychic" be used only where there is evidence of a will capable of modifying reflex or instinctual processes. Here I must refer the reader to my paper "On the Nature of the Psyche," [1] where I have discussed this definition of the "psychic" at somewhat greater length.

4   The somatic basis of the ego consists, then, of conscious and unconscious factors. The same is true of the psychic basis: on the one hand the ego rests on the *total field of consciousness*, and on the other, on the *sum total of unconscious contents*. These fall into three groups: first, temporarily subliminal contents that can be reproduced voluntarily (memory); second, unconscious contents that cannot be reproduced voluntarily; third, contents that are not capable of becoming conscious at all. Group two can be inferred from the spontaneous irruption of subliminal contents into consciousness. Group three is hypothetical; it is a logical inference from the facts underlying group two. It contains contents which have *not yet* irrupted into consciousness, or which never will.

5   When I said that the ego "rests" on the total field of consciousness I do not mean that it *consists* of this. Were that so, it would be indistinguishable from the field of consciousness as a whole. The ego is only the latter's point of reference, grounded on and limited by the somatic factor described above.

1 Pars. 371ff.

4

6　　Although its bases are in themselves relatively unknown and unconscious, the ego is a conscious factor par excellence. It is even acquired, empirically speaking, during the individual's lifetime. It seems to arise in the first place from the collision between the somatic factor and the environment, and, once established as a subject, it goes on developing from further collisions with the outer world and the inner.

7　　Despite the unlimited extent of its bases, the ego is never more and never less than consciousness as a whole. As a conscious factor the ego could, theoretically at least, be described completely. But this would never amount to more than a picture of the *conscious personality;* all those features which are unknown or unconscious to the subject would be missing. A total picture would have to include these. But a total description of the personality is, even in theory, absolutely impossible, because the unconscious portion of it cannot be grasped cognitively. This unconscious portion, as experience has abundantly shown, is by no means unimportant. On the contrary, the most decisive qualities in a person are often unconscious and can be perceived only by others, or have to be laboriously discovered with outside help.

8　　Clearly, then, the *personality as a total phenomenon* does not coincide with the ego, that is, with the conscious personality, but forms an entity that has to be distinguished from the ego. Naturally the need to do this is incumbent only on a psychology that reckons with the fact of the unconscious, but for such a psychology the distinction is of paramount importance. Even for jurisprudence it should be of some importance whether certain psychic facts are conscious or not—for instance, in adjudging the question of responsibility.

9　　I have suggested calling the total personality which, though present, cannot be fully known, the *self.* The ego is, by definition, subordinate to the self and is related to it like a part to the whole. Inside the field of consciousness it has, as we say, free will. By this I do not mean anything philosophical, only the well-known psychological fact of "free choice," or rather the subjective feeling of freedom. But, just as our free will clashes with necessity in the outside world, so also it finds its limits outside the field of consciousness in the subjective inner world, where it comes into conflict with the facts of the self. And just as circumstances or outside events "happen" to us and limit our freedom, so the self acts upon the ego like an *objective occurrence* which free will can do very little to alter. It is, indeed, well known that the ego not only can do nothing against the self, but is sometimes actually assimilated by unconscious components of the personality that are in the process of development and is greatly altered by them.

10   It is, in the nature of the case, impossible to give any general description of the ego except a formal one. Any other mode of observation would have to take account of the *individuality* which attaches to the ego as one of its main characteristics. Although the numerous elements composing this complex factor are, in themselves, everywhere the same, they are infinitely varied as regards clarity, emotional colouring, and scope. The result of their combination—the ego—is therefore, so far as one can judge, individual and unique, and retains its identity up to a certain point. Its stability is relative, because far-reaching changes of personality can sometimes occur. Alterations of this kind need not always be pathological; they can also be developmental and hence fall within the scope of the normal.

11   Since it is the point of reference for the field of consciousness, the ego is the subject of all successful attempts at adaptation so far as these are achieved by the will. The ego therefore has a significant part to play in the psychic economy. Its position there is so important that there are good grounds for the prejudice that the ego is the centre of the personality, and that the field of consciousness is the psyche *per se*. If we discount certain suggestive ideas in Leibniz, Kant, Schelling, and Schopenhauer, and the philosophical excursions of Carus and von Hartmann, it is only since the end of the nineteenth century that modern psychology, with its inductive methods, has discovered the foundations of consciousness and proved empirically the existence of a psyche outside consciousness. With this discovery the position of the ego, till then absolute, became relativized; that is to say, though it retains its quality as the centre of the field of consciousness, it is questionable whether it is the centre of the personality. It is part of the personality but not the whole of it. As I have said, it is simply impossible to estimate how large or how small its share is; how free or how dependent it is on the qualities of this "extra-conscious" psyche. We can only say that

its freedom is limited and its dependence proved in ways that are often decisive. In my experience one would do well not to underestimate its dependence on the unconscious. Naturally there is no need to say this to persons who already overestimate the latter's importance. Some criterion for the right measure is afforded by the psychic consequences of a wrong estimate, a point to which we shall return later on.

12   We have seen that, from the standpoint of the psychology of consciousness, the unconscious can be divided into three groups of contents. But from the standpoint of the psychology of the personality a twofold division ensues: an "extra-conscious" psyche whose contents are *personal*, and an "extra-conscious" psyche whose contents are *impersonal* and *collective*. The first group comprises contents which are integral components of the individual personality and could therefore just as well be conscious; the second group forms, as it were, an omnipresent, unchanging, and everywhere identical *quality or substrate of the psyche per se*. This is, of course, no more than a hypothesis. But we are driven to it by the peculiar nature of the empirical material, not to mention the high probability that the general similarity of psychic processes in all individuals must be based on an equally general and impersonal principle that conforms to law, just as the instinct manifesting itself in the individual is only the partial manifestation of an instinctual substrate common to all men.

II

THE SHADOW

13   Whereas the contents of the personal unconscious are acquired during the individual's lifetime, the contents of the collective unconscious are invariably archetypes that were present from the beginning. Their relation to the instincts has been discussed elsewhere.[1] The archetypes most clearly characterized from the empirical point of view are those which have the most frequent and the most disturbing influence on the ego. These are the *shadow,* the *anima,* and the *animus.*[2] The most accessible of these, and the easiest to experience, is the shadow, for its nature can in large measure be inferred from the contents of the personal unconscious. The only exceptions to this rule are those rather rare cases where the positive qualities of the personality are repressed, and the ego in consequence plays an essentially negative or unfavourable role.

14   The shadow is a moral problem that challenges the whole ego-personality, for no one can become conscious of the shadow without considerable moral effort. To become conscious of it involves recognizing the dark aspects of the personality as present and real. This act is the essential condition for any kind of self-knowledge, and it therefore, as a rule, meets with considerable resistance. Indeed, self-knowledge as a psychotherapeutic measure frequently requires much painstaking work extending over a long period.

15   Closer examination of the dark characteristics—that is, the inferiorities constituting the shadow—reveals that they have an *emotional* nature, a kind of autonomy, and accordingly an obsessive or, better, possessive quality. Emotion, incidentally, is

---

1 "Instinct and the Unconscious" and "On the Nature of the Psyche," pars. 397ff.
2 The contents of this and the following chapter are taken from a lecture delivered to the Swiss Society for Practical Psychology, in Zurich, 1948. The material was first published in the *Wiener Zeitschrift für Nervenheilkunde und deren Grenzgebiete,* I (1948) : 4.

not an activity of the individual but something that happens to him. Affects occur usually where adaptation is weakest, and at the same time they reveal the reason for its weakness, namely a certain degree of inferiority and the existence of a lower level of personality. On this lower level with its uncontrolled or scarcely controlled emotions one behaves more or less like a primitive, who is not only the passive victim of his affects but also singularly incapable of moral judgment.

16   Although, with insight and good will, the shadow can to some extent be assimilated into the conscious personality, experience shows that there are certain features which offer the most obstinate resistance to moral control and prove almost impossible to influence. These resistances are usually bound up with *projections,* which are not recognized as such, and their recognition is a moral achievement beyond the ordinary. While some traits peculiar to the shadow can be recognized without too much difficulty as one's own personal qualities, in this case both insight and good will are unavailing because the cause of the emotion appears to lie, beyond all possibility of doubt, in the *other person.* No matter how obvious it may be to the neutral observer that it is a matter of projections, there is little hope that the subject will perceive this himself. He must be convinced that he throws a very long shadow before he is willing to withdraw his emotionally-toned projections from their object.

17   Let us suppose that a certain individual shows no inclination whatever to recognize his projections. The projection-making factor then has a free hand and can realize its object—if it has one—or bring about some other situation characteristic of its power. As we know, it is not the conscious subject but the unconscious which does the projecting. Hence one meets with projections, one does not make them. The effect of projection is to isolate the subject from his environment, since instead of a real relation to it there is now only an illusory one. Projections change the world into the replica of one's own unknown face. In the last analysis, therefore, they lead to an autoerotic or autistic condition in which one dreams a world whose reality remains forever unattainable. The resultant *sentiment d'incomplétude* and the still worse feeling of sterility are in their turn explained by projection as the malevolence of the environment, and by means of this vicious circle the isolation is intensified. The more

projections are thrust in between the subject and the environment, the harder it is for the ego to see through its illusions. A forty-five-year-old patient who had suffered from a compulsion neurosis since he was twenty and had become completely cut off from the world once said to me: "But I can never admit to myself that I've wasted the best twenty-five years of my life!"

18   It is often tragic to see how blatantly a man bungles his own life and the lives of others yet remains totally incapable of seeing how much the whole tragedy originates in himself, and how he continually feeds it and keeps it going. Not *consciously,* of course—for consciously he is engaged in bewailing and cursing a faithless world that recedes further and further into the distance. Rather, it is an unconscious factor which spins the illusions that veil his world. And what is being spun is a cocoon, which in the end will completely envelop him.

19   One might assume that projections like these, which are so very difficult if not impossible to dissolve, would belong to the realm of the shadow—that is, to the negative side of the personality. This assumption becomes untenable after a certain point, because the symbols that then appear no longer refer to the same but to the opposite sex, in a man's case to a woman and vice versa. The source of projections is no longer the shadow—which is always of the same sex as the subject—but a contrasexual figure. Here we meet the animus of a woman and the anima of a man, two corresponding archetypes whose autonomy and unconsciousness explain the stubbornness of their projections. Though the shadow is a motif as well known to mythology as anima and animus, it represents first and foremost the personal unconscious, and its content can therefore be made conscious without too much difficulty. In this it differs from anima and animus, for whereas the shadow can be seen through and recognized fairly easily, the anima and animus are much further away from consciousness and in normal circumstances are seldom if ever realized. With a little self-criticism one can see through the shadow—so far as its nature is personal. But when it appears as an archetype, one encounters the same difficulties as with anima and animus. In other words, it is quite within the bounds of possibility for a man to recognize the relative evil of his nature, but it is a rare and shattering experience for him to gaze into the face of absolute evil.

III

THE SYZYGY: ANIMA AND ANIMUS

20   What, then, is this projection-making factor? The East calls it the "Spinning Woman" [1]—Maya, who creates illusion by her dancing. Had we not long since known it from the symbolism of dreams, this hint from the Orient would put us on the right track: the enveloping, embracing, and devouring element points unmistakably to the mother,[2] that is, to the son's relation to the real mother, to her imago, and to the woman who is to become a mother for him. His Eros is passive like a child's; he hopes to be caught, sucked in, enveloped, and devoured. He seeks, as it were, the protecting, nourishing, charmed circle of the mother, the condition of the infant released from every care, in which the outside world bends over him and even forces happiness upon him. No wonder the real world vanishes from sight!

21   If this situation is dramatized, as the unconscious usually dramatizes it, then there appears before you on the psychological stage a man living regressively, seeking his childhood and his mother, fleeing from a cold cruel world which denies him understanding. Often a mother appears beside him who apparently shows not the slightest concern that her little son should become a man, but who, with tireless and self-immolating effort, neglects nothing that might hinder him from growing up and marrying. You behold the secret conspiracy between mother and son, and how each helps the other to betray life.

22   Where does the guilt lie? With the mother, or with the son? Probably with both. The unsatisfied longing of the son for life and the world ought to be taken seriously. There is in him a

1 Erwin Rousselle, "Seelische Führung im lebenden Taoismus," Pl. I, pp. 150, 170. Rousselle calls the spinning woman the "animal soul." There is a saying that runs, "The spinner sets in motion." I have defined the anima as a personification of the unconscious.

2 Here and in what follows, the word "mother" is not meant in the literal sense but as a symbol of everything that functions as a mother.

desire to touch reality, to embrace the earth and fructify the field of the world. But he makes no more than a series of fitful starts, for his initiative as well as his staying power are crippled by the secret memory that the world and happiness may be had as a gift—from the mother. The fragment of world which he, like every man, must encounter again and again is never quite the right one, since it does not'fall into his lap, does not meet him half way, but remains resistant, has to be conquered, and submits only to force. It makes demands on the masculinity of a man, on his ardour, above all on his courage and resolution when it comes to throwing his whole being into the scales. For this he would need a faithless Eros, one capable of forgetting his mother and undergoing the pain of relinquishing the first love of his life. The mother, foreseeing this danger, has carefully inculcated into him the virtues of faithfulness, devotion, loyalty, so as to protect him from the moral disruption which is the risk of every life adventure. He has learnt these lessons only too well, and remains true to his mother. This naturally causes her the deepest anxiety (when, to her greater glory, he turns out to be a homosexual, for example) and at the same time affords her an unconscious satisfaction that is positively mythological. For, in the relationship now reigning between them, there is consummated the immemorial and most sacred archetype of the marriage of mother and son. What, after all, has commonplace reality to offer, with its registry offices, pay envelopes, and monthly rent, that could outweigh the mystic awe of the *hieros gamos*? Or the star-crowned woman whom the dragon pursues, or the pious obscurities veiling the marriage of the Lamb?

23   This myth, better than any other, illustrates the nature of the collective unconscious. At this level the mother is both old and young, Demeter and Persephone, and the son is spouse and sleeping suckling rolled into one. The imperfections of real life, with its laborious adaptations and manifold disappointments, naturally cannot compete with such a state of indescribable fulfilment.

24   In the case of the son, the projection-making factor is identical with the mother-imago, and this is consequently taken to be the real mother. The projection can only be dissolved when the son sees that in the realm of his psyche there is an imago not only of the mother but of the daughter, the sister, the beloved,

the heavenly goddess, and the chthonic Baubo. Every mother and every beloved is forced to become the carrier and embodiment of this omnipresent and ageless image, which corresponds to the deepest reality in a man. It belongs to him, this perilous image of Woman; she stands for the loyalty which in the interests of life he must sometimes forgo; she is the much needed compensation for the risks, struggles, sacrifices that all end in disappointment; she is the solace for all the bitterness of life. And, at the same time, she is the great illusionist, the seductress, who draws him into life with her Maya—and not only into life's reasonable and useful aspects, but into its frightful paradoxes and ambivalences where good and evil, success and ruin, hope and despair, counterbalance one another. Because she is his greatest danger she demands from a man his greatest, and if he has it in him she will receive it.

25   This image is "My Lady Soul," as Spitteler called her. I have suggested instead the term "anima," as indicating something specific, for which the expression "soul" is too general and too vague. The empirical reality summed up under the concept of the anima forms an extremely dramatic content of the unconscious. It is possible to describe this content in rational, scientific language, but in this way one entirely fails to express its living character. Therefore, in describing the living processes of the psyche, I deliberately and consciously give preference to a dramatic, mythological way of thinking and speaking, because this is not only more expressive but also more exact than an abstract scientific terminology, which is wont to toy with the notion that its theoretic formulations may one fine day be resolved into algebraic equations.

26   The projection-making factor is the anima, or rather the unconscious as represented by the anima. Whenever she appears, in dreams, visions, and fantasies, she takes on personified form, thus demonstrating that the factor she embodies possesses all the outstanding characteristics of a feminine being.[3] She is not an invention of the conscious, but a spontaneous product of the

3 Naturally, she is a typical figure in *belles-lettres*. Recent publications on the subject of the anima include Linda Fierz-David, *The Dream of Poliphilo*, and my "Psychology of the Transference." The anima as a psychological idea first appears in the 16th-cent. humanist Richardus Vitus. Cf. my *Mysterium Coniunctionis*, pars. 91ff.

unconscious. Nor is she a substitute figure for the mother. On the contrary, there is every likelihood that the numinous qualities which make the mother-imago so dangerously powerful derive from the collective archetype of the anima, which is incarnated anew in every male child.

27   Since the anima is an archetype that is found in men, it is reasonable to suppose that an equivalent archetype must be present in women; for just as the man is compensated by a feminine element, so woman is compensated by a masculine one. I do not, however, wish this argument to give the impression that these compensatory relationships were arrived at by deduction. On the contrary, long and varied experience was needed in order to grasp the nature of anima and animus empirically. Whatever we have to say about these archetypes, therefore, is either directly verifiable or at least rendered probable by the facts. At the same time, I am fully aware that we are discussing pioneer work which by its very nature can only be provisional.

28   Just as the mother seems to be the first carrier of the projection-making factor for the son, so is the father for the daughter. Practical experience of these relationships is made up of many individual cases presenting all kinds of variations on the same basic theme. A concise description of them can, therefore, be no more than schematic.

29   Woman is compensated by a masculine element and therefore her unconscious has, so to speak, a masculine imprint. This results in a considerable psychological difference between men and women, and accordingly I have called the projection-making factor in women the animus, which means mind or spirit. The animus corresponds to the paternal Logos just as the anima corresponds to the maternal Eros. But I do not wish or intend to give these two intuitive concepts too specific a definition. I use Eros and Logos merely as conceptual aids to describe the fact that woman's consciousness is characterized more by the connective quality of Eros than by the discrimination and cognition associated with Logos. In men, Eros, the function of relationship, is usually less developed than Logos. In women, on the other hand, Eros is an expression of their true nature, while their Logos is often only a regrettable accident. It gives rise to misunderstandings and annoying interpretations in the family

14

circle and among friends. This is because it consists of *opinions* instead of reflections, and by opinions I mean *a priori* assumptions that lay claim to absolute truth. Such assumptions, as everyone knows, can be extremely irritating. As the animus is partial to argument, he can best be seen at work in disputes where both parties know they are right. Men can argue in a very womanish way, too, when they are anima-possessed and have thus been transformed into the animus of their own anima. With them the question becomes one of personal vanity and touchiness (as if they were females); with women it is a question of *power*, whether of truth or justice or some other "ism"—for the dressmaker and hairdresser have already taken care of their vanity. The "Father" (i.e., the sum of conventional opinions) always plays a great role in female argumentation. No matter how friendly and obliging a woman's Eros may be, no logic on earth can shake her if she is ridden by the animus. Often the man has the feeling—and he is not altogether wrong—that only seduction or a beating or rape would have the necessary power of persuasion. He is unaware that this highly dramatic situation would instantly come to a banal and unexciting end if he were to quit the field and let a second woman carry on the battle (his wife, for instance, if she herself is not the fiery war horse). This sound idea seldom or never occurs to him, because no man can converse with an animus for five minutes without becoming the victim of his own anima. Anyone who still had enough sense of humour to listen objectively to the ensuing dialogue would be staggered by the vast number of commonplaces, misapplied truisms, clichés from newspapers and novels, shopsoiled platitudes of every description interspersed with vulgar abuse and brain-splitting lack of logic. It is a dialogue which, irrespective of its participants, is repeated millions and millions of times in all the languages of the world and always remains essentially the same.

30   This singular fact is due to the following circumstance: when animus and anima meet, the animus draws his sword of power and the anima ejects her poison of illusion and seduction. The outcome need not always be negative, since the two are equally likely to fall in love (a special instance of love at first sight). The language of love is of astonishing uniformity, using the well-worn formulas with the utmost devotion and fidelity,

so that once again the two partners find themselves in a banal collective situation. Yet they live in the illusion that they are related to one another in a most individual way.

31   In both its positive and its negative aspects the anima/animus relationship is always full of "animosity," i.e., it is emotional, and hence collective. Affects lower the level of the relationship and bring it closer to the common instinctual basis, which no longer has anything individual about it. Very often the relationship runs its course heedless of its human performers, who afterwards do not know what happened to them.

32   Whereas the cloud of "animosity" surrounding the man is composed chiefly of sentimentality and resentment, in woman it expresses itself in the form of opinionated views, interpretations, insinuations, and misconstructions, which all have the purpose (sometimes attained) of severing the relation between two human beings. The woman, like the man, becomes wrapped in a veil of illusions by her demon-familiar, and, as the daughter who alone understands her father (that is, is eternally right in everything), she is translated to the land of sheep, where she is put to graze by the shepherd of her soul, the animus.

33   Like the anima, the animus too has a positive aspect. Through the figure of the father he expresses not only conventional opinion but—equally—what we call "spirit," philosophical or religious ideas in particular, or rather the attitude resulting from them. Thus the animus is a psychopomp, a mediator between the conscious and the unconscious and a personification of the latter. Just as the anima becomes, through integration, the Eros of consciousness, so the animus becomes a Logos; and in the same way that the anima gives relationship and relatedness to a man's consciousness, the animus gives to woman's consciousness a capacity for reflection, deliberation, and self-knowledge.

34   The effect of anima and animus on the ego is in principle the same. This effect is extremely difficult to eliminate because, in the first place, it is uncommonly strong and immediately fills the ego-personality with an unshakable feeling of rightness and righteousness. In the second place, the cause of the effect is projected and appears to lie in objects and objective situations. Both these characteristics can, I believe, be traced back to the peculiarities of the archetype. For the archetype, of course, exists

16

a priori. This may possibly explain the often totally irrational yet undisputed and indisputable existence of certain moods and opinions. Perhaps these are so notoriously difficult to influence because of the powerfully suggestive effect emanating from the archetype. Consciousness is fascinated by it, held captive, as if hypnotized. Very often the ego experiences a vague feeling of moral defeat and then behaves all the more defensively, defiantly, and self-righteously, thus setting up a vicious circle which only increases its feeling of inferiority. The bottom is then knocked out of the human relationship, for, like megalomania, a feeling of inferiority makes mutual recognition impossible, and without this there is no relationship.

35   As I said, it is easier to gain insight into the shadow than into the anima or animus. With the shadow, we have the advantage of being prepared in some sort by our education, which has always endeavoured to convince people that they are not one-hundred-per-cent pure gold. So everyone immediately understands what is meant by "shadow," "inferior personality," etc. And if he has forgotten, his memory can easily be refreshed by a Sunday sermon, his wife, or the tax collector. With the anima and animus, however, things are by no means so simple. Firstly, there is no moral education in this respect, and secondly, most people are content to be self-righteous and prefer mutual vilification (if nothing worse!) to the recognition of their projections. Indeed, it seems a very natural state of affairs for men to have irrational moods and women irrational opinions. Presumably this situation is grounded on instinct and must remain as it is to ensure that the Empedoclean game of the hate and love of the elements shall continue for all eternity. Nature is conservative and does not easily allow her courses to be altered; she defends in the most stubborn way the inviolability of the preserves where anima and animus roam, Hence it is much more difficult to become conscious of one's anima/animus projections than to acknowledge one's shadow side. One has, of course, to overcome certain moral obstacles, such as vanity, ambition, conceit, resentment, etc., but in the case of projections all sorts of purely intellectual difficulties are added, quite apart from the contents of the projection which one simply doesn't know how to cope with. And on top of all this there arises a profound doubt as to whether one is not meddling too much with nature's

business by prodding into consciousness things which it would have been better to leave asleep.

36 Although there are, in my experience, a fair number of people who can understand without special intellectual or moral difficulties what is meant by anima and animus, one finds very many more who have the greatest trouble in visualizing these empirical concepts as anything concrete. This shows that they fall a little outside the usual range of experience. They are unpopular precisely because they seem unfamiliar. The consequence is that they mobilize prejudice and become taboo like everything else that is unexpected.

37 So if we set it up as a kind of requirement that projections should be dissolved, because it is wholesomer that way and in every respect more advantageous, we are entering upon new ground. Up till now everybody has been convinced that the idea "my father," "my mother," etc., is nothing but a faithful reflection of the real parent, corresponding in every detail to the original, so that when someone says "my father" he means no more and no less than what his father is in reality. This is actually what he supposes he does mean, but a supposition of identity by no means brings that identity about. This is where the fallacy of the *enkekalymmenos* ('the veiled one') comes in.[4] If one includes in the psychological equation X's picture of his father, which he takes for the real father, the equation will not work out, because the unknown quantity he has introduced does not tally with reality. X has overlooked the fact that his idea of a person consists, in the first place, of the possibly very incomplete picture he has received of the real person and, in the second place, of the subjective modifications he has imposed upon this picture. X's idea of his father is a complex quantity for which the real father is only in part responsible, an indefinitely larger share falling to the son. So true is this that every time he criticizes or praises his father he is unconsciously hitting back at himself, thereby bringing about those psychic consequences that overtake people who habitually disparage or overpraise themselves. If, however, X carefully compares his reactions with reality, he stands a chance of noticing that he has miscalculated

4 The fallacy, which stems from Eubulides the Megarian, runs: "Can you recognize your father?" Yes. "Can you recognize this veiled one?" No. "This veiled one is your father. Hence you can recognize your father and not recognize him."

somewhere by not realizing long ago from his father's behaviour that the picture he has of him is a false one. But as a rule X is convinced that he is right, and if anybody is wrong it must be the other fellow. Should X have a poorly developed Eros, he will be either indifferent to the inadequate relationship he has with his father or else annoyed by the inconsistency and general incomprehensibility of a father whose behaviour never really corresponds to the picture X has of him. Therefore X thinks he has every right to feel hurt, misunderstood, and even betrayed.

38   One can imagine how desirable it would be in such cases to dissolve the projection. And there are always optimists who believe that the golden age can be ushered in simply by telling people the right way to go. But just let them try to explain to these people that they are acting like a dog chasing its own tail. To make a person see the shortcomings of his attitude considerably more than mere "telling" is needed, for more is involved than ordinary common sense can allow. What one is up against here is the kind of fateful misunderstanding which, under ordinary conditions, remains forever inaccessible to insight. It is rather like expecting the average respectable citizen to recognize himself as a criminal.

39   I mention all this just to illustrate the order of magnitude to which the anima/animus projections belong, and the moral and intellectual exertions that are needed to dissolve them. Not all the contents of the anima and animus are projected, however. Many of them appear spontaneously in dreams and so on, and many more can be made conscious through active imagination. In this way we find that thoughts, feelings, and affects are alive in us which we would never have believed possible. Naturally, possibilities of this sort seem utterly fantastic to anyone who has not experienced them himself, for a normal person "knows what he thinks." Such a childish attitude on the part of the "normal person" is simply the rule, so that no one without experience in this field can be expected to understand the real nature of anima and animus. With these reflections one gets into an entirely new world of psychological experience, provided of course that one succeeds in realizing it in practice. Those who do succeed can hardly fail to be impressed by all that the ego does not know and never has known. This increase in self-knowledge is still very rare nowadays and is usually

paid for in advance with a neurosis, if not with something worse.

40   The autonomy of the collective unconscious expresses itself in the figures of anima and animus. They personify those of its contents which, when withdrawn from projection, can be integrated into consciousness. To this extent, both figures represent *functions* which filter the contents of the collective unconscious through to the conscious mind. They appear or behave as such, however, only so long as the tendencies of the conscious and unconscious do not diverge too greatly. Should any tension arise, these functions, harmless till then, confront the conscious mind in personified form and behave rather like systems split off from the personality, or like part souls. This comparison is inadequate in so far as nothing previously belonging to the ego-personality has split off from it; on the contrary, the two figures represent a disturbing accretion. The reason for their behaving in this way is that though the *contents* of anima and animus can be integrated they themselves cannot, since they are archetypes. As such they are the foundation stones of the psychic structure, which in its totality exceeds the limits of consciousness and therefore can never become the object of direct cognition. Though the effects of anima and animus can be made conscious, they themselves are factors transcending consciousness and beyond the reach of perception and volition. Hence they remain autonomous despite the integration of their contents, and for this reason they should be borne constantly in mind. This is extremely important from the therapeutic standpoint, because constant observation pays the unconscious a tribute that more or less guarantees its co-operation. The unconscious as we know can never be "done with" once and for all. It is, in fact, one of the most important tasks of psychic hygiene to pay continual attention to the symptomatology of unconscious contents and processes, for the good reason that the conscious mind is always in danger of becoming one-sided, of keeping to well-worn paths and getting stuck in blind alleys. The complementary and compensating function of the unconscious ensures that these dangers, which are especially great in neurosis, can in some measure be avoided. It is only under ideal conditions, when life is still simple and unconscious enough to follow the serpentine path of instinct without hesitation or misgiving, that the compensation works with entire success. The more civilized, the more con-

scious and complicated a man is, the less he is able to follow his instincts. His complicated living conditions and the influence of his environment are so strong that they drown the quiet voice of nature. Opinions, beliefs, theories, and collective tendencies appear in its stead and back up all the aberrations of the conscious mind. Deliberate attention should then be given to the unconscious so that the compensation can set to work. Hence it is especially important to picture the archetypes of the unconscious not as a rushing phantasmagoria of fugitive images but as constant, autonomous factors, which indeed they are.

41   Both these archetypes, as practical experience shows, possess a fatality that can on occasion produce tragic results. They are quite literally the father and mother of all the disastrous entanglements of fate and have long been recognized as such by the whole world. Together they form a divine pair,[5] one of whom, in accordance with his Logos nature, is characterized by *pneuma* and *nous,* rather like Hermes with his ever-shifting hues, while the other, in accordance with her Eros nature, wears the features of Aphrodite, Helen (Selene), Persephone, and Hecate. Both of them are unconscious powers, "gods" in fact, as the ancient world quite rightly conceived them to be. To call them by this name is to give them that central position in the scale of psychological values which has always been theirs whether consciously acknowledged or not; for their power grows in proportion to the degree that they remain unconscious. Those who do not see them are in their hands, just as a typhus epidemic flourishes best when its source is undiscovered. Even in Christianity the divine syzygy has not become obsolete, but occupies the highest place as Christ and his bride the Church.[6] Parallels like these prove extremely helpful in our attempts to find the right

---

[5] Naturally this is not meant as a psychological definition, let alone a metaphysical one. As I pointed out in "The Relations between the Ego and the Unconscious" (pars. 296ff.), the syzygy consists of three elements: the femininity pertaining to the man and the masculinity pertaining to the woman; the experience which man has of woman and vice versa; and, finally, the masculine and feminine archetypal image. The first element can be integrated into the personality by the process of conscious realization, but the last one cannot.

[6] "For the Scripture says, God made man male and female; the male is Christ, the female is the Church."—Second Epistle of Clement to the Corinthians, xiv, 2 (trans. by Lake, I, p. 151). In pictorial representations, Mary often takes the place of the Church.

criterion for gauging the significance of these two archetypes. What we can discover about them from the conscious side is so slight as to be almost imperceptible. It is only when we throw light into the dark depths of the psyche and explore the strange and tortuous paths of human fate that it gradually becomes clear to us how immense is the influence wielded by these two factors that complement our conscious life.

42   Recapitulating, I should like to emphasize that the integration of the shadow, or the realization of the personal unconscious, marks the first stage in the analytic process, and that without it a recognition of anima and animus is impossible. The shadow can be realized only through a relation to a partner, and anima and animus only through a relation to a partner of the opposite sex, because only in such a relation do their projections become operative. The recognition of the anima gives rise, in a man, to a triad, one third of which is transcendent: the masculine subject, the opposing feminine subject, and the transcendent anima. With a woman the situation is reversed. The missing fourth element that would make the triad a quaternity is, in a man, the archetype of the Wise Old Man, which I have not discussed here, and in a woman the Chthonic Mother. These four constitute a half immanent and half transcendent quaternity, an archetype which I have called the *marriage quaternio*.[7] The marriage quaternio provides a schema not only for the self but also for the structure of primitive society with its cross-cousin marriage, marriage classes, and division of settlements into quarters. The self, on the other hand, is a God-image, or at least cannot be distinguished from one. Of this the early Christian spirit was not ignorant, otherwise Clement of Alexandria could never have said that he who knows himself knows God.[8]

[7] "The Psychology of the Transference," pars. 425ff. Cf. infra, pars. 358ff., the Naassene *quaternio*.
[8] Cf. infra, par. 347.

IV

THE SELF [1]

43   We shall now turn to the question of whether the increase in self-knowledge resulting from the withdrawal of impersonal projections—in other words, the integration of the contents of the collective unconscious—exerts a specific influence on the ego-personality. To the extent that the integrated contents are *parts of the self,* we can expect this influence to be considerable. Their assimilation augments not only the area of the field of consciousness but also the importance of the ego, especially when, as usually happens, the ego lacks any critical approach to the unconscious. In that case it is easily overpowered and becomes identical with the contents that have been assimilated. In this way, for instance, a masculine consciousness comes under the influence of the anima and can even be possessed by her.

44   I have discussed the wider effects of the integration of unconscious contents elsewhere [2] and can therefore omit going into details here. I should only like to mention that the more numerous and the more significant the unconscious contents which are assimilated to the ego, the closer the approximation of the ego to the self, even though this approximation must be a never-ending process. This inevitably produces an inflation of the ego, [3] unless a critical line of demarcation is drawn between it and the unconscious figures. But this act of discrimination yields practical results only if it succeeds in fixing reasonable boundaries to the ego and in granting the figures of the unconscious—the self, anima, animus, and shadow—relative autonomy and reality

---

1 The material for this chapter is drawn from a paper, "Über das Selbst," published in the *Eranos-Jahrbuch 1948.*
2 "The Relations between the Ego and the Unconscious."
3 In the sense of the words used in I Cor. 5 : 2: "Inflati estis [πεφυσιωμένοι] et non magis luctum habuistis" (And you are puffed up, and have not rather mourned)—with reference to a case of tolerated incest with the mother ("that a man should have his father's wife").

(of a psychic nature). To psychologize this reality out of existence either is ineffectual, or else merely increases the inflation of the ego. One cannot dispose of facts by declaring them unreal. The projection-making factor, for instance, has undeniable reality. Anyone who insists on denying it becomes identical with it, which is not only dubious in itself but a positive danger to the well-being of the individual. Everyone who has dealings with such cases knows how perilous an inflation can be. No more than a flight of steps or a smooth floor is needed to precipitate a fatal fall. Besides the "pride goeth before a fall" motif there are other factors of a no less disagreeable psychosomatic and psychic nature which serve to reduce "puffed-up-ness." This condition should not be interpreted as one of conscious self-aggrandizement. Such is far from being the rule. In general we are not directly conscious of this condition at all, but can at best infer its existence indirectly from the symptoms. These include the reactions of our immediate environment. Inflation magnifies the blind spot in the eye, and the more we are assimilated by the projection-making factor, the greater becomes the tendency to identify with it. A clear symptom of this is our growing disinclination to take note of the reactions of the environment and pay heed to them.

45   It must be reckoned a psychic catastrophe when the *ego is assimilated by the self.* The image of wholeness then remains in the unconscious, so that on the one hand it shares the archaic nature of the unconscious and on the other finds itself in the psychically relative space-time continuum that is characteristic of the unconscious as such.[4] Both these qualities are numinous and hence have an unlimited determining effect on ego-consciousness, which is differentiated, i.e., separated, from the unconscious and moreover exists in an absolute space and an absolute time. It is a vital necessity that this should be so. If, therefore, the ego falls for any length of time under the control of an unconscious factor, its adaptation is disturbed and the way opened for all sorts of possible accidents.

46   Hence it is of the greatest importance that the ego should be anchored in the world of consciousness and that consciousness should be reinforced by a very precise adaptation. For this, certain virtues like attention, conscientiousness, patience, etc.,

4 Cf. "On the Nature of the Psyche," pars. 414ff., 439ff.

are of great value on the moral side, just as accurate observation of the symptomatology of the unconscious and objective self-criticism are valuable on the intellectual side.

47   However, accentuation of the ego personality and the world of consciousness may easily assume such proportions that the figures of the unconscious are psychologized and the self consequently becomes assimilated to the ego. Although this is the exact opposite of the process we have just described it is followed by the same result: inflation. The world of consciousness must now be levelled down in favour of the reality of the unconscious. In the first case, reality had to be protected against an archaic, "eternal" and "ubiquitous" dream-state; in the second, room must be made for the dream at the expense of the world of consciousness. In the first case, mobilization of all the virtues is indicated; in the second, the presumption of the ego can only be damped down by moral defeat. This is necessary, because otherwise one will never attain that median degree of modesty which is essential for the maintenance of a balanced state. It is not a question, as one might think, of relaxing morality itself but of making a moral effort in a different direction. For instance, a man who is not conscientious enough has to make a moral effort in order to come up to the mark; while for one who is sufficiently rooted in the world through his own efforts it is no small moral achievement to inflict defeat on his virtues by loosening his ties with the world and reducing his adaptive performance. (One thinks in this connection of Brother Klaus, now canonized, who for the salvation of his soul left his wife to her own devices, along with numerous progeny.)

48   Since real moral problems all begin where the penal code leaves off, their solution can seldom or never depend on precedent, much less on precepts and commandments. The real moral problems spring from conflicts of duty. Anyone who is sufficiently humble, or easy-going, can always reach a decision with the help of some outside authority. But one who trusts others as little as himself can never reach a decision at all, unless it is brought about in the manner which Common Law calls an "Act of God." The Oxford Dictionary defines this concept as the "action of uncontrollable natural forces." In all such cases there is an unconscious authority which puts an end to doubt by creating a *fait accompli*. (In the last analysis this is true also of

25

those who get their decision from a higher authority, only in more veiled form.) One can describe this authority either as the "will of God" or as an "action of uncontrollable natural forces," though psychologically it makes a good deal of difference how one thinks of it. The rationalistic interpretation of this inner authority as "natural forces" or the instincts satisfies the modern intellect but has the great disadvantage that the apparent victory of instinct offends our moral self-esteem; hence we like to persuade ourselves that the matter has been decided solely by the rational motions of the will. Civilized man has such a fear of the "crimen laesae maiestatis humanae" that whenever possible he indulges in a retrospective coloration of the facts in order to cover up the feeling of having suffered a moral defeat. He prides himself on what he believes to be his self-control and the omnipotence of his will, and despises the man who lets himself be outwitted by mere nature.

49   If, on the other hand, the inner authority is conceived as the "will of God" (which implies that "natural forces" are divine forces), our self-esteem is benefited because the decision then appears to be an act of obedience and the result a divine intention. This way of looking at it can, with some show of justice, be accused not only of being very convenient but of cloaking moral laxity in the mantle of virtue. The accusation, however, is justified only when one is in fact knowingly hiding one's own egoistic opinion behind a hypocritical façade of words. But this is by no means the rule, for in most cases instinctive tendencies assert themselves for or against one's subjective interests no matter whether an outside authority approves or not. The inner authority does not need to be consulted first, as it is present at the outset in the intensity of the tendencies struggling for decision. In this struggle the individual is never a spectator only; he takes part in it more or less "voluntarily" and tries to throw the weight of his feeling of moral freedom into the scales of decision. Nevertheless, it remains a matter of doubt how much his seemingly free decision has a causal, and possibly unconscious, motivation. This may be quite as much an "act of God" as any natural cataclysm. The problem seems to me unanswerable, because we do not know where the roots of the feeling of moral freedom lie; and yet they exist no less surely than the instincts, which are felt as compelling forces.

50   All in all, it is not only more beneficial but more "correct" psychologically to explain as the "will of God" the natural forces that appear in us as instincts. In this way we find ourselves living in harmony with the *habitus* of our ancestral psychic life; that is, we function as man has functioned at all times and in all places. The existence of this habitus is proof of its viability, for, if it were not viable, all those who obeyed it would long since have perished of maladaptation. On the other hand, by conforming to it one has a reasonable life expectancy. When an habitual way of thinking guarantees as much as this there is not only no ground for declaring it incorrect but, on the contrary, every reason to take it as "true" or "correct" in the psychological sense. Psychological truths are not metaphysical insights; they are habitual modes of thinking, feeling, and behaving which experience has proved appropriate and useful.

51   So when I say that the impulses which we find in ourselves should be understood as the "will of God," I wish to emphasize that they ought not to be regarded as an arbitrary wishing and willing, but as absolutes which one must learn how to handle correctly. The will can control them only in part. It may be able to suppress them, but it cannot alter their nature, and what is suppressed comes up again in another place in altered form, but this time loaded with a resentment that makes the otherwise harmless natural impulse our enemy. I should also like the term "God" in the phrase "the will of God" to be understood not so much in the Christian sense as in the sense intended by Diotima, when she said: "Eros, dear Socrates, is a mighty daemon." The Greek words *daimon* and *daimonion* express a determining power which comes upon man from outside, like providence or fate, though the ethical decision is left to man. He must know, however, what he is deciding about and what he is doing. Then, if he obeys he is following not just his own opinion, and if he rejects he is destroying not just his own invention.

52   The purely biological or scientific standpoint falls short in psychology because it is, in the main, intellectual only. That this should be so is not a disadvantage, since the methods of natural science have proved of great heuristic value in psychological research. But the psychic phenomenon cannot be grasped in its totality by the intellect, for it consists not only of *meaning* but also of *value*, and this depends on the intensity of the

accompanying feeling-tones. Hence at least the two "rational" functions [5] are needed in order to map out anything like a complete diagram of a given psychic content.

53   If, therefore, in dealing with psychic contents one makes allowance not only for intellectual judgments but for value judgments as well, not only is the result a more complete picture of the content in question, but one also gets a better idea of the particular position it holds in the hierarchy of psychic contents in general. The feeling-value is a very important criterion which psychology cannot do without, because it determines in large measure the role which the content will play in the psychic economy. That is to say, the affective value gives the measure of the intensity of an idea, and the intensity in its turn expresses that idea's energic tension, its effective potential. The shadow, for instance, usually has a decidedly negative feeling-value, while the anima, like the animus, has more of a positive one. Whereas the shadow is accompanied by more or less definite and describable feeling-tones, the anima and animus exhibit feeling qualities that are harder to define. Mostly they are felt to be fascinating or numinous. Often they are surrounded by an atmosphere of sensitivity, touchy reserve, secretiveness, painful intimacy, and even absoluteness. The relative autonomy of the anima- and animus-figures expresses itself in these qualities. In order of affective rank they stand to the shadow very much as the shadow stands in relation to ego-consciousness. The main affective emphasis seems to lie on the latter; at any rate it is able, by means of a considerable expenditure of energy, to repress the shadow, at least temporarily. But if for any reason the unconscious gains the upper hand, then the valency of the shadow and of the other figures increases proportionately, so that the scale of values is reversed. What lay furthest away from waking consciousness and seemed unconscious assumes, as it were, a threatening shape, and the affective value increases the higher up the scale you go: ego-consciousness, shadow, anima, self. This reversal of the conscious waking state occurs regularly during the transition from waking to sleeping, and what then emerge most vividly are the very things that were unconscious by day. Every *abaissement du niveau mental* brings about a relative reversal of values.

[5] Cf. *Psychological Types,* Defs., "Rational" and "Irrational."

54   I am speaking here of the *subjective* feeling-value, which is subject to the more or less periodic changes described above. But there are also *objective* values which are founded on a *consensus omnium*—moral, aesthetic, and religious values, for instance, and these are universally recognized ideals or feeling-toned collective ideas (Lévy-Bruhl's "représentations collectives").[6] The subjective feeling-tones or "value quanta" are easily recognized by the kind and number of constellations, or symptoms of disturbance,[7] they produce. Collective ideals often have no subjective feeling-tone, but nevertheless retain their feeling-value. This value, therefore, cannot be demonstrated by subjective symptoms, though it may be by the attributes attaching to these collective ideas and by their characteristic symbolism, quite apart from their suggestive effect.

55   The problem has a practical aspect, since it may easily happen that a collective idea, though significant in itself, is—because of its lack of subjective feeling-tone—represented in a dream only by a subsidiary attribute, as when a god is represented by his theriomorphic attribute, etc. Conversely, the idea may appear in consciousness lacking the affective emphasis that properly belongs to it, and must then be transposed back into its archetypal context—a task that is usually discharged by poets and prophets. Thus Hölderlin, in his "Hymn to Liberty," lets this concept, worn stale by frequent use and misuse, rise up again in its pristine splendour:

> Since her arm out of the dust has raised me,
> Beats my heart so boldly and serene;
> And my cheek still tingles with her kisses,
> Flushed and glowing where her lips have been.
> Every word she utters, by her magic
> Rises new-created, without flaw;
> Hearken to the tidings of my goddess,
> Hearken to the Sovereign, and adore! [8]

56   It is not difficult to see here that the idea of liberty has been changed back to its original dramatic state—into the shining

---

6 *Les Fonctions mentales dans les sociétés inférieures.*
7 "On Psychic Energy," pars. 14ff., 20ff.
8 *Sämtliche Werke*, I, p. 126.

figure of the anima, freed from the weight of the earth and the
tyranny of the senses, the psychopomp who leads the way to the
Elysian fields.

57   The first case we mentioned, where the collective idea is
represented in a dream by a lowly aspect of itself, is certainly the
more frequent: the "goddess" appears as a black cat, and the
Deity as the *lapis exilis* (stone of no worth). Interpretation then
demands a knowledge of certain things which have less to do
with zoology and mineralogy than with the existence of an historical *consensus omnium* in regard to the object in question.
These "mythological" aspects are always present, even though
in a given case they may be unconscious. If for instance one
doesn't happen to recall, when considering whether to paint the
garden gate green or white, that green is the colour of life and
hope, the symbolic aspect of "green" is nevertheless present as
an unconscious *sous-entendu*. So we find something which has
the highest significance for the life of the unconscious standing
lowest on the scale of conscious values, and vice versa. The figure of the shadow already belongs to the realm of bodiless phan-
toms—not to speak of anima and animus, which do not seem to
appear at all except as projections upon our fellow human beings. As for the self, it is completely outside the personal sphere,
and appears, if at all, only as a religious mythologem, and its
symbols range from the highest to the lowest. Anyone who identifies with the daylight half of his psychic life will therefore
declare the dreams of the night to be null and void, notwithstanding that the night is as long as the day and that all consciousness is manifestly founded on unconsciousness, is rooted
in it and every night is extinguished in it. What is more, psychopathology knows with tolerable certainty what the unconscious
can do to the conscious, and for this reason devotes to the unconscious an attention that often seems incomprehensible to the
layman. We know, for instance, that what is small by day is big
at night, and the other way round; thus we also know that
besides the small by day there always looms the big by night,
even when it is invisible.

58   This knowledge is an essential prerequisite for any integration—that is to say a content can only be integrated when its
double aspect has become conscious and when it is grasped not
merely intellectually but understood according to its feeling-

value. Intellect and feeling, however, are difficult to put into
one harness—they conflict with one another by definition. Whoever identifies with an intellectual standpoint will occasionally
find his feeling confronting him like an enemy in the guise of
the anima; conversely, an intellectual animus will make violent
attacks on the feeling standpoint. Therefore, anyone who wants
to achieve the difficult feat of realizing something not only intellectually, but also according to its feeling-value, must for better
or worse come to grips with the anima/animus problem in order
to open the way for a higher union, a *coniunctio oppositorum*.
This is an indispensable prerequisite for wholeness.

59   Although "wholeness" seems at first sight to be nothing but
an abstract idea (like anima and animus), it is nevertheless empirical in so far as it is anticipated by the psyche in the form of
spontaneous or autonomous symbols. These are the quaternity
or mandala symbols, which occur not only in the dreams of
modern people who have never heard of them, but are widely
disseminated in the historical records of many peoples and many
epochs. Their significance as *symbols of unity and totality* is
amply confirmed by history as well as by empirical psychology.
What at first looks like an abstract idea stands in reality for
something that exists and can be experienced, that demonstrates
its *a priori* presence spontaneously. Wholeness is thus an objective factor that confronts the subject independently of him, like
anima or animus; and just as the latter have a higher position in
the hierarchy than the shadow, so wholeness lays claim to a position and a value superior to those of the syzygy. The syzygy
seems to represent at least a substantial portion of it, if not actually two halves of the totality formed by the royal brother-
sister pair, and hence the tension of opposites from which the
divine child [9] is born as the symbol of unity.

60   Unity and totality stand at the highest point on the scale of
objective values because their symbols can no longer be distinguished from the *imago Dei*. Hence all statements about the
God-image apply also to the empirical symbols of totality. Experience shows that individual mandalas are symbols of *order,* and
that they occur in patients principally during times of psychic

[9] Cf. my "Psychology of the Child Archetype"; also *Psychology and Alchemy,*
index, s.v. "filius Philosophorum," "child," "hermaphrodite."

disorientation or re-orientation. As magic circles they bind and subdue the lawless powers belonging to the world of darkness, and depict or create an order that transforms the chaos into a cosmos.[10] The mandala at first comes into the conscious mind as an unimpressive point or dot,[11] and a great deal of hard and painstaking work as well as the integration of many projections are generally required before the full range of the symbol can be anything like completely understood. If this insight were purely intellectual it could be achieved without much difficulty, for the world-wide pronouncements about the God within us and above us, about Christ and the *corpus mysticum,* the personal and suprapersonal atman, etc., are all formulations that can easily be mastered by the philosophic intellect. This is the common source of the illusion that one is then in possession of the thing itself. But actually one has acquired nothing more than its name, despite the age-old prejudice that the name magically represents the thing, and that it is sufficient to pronounce the name in order to posit the thing's existence. In the course of the millennia the reasoning mind has been given every opportunity to see through the futility of this conceit, though that has done nothing to prevent the intellectual mastery of a thing from being accepted at its face value. It is precisely our experiences in psychology which demonstrate as plainly as could be wished that the intellectual "grasp" of a psychological fact produces no more than a concept of it, and that a concept is no more than a name, a *flatus vocis.* These intellectual counters can be bandied about easily enough. They pass lightly from hand to hand, for they have no weight or substance. They sound full but are hollow; and though purporting to designate a heavy task and obligation, they commit us to nothing. The intellect is undeniably useful in its own field, but is a great cheat and illusionist outside of it whenever it tries to manipulate values.

61   It would seem that one can pursue any science with the intellect alone except psychology, whose subject—the psyche—has more than the two aspects mediated by sense-perception and thinking. The function of value—feeling—is an integral part of our conscious orientation and ought not to be missing in a psychological judgment of any scope, otherwise the model we are trying to build of the real process will be incomplete. Every

10 Cf. *Psychology and Alchemy,* Part II, ch. 3.   11 [Cf. infra, par. 340.]

psychic process has a value quality attached to it, namely its feeling-tone. This indicates the degree to which the subject is *affected* by the process or how much it means to him (in so far as the process reaches consciousness at all). It is through the "affect" that the subject becomes involved and so comes to feel the whole weight of reality. The difference amounts roughly to that between a severe illness which one reads about in a textbook and the real illness which one has. In psychology one possesses nothing unless one has experienced it in reality. Hence a purely intellectual insight is not enough, because one knows only the words and not the substance of the thing from inside.

62   There are far more people who are afraid of the unconscious than one would expect. They are even afraid of their own shadow. And when it comes to the anima and animus, this fear turns to panic. For the syzygy does indeed represent the psychic contents that irrupt into consciousness in a psychosis (most clearly of all in the paranoid forms of schizophrenia).[12] The overcoming of this fear is often a moral achievement of unusual magnitude, and yet it is not the only condition that must be fulfilled on the way to a real experience of the self.

63   The shadow, the syzygy, and the self are psychic factors of which an adequate picture can be formed only on the basis of a fairly thorough experience of them. Just as these concepts arose out of an experience of reality, so they can be elucidated only by further experience. Philosophical criticism will find everything to object to in them unless it begins by recognizing that they are concerned with *facts,* and that the "concept" is simply an abbreviated description or definition of these facts. Such criticism has as little effect on the object as zoological criticism on a duck-billed platypus. It is not the concept that matters; the concept is only a word, a counter, and it has meaning and use only because it stands for a certain sum of experience. Unfortunately I cannot pass on this experience to my public. I have tried in a number of publications, with the help of case material, to present the nature of these experiences and also the method of obtaining them. Wherever my methods were really applied the facts I give have been confirmed. One could see the

12 A classic case is the one published by Nelken: "Analytische Beobachtungen über Phantasien eines Schizophrenen." Another is Schreber's *Memoirs of My Nervous Illness.*

moons of Jupiter even in Galileo's day if one took the trouble to use his telescope.

64   Outside the narrower field of professional psychology these figures meet with understanding from all who have any knowledge of comparative mythology. They have no difficulty in recognizing the shadow as the adverse representative of the dark chthonic world, a figure whose characteristics are universal. The syzygy is immediately comprehensible as the psychic prototype of all divine couples. Finally the self, on account of its empirical peculiarities, proves to be the *eidos* behind the supreme ideas of unity and totality that are inherent in all monotheistic and monistic systems.

65   I regard these parallels as important because it is possible, through them, to relate so-called *metaphysical* concepts, which have lost their root connection with natural experience, to living, universal psychic processes, so that they can recover their true and original meaning. In this way the connection is reestablished between the ego and projected contents now formulated as "metaphysical" ideas. Unfortunately, as already said, the fact that metaphysical ideas exist and are believed in does nothing to prove the actual existence of their content or of the object they refer to, although the coincidence of idea and reality in the form of a special psychic state, a state of grace, should not be deemed impossible, even if the subject cannot bring it about by an act of will. Once metaphysical ideas have lost their capacity to recall and evoke the original experience they have not only become useless but prove to be actual impediments on the road to wider development. One clings to possessions that have once meant wealth; and the more ineffective, incomprehensible, and lifeless they become the more obstinately people cling to them. (Naturally it is only sterile ideas that they cling to; living ideas have content and riches enough, so there is no need to cling to them.) Thus in the course of time the meaningful turns into the meaningless. This is unfortunately the fate of metaphysical ideas.

66   Today it is a real problem what on earth such ideas can mean. The world—so far as it has not completely turned its back on tradition—has long ago stopped wanting to hear a "message"; it would rather be told what the message means. The words that resound from the pulpit are incomprehensible and cry for an

explanation. How has the death of Christ brought us redemption when no one feels redeemed? In what way is Jesus a God-man and what is such a being? What is the Trinity about, and the parthenogenesis, the eating of the body and the drinking of the blood, and all the rest of it? What connection can there be between the world of such concepts and the everyday world, whose material reality is the concern of natural science on the widest possible scale? At least sixteen hours out of twenty-four we live exclusively in this everyday world, and the remaining eight we spend preferably in an unconscious condition. Where and when does anything take place to remind us even remotely of phenomena like angels, miraculous feedings, beatitudes, the resurrection of the dead, etc.? It was therefore something of a discovery to find that during the unconscious state of sleep intervals occur, called "dreams," which occasionally contain scenes having a not inconsiderable resemblance to the motifs of mythology. For myths are miracle tales and treat of all those things which, very often, are also objects of belief.

67   In the everyday world of consciousness such things hardly exist; that is to say, until 1933 only lunatics would have been found in possession of living fragments of mythology. After this date the world of heroes and monsters spread like a devastating fire over whole nations, proving that the strange world of myth had suffered no loss of vitality during the centuries of reason and enlightenment. If metaphysical ideas no longer have such a fascinating effect as before, this is certainly not due to any lack of primitivity in the European psyche, but simply and solely to the fact that the erstwhile symbols no longer express what is now welling up from the unconscious as the end-result of the development of Christian consciousness through the centuries. This end-result is a true *antimimon pneuma*, a false spirit of arrogance, hysteria, woolly-mindedness, criminal amorality, and doctrinaire fanaticism, a purveyor of shoddy spiritual goods, spurious art, philosophical stutterings, and Utopian humbug, fit only to be fed wholesale to the mass man of today. That is what the post-Christian spirit looks like.

35

V

CHRIST, A SYMBOL OF THE SELF

⁶⁸ The dechristianization of our world, the Luciferian develop-
ment of science and technology, and the frightful material and
moral destruction left behind by the second World War have
been compared more than once with the *eschatological* events
foretold in the New Testament. These, as we know, are concerned with the coming of the Antichrist: "This is Antichrist,
who denieth the Father and the Son." [1] "Every spirit that dis-
solveth Jesus . . . is Antichrist . . . of whom you have heard
that he cometh." [2] The Apocalypse is full of expectations of terrible things that will take place at the end of time, before the
marriage of the Lamb. This shows plainly that the *anima chris-
tiana* has a sure knowledge not only of the existence of an
adversary but also of his future usurpation of power.

⁶⁹ Why—my reader will ask—do I discourse here upon Christ
and his adversary, the Antichrist? Our discourse necessarily
brings us to Christ, because he is the still living myth of our
culture. He is our culture hero, who, regardless of his historical
existence, embodies the myth of the divine Primordial Man, the
mystic Adam. It is he who occupies the centre of the Christian
mandala, who is the Lord of the Tetramorph, i.e., the four symbols of the evangelists, which are like the four columns of his
throne. He is in us and we in him. His kingdom is the pearl of
great price, the treasure buried in the field, the grain of mus-
tard seed which will become a great tree, and the heavenly

1 I John 2 : 22 (DV).
2 I John 4 : 3 (DV). The traditional view of the Church is based on II Thessalo-
nians 2 : 3ff., which speaks of the apostasy, of the ἄνθρωπος τῆς ἀνομίας (man of
lawlessness) and the υἱὸς τῆς ἀπωλείας (son of perdition) who herald the coming of
the Lord. This "lawless one" will set himself up in the place of God, but will
finally be slain by the Lord Jesus "with the breath of his mouth." He will work
wonders κατ' ἐνέργειαν τοῦ σατανᾶ (according to the working of Satan). Above all,
he will reveal himself by his *lying and deceitfulness*. Daniel 11 : 36ff. is regarded
as a prototype.

city.³ As Christ is in us, so also is his heavenly kingdom.⁴

70   These few, familiar references should be sufficient to make the psychological position of the Christ symbol quite clear. *Christ exemplifies the archetype of the self*.⁵ He represents a totality of a divine or heavenly kind, a glorified man, a son of God *sine macula peccati*, unspotted by sin. As *Adam secundus* he corresponds to the first Adam before the Fall, when the latter was still a pure image of God, of which Tertullian (d. 222) says: "And this therefore is to be considered as the image of God in man, that the human spirit has the same motions and senses as God has, though not in the same way as God has them." ⁶ Origen (185–254) is very much more explicit: The *imago Dei* imprinted on the soul, not on the body,⁷ is an image of an image, "for my soul is not directly the image of God, but is made after the likeness of the former image." ⁸ Christ, on the other hand, is the

---

3 For "city" cf. *Psychology and Alchemy*, pp. 104ff.

4 Ἡ βασιλεία τοῦ θεοῦ ἐντὸς ὑμῶν ἔστιν (The kingdom of God is within you [or "among you"]). "The kingdom of God cometh not with observation: neither shall they say, Lo here! or, lo there!" for it is within and everywhere. (Luke 17 : 20f.) "It is not of this [external] world." (John 18 : 36.) The likeness of the kingdom of God to man is explicitly stated in the parable of the sower (Matthew 13 : 24. Cf. also Matthew 13 : 45, 18 : 23, 22 : 2). The papyrus fragments from Oxyrhynchus say: . . . ἡ βασ[ιλεία τῶν οὐρανῶν] ἐντὸς ὑμῶν [ἐ]στι [καὶ ὅστις ἂν ἑαυτὸν] γνῶ ταύτην εὑρή[σει] ἑαυτοὺς γνώσεσθε κτλ. (The kingdom of heaven is within you, and whosoever knoweth himself shall find it. Know yourselves.) Cf. James, *The Apocryphal New Testament*, p. 26, and Grenfell and Hunt, *New Sayings of Jesus*, p. 15.

5 Cf. my observations on Christ as archetype in "A Psychological Approach to the Dogma of the Trinity," pars. 226ff.

6 "Et haec ergo imago censenda est Dei in homine, quod eosdem motus et sensus habeat humanus animus, quos et Deus, licet non tales quales Deus" (*Adv. Marcion.*, II, xvi; in Migne, *P.L.*, vol. 2, col. 304).

7 *Contra Celsum*, VIII, 49 (Migne, *P.G.*, vol. 11, col. 1590): "In anima, non in corpore impressus sit imaginis conditoris character" (The character of the image of the Creator is imprinted on the soul, not on the body). (Cf. trans. by H. Chadwick, p. 488.)

8 *In Lucam homilia*, VIII (Migne, *P.G.*, vol. 13, col. 1820): "Si considerem Dominum Salvatorem imaginem esse invisibilis Dei, et videam animam meam factam ad imaginem conditoris, ut imago esset imaginis: neque enim anima mea specialiter imago est Dei, sed ad similitudinem imaginis prioris effecta est" (If I consider that the Lord and Saviour is the image of the invisible God, I see that my soul is made after the image of the Creator, so as to be an image of an image; for my soul is not directly the image of God, but is made after the likeness of the former image).

true image of God,[9] after whose likeness our inner man is made, invisible, incorporeal, incorrupt, and immortal.[10] The God-image in us reveals itself through "prudentia, iustitia, moderatio, virtus, sapientia et disciplina." [11]

71 St. Augustine (354–430) distinguishes between the God-image which is Christ and the image which is implanted in man as a means or possibility of becoming like God.[12] The God-image is not in the corporeal man, but in the *anima rationalis*, the possession of which distinguishes man from animals. "The God-image is within, not in the body. . . . Where the understanding is, where the mind is, where the power of investigating truth is, there God has his image." [13] Therefore we should remind ourselves, says Augustine, that we are fashioned after the image of God nowhere save in the understanding: ". . . but where man knows himself to be made after the image of God,

[9] *De principiis*, I, ii, 8 (Migne, *P.G.*, vol. 11, col. 156): "Salvator figura est substantiae vel subsistentiae Dei" (The Saviour is the figure of the substance or subsistence of God). *In Genesim homilia*, I, 13 (Migne, *P.G.*, vol. 12, col. 156): "Quae est ergo alia imago Dei ad cuius imaginis similitudinem factus est homo, nisi Salvator noster, qui est primogenitus omnis creaturae?" (What else therefore is the image of God after the likeness of which image man was made, but our Saviour, who is the first born of every creature?) *Selecta in Genesim*, IX, 6 (Migne, *P.G.*, vol. 12, col. 107): "Imago autem Dei invisibilis salvator" (But the image of the invisible God is the saviour).

[10] *In Gen. hom.*, I, 13 (Migne, *P.G.*, vol. 12, col. 155): "Is autem qui ad imaginem Dei factus est et ad similitudinem, interior homo noster est, invisibilis et incorporalis, et incorruptus atque immortalis" (But that which is made after the image and similitude of God is our inner man, invisible, incorporeal, incorrupt, and immortal).

[11] *De princip.*, IV, 37 (Migne, *P.G.*, vol. 11, col. 412).

[12] *Retractationes*, I, xxvi (Migne, *P.L.*, vol. 32, col. 626): "(Unigenitus) . . . tantummodo imago est, non ad imaginem" (The Only-Begotten . . . alone is the image, not after the image).

[13] *Enarrationes in Psalmos*, XLVIII, Sermo II (Migne, *P.L.*, vol. 36, col. 564): "Imago Dei intus est, non est in corpore . . . ubi est intellectus, ubi est mens, ubi ratio investigandae veritatis etc. ibi habet Deus imaginem suam." Also ibid., Psalm XLII, 6 (Migne, *P.L.*, vol. 36, col. 480): "Ergo intelligimus habere nos aliquid ubi imago Dei est, mentem scilicet atque rationem" (Therefore we understand that we have something in which the image of God is, namely mind and reason). Sermo XC, 10 (Migne, *P.L.*, vol. 38, col. 566): "Veritas quaeritur in Dei imagine" (Truth is sought in the image of God), but against this the *Liber de vera religione* says: "in interiore homine habitat veritas" (truth dwells in the inner man). From this it is clear that the *imago Dei* coincides with the *interior homo*.

there he knows there is something more in him than is given to the beasts."[14] From this it is clear that the God-image is, so to speak, identical with the *anima rationalis*. The latter is the higher spiritual man, the *homo coelestis* of St Paul.[15] Like Adam before the Fall, Christ is an embodiment of the God-image,[16] whose totality is specially emphasized by St. Augustine. "The Word," he says, "took on complete manhood, as it were in its fulness: the soul and body of a man. And if you would have me put it more exactly—since even a beast of the field has a 'soul' and a body—when I say a human soul and human flesh, I mean he took upon him a complete human soul."[17]

72   The God-image in man was not destroyed by the Fall but was only damaged and corrupted ("deformed"), and can be restored through God's grace. The scope of the integration is suggested by the *descensus ad inferos,* the descent of Christ's soul to hell, its work of redemption embracing even the dead. The psychological equivalent of this is the integration of the collective unconscious which forms an essential part of the individuation process. St. Augustine says: "Therefore our end must be our perfection, but our perfection is Christ,"[18] since he is the perfect God-image. For this reason he is also called "King." His bride (*sponsa*) is the human soul, which "in an inwardly hidden spiritual mystery is joined to the Word, that two may be in one flesh," to correspond with the mystic marriage of Christ and the Church.[19] Concurrently with the continuance of this *hieros*

14 *Enarr. in Ps.,* LIV, 3 (Migne, *P.L.,* vol. 36, col. 629): ". . . ubi autem homo ad imaginem Dei factum se novit, ibi aliquid in se agnoscit amplius esse quam datum est pecoribus."

15 I Cor. 15 : 47.

16 *In Joannis Evangelium,* Tract. LXXVIII, 3 (Migne, *P.L.,* vol. 35, col. 1836): "Christus est Deus, anima rationalis et caro" (Christ is God, a rational soul and a body).

17 Sermo CCXXXVII, 4 (Migne, *P.L.,* vol. 38, col. 1124): "(Verbum) suscepit totum quasi plenum hominem, animam et corpus hominis. Et si aliquid scrupulosius vis audire; quia animam et carnem habet et pecus, cum dico animam humanam et carnem humanam, totam animam humanam accepit."

18 *Enarr. in Ps.,* LIV, 1 (Migne, *P.L.,* vol. 36, col. 628).

19 *Contra Faustum,* XXII, 38 (Migne, *P.L.,* vol. 42, col. 424): "Est enim et sancta Ecclesia Domino Jesu Christo in occulto uxor. Occulte quippe atque intus in abscondito secreto spirituali anima humana inhaeret Verbo Dei, ut sint duo in carne una." Cf. St. Augustine's *Reply to Faustus the Manichaean* (trans. by P.ichard Stothert, p. 433): "The holy Church, too, is in secret the spouse of the

gamos in the dogma and rites of the Church, the symbolism developed in the course of the Middle Ages into the alchemical conjunction of opposites, or "chymical wedding," thus giving rise on the one hand to the concept of the *lapis philosophorum,* signifying totality, and on the other hand to the concept of chemical combination.

73   The God-image in man that was damaged by the first sin can be "reformed" [20] with the help of God, in accordance with Romans 12 : 2: "And be not conformed to this world, but be transformed by the renewal of your mind, that you may prove what is . . . the will of God" (RSV). The totality images which the unconscious produces in the course of an individuation process are similar "reformations" of an *a priori* archetype (the mandala). [21] As I have already emphasized, the spontaneous symbols of the self, or of wholeness, cannot in practice be distinguished from a God-image. Despite the word μεταμορφοῦσθε ('be transformed') in the Greek text of the above quotation, the "renewal" (ἀνακαίνωσις, *reformatio*) of the mind is not meant as an actual alteration of consciousness, but rather as the restoration of an original condition, an apocatastasis. This is in exact agreement with the empirical findings of psychology, that there is an ever-present archetype of wholeness [22] which may easily disappear from the purview of consciousness or may never be perceived at all until a consciousness illuminated by conversion recognizes it in the figure of Christ. As a result of this "anamnesis" the original state of oneness with the God-image is restored. It brings about an integration, a bridging of the split in the personality caused by the instincts striving apart in different and mutually contradictory directions. The only time the split

---

Lord Jesus Christ. For it is secretly, and in the hidden depths of the spirit, that the soul of man is joined to the word of God, so that they are two in one flesh." St. Augustine is referring here to Eph. 5 : 31f.: "For this cause shall a man leave his father and mother, and shall be joined unto his wife, and they two shall be one flesh. This is a great mystery: but I speak concerning Christ and the Church."
[20] Augustine, *De Trinitate,* XIV, 22 (Migne, *P.L.,* vol. 42, col. 1053): "Reformamini in novitate mentis vostrae, ut incipiat illa imago ab illo reformari, a quo formata est" (Be reformed in the newness of your mind; the beginning of the image's reforming must come from him who first formed it) (trans. by John Burnaby, p. 120).
[21] Cf. "Concerning Mandala Symbolism," in Part I of vol. 9.
[22] *Psychology and Alchemy,* pars. 323ff.

does not occur is when a person is still as legitimately unconscious of his instinctual life as an animal. But it proves harmful and impossible to endure when an artificial unconsciousness—a repression—no longer reflects the life of the instincts.

74   There can be no doubt that the original Christian conception of the *imago Dei* embodied in Christ meant an all-embracing totality that even includes the animal side of man. Nevertheless the Christ-symbol lacks wholeness in the modern psychological sense, since it does not include the dark side of things but specifically excludes it in the form of a Luciferian opponent. Although the exclusion of the power of evil was something the Christian consciousness was well aware of, all it lost in effect was an insubstantial shadow, for, through the doctrine of the *privatio boni* first propounded by Origen, evil was characterized as a mere diminution of good and thus deprived of substance. According to the teachings of the Church, evil is simply "the accidental lack of perfection." This assumption resulted in the proposition "omne bonum a Deo, omne malum ab homine." Another logical consequence was the subsequent elimination of the devil in certain Protestant sects.

75   Thanks to the doctrine of the *privatio boni,* wholeness seemed guaranteed in the figure of Christ. One must, however, take evil rather more substantially when one meets it on the plane of empirical psychology. There it is simply the opposite of good. In the ancient world the Gnostics, whose arguments were very much influenced by psychic experience, tackled the problem of evil on a broader basis than the Church Fathers. For instance, one of the things they taught was that Christ "cast off his shadow from himself." [23] If we give this view the weight it

23 Irenaeus (*Adversus haereses*, II, 5, 1) records the Gnostic teaching that when Christ, as the demiurgic Logos, created his mother's being, he "cast her out of the Pleroma—that is, he cut her off from knowledge." For creation took place outside the pleroma, in the shadow and the void. According to Valentinus (*Adv. haer.*, I, 11, 1), Christ did not spring from the Aeons of the pleroma, but from the mother who was outside it. She bore him, he says, "not without a kind of shadow." But he, "being masculine,' cast off the shadow from himself and returned to the Pleroma (καὶ τοῦτον [Χριστὸν] μὲν ἅτε ἄρρενα ὑπάρχοντα ἀποκόψαντα ἀφ' ἑαυτοῦ τὴν σκιάν, ἀναδραμεῖν εἰς τὸ Πλήρωμα κτλ.), while his mother, "being left behind in the shadow, and deprived of spiritual substance,' there gave birth to the real "Demiurge and Pantokrator of the lower world.' But the shadow which lies over the world is, as we know from the Gospels, the *princeps huius mundi,* the devil. Cf. *The Writings of Irenaeus,* I, pp. 45f.

41

deserves, we can easily recognize the cut-off counterpart in the figure of Antichrist. The Antichrist develops in legend as a perverse imitator of Christ's life. He is a true ἀντίμιμον πνεῦμα, an imitating spirit of evil who follows in Christ's footsteps like a shadow following the body. This complementing of the bright but one-sided figure of the Redeemer—we even find traces of it in the New Testament—must be of especial significance. And indeed, considerable attention was paid to it quite early.

76   If we see the traditional figure of Christ as a parallel to the psychic manifestation of the self, then the Antichrist would correspond to the shadow of the self, namely the dark half of the human totality, which ought not to be judged too optimistically. So far as we can judge from experience, light and shadow are so evenly distributed in man's nature that his psychic totality appears, to say the least of it, in a somewhat murky light. The psychological concept of the self, in part derived from our knowledge of the whole man, but for the rest depicting itself spontaneously in the products of the unconscious as an archetypal quaternity bound together by inner antinomies, cannot omit the shadow that belongs to the light figure, for without it this figure lacks body and humanity. In the empirical self, light and shadow form a paradoxical unity. In the Christian concept, on the other hand, the archetype is hopelessly split into two irreconcilable halves, leading ultimately to a metaphysical dualism—the final separation of the kingdom of heaven from the fiery world of the damned.

77   For anyone who has a positive attitude towards Christianity the problem of the Antichrist is a hard nut to crack. It is nothing less than the counterstroke of the devil, provoked by God's Incarnation; for the devil attains his true stature as the adversary of Christ, and hence of God, only after the rise of Christianity, while as late as the Book of Job he was still one of God's sons and on familiar terms with Yahweh.[24] Psychologically the case is clear, since the dogmatic figure of Christ is so sublime and spotless that everything else turns dark beside it. It is, in fact, so one-sidedly perfect that it demands a psychic complement to restore the balance. This inevitable opposition led very early to the doctrine of the two sons of God, of whom the elder

24 Cf. R. Schärf, "Die Gestalt des Satans im Alten Testament."

was called Satanaël.[25] The coming of the Antichrist is not just a prophetic prediction—it is an inexorable psychological law whose existence, though unknown to the author of the Johannine Epistles, brought him a sure knowledge of the impending enantiodromia. Consequently he wrote as if he were conscious of the inner necessity for this transformation, though we may be sure that the idea seemed to him like a divine revelation. In reality every intensified differentiation of the Christ-image brings about a corresponding accentuation of its unconscious complement, thereby increasing the tension between above and below.

78   In making these statements we are keeping entirely within the sphere of Christian psychology and symbolism. A factor that no one has reckoned with, however, is the fatality inherent in the Christian disposition itself, which leads inevitably to a reversal of its spirit—not through the obscure workings of chance but in accordance with psychological law. The ideal of spirituality striving for the heights was doomed to clash with the materialistic earth-bound passion to conquer matter and master the world. This change became visible at the time of the "Renaissance." The word means "rebirth," and it referred to the renewal of the antique spirit. We know today that this spirit was chiefly a mask; it was not the spirit of antiquity that was reborn, but the spirit of medieval Christianity that underwent strange pagan transformations, exchanging the heavenly goal for an earthly one, and the vertical of the Gothic style for a horizontal perspective (voyages of discovery, exploration of the world and of nature). The subsequent developments that led to the Enlightenment and the French Revolution have produced a worldwide situation today which can only be called "antichristian" in a sense that confirms the early Christian anticipation of the "end of time." It is as if, with the coming of Christ, opposites that were latent till then had become manifest, or as if a pendulum had swung violently to one side and were now carrying out the complementary movement in the opposite direction. No tree, it is said, can grow to heaven unless its roots reach down to hell. The double meaning of this movement lies in the nature of the pendulum. Christ is without spot, but right at the beginning of his career there occurs the encounter with Satan, the

25 "The Spirit Mercurius," par. 271.

Adversary, who represents the counterpole of that tremendous tension in the world psyche which Christ's advent signified. He is the "mysterium iniquitatis" that accompanies the "sol iustitiae" as inseparably as the shadow belongs to the light, in exactly the same way, so the Ebionites [26] and Euchites [27] thought, that one brother cleaves to the other. Both strive for a kingdom: one for the kingdom of heaven, the other for the "principatus huius mundi." We hear of a reign of a "thousand years" and of a "coming of the Antichrist," just as if a partition of worlds and epochs had taken place between two royal brothers. The meeting with Satan was therefore more than mere chance; it was a link in the chain.

79   Just as we have to remember the gods of antiquity in order to appreciate the psychological value of the anima/animus archetype, so Christ is our nearest analogy of the self and its meaning. It is naturally not a question of a collective value artificially manufactured or arbitrarily awarded, but of one that is effective and present *per se,* and that makes its effectiveness felt whether the subject is conscious of it or not. Yet, although the attributes of Christ (consubstantiality with the Father, co-eternity, filiation, parthenogenesis, crucifixion, Lamb sacrificed between opposites, One divided into Many, etc.) undoubtedly mark him out as an embodiment of the self, looked at from the psychological angle he corresponds to only one half of the archetype. The other half appears in the Antichrist. The latter is just as much a manifestation of the self, except that he consists of its dark aspect. Both are Christian symbols, and they have the same meaning as the image of the Saviour crucified between two thieves. This great symbol tells us that the progressive development and differentiation of consciousness leads to an ever more menacing awareness of the conflict and involves nothing less than a crucifixion of the ego, its agonizing suspension between irreconcilable opposites.[28] Naturally there can be no question

26 Jewish Christians who formed a Gnostic-syncretistic party.

27 A Gnostic sect mentioned in Epiphanius, *Panarium adversus octoginta haereses,* LXXX, 1–3, and in Michael Psellus, *De daemonibus* (in Marsilius Ficinus, *Auctores Platonici* [*Iamblichus de mysteriis Aegyptiorum*], Venice, 1497).

28 "Oportuit autem ut alter illorum extremorum isque optimus appellaretur Dei filius propter suam excellentiam; alter vero ipsi *ex diametro oppositus,* mali daemonis, Satanae diabolique filius diceretur" (But it is fitting that one of these two extremes, and that the best, should be called the Son of God because of his excel-

of a total extinction of the ego, for then the focus of consciousness would be destroyed, and the result would be complete unconsciousness. The relative abolition of the ego affects only those supreme and ultimate decisions which confront us in situations where there are insoluble conflicts of duty. This means, in other words, that in such cases the ego is a suffering bystander who decides nothing but must submit to a decision and surrender unconditionally. The "genius" of man, the higher and more spacious part of him whose extent no one knows, has the final word. It is therefore well to examine carefully the psychological aspects of the individuation process in the light of Christian tradition, which can describe it for us with an exactness and impressiveness far surpassing our feeble attempts, even though the Christian image of the self—Christ—lacks the shadow that properly belongs to it.

80   The reason for this, as already indicated, is the doctrine of the Summum Bonum. Irenaeus says very rightly, in refuting the

---

lence, and the other, *diametrically opposed* to him, the son of the evil demon, of Satan and the devil) (Origen, *Contra Celsum*, VI, 45; in Migne, *P.G.*, vol. 11, col. 1367; cf. trans. by Chadwick, p. 362). The opposites even condition one another: "Ubi quid malum est . . . ibi necessario bonum esse malo contrarium. . . . Alterum ex altero sequitur: proinde aut utrumque tollendum est negandumque bona et mala esse; aut admisso altero maximeque malo, bonum quoque admissum oportet." (Where there is evil . . . there must needs be good contrary to the evil. . . . The one follows from the other; hence we must either do away with both, and deny that good and evil exist, or if we admit the one, and particularly evil, we must also admit the good.) (*Contra Celsum*, II, 51; in Migne, *P.G.*, vol. 11, col. 878; cf. trans. by Chadwick, p. 106.) In contrast to this clear, logical statement Origen cannot help asserting elsewhere that the "Powers, Thrones, and Principalities" down to the evil spirits and impure demons "do not have it—the contrary virtue—substantially" ("non substantialiter id habeant scl. virtus adversaria"), and that they were not created evil but chose the condition of wickedness ("malitiae gradus") of their own free will. (*De principiis*, I, VIII, 4; in Migne, *P.G.*, vol. 11, col. 179.) Origen is already committed, at least by implication, to the definition of God as the Summum Bonum, and hence betrays the inclination to deprive evil of substance. He comes very close to the Augustinian conception of the *privatio boni* when he says: "Certum namque est malum esse bono carere" (For it is certain that to be evil means to be deprived of good). But this sentence is immediately preceded by the following: "Recedere autem a bono, non aliud est quam effici in malo" (To turn aside from good is nothing other than to be perfected in evil) (*De principiis*, II, IX, 2; in Migne, *P.G.*, vol. 11, cols. 226–27). This shows clearly that an increase in the one means a diminution of the other, so that good and evil represent equivalent halves of an opposition.

Gnostics, that exception must be taken to the "light of their Father," because it "could not illuminate and fill even those things which were within it," [29] namely the shadow and the void. It seemed to him scandalous and reprehensible to suppose that within the pleroma of light there could be a "dark and formless void." For the Christian neither God nor Christ could be a paradox; they had to have a single meaning, and this holds true to the present day. No one knew, and apparently (with a few commendable exceptions) no one knows even now, that the hybris of the speculative intellect had already emboldened the ancients to propound a philosophical definition of God that more or less obliged him to be the Summum Bonum. A Protestant theologian has even had the temerity to assert that "God *can* only be good." Yahweh could certainly have taught him a thing or two in this respect, if he himself is unable to see his intellectual trespass against God's freedom and omnipotence. This forcible usurpation of the Summum Bonum naturally has its reasons, the origins of which lie far back in the past (though I cannot enter into this here). Nevertheless, it is the effective source of the concept of the *privatio boni,* which nullifies the reality of evil and can be found as early as Basil the Great (330–79) and Dionysius the Areopagite (2nd half of the 4th century), and is fully developed in Augustine.

81   The earliest authority of all for the later axiom "Omne bonum a Deo, omne malum ab homine" is Tatian (2nd century), who says: "Nothing evil was created by God; we ourselves have produced all wickedness." [30] This view is also adopted by Theophilus of Antioch (2nd century) in his treatise *Ad Autolycum.*[31]

82   Basil says:

You must not look upon God as the author of the existence of evil, nor consider that evil has any subsistence in itself [ἰδίαν ὑπόστασιν τοῦ κακοῦ εἶναι]. For evil does not subsist as a living being does, nor can we set before our eyes any substantial essence [οὐσίαν ἐνυπόστατον] thereof. For evil is the privation [στέρησις] of good. . . . And thus evil does not inhere in its own substance [ἐν ἰδίᾳ ὑπάρξει], but arises

---

[29] *Adv. haer.,* II, 4, 3.   [30] *Oratio ad Graecos* (Migne, *P.G.,* vol. 6, col. 829). [31] Migne, *P.G.,* vol. 6, col. 1080.

from the mutilation [πηρώμασιν] of the soul.[32] Neither is it uncreated, as the wicked say who set up evil for the equal of good . . . nor is it created. For if all things are of God, how can evil arise from good?[33]

83   Another passage sheds light on the logic of this statement. In the second homily of the *Hexaemeron*, Basil says:

It is equally impious to say that evil has its origin from God, because the contrary cannot proceed from the contrary. Life does not engender death, darkness is not the origin of light, sickness is not the maker of health. . . . Now if evil is neither uncreated nor created by God, whence comes its nature? That evil exists no one living in the world will deny. What shall we say, then? That evil is not a living and animated entity, but a condition [διάθεσις] of the soul opposed to virtue, proceeding from light-minded [ῥαθύμοις] persons on account of their falling away from good. . . . Each of us should acknowledge that he is the first author of the wickedness in him.[34]

84   The perfectly natural fact that when you say "high" you immediately postulate "low" is here twisted into a causal relationship and reduced to absurdity, since it is sufficiently obvious that darkness produces no light and light produces no darkness. The idea of good and evil, however, is the premise for any moral judgment. They are a logically equivalent pair of opposites and, as such, the *sine qua non* of all acts of cognition. From the empirical standpoint we cannot say more than this. And from this standpoint we would have to assert that good and evil, being coexistent halves of a moral judgment, do not derive from one another but are always there together. Evil, like good, belongs to the category of human values, and we are the authors of moral value judgments, but only to a limited degree are we authors of the facts submitted to our moral judgment. These facts are called by one person good and by another evil. Only in capital cases is there anything like a *consensus generalis*. If we hold with Basil that man is the author of evil, we are saying in the same breath that he is also the author of good. But man is first and

32 Basil thought that the darkness of the world came from the shadow cast by the body of heaven. *Hexaemeron*, II, 5 (Migne, *P.G.*, vol. 29, col. 40).
33 *Homilia: Quod Deus non est auctor malorum* (Migne, *P.G.*, vol. 31, col. 341).
34 *De spiritu sancto* (Migne, *P.G.*, vol. 29, col. 37). Cf. *Nine Homilies of the Hexaemeron*, trans. by Blomfield Jackson, pp. 61f.

foremost the author merely of judgments; in relation to the facts judged, his responsibility is not so easy to determine. In order to do this, we would have to give a clear definition of the extent of his free will. The psychiatrist knows what a desperately difficult task this is.

85   For these reasons the psychologist shrinks from metaphysical assertions but must criticize the admittedly human foundations of the *privatio boni*. When therefore Basil asserts on the one hand that evil has no substance of its own but arises from a "mutilation of the soul," and if on the other hand he is convinced that evil really exists, then the relative reality of evil is grounded on a real "mutilation" of the soul which must have an equally real cause. If the soul was originally created good, then it has really been corrupted and by something that is real, even if this is nothing more than carelessness, indifference, and frivolity, which are the meaning of the word ῥαθυμία. When something —I must stress this with all possible emphasis—is traced back to a psychic condition or fact, it is very definitely not reduced to nothing and thereby nullified, but is shifted on to the plane of *psychic reality*, which is very much easier to establish empirically than, say, the reality of the devil in dogma, who according to the authentic sources was not invented by man at all but existed long before he did. If the devil fell away from God of his own free will, this proves firstly that evil was in the world before man, and therefore that man cannot be the sole author of it, and secondly that the devil already had a "mutilated" soul for which we must hold a real cause responsible. The basic flaw in Basil's argument is the *petitio principii* that lands him in insoluble contradictions: it is laid down from the start that the independent existence of evil must be denied even in face of the eternity of the devil as asserted by dogma. The historical reason for this was the threat presented by Manichaean dualism. This is especially clear in the treatise of Titus of Bostra (d. *c.* 370), entitled *Adversus Manichaeos*,[35] where he states in refutation of the Manichaeans that, so far as substance is concerned, there is no such thing as evil.

86   John Chrysostom (*c.* 344–407) uses, instead of στέρησις (*privatio*), the expression ἐκτροπὴ τοῦ καλοῦ (deviation, or turning away,

35 Migne, *P.G.*, vol. 18, cols. 1132f.

from good). He says: "Evil is nothing other than a turning away from good, and therefore evil is secondary in relation to good." [36]

87   Dionysius the Areopagite gives a detailed explanation of evil in the fourth chapter of *De divinis nominibus*. Evil, he says, cannot come from good, because if it came from good it would not be evil. But since everything that exists comes from good, everything is in some way good, but "evil does not exist at all" (τὸ δὲ κακὸν οὔτε ὄν ἐστιν).

88   Evil in its nature is neither a thing nor does it bring anything forth.

Evil does not exist at all and is neither good nor productive of good [οὐκ ἔστι καθόλου τὸ κακὸν οὔτε ἀγαθὸν οὔτε ἀγαθοποιόν].

All things which are, by the very fact that they are, are good and come from good; but in so far as they are deprived of good, they are neither good nor do they exist.

That which has no existence is not altogether evil, for the absolutely non-existent will be nothing, unless it be thought of as subsisting in the good superessentially [κατὰ τὸ ὑπερούσιον]. Good, then, as absolutely existing and as absolutely non-existing, will stand in the foremost and highest place [πολλῷ πρότερον ὑπεριδρύμενον], while evil is neither in that which exists nor in that which does not exist [τὸ δὲ κακὸν οὔτε ἐν τοῖς οὖσιν, οὔτε ἐν τοῖς μὴ οὖσιν].[37]

89   These quotations show with what emphasis the reality of evil was denied by the Church Fathers. As already mentioned, this hangs together with the Church's attitude to Manichaean dualism, as can plainly be seen in St. Augustine. In his polemic against the Manichaeans and Marcionites he makes the following declaration:

For this reason all things are good, since some things are better than others and the goodness of the less good adds to the glory of the better. . . . Those things we call evil, then, are defects in good things, and quite incapable of existing in their own right outside good things. . . . But those very defects testify to the natural goodness of things. For what is evil by reason of a defect must obviously be good of its own nature. For a defect is something contrary to nature, something which damages the nature of a thing—and it can

[36] *Responsiones ad orthodoxas* (Migne, *P.G.*, vol. 6, cols. 1313–14).
[37] Migne, *P.G.*, vol. 3, cols. 716–18. Cf. the *Works of Dionysius the Areopagite*, trans. by John Parker, I, pp. 53ff.

do so only by diminishing that thing's goodness. *Evil therefore is nothing but the privation of good.* And thus it can have no existence anywhere except in some good thing. . . . So there can be things which are good without any evil in them, such as God himself, and the higher celestial beings; but there can be no evil things without good. For if evils cause no damage to anything, they are not evils; if they do damage something, they diminish its goodness; and if they damage it still more, it is because it still has some goodness which they diminish; and if they swallow it up altogether, nothing of its nature is left to be damaged. And so there will be no evil by which it can be damaged, since there is then no nature left whose goodness any damage can diminish.[38]

90   The *Liber Sententiarum ex Augustino* says (CLXXVI): "Evil is not a substance,[39] for as it has not God for its author, it

[38] "Nunc vero ideo sunt omnia bona, quia sunt aliis alia meliora, et bonitas inferiorum addit laudibus meliorum. . . . Ea vero quae dicuntur mala, aut vitia sunt rerum bonarum, quae omnino extra res bonas per se ipsa alicubi esse non possunt. . . . Sed ipsa quoque vitia testimonium perhibent bonitati naturarum. Quod enim malum est per vitium, profecto bonum est per naturam. Vitium quippe contra naturam est, quia naturae nocet; nec noceret, nisi bonum eius minueret. *Non est ergo malum nisi privatio boni.* Ac per hoc nusquam est nisi in re aliqua bona. . . . Ac per hoc bona sine malis esse possunt, sicut ipse Deus, et quaeque superiora coelestia; mala vero sine bonis esse non possunt. Si enim nihil nocent, mala non sunt; si autem nocent, bonum minuunt; et si amplius nocent, habent adhuc bonum quod minuant; et si totum consumunt, nihil naturae remanebit qui noceatur; ac per hoc nec malum erit a quo noceatur, quando natura defuerit, cuius bonum nocendo minuatur." (*Contra adversarium legis et prophetarum,* I, 4f.; in Migne, *P.L.,* vol. 42, cols. 606–7.) Although the *Dialogus Quaestionum LXV* is not an authentic writing of Augustine's, it reflects his standpoint very clearly. Quaest. XVI: "Cum Deus omnia bona creaverit, nihilque sit quod non ab illo conditum sit, unde malum? Resp. Malum natura non est; sed *privatio boni* hoc nomen accepit. Denique bonum potest esse sine malo, sed malum non potest esse sine bono, nec potest esse malum ubi non fuerit bonum. . . . Ideoque quando dicimus bonum, naturam laudamus; quando dicimus malum, non naturam sed vitium, quod est bonae naturae contrarium reprehendimus." (Question XVI: Since God created all things good and there is nothing which was not created by him, whence arises evil? Answer: Evil is not a natural thing, it is rather the name given to the privation of good. Thus there can be good without evil, but there cannot be evil without good, nor can there be evil where there is no good. . . . Therefore, when we call a thing good, we praise its inherent nature; when we call a thing evil, we blame not its nature, but some defect in it contrary to its nature, which is good.)

[39] "Iniquity has no substance" (CCXXVIII). "There is a nature in which there is no evil—in which, indeed, there can be no evil. But it is impossible for a nature to exist in which there is no good" (CLX).

does not exist; and so the defect of corruption is nothing else than the desire or act of a misdirected will." [40] Augustine agrees with this when he says: "The steel is not evil; but the man who uses the steel for a criminal purpose, he is evil." [41]

91   These quotations clearly exemplify the standpoint of Dionysius and Augustine: evil has no substance or existence in itself, since it is merely a diminution of good, which alone has substance. Evil is a *vitium,* a bad use of things as a result of erroneous decisions of the will (blindness due to evil desire, etc.). Thomas Aquinas, the great theoretician of the Church, says with reference to the above quotation from Dionysius:

> One opposite is known through the other, as darkness is known through light. Hence also what evil is must be known from the nature of good. Now we have said above that good is everything appetible; and thus, since every nature desires its own being and its own perfection, it must necessarily be said that the being and perfection of every created thing is essentially good. Hence it cannot be that evil signifies a being, or any form or nature. Therefore it must be that by the name of evil is signified the absence of good.[42]
>
> Evil is not a being, whereas good is a being.[43]
>
> That every agent works for an end clearly follows from the fact that every agent tends to something definite. Now that to which an agent tends definitely must needs be befitting to that agent, since the latter would not tend to it save on account of some fittingness thereto. But that which is befitting to a thing is good for it. Therefore every agent works for a good.[44]

92   St. Thomas himself recalls the saying of Aristotle that "the thing is the whiter, the less it is mixed with black," [45] without mentioning, however, that the reverse proposition: "the thing is the blacker, the less it is mixed with white," not only has the same validity as the first but is also its logical equivalent. He

---

[40] *Augustini Opera omnia,* Maurist edn., X, Part 2, cols. 2561–2618.

[41] *Sermones supposititii,* Sermo I, 3, Maurist edn., V, col. 2287.

[42] *Summa theologica,* I, q. 48, ad 1 (trans. by the Fathers of the English Dominican Province, II, p. 264).   [43] Ibid., I, q. 48, ad 3 (trans., p. 268).

[44] ". . . Quod autem conveniens est alicui est illi bonum. Ergo omne agens agit propter bonum" (*Summa contra Gentiles,* III, ch. 3, trans. by the English Dominican Fathers, vol. III, p. 7).

[45] *Summa theologica,* I, q. 48, ad 2 (trans., II, p. 266, citing Aristotle's *Topics,* iii, 4).

might also have mentioned that not only darkness is known through light, but that, conversely, light is known through darkness.

93   As only that which works is real, so, according to St. Thomas, only good is real in the sense of "existing." His argument, however, introduces a good that is tantamount to "convenient, sufficient, appropriate, suitable." One ought therefore to translate "omne agens agit propter bonum" as: "Every agent works for the sake of what suits it." That's what the devil does too, as we all know. He too has an "appetite" and strives after perfection—not in good but in evil. Even so, one could hardly conclude from this that his striving is "essentially good."

94   Obviously evil can be represented as a diminution of good, but with this kind of logic one could just as well say: The temperature of the Arctic winter, which freezes our noses and ears, is relatively speaking only a little below the heat prevailing at the equator. For the Arctic temperature seldom falls much lower than 230° C. above absolute zero. All things on earth are "warm" in the sense that nowhere is absolute zero even approximately reached. Similarly, all things are more or less "good," and just as cold is nothing but a diminution of warmth, so evil is nothing but a diminution of good. The *privatio boni* argument remains a euphemistic *petitio principii* no matter whether evil is regarded as a lesser good or as an effect of the finiteness and limitedness of created things. The false conclusion necessarily follows from the premise "Deus = Summum Bonum," since it is unthinkable that the perfect good could ever have created evil. It merely created the good and the less good (which last is simply called "worse" by laymen).[46] Just as we freeze miserably despite a temperature of 230° above absolute zero, so there are people and things that, although created by God, are good only to the minimal and bad to the maximal degree.

95   It is probably from this tendency to deny any reality to evil that we get the axiom "Omne bonum a Deo, omne malum ab homine." This is a contradiction of the truth that he who created the heat is also responsible for the cold ("the goodness of the less good"). We can certainly hand it to Augustine that

---

46 In the Decrees of the 4th Lateran Council we read: "For the devil and the other demons as created by God were naturally good, but became evil of their own motion." Denzinger and Bannwart, *Enchiridion symbolorum*, p. 189.

all natures are good, yet just not good enough to prevent their badness from being equally obvious.

*

96   One could hardly call the things that have happened, and still happen, in the concentration camps of the dictator states an "accidental lack of perfection"—it would sound like mockery.

97   Psychology does not know what good and evil are in themselves; it knows them only as judgments about relationships. "Good" is what seems suitable, acceptable, or valuable from a certain point of view; evil is its opposite. If the things we call good are "really" good, then there must be evil things that are "real" too. It is evident that psychology is concerned with a more or less subjective judgment, i.e., with a psychic antithesis that cannot be avoided in naming value relationships: "good" denotes something that is not bad, and "bad" something that is not good. There are things which from a certain point of view are extremely evil, that is to say dangerous. There are also things in human nature which are very dangerous and which therefore seem proportionately evil to anyone standing in their line of fire. It is pointless to gloss over these evil things, because that only lulls one into a sense of false security. Human nature is capable of an infinite amount of evil, and the evil deeds are as real as the good ones so far as human experience goes and so far as the psyche judges and differentiates between them. Only unconsciousness makes no difference between good and evil. Inside the psychological realm one honestly does not know which of them predominates in the world. We hope, merely, that good does—i.e., what seems suitable to us. No one could possibly say what the general good might be. No amount of insight into the relativity and fallibility of our moral judgment can deliver us from these defects, and those who deem themselves beyond good and evil are usually the worst tormentors of mankind, because they are twisted with the pain and fear of their own sickness.

98   Today as never before it is important that human beings should not overlook the danger of the evil lurking within them. It is unfortunately only too real, which is why psychology must insist on the reality of evil and must reject any definition that regards it as insignificant or actually non-existent. Psychology is an empirical science and deals with realities. As a psychologist,

therefore, I have neither the inclination nor the competence to mix myself up with metaphysics. Only, I have to get polemical when metaphysics encroaches on experience and interprets it in a way that is not justified empirically. My criticism of the *privatio boni* holds only so far as psychological experience goes. From the scientific point of view the *privatio boni,* as must be apparent to everyone, is founded on a *petitio principii,* where what invariably comes out at the end is what you put in at the beginning. Arguments of this kind have no power of conviction. But the fact that such arguments are not only used but are undoubtedly believed is something that cannot be disposed of so easily. It proves that there is a tendency, existing right from the start, to give priority to "good," and to do so with all the means in our power, whether suitable or unsuitable. So if Christian metaphysics clings to the *privatio boni,* it is giving expression to the tendency always to increase the good and diminish the bad. The *privatio boni* may therefore be a metaphysical truth. I presume to no judgment on this matter. I must only insist that in our field of experience white and black, light and dark, good and bad, are equivalent opposites which always predicate one another.

99   This elementary fact was correctly appreciated in the so-called Clementine Homilies,[47] a collection of Gnostic-Christian writings dating from about A.D. 150. The unknown author understands good and evil as the right and left hand of God, and views the whole of creation in terms of syzygies, or pairs of opposites. In much the same way the follower of Bardesanes, Marinus, sees good as "light" and pertaining to the right hand (δεξιόν), and evil as "dark" and pertaining to the left hand (ἀριστερόν).[48] The left also corresponds to the feminine. Thus in Irenaeus (*Adv. haer.,* I, 30, 3), Sophia Prounikos is called Sinistra. Clement finds this altogether compatible with the idea of God's unity.

[47] Harnack (*Lehrbuch der Dogmengeschichte,* p. 332) ascribes the Clementine Homilies to the beginning of the 4th cent. and is of the opinion that they contain "no source that could be attributed with any certainty to the 2nd century." He thinks that Islam is far superior to this theology. Yahweh and Allah are unreflected God-images, whereas in the Clementine Homilies there is a psychological and reflective spirit at work. It is not immediately evident why this should bring about a disintegration of the God-concept, as Harnack thinks. Fear of psychology should not be carried too far.
[48] *Der Dialog des Adamantius,* III, 4 (ed. by van de Sande Bakhuyzen, p. 119).

Provided that one has an anthropomorphic God-image—and every God-image is anthropomorphic in a more or less subtle way—the logic and naturalness of Clement's view can hardly be contested. At all events this view, which may be some two hundred years older than the quotations given above, proves that the reality of evil does not necessarily lead to Manichaean dualism and so does not endanger the unity of the God-image. As a matter of fact, it guarantees that unity on a plane beyond the crucial difference between the Yahwistic and the Christian points of view. Yahweh is notoriously unjust, and injustice is not good. The God of Christianity, on the other hand, is *only* good. There is no denying that Clement's theology helps us to get over this contradiction in a way that fits the psychological facts.

100   It is therefore worth following up Clement's line of thought a little more closely. "God," he says, "appointed two kingdoms [βασιλείας] and two ages [αἰῶνας], determining that the present world should be given over to evil [πονηρῷ], because it is small and passes quickly away. But he promised to preserve the future world for good, because it is great and eternal." Clement goes on to say that this division into two corresponds to the structure of man: the body comes from the female, who is characterized by emotionality; the spirit comes from the male, who stands for rationality. He calls body and spirit the "two triads." [49]

Man is a compound of two mixtures [φυραμάτων, lit. 'pastes'], the female and the male. Wherefore also two ways have been laid before him—those of obedience and of disobedience to law; and two kingdoms have been established—the one called the kingdom of heaven, and the other the kingdom of those who are now rulers upon earth. . . . Of these two, the one does violence to the other. Moreover these two rulers are the swift hands of God.

That is a reference to Deuteronomy 32 : 39: "I will kill and I will make to live" (DV). He kills with the left hand and saves with the right.

---

49 The female or somatic triad consist of ἐπιθυμία (desire), ὀργή (anger), and λύπη (grief); the male, of λογισμός (reflection), γνῶσις (knowledge), and φόβος (fear). Cf. the triad of functions in "The Phenomenology of the Spirit in Fairytales," Part I of vol. 9, pars. 425ff.

These two principles have not their substance outside of God, for there is no other primal source [ἀρχή]. Nor have they been sent forth from God as animals, for they were of the same mind [ὁμόδοξοι] with him. . . . But from God were sent forth the four first elements— hot and cold, moist and dry. In consequence of this, he is the Father of every substance [οὐσίας], but not of the knowledge which arises from the mixing of the elements.[50] For when these were combined from without, choice [προαίρεσις] was begotten in them as a child.[51]

That is to say, through the mixing of the four elements inequalities arose which caused uncertainty and so necessitated decisions or acts of choice. The four elements form the fourfold substance of the body (τετραγενὴς τοῦ σώματος οὐσία) and also of evil (τοῦ πονηροῦ). This substance was "carefully discriminated and sent forth from God, but when it was combined from without, according to the will of him who sent it forth, there arose, as a result of the combination, the preference which rejoices in evils [ἡ κακοῖς χαίρουσα προαίρεσις]." [52]

101 The last sentence is to be understood as follows: The fourfold substance is eternal (οὖσα ἀεί) and God's child. But the tendency to evil was added from outside to the mixture willed by God (κατὰ τὴν τοῦ θεοῦ βούλησιν ἔξω τῇ κράσει συμβέβηκεν). Thus evil is not created by God or by any one else, nor was it projected out of him, nor did it arise of itself. Peter, who is engaged in these reflections, is evidently not quite sure how the matter stands.

102 It seems as if, without God's intending it (and possibly without his knowing it) the mixture of the four elements took a wrong turning, though this is rather hard to square with Clement's idea of the opposite hands of God "doing violence to one another." Obviously Peter, the leader of the dialogue, finds it rather difficult to attribute the cause of evil to the Creator in so many words.

103 The author of the Homilies espouses a Petrine Christianity distinctly "High Church" or ritualistic in flavour. This, taken

[50] P. de Lagarde (Clementina, p. 190) has here . . . πάσης οὐσίας . . . οὔσης γνώμης. The reading οὐ τῆς seems to me to make more sense.
[51] Ch. III: τῆς μετὰ τὴν κρᾶσιν.
[52] The Clementine Homilies and the Apostolical Constitutions, trans. by Thomas Smith et al., pp. 312ff. (slightly modified).

together with his doctrine of the dual aspect of God, brings him into close relationship with the early Jewish-Christian Church, where, according to the testimony of Epiphanius, we find the Ebionite notion that God had two sons, an elder one, Satan, and a younger one, Christ.[53] Michaias, one of the speakers in the dialogue, suggests as much when he remarks that if good and evil were begotten in the same way they must be brothers.[54]

104   In the (Jewish-Christian?) apocalypse, the "Ascension of Isaiah," we find, in the middle section, Isaiah's vision of the seven heavens through which he was rapt.[55] First he saw Sammaël and his hosts, against whom a "great battle" was raging in the firmament. The angel then wafted him beyond this into the first heaven and led him before a throne. On the right of the throne stood angels who were more beautiful than the angels on the left. Those on the right "all sang praises with *one* voice," but the ones on the left sang *after* them, and their singing was not like the singing of the first. In the second heaven all the angels were more beautiful than in the first heaven, and there was no difference between them, either here or in any of the higher heavens. Evidently Sammaël still has a noticeable influence on the first heaven, since the angels on the left are not so beautiful there. Also, the lower heavens are not so splendid as the upper ones, though each surpasses the other in splendour. The devil, like the Gnostic archons, dwells in the firmament, and he and his angels presumably correspond to astrological gods and influences. The gradation of splendour, going all the way up to the topmost heaven, shows that his sphere interpenetrates with the divine sphere of the Trinity, whose light in turn filters down as far as the lowest heaven. This paints a picture of complementary opposites balancing one another like right and left hands. Significantly enough, this vision, like the Clementine Homilies, belongs to the pre-Manichaean period (second century), when there was as yet no need for Christianity to fight against its Manichaean competitors. It might easily be a descrip-

53 *Panarium*, ed. by Oehler, I, p. 267.
54 *Clement. Hom.* XX, ch. VII. Since there is no trace in pseudo-Clement of the defensive attitude towards Manichaean dualism which is so characteristic of the later writers, it is possible that the Homilies date back to the beginning of the 3rd cent., if not earlier.
55 Hennecke, *Neutestamentliche Apokryphen,* pp. 309ff.

tion of a genuine yang-yin relationship, a picture that comes closer to the actual truth than the *privatio boni*. Moreover, it does not damage monotheism in any way, since it unites the opposites just as yang and yin are united in Tao (which the Jesuits quite logically translated as "God"). It is as if Manichaean dualism first made the Fathers conscious of the fact that until then, without clearly realizing it, they had always believed firmly in the substantiality of evil. This sudden realization might well have led them to the dangerously anthropomorphic assumption that what man cannot unite, God cannot unite either. The early Christians, thanks to their greater unconsciousness, were able to avoid this mistake.

105   Perhaps we may risk the conjecture that the problem of the Yahwistic God-image, which had been constellated in men's minds ever since the Book of Job, continued to be discussed in Gnostic circles and in syncretistic Judaism generally, all the more eagerly as the Christian answer to this question—namely the unanimous decision in favour of God's goodness [56]—did not satisfy the conservative Jews. In this respect, therefore, it is significant that the doctrine of the two antithetical sons of God originated with the Jewish Christians living in Palestine. Inside Christianity itself the doctrine spread to the Bogomils and Cathars; in Judaism it influenced religious speculation and found lasting expression in the two sides of the cabalistic Tree of the Sephiroth, which were named *hesed* (love) and *din* (justice). A rabbinical scholar, Zwi Werblowsky, has been kind enough to put together for me a number of passages from Hebrew literature which have bearing on this problem.

106   R. Joseph taught: "What is the meaning of the verse, 'And none of you shall go out at the door of his house until the morning?' (Exodus 12 : 22.) [57] Once permission has been granted to the destroyer, he does not distinguish between the righteous and the wicked. Indeed, he even begins with the righteous." [58] Commenting on Exodus 33 : 5 ("If for a single moment I should go up among you, I would consume you"), the midrash says: "Yahweh means he could wax wroth with you for a moment—

[56] Cf. Matt. 19 : 17 and Mark 10 : 18.
[57] A reference to the slaying of the first-born in Egypt.
[58] *Nezikin* I, Baba Kamma 60 (in *The Babylonian Talmud,* trans. and ed. by Isidore Epstein, p. 348 [hereafter abbr. *BT*]; slightly modified).

for that is the length of his wrath, as is said in Isaiah 26 : 20, 'Hide yourselves for a little moment until the wrath is past'— and destroy you." Yahweh gives warning here of his unbridled irascibility. If in this moment of divine wrath a curse is uttered, it will indubitably be effective. That is why Balaam, "who knows the thoughts of the Most High,"[59] when called upon by Balak to curse Israel, was so dangerous an enemy, because he knew the moment of Yahweh's wrath.[60]

107   God's love and mercy are named his right hand, but his justice and his administration of it are named his left hand. Thus we read in I Kings 22 : 19: "I saw the Lord sitting on his throne, and all the host of heaven standing beside him on his right hand and on his left." The midrash comments: "Is there right and left on high? This means that the intercessors stand on the right and the accusers on the left."[61] The comment on Exodus 15 : 6 ("Thy right hand, O Lord, glorious in power, thy right hand, O Lord, shatters the enemy") runs: "When the children of Israel perform God's will, they make the left hand his right hand. When they do not do his will, they make even the right hand his left hand."[62] "God's left hand dashes to pieces; his right hand is glorious to save."[63]

108   The dangerous aspect of Yahweh's justice comes out in the following passage: "Even so said the Holy One, blessed be He: If I create the world on the basis of mercy alone, its sins will be great; but on the basis of justice alone the world cannot exist. Hence I will create it on the basis of justice and mercy, and may it then stand!"[64] The midrash on Genesis 18 : 23 (Abraham's plea for Sodom) says (Abraham speaking): "If thou desirest the world to endure, there can be no absolute justice, while if thou desirest absolute justice, the world cannot endure. Yet thou wouldst hold the cord by both ends, desiring both the world and absolute justice. Unless thou forgoest a little, the world cannot endure."[65]

59 Numbers 24 : 16.   60 Zera'im I, Berakoth 7a (BT, p. 31).
61 Midrash Tanchuma Shemoth XVII.
62 Cf. Pentateuch with Targum Onkelos . . . and Rashi's Commentary, trans. by M. Rosenbaum and A. M. Silbermann, II, p. 76.
63 Midrash on Song of Sol. 2 : 6.
64 Bereshith Rabba XII, 15 (Midrash Rabbah translated into English, ed. by H. Freedman and M. Simon, I, p. 99; slightly modified).
65 Ibid. XXXIX, 6 (p. 315).

¹⁰⁹   Yahweh prefers the repentant sinners even to the righteous, and protects them from his justice by covering them with his hand or by hiding them under his throne.⁶⁶

¹¹⁰   With reference to Habakkuk 2 : 3 ("For still the vision awaits its time. . . . If it seem slow, wait for it"), R. Jonathan says: "Should you say, *We* wait [for his coming] but *He* does not, it stands written (Isaiah 30 : 18), 'Therefore will the Lord wait, that he may be gracious unto you.' . . . But since we wait and he waits too, what delays his coming? Divine justice delays it." ⁶⁷ It is in this sense that we have to understand the prayer of R. Jochanan: "May it be thy will, O Lord our God, to look upon our shame and behold our evil plight. Clothe thyself in thy mercies, cover thyself in thy strength, wrap thyself in thy loving-kindness, and gird thyself with thy graciousness, and may thy goodness and gentleness come before thee." ⁶⁸ God is properly exhorted to remember his good qualities. There is even a tradition that God prays to himself: "May it be My will that My mercy may suppress My anger, and that My compassion may prevail over My other attributes." ⁶⁹ This tradition is borne out by the following story:

R. Ishmael the son of Elisha said: I once entered the innermost sanctuary to offer incense, and there I saw Akathriel ⁷⁰ Jah Jahweh Zebaoth ⁷¹ seated upon a high and exalted throne. He said to me, Ishmael, my son, bless me! And I answered him: May it be Thy will that Thy mercy may suppress Thy anger, and that Thy compassion may prevail over Thy other attributes, so that Thou mayest deal with Thy children according to the attribute of mercy and stop short of the limit of strict justice! And He nodded to me with His head.⁷²

¹¹¹   It is not difficult to see from these quotations what was the effect of Job's contradictory God-image. It became a subject for religious speculation inside Judaism and, through the medium

⁶⁶ *Mo'ed* IV, Pesahim 119 (*BT*, p. 613); *Nezikin* VI, Sanhedrin II, 103 (*BT*, pp. 698ff.).   ⁶⁷ *Nezikin* VI, Sanhedrin II, 97 (*BT*, p. 659; modified).
⁶⁸ *Zera'im* I, Berakoth 16b (*BT*, p. 98; slightly modified).   ⁶⁹ Ibid. 7a (p. 30).
⁷⁰ "Akathriel" is a made-up word composed of *ktr* = *kether* (throne) and *el*, the name of God.
⁷¹ A string of numinous God names, usually translated as "the Lord of Hosts."
⁷² *Zera'im* I, Berakoth 7 (*BT*, p. 30; slightly modified).

of the Cabala, it evidently had an influence on Jakob Böhme. In his writings we find a similar ambivalence, namely the love and the "wrath-fire" of God, in which Lucifer burns for ever.[73]

112   Since psychology is not metaphysics, no metaphysical dualism can be derived from, or imputed to, its statements concerning the equivalence of opposites.[74] It knows that equivalent opposites are necessary conditions inherent in the act of cognition, and that without them no discrimination would be possible. It is not exactly probable that anything so intrinsically bound up with the act of cognition should be at the same time a property of the object. It is far easier to suppose that it is primarily our consciousness which names and evaluates the differences between things, and perhaps even creates distinctions where no differences are discernible.

113   I have gone into the doctrine of the *privatio boni* at such length because it is in a sense responsible for a too optimistic conception of the evil in human nature and for a too pessimistic view of the human soul. To offset this, early Christianity, with unerring logic, balanced Christ against an Antichrist. For how can you speak of "high" if there is no "low," or "right" if there is no "left," of "good" if there is no "bad," and the one is as real as the other? Only with Christ did a devil enter the world as the real counterpart of God, and in early Jewish-Christian circles Satan, as already mentioned, was regarded as Christ's elder brother.

114   But there is still another reason why I must lay such critical stress on the *privatio boni*. As early as Basil we meet with the tendency to attribute evil to the disposition (διάθεσις) of the soul, and at the same time to give it a "non-existent" character. Since, according to this author, evil originates in human frivolity

---

73 *Aurora*, trans. by John Sparrow, p. 423.
74 My learned friend Victor White, O.P., in his *Dominican Studies* (II, p. 399), thinks he can detect a Manichaean streak in me. I don't go in for metaphysics, but ecclesiastical philosophy undoubtedly does, and for this reason I must ask what are we to make of hell, damnation, and the devil, if these things are eternal? Theoretically they consist of nothing, and how does that square with the dogma of eternal damnation? But if they consist of something, that something can hardly be good. So where is the danger of dualism? In addition to this my critic should know how very much I stress the unity of the self, this central archetype which is a *complexio oppositorum* par excellence, and that my leanings are therefore towards the very reverse of dualism.

and therefore owes its existence to mere negligence, it exists, so to speak, only as a by-product of psychological oversight, and this is such a *quantité négligeable* that evil vanishes altogether in smoke. Frivolity as a cause of evil is certainly a factor to be taken seriously, but it is a factor that can be got rid of by a change of attitude. We *can* act differently, if we want to. Psychological causation is something so elusive and seemingly unreal that everything which is reduced to it inevitably takes on the character of futility or of a purely accidental mistake and is thereby minimized to the utmost. It is an open question how much of our modern undervaluation of the psyche stems from this prejudice. This prejudice is all the more serious in that it causes the psyche to be suspected of being the birthplace of all evil. The Church Fathers can hardly have considered what a fatal power they were ascribing to the soul. One must be positively blind not to see the colossal role that evil plays in the world. Indeed, it took the intervention of God himself to deliver humanity from the curse of evil, for without his intervention man would have been lost. If this paramount power of evil is imputed to the soul, the result can only be a negative inflation —i.e., a daemonic claim to power on the part of the unconscious which makes it all the more formidable. This unavoidable consequence is anticipated in the figure of the Antichrist and is reflected in the course of contemporary events, whose nature is in accord with the Christian aeon of the Fishes, now running to its end.

115   In the world of Christian ideas Christ undoubtedly represents the self.[75] As the apotheosis of individuality, the self has the attributes of uniqueness and of occurring once only in time. But since the psychological self is a transcendent concept, expressing the totality of conscious and unconscious contents, it

[75] It has been objected that Christ cannot have been a valid symbol of the self, or was only an illusory substitute for it. I can agree with this view only if it refers strictly to the present time, when psychological criticism has become possible, but not if it pretends to judge the pre-psychological age. Christ did not merely *symbolize* wholeness, but, as a psychic phenomenon, he *was* wholeness. This is proved by the symbolism as well as by the phenomenology of the past, for which— be it noted—evil was a *privatio boni*. The idea of totality is, at any given time, as total as one is oneself. Who can guarantee that our conception of totality is not equally in need of completion? The mere concept of totality does not by any means posit it.

can only be described in antinomial terms; [76] that is, the a attributes must be supplemented by their opposites if the scendental situation is to be characterized correctly. We can ao this most simply in the form of a quaternion of opposites:

116   This formula expresses not only the psychological self but also the dogmatic figure of Christ. As an historical personage Christ is unitemporal and unique; as God, universal and eternal. Likewise the self: as the essence of individuality it is unitemporal and unique; as an archetypal symbol it is a God-image and therefore universal and eternal.[77] Now if theology describes Christ as simply "good" and "spiritual," something "evil" and "material"—or "chthonic"—is bound to arise on the other side, to represent the Antichrist. The resultant quaternion of opposites is united on the psychological plane by the fact that the self is not deemed exclusively "good" and "spiritual"; consequently its shadow turns out to be much less black. A further result is that the opposites of "good" and "spiritual" need no longer be separated from the whole:

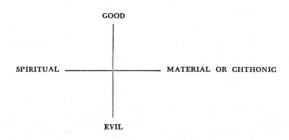

[76] Just as the transcendent nature of light can only be expressed through the image of waves *and* particles.
[77] Cf. *Psychology and Alchemy,* pars. 323ff., and "The Relations between the Ego and the Unconscious," pars. 398ff.

117   This *quaternio* characterizes the psychological self. Being a totality, it must by definition include the light and dark aspects, in the same way that the self embraces both masculine and feminine and is therefore symbolized by the marriage *quaternio*.[78] This last is by no means a new discovery, since according to Hippolytus it was known to the Naassenes.[79] Hence individuation is a "mysterium coniunctionis," the self being experienced as a nuptial union of opposite halves [80] and depicted as a composite whole in mandalas that are drawn spontaneously by patients.

118   It was known, and stated, very early that the man Jesus, the son of Mary, was the *principium individuationis*. Thus Basilides [81] is reported by Hippolytus as saying: "Now Jesus became the first sacrifice in the discrimination of the natures [φυλοκρίνησις], and the Passion came to pass for no other reason than the discrimination of composite things. For in this manner, he says, the sonship that had been left behind in a formless state [ἀμορφία] . . . , needed separating into its components [φυλοκρινηθῆναι], in the same way that Jesus was separated." [82] According to the rather complicated teachings of Basilides, the "non-existent" God begot a threefold sonship (υἱότης). The first "son," whose nature was the finest and most subtle, remained up above with the Father. The second son, having a grosser (παχυμερέστερα) nature, descended a bit lower, but received "some such wing as that with which Plato . . . equips the soul in his *Phaedrus*." [83] The third son, as his nature needed purifying (ἀποκαθάρσις), fell deepest into "formlessness." This third "sonship" is obviously the grossest and heaviest because of its impurity. In these three emanations or manifestations of the non-existent God it is not hard to see the trichotomy of spirit, soul, and body (πνευματικόν, ψυχικόν, σαρκικόν). Spirit is the finest and highest; soul, as the *ligamentum spiritus et corporis*, is grosser than spirit, but has "the wings of an eagle," [84] so that it may lift its heaviness up to

---

78 Cf. "The Psychology of the Transference," pars. 425ff.

79 *Elenchos*, V, 8, 2 (trans. by F. Legge, I, p. 131). Cf. infra, pars. 358ff.

80 *Psychology and Alchemy*, par. 334, and "The Psychology of the Transference," pars. 457ff.   81 Basilides lived in the 2nd cent.

82 *Elenchos*, VII, 27, 12 (cf. Legge trans., II, p. 79).

83 Ibid., VII, 22, 10 (cf. II, pp. 69–70).

84 Ibid., VII, 22, 15 (II, p. 70). The eagle has the same significance in alchemy.

the higher regions. Both are of a "subtle" nature and dwell, like the ether and the eagle, in or near the region of light, whereas the body, being heavy, dark, and impure, is deprived of the light but nevertheless contains the divine seed of the third sonship, though still *unconscious and formless.* This seed is as it were awakened by Jesus, purified and made capable of ascension (ἀναδρομή),[85] by virtue of the fact that the opposites were separated in Jesus through the Passion (i.e., through his division into four).[86] Jesus is thus the prototype for the awakening of the third sonship slumbering in the darkness of humanity. He is the "spiritual inner man." [87] He is also a complete trichotomy in himself, for Jesus the son of Mary represents the incarnate man, but his immediate predecessor is the second Christ, the son of the highest archon of the hebdomad, and his first prefiguration is Christ the son of the highest archon of the ogdoad, the demiurge Yahweh.[88] This trichotomy of Anthropos figures corresponds exactly to the three sonships of the non-existing God and to the division of human nature into three parts. We have therefore three trichotomies:

[85] This word also occurs in the well-known passage about the *krater* in Zosimos. (Berthelot, *Alch. grecs*, III, li, 8: ἀναδραμε ἐπὶ τὸ γένος τὸ σόν.

[86] I must say a word here about the *horos* doctrine of the Valentinians in Irenaeus (*Adv. haer*, I, 2, 2ff.) *Horos* (boundary) is a "power" or numen identical with Christ, or at least proceeding from him. It has the following synonyms: ὁροθέτης (boundary-fixer), μεταγωγεύς (he who leads across), καρπιστής (emancipator), λυτρώτης (redeemer), σταυρός (cross). In this capacity he is the regulator and mainstay of the universe, like Jesus. When Sophia was "formless and shapeless as an embryo, Christ took pity on her, stretched her out through his Cross and gave her form through his power," so that at least she acquired substance (*Adv. haer.*, I, 4). He also left behind for her an "intimation of immortality." The identity of the Cross with Horos, or with Christ, is clear from the text, an image that we find also in Paulinus of Nola:

> ". . . regnare deum super omnia Christum,
> qui cruce dispensa per quattuor extima ligni
> quattuor adtingit dimensum partibus orbem,
> ut trahat ad uitam populos ex omnibus oris."

(Christ reigns over all things as God, who, on the outstretched cross, reaches out through the four extremities of the wood to the four parts of the wide world, that he may draw unto life the peoples from all lands.) (*Carmina*, ed. by Wilhelm Hartel, Carm. XIX, 639ff., p. 140.) For the Cross as God's "lightning" cf. "A Study in the Process of Individuation," pars. 535f.

[87] *Elenchos*, VII, 27, 5 (Legge trans., II, p. 78).

[88] Ibid., VII, 26, 5 (II, p. 75).

I	II	III
First sonship	*Christ of the Ogdoad*	*Spirit*
Second sonship	*Christ of the Hebdomad*	*Soul*
Third sonship	*Jesus the Son of Mary*	*Body*

¹¹⁹   It is in the sphere of the dark, heavy body that we must look for the ἀμορφία, the "formlessness" wherein the third sonship lies hidden. As suggested above, this formlessness seems to be practically the equivalent of "unconsciousness." G. Quispel has drawn attention to the concepts of ἀγνωσία in Epiphanius ⁸⁹ and ἀνόητον in Hippolytus,⁹⁰ which are best translated by "unconscious." Ἀμορφία, ἀγνωσία, and ἀνόητον all refer to the initial state of things, to the potentiality of unconscious contents, aptly formulated by Basilides as οὐκ ὂν σπέρμα τοῦ κόσμου πολύμορφον ὁμοῦ καὶ πολυούσιον (the non-existent, many-formed, and all-empowering seed of the world).⁹¹

¹²⁰   This picture of the third sonship has certain analogies with the medieval *filius philosophorum* and the *filius macrocosmi*, who also symbolize the world-soul slumbering in matter.⁹² Even with Basilides the body acquires a special and unexpected significance, since in it and its materiality is lodged a third of the revealed Godhead. This means nothing less than that matter is predicated as having considerable numinosity in itself, and I see this as an anticipation of the "mystic" significance which matter subsequently assumed in alchemy and—later on—in natural science. From a psychological point of view it is par-

---

⁸⁹ *Panarium*, XXXI, 5 (Oehler edn., I, p. 314).

⁹⁰ *Elenchos*, VII, 22, 16 (Legge trans., II, p. 71). Cf. infra, pars. 298ff.

⁹¹ Ibid., 20, 5 (cf. II, p. 66). Quispel, "Note sur 'Basilide'."

⁹² With reference to the psychological nature of Gnostic sayings, see Quispel's "Philo und die altchristliche Häresie," p. 432, where he quotes Irenaeus (*Adv. haer.*, II, 4, 2): "Id quod extra et quod intus dicere eos secundum agnitionem et ignorantiam, sed non secundum localem sententiam" (In speaking of what is outward and what is inward, they refer, not to place, but to what is known and what is not known). (Cf. Legge, I, p. 127.) The sentence that follows immediately after this—"But in the Pleroma, or in that which is contained by the Father, everything that the demiurge or the angels have created is contained by the unspeakable greatness, as the centre in a circle"—is therefore to be taken as a description of unconscious contents. Quispel's view of projection calls for the critical remark that projection does not do away with the *reality* of a psychic content. Nor can a fact be called "unreal" merely because it cannot be described as other than "psychic." Psyche is reality par excellence.

ticularly important that Jesus corresponds to the third sonship and is the prototype of the "awakener" because the opposites were separated in him through the Passion and so became conscious, whereas in the third sonship itself they remain unconscious so long as the latter is formless and undifferentiated. This amounts to saying that in unconscious humanity there is a latent seed that corresponds to the prototype Jesus. Just as the man Jesus became conscious only through the light that emanated from the higher Christ and separated the natures in him, so the seed in unconscious humanity is awakened by the light emanating from Jesus, and is thereby impelled to a similar discrimination of opposites. This view is entirely in accord with the psychological fact that the archetypal image of the self has been shown to occur in dreams even when no such conceptions exist in the conscious mind of the dreamer.[93]

*

121   I would not like to end this chapter without a few final remarks that are forced on me by the importance of the material we have been discussing. The standpoint of a psychology whose subject is the phenomenology of the psyche is evidently something that is not easy to grasp and is very often misunderstood. If, therefore, at the risk of repeating myself, I come back to fundamentals, I do so only in order to forestall certain wrong impressions which might be occasioned by what I have said, and to spare my reader unnecessary difficulties.

122   The parallel I have drawn here between Christ and the self is not to be taken as anything more than a psychological one, just as the parallel with the fish is mythological. There is no question of any intrusion into the sphere of metaphysics, i.e., of faith. The images of God and Christ which man's religious fantasy projects cannot avoid being anthropomorphic and are admitted to be so; hence they are capable of psychological elucidation like any other symbols. Just as the ancients believed that they had said something important about Christ with their fish symbol, so it seemed to the alchemists that their parallel with the stone served to illuminate and deepen the meaning of the Christ-image. In the course of time, the fish symbolism

93 Cf. *Psychology and Alchemy*, pars. 52ff., 122ff., and "A Study in the Process of Individuation," pars. 542, 550, 581f.

disappeared completely, and so likewise did the *lapis philoso-phorum*. Concerning this latter symbol, however, there are plenty of statements to be found which show it in a special light —views and ideas which attach such importance to the stone that one begins to wonder whether, in the end, it was Christ who was taken as a symbol of the stone rather than the other way round. This marks a development which—with the help of certain ideas in the epistles of John and Paul—includes Christ in the realm of immediate inner experience and makes him appear as the figure of the total man. It also links up directly with the psychological evidence for the existence of an archetypal content possessing all those qualities which are characteristic of the Christ-image in its archaic and medieval forms. Modern psychology is therefore confronted with a question very like the one that faced the alchemists: Is the self a symbol of Christ, or is Christ a symbol of the self?

¹²³ In the present study I have affirmed the latter alternative. I have tried to show how the traditional Christ-image concentrates upon itself the characteristics of an archetype—the archetype of the self. My aim and method do not purport to be anything more in principle than, shall we say, the efforts of an art historian to trace the various influences which have contributed towards the formation of a particular Christ-image. Thus we find the concept of the archetype in the history of art as well as in philology and textual criticism. The psychological archetype differs from its parallels in other fields only in one respect: it refers to a living and ubiquitous psychic fact, and this naturally shows the whole situation in a rather different light. One is then tempted to attach greater importance to the immediate and living presence of the archetype than to the idea of the historical Christ. As I have said, there is among certain of the alchemists, too, a tendency to give the *lapis* priority over Christ. Since I am far from cherishing any missionary intentions, I must expressly emphasize that I am not concerned here with confessions of faith but with proven scientific facts. If one inclines to regard the archetype of the self as the real agent and hence takes Christ as a symbol of the self, one must bear in mind that there is a considerable difference between *perfection* and *completeness*. The Christ-image is as good as perfect (at least it is meant to be so), while the archetype (so far as known) denotes completeness

but is far from being perfect. It is a paradox, a statement about something indescribable and transcendental. Accordingly the realization of the self, which would logically follow from a recognition of its supremacy, leads to a fundamental conflict, to a real suspension between opposites (reminiscent of the crucified Christ hanging between two thieves), and to an approximate state of wholeness that lacks perfection. To strive after teleiosis in the sense of perfection is not only legitimate but is inborn in man as a peculiarity which provides civilization with one of its strongest roots. This striving is so powerful, even, that it can turn into a passion that draws everything into its service. Natural as it is to seek perfection in one way or another, the archetype fulfils itself in completeness, and this is a τελείωσις of quite another kind. Where the archetype predominates, completeness is *forced* upon us against all our conscious strivings, in accordance with the archaic nature of the archetype. The individual may strive after perfection ("Be you therefore perfect—τέλειοι— as also your heavenly Father is perfect." [94]) but must suffer from the opposite of his intentions for the sake of his completeness. "I find then a law, that, when I would do good, evil is present with me." [95]

124   The Christ-image fully corresponds to this situation: Christ is the perfect man who is crucified. One could hardly think of a truer picture of the goal of ethical endeavour. At any rate the transcendental idea of the self that serves psychology as a working hypothesis can never match that image because, although it is a symbol, it lacks the character of a revelatory historical event. Like the related ideas of *atman* and *tao* in the East, the idea of the self is at least in part a product of cognition, grounded neither on faith nor on metaphysical speculation but on the experience that under certain conditions the unconscious spontaneously brings forth an archetypal symbol of wholeness. From this we must conclude that some such archetype occurs universally and is endowed with a certain numinosity. And there is in fact any amount of historical evidence as well as modern case material to prove this.[96] These naïve and completely uninfluenced pictorial representations of the symbol show that it is given central and supreme importance precisely because it

94 Matt. 5 : 48 (DV).   95 Rom. 7 : 21 (AV).
96 Cf. the last two papers in Part I of vol. 9.

stands for the conjunction of opposites. Naturally the conjunction can only be understood as a paradox, since a union of opposites can be thought of only as their annihilation. Paradox is a characteristic of all transcendental situations because it alone gives adequate expression to their indescribable nature.

125   Whenever the archetype of the self predominates, the inevitable psychological consequence is a state of conflict vividly exemplified by the Christian symbol of crucifixion—that acute state of unredeemedness which comes to an end only with the words "consummatum est." Recognition of the archetype, therefore, does not in any way circumvent the Christian mystery; rather, it forcibly creates the psychological preconditions without which "redemption" would appear meaningless. "Redemption" does not mean that a burden is taken from one's shoulders which one was never meant to bear. Only the "complete" person knows how unbearable man is to himself. So far as I can see, no relevant objection could be raised from the Christian point of view against anyone accepting the task of individuation imposed on us by nature, and the recognition of our wholeness or completeness, as a binding personal commitment. If he does this consciously and intentionally, he avoids all the unhappy consequences of repressed individuation. In other words, if he voluntarily takes the burden of completeness on himself, he need not find it "happening" to him against his will in a negative form. This is as much as to say that anyone who is destined to descend into a deep pit had better set about it with all the necessary precautions rather than risk falling into the hole backwards.

126   The irreconcilable nature of the opposites in Christian psychology is due to their moral accentuation. This accentuation seems natural to us, although, looked at historically, it is a legacy from the Old Testament with its emphasis on righteousness in the eyes of the law. Such an influence is notably lacking in the East, in the philosophical religions of India and China. Without stopping to discuss the question of whether this exacerbation of the opposites, much as it increases suffering, may not after all correspond to a higher degree of truth, I should like merely to express the hope that the present world situation may be looked upon in the light of the psychological rule alluded to above. Today humanity, as never before, is split into two apparently irrec-

oncilable halves. The psychological rule says that when an inner situation is not made conscious, it happens outside, as fate. That is to say, when the individual remains undivided and does not become conscious of his inner opposite, the world must perforce act out the conflict and be torn into opposing halves.

II

THE PHENOMENOLOGY OF THE
SPIRIT IN FAIRY TALES

THE PHENOMENOLOGY OF THE SPIRIT
IN FAIRYTALES [1]

384   One of the unbreakable rules in scientific research is to take an object as known only so far as the inquirer is in a position to make scientifically valid statements about it. "Valid" in this sense simply means what can be verified by facts. The object of inquiry is the natural phenomenon. Now in psychology, one of the most important phenomena is the *statement,* and in particular its form and content, the latter aspect being perhaps the more significant with regard to the nature of the psyche. The first task that ordinarily presents itself is the description and arrangement of events, then comes the closer examination into the laws of their living behaviour. To inquire into the *substance* of what has been observed is possible in natural science only where there is an Archimedean point outside. For the psyche, no such outside standpoint exists—only the psyche can observe the psyche. Consequently, knowledge of the psychic substance is impossible for us, at least with the means at present available. This does not rule out the possibility that the atomic physics of the future may supply us with the said Archimedean point. For the time being, however, our subtlest lucubrations can establish no more than is expressed in the statement: this is how the psyche behaves. The honest investigator will piously refrain from meddling with questions of substance. I do not think it superfluous to acquaint my reader with the necessary limitations that psychology voluntarily imposes on itself, for he will then be in a position to appreciate the phenomenological standpoint of modern psychology, which is not always understood. This

---

1 [First published as a lecture, "Zur Psychologie des Geistes," in the *Eranos-Jahr-buch 1945.* Revised and published as "Zur Phänomenologie des Geistes im Märchen," in *Symbolik des Geistes* (Zurich, 1948), from which the present translation was made. This translation was published in a slightly different form in *Spirit and Nature* (Papers from the Eranos Yearbooks, 1; New York, 1953; London, 1954).—EDITORS.]

standpoint does not exclude the existence of faith, conviction, and experienced certainties of whatever description, nor does it contest their possible validity. Great as is their importance for the individual and for collective life, psychology completely lacks the means to prove their validity in the scientific sense. One may lament this incapacity on the part of science, but that does not enable it to jump over its own shadow.

I. CONCERNING THE WORD 'SPIRIT'

385   The word "spirit" possesses such a wide range of application that it requires considerable effort to make clear to oneself all the things it can mean. Spirit, we say, is the principle that stands in opposition to matter. By this we understand an immaterial substance or form of existence which on the highest and most universal level is called "God." We imagine this immaterial substance also as the vehicle of psychic phenomena or even of life itself. In contradiction to this view there stands the antithesis: spirit and nature. Here the concept of spirit is restricted to the supernatural or anti-natural, and has lost its substantial connection with psyche and life. A similar restriction is implied in Spinoza's view that spirit is an attribute of the One Substance. Hylozoism goes even further, taking spirit to be a quality of matter.

386   A very widespread view conceives spirit as a higher and psyche as a lower principle of activity, and conversely the alchemists thought of spirit as the *ligamentum animae et corporis*, obviously regarding it as a *spiritus vegetativus* (the later life-spirit or nerve-spirit). Equally common is the view that spirit and psyche are essentially the same and can be separated only arbitrarily. Wundt takes spirit as "the inner being, regardless of any connection with an outer being." Others restrict spirit to certain psychic capacities or functions or qualities, such as the capacity to think and reason in contradistinction to the more "soulful" sentiments. Here spirit means the sum-total of all the phenomena of rational thought, or of the intellect, including the will, memory, imagination, creative power, and aspirations motivated by ideals. Spirit has the further connotation of *sprightliness*, as when we say that a person is "spirited," mean-

ing that he is versatile and full of ideas, with a brilliant, witty, and surprising turn of mind. Again, spirit denotes a certain attitude or the principle underlying it, for instance, one is "educated in the spirit of Pestalozzi," or one says that the "spirit of Weimar is the immortal German heritage." A special instance is the time-spirit, or spirit of the age, which stands for the principle and motive force behind certain views, judgments, and actions of a collective nature. Then there is the "objective spirit," [2] by which is meant the whole stock of man's cultural possessions with particular regard to his intellectual and religious achievements.

387   As linguistic usage shows, spirit in the sense of an attitude has unmistakable leanings towards personification: the spirit of Pestalozzi can also be taken concretistically as his ghost or imago, just as the spirits of Weimar are the personal spectres of Goethe and Schiller; for spirit still has the spookish meaning of the soul of one departed. The "cold breath of the spirits" points on the one hand to the ancient affinity of $\psi v\chi\dot\eta$ with $\psi v\chi\rho\dot o s$ and $\psi\bar v\chi o s$, which both mean 'cold,' and on the other hand to the original meaning of $\pi v\epsilon\bar v\mu a$, which simply denoted 'air in motion'; and in the same way animus and anima were connected with $\check a v\epsilon\mu o s$, 'wind.' The German word Geist probably has more to do with something frothing, effervescing, or fermenting; hence affinities with Gischt (foam), Gäscht (yeast), ghost, and also with the emotional ghastly and aghast, are not to be rejected. From time immemorial emotion has been regarded as possession, which is why we still say today, of a hot-tempered person, that he is possessed of a devil or that an evil spirit has entered into him.[3] Just as, according to the old view, the spirits or souls of the dead are of a subtle disposition like a vapour or a smoke, so to the alchemist spiritus was a subtle, volatile, active, and vivifying essence, such as alcohol was understood to be, and all the arcane substances. On this level, spirit includes spirits of salts, spirits of ammonia, formic spirit, etc.

388   This score or so of meanings and shades of meaning attributable to the word "spirit" make it difficult for the psychologist to delimit his subject conceptually, but on the other hand they lighten the task of describing it, since the many different aspects

2 [An Hegelian term, roughly equivalent to our "spirit of man."—TRANS.]
3 See my "Spirit and Life."

go to form a vivid and concrete picture of the phenomenon in question. We are concerned with a functional complex which originally, on the primitive level, was felt as an invisible, breath-like "presence." William James has given us a lively account of this primordial phenomenon in his *Varieties of Religious Experience*. Another well-known example is the wind of the Pentecostal miracle. The primitive mentality finds it quite nat-ural to personify the invisible presence as a ghost or demon. The souls or spirits of the dead are identical with the psychic activity of the living; they merely continue it. The view that the psyche is a spirit is implicit in this. When therefore some-thing psychic happens in the individual which he feels as belong-ing to himself, that something is his own spirit. But if anything psychic happens which seems to him strange, then it is some-body else's spirit, and it may be causing a possession. The spirit in the first case corresponds to the subjective attitude, in the latter case to public opinion, to the time-spirit, or to the origi-nal, not yet human, anthropoid disposition which we also call the *unconscious*.

389   In keeping with its original wind-nature, spirit is always an active, winged, swift-moving being as well as that which vivifies, stimulates, incites, fires, and inspires. To put it in modern lan-guage, spirit is the dynamic principle, forming for that very reason the classical antithesis of matter—the antithesis, that is, of its stasis and inertia. Basically it is the contrast between life and death The subsequent differentiation of this contrast leads to the actually very remarkable opposition of spirit and nature. Even though spirit is regarded as essentially alive and enliven-ing, one cannot really feel nature as unspiritual and dead. We must therefore be dealing here with the (Christian) postulate of a spirit whose life is so vastly superior to the life of nature that in comparison with it the latter is no better than death.

390   This special development in man's idea of spirit rests on the recognition that its invisible presence is a psychic phenomenon, i.e., one's own spirit, and that this consists not only of uprushes of life but of formal products too. Among the first, the most prominent are the images and shadowy presentations that oc-cupy our inner field of vision; among the second, thinking and reason, which organize the world of images. In this way a tran-

scendent spirit superimposed itself upon the original, natural life-spirit and even swung over to the opposite position, as though the latter were merely naturalistic. The transcendent spirit became the supranatural and transmundane cosmic principle of order and as such was given the name of "God," or at least it became an attribute of the One Substance (as in Spinoza) or one Person of the Godhead (as in Christianity).

391   The corresponding development of spirit in the reverse, hylozoistic direction—*a maiori ad minus*—took place under anti-Christian auspices in materialism. The premise underlying this reaction is the exclusive certainty of the spirit's identity with psychic functions, whose dependence upon brain and metabolism became increasingly clear. One had only to give the One Substance another name and call it "matter" to produce the idea of a spirit which was entirely dependent on nutrition and environment, and whose highest form was the intellect or reason. This meant that the original pneumatic presence had taken up its abode in man's physiology, and a writer like Klages could arraign the spirit as the "adversary of the soul." [4] For it was into this latter concept that the original spontaneity of the spirit withdrew after it had been degraded to a servile attribute of matter. Somewhere or other the *deus ex machina* quality of spirit had to be preserved—if not in the spirit itself, then in its synonym the soul, that glancing, Aeolian [5] thing, elusive as a butterfly (anima, $\psi\nu\chi\eta$).

392   Even though the materialistic conception of the spirit did not prevail everywhere, it still persisted, outside the sphere of religion, in the realm of conscious phenomena. Spirit as "subjective spirit" came to mean a purely endopsychic phenomenon, while "objective spirit" did not mean the universal spirit, or God, but merely the sum total of intellectual and cultural possessions which make up our human institutions and the content of our libraries. Spirit had forfeited its original nature, its autonomy and spontaneity over a very wide area, with the solitary exception of the religious field, where, at least in principle, its pristine character remained unimpaired.

[4] Ludwig Klages, *Der Geist als Widersacher der Seele*.
[5] *Soul*, from Old German *saiwalô*, may be cognate with αἰόλος, 'quick-moving, changeful of hue, shifting.' It also has the meaning of 'wily' or 'shifty'; hence an air of probability attaches to the alchemical definition of *anima* as Mercurius.

In this résumé we have described an entity which presents itself to us as an immediate psychic phenomenon distinguished from other psychisms whose existence is naïvely believed to be causally dependent upon physical influences. A connection between spirit and physical conditions is not immediately apparent, and for this reason it was credited with immateriality to a much higher degree than was the case with psychic phenomena in the narrower sense. Not only is a certain physical dependence attributed to the latter, but they are themselves thought of as possessing a kind of materiality, as the idea of the subtle body and the Chinese *kuei*-soul clearly show. In view of the intimate connection that exists between certain psychic processes and their physical parallels we cannot very well accept the total immateriality of the psyche. As against this, the *consensus omnium* insists on the immateriality of spirit, though not everyone would agree that it also has a reality of its own. It is, however, not easy to see why our hypothetical "matter," which looks quite different from what it did even thirty years ago, alone should be real, and spirit not. Although the idea of immateriality does not in itself exclude that of reality, popular opinion invariably associates reality with materiality. Spirit and matter may well be forms of one and the same transcendental being. For instance the Tantrists, with as much right, say that matter is nothing other than the concreteness of God's thoughts. The sole immediate reality is the psychic reality of conscious contents, which are as it were labelled with a spiritual or material origin as the case may be.

393   The hallmarks of spirit are, firstly, the principle of spontaneous movement and activity; secondly, the spontaneous capacity to produce images independently of sense perception; and thirdly, the autonomous and sovereign manipulation of these images. This spiritual entity approaches primitive man from outside; but with increasing development it gets lodged in man's consciousness and becomes a subordinate function, thus apparently forfeiting its original character of autonomy. That character is now retained only in the most conservative views, namely in the religions. The descent of spirit into the sphere of human consciousness is expressed in the myth of the divine νοῦς caught in the embrace of φύσις. This process, con-

tinuing over the ages, is probably an unavoidable necessity, and the religions would find themselves in a very forlorn situation if they believed in the attempt to hold up evolution. Their task, if they are well advised, is not to impede the ineluctable march of events, but to guide it in such a way that it can proceed without fatal injury to the soul. The religions should therefore constantly recall to us the origin and original character of the spirit, lest man should forget what he is drawing into himself and with what he is filling his consciousness. He himself did not create the spirit, rather the spirit makes *him* creative, always spurring him on, giving him lucky ideas, staying power, "enthusiasm" and "inspiration." So much, indeed, does it permeate his whole being that he is in gravest danger of thinking that he actually created the spirit and that he "has" it. In reality, however, the primordial phenomenon of the spirit takes possession of *him,* and, while appearing to be the willing object of human intentions, it binds his freedom, just as the physical world does, with a thousand chains and becomes an obsessive *idée-force.* Spirit threatens the naïve-minded man with inflation, of which our own times have given us the most horribly instructive examples. The danger becomes all the greater the more our interest fastens upon external objects and the more we forget that the differentiation of our relation to nature should go hand in hand with a correspondingly differentiated relation to the spirit, so as to establish the necessary balance. If the outer object is not offset by an inner, unbridled materialism results, coupled with maniacal arrogance or else the extinction of the autonomous personality, which is in any case the ideal of the totalitarian mass state.

394   As can readily be seen, the common modern idea of spirit ill accords with the Christian view, which regards it as the *summum bonum,* as God himself. To be sure, there is also the idea of an evil spirit. But the modern idea cannot be equated with that either, since for us spirit is not necessarily evil; we would have to call it morally indifferent or neutral. When the Bible says "God is spirit," it sounds more like the definition of a substance, or like a qualification. But the devil too, it seems, is endowed with the same peculiar spiritual substance, albeit an evil and corrupt one. The original identity of substance is

81

still expressed in the idea of the fallen angel, as well as in the close connection between Jehovah and Satan in the Old Testament. There may be an echo of this primitive connection in the Lord's Prayer, where we say "Lead us not into temptation"—for is not this really the business of the *tempter,* the devil himself?

395   This brings us to a point we have not considered at all in the course of our observations so far. We have availed ourselves of cultural and everyday conceptions which are the product of human consciousness and its reflections, in order to form a picture of the psychic modes of manifestation of the factor "spirit." But we have yet to consider that because of its original autonomy,[6] about which there can be no doubt in the psychological sense, the spirit is quite capable of staging its own manifestations spontaneously.

II. SELF-REPRESENTATION OF THE SPIRIT IN DREAMS

396   The psychic manifestations of the spirit indicate at once that they are of an archetypal nature—in other words, the phenomenon we call spirit depends on the existence of an autonomous primordial image which is universally present in the preconscious makeup of the human psyche. As usual, I first came up against this problem when investigating the dreams of my patients. It struck me that a certain kind of father-complex has a "spiritual" character, so to speak, in the sense that the father-image gives rise to statements, actions, tendencies, impulses, opinions, etc., to which one could hardly deny the attribute "spiritual." In men, a positive father-complex very often produces a certain credulity with regard to authority and a distinct willingness to bow down before all spiritual dogmas and values; while in women, it induces the liveliest spiritual aspirations and interests. In dreams, it is always the father-figure from whom the decisive convictions, prohibitions, and wise counsels ema-

6 Even if one accepts the view that a self-revelation of spirit—an apparition for instance—is nothing but an hallucination, the fact remains that this is a spontaneous psychic event not subject to our control. At any rate it is an autonomous complex, and that is quite sufficient for our purpose.

nate. The invisibility of this source is frequently emphasized by the fact that it consists simply of an authoritative voice which passes final judgments.[7] Mostly, therefore, it is the figure of a "wise old man" who symbolizes the spiritual factor. Sometimes the part is played by a "real" spirit, namely the ghost of one dead, or, more rarely, by grotesque gnomelike figures or talking animals. The dwarf forms are found, at least in my experience, mainly in women; hence it seems to me logical that in Ernst Barlach's play *Der tote Tag* (1912), the gnomelike figure of Steissbart ("Rumpbeard") is associated with the mother, just as Bes is associated with the mother-goddess at Karnak. In both sexes the spirit can also take the form of a boy or a youth. In women he corresponds to the so-called "positive" animus who indicates the possibility of conscious spiritual effort. In men his meaning is not so simple. He can be positive, in which case he signifies the "higher" personality, the self or *filius regius* as conceived by the alchemists.[8] But he can also be negative, and then he signifies the infantile shadow.[9] In both cases the boy means some form of spirit.[10] Graybeard and boy belong together. The pair of them play a considerable role in alchemy as symbols of Mercurius.

397   It can never be established with one-hundred-per-cent certainty whether the spirit-figures in dreams are morally good. Very often they show all the signs of duplicity, if not of outright malice. I must emphasize, however, that the grand plan on which the unconscious life of the psyche is constructed is so inaccessible to our understanding that we can never know what evil may not be necessary in order to produce good by enantiodromia, and what good may very possibly lead to evil. Sometimes the *probate spiritus* recommended by John cannot, with the best will in the world, be anything other than a cautious and patient waiting to see how things will finally turn out.

398   The figure of the wise old man can appear so plastically, not only in dreams but also in visionary meditation (or what we call

---

[7] Cf. *Psychology and Alchemy*, par. 115.

[8] Cf. the vision of the "naked boy" in Meister Eckhart (trans. by Evans, I, p. 438).

[9] I would remind the reader of the "boys" in Bruno Goetz's novel *Das Reich ohne Raum*.

[10] Cf. the paper on the "Child Archetype" in this volume, pars. 268f.

"active imagination"), that, as is sometimes apparently the case in India, it takes over the role of a guru.[11] The wise old man appears in dreams in the guise of a magician, doctor, priest, teacher, professor, grandfather, or any other person possessing authority. The archetype of spirit in the shape of a man, hobgoblin, or animal always appears in a situation where insight, understanding, good advice, determination, planning, etc., are needed but cannot be mustered on one's own resources. The archetype compensates this state of spiritual deficiency by contents designed to fill the gap. An excellent example of this is the dream about the white and black magicians, which tried to compensate the spiritual difficulties of a young theological student. I did not know the dreamer myself, so the question of my personal influence is ruled out. He dreamed *he was standing in the presence of a sublime hieratic figure called the "white magician," who was nevertheless clothed in a long black robe. This magician had just ended a lengthy discourse with the words "And for that we require the help of the black magician." Then the door suddenly opened and another old man came in, the "black magician," who however was dressed in a white robe. He too looked noble and sublime. The black magician evidently wanted to speak with the white, but hesitated to do so in the presence of the dreamer. At that the white magician, pointing to the dreamer, said, "Speak, he is an innocent." So the black magician began to relate a strange story of how he had found the lost keys of Paradise and did not know how to use them. He had, he said, come to the white magician for an explanation of the secret of the keys. He told him that the king of the country in which he lived was seeking a suitable tomb for himself. His subjects had chanced to dig up an old sarcophagus containing the mortal remains of a virgin. The king opened the sarcophagus, threw away the bones, and had the empty sarcophagus buried again for later use. But no sooner had the bones seen the light of day than the being to whom they once had belonged*

---

[11] Hence the many miraculous stories about rishis and mahatmas. A cultured Indian with whom I once conversed on the subject of gurus told me. when I asked him who his guru had been, that it was Shankaracharya (who lived in the 8th and 9th cents.) "But that's the celebrated commentator," I remarked in amazement. Whereupon he replied, "Yes, so he was; but naturally it was his spirit," not in the least perturbed by my Western bewilderment.

—the virgin—changed into a black horse that galloped off into the desert. The black magician pursued it across the sandy wastes and beyond, and there after many vicissitudes and difficulties he found the lost keys of Paradise. That was the end of his story, and also, unfortunately, of the dream.

399   Here the compensation certainly did not fall out as the dreamer would wish, by handing him a solution on a plate; rather it confronted him with a problem to which I have already alluded, and one which life is always bringing us up against: namely, the uncertainty of all moral valuation, the bewildering interplay of good and evil, and the remorseless concatenation of guilt, suffering, and redemption. This path to the primordial religious experience is the right one, but how many can recognize it? It is like a still small voice, and it sounds from afar. It is ambiguous, questionable, dark, presaging danger and hazardous adventure; a razor-edged path, to be trodden for God's sake only, without assurance and without sanction.

III. THE SPIRIT IN FAIRYTALES

400   I would gladly present the reader with some more modern dream-material, but I fear that the individualism of dreams would make too high a demand upon our exposition and would claim more space than is here at our disposal. We shall therefore turn to folklore, where we need not get involved in the grim confrontations and entanglements of individual case histories and can observe the variations of the spirit motif without having to consider conditions that are more or less unique. In myths and fairytales, as in dreams, the psyche tells its own story, and the interplay of the archetypes is revealed in its natural setting as "formation, transformation / the eternal Mind's eternal recreation."

401   The frequency with which the spirit-type appears as an old man is about the same in fairytales as in dreams.[12] The old man always appears when the hero is in a hopeless and desperate situation from which only profound reflection or a lucky idea —in other words, a spiritual function or an endopsychic autom-

[12] I am indebted to Mrs. H. von Roques and Dr. Marie-Louise von Franz for the fairytale material used here.

atism of some kind—can extricate him. But since, for internal and external reasons, the hero cannot accomplish this himself, the knowledge needed to compensate the deficiency comes in the form of a personified thought, i.e., in the shape of this sagacious and helpful old man. An Estonian fairytale,[13] for instance, tells how an ill-treated little orphan boy who had let a cow escape was afraid to return home again for fear of more punishment. So he ran away, chancing to luck. He naturally got himself into a hopeless situation, with no visible way out. Exhausted, he fell into a deep sleep. When he awoke, "it seemed to him that he had something liquid in his mouth, and he saw a little old man with a long grey beard standing before him, who was in the act of replacing the stopper in his little milk-flask. 'Give me some more to drink,' begged the boy. 'You have had enough for today,' replied the old man. 'If my path had not chanced to lead me to you, that would assuredly have been your last sleep, for when I found you, you were half dead.' Then the old man asked the boy who he was and where he wanted to go. The boy recounted everything he could remember happening to him up to the beating he had received the previous evening. 'My dear child,' said the old man, 'you are no better and no worse off than many others whose dear protectors and comforters rest in their coffins under the earth. You can no longer turn back. Now that you have run away, you must seek a new fortune in the world. As I have neither house nor home, nor wife nor child, I cannot take further care of you, but I will give you some good advice for nothing.' "

402   So far the old man has been expressing no more than what the boy, the hero of the tale, could have thought out for himself. Having given way to the stress of emotion and simply run off like that into the blue, he would at least have had to reflect that he needed food. It would also have been necessary, at such a moment, to consider his position. The whole story of his life up to the recent past would then have passed before his mind, as is usual in such cases. An anamnesis of this kind is a purpose-

13 *Finnische und estnische Volksmärchen*, No. 68, p. 208 ["How an Orphan Boy Unexpectedly Found His Luck"]. [All German collections of tales here cited are listed under "Folktales" in the bibliography, q.v. English titles of tales are given in brackets, though no attempt has been made to locate published translations. —EDITORS.]

ful process whose aim is to gather the assets of the whole personality together at the critical moment, when all one's spiritual and physical forces are challenged, and with this united strength to fling open the door of the future. No one can help the boy to do this; he has to rely entirely on himself. There is no going back. This realization will give the necessary resolution to his actions. By forcing him to face the issue, the old man saves him the trouble of making up his mind. Indeed the old man is himself this purposeful reflection and concentration of moral and physical forces that comes about spontaneously in the psychic space outside consciousness when conscious thought is not yet—or is no longer—possible. The concentration and tension of psychic forces have something about them that always looks like magic: they develop an unexpected power of endurance which is often superior to the conscious effort of will. One can observe this experimentally in the artificial concentration induced by hypnosis: in my demonstrations I used regularly to put an hysteric, of weak bodily build, into a deep hypnotic sleep and then get her to lie with the back of her head on one chair and her heels resting on another, stiff as a board, and leave her there for about a minute. Her pulse would gradually go up to 90. A husky young athlete among the students tried in vain to imitate this feat with a conscious effort of will. He collapsed in the middle with his pulse racing at 120.

403   When the clever old man had brought the boy to this point he could begin his good advice, i.e., the situation no longer looked hopeless. He advised him to continue his wanderings, always to the eastward, where after seven years he would reach the great mountain that betokened his good fortune. The bigness and tallness of the mountain are allusions to his adult personality.[14] Concentration of his powers brings assurance and is therefore the best guarantee of success.[15] From now on he will

[14] The mountain stands for the goal of the pilgrimage and ascent, hence it often has the psychological meaning of the self. The *I Ching* describes the goal thus: "The king introduces him / To the Western Mountain" (Wilhelm/Baynes trans., 1967, p. 74—Hexagram 17, *Sui*, "Following"). Cf. Honorius of Autun (*Expositio in Cantica canticorum*, col. 389): "The mountains are prophets." Richard of St. Victor says: "Vis videre Christum transfiguratum? Ascende in montem istum, disce cognoscere te ipsum" (Do you wish to see the transfigured Christ? Ascend that mountain and learn to know yourself). (*Benjamin minor*, cols. 53–56.)
[15] In this respect we would call attention to the phenomenology of yoga.

lack for nothing. "Take my scrip and my flask," says the old man, "and each day you will find in them all the food and drink you need." At the same time he gave him a burdock leaf that could change into a boat whenever the boy had to cross water.

404   Often the old man in fairytales asks questions like who? why? whence? and whither?[16] for the purpose of inducing self-reflection and mobilizing the moral forces, and more often still he gives the necessary magical talisman,[17] the unexpected and improbable power to succeed, which is one of the peculiarities of the unified personality in good or bad alike. But the intervention of the old man—the spontaneous objectivation of the archetype—would seem to be equally indispensable, since the conscious will by itself is hardly ever capable of uniting the personality to the point where it acquires this extraordinary power to succeed. For that, not only in fairytales but in life generally, the objective intervention of the archetype is needed, which checks the purely affective reactions with a chain of inner confrontations and realizations. These cause the who? where? how? why? to emerge clearly and in this wise bring knowledge of the immediate situation as well as of the goal. The resultant enlightenment and untying of the fatal tangle often has something positively magical about it—an experience not unknown to the psychotherapist.

405   The tendency of the old man to set one thinking also takes the form of urging people to "sleep on it." Thus he says to the girl who is searching for her lost brothers: "Lie down:

16 There are numerous examples of this: *Spanische und Portugiesische Volksmärchen*, pp. 158, 199 ["The White Parrot" and "Queen Rose, or Little Tom"]; *Russische Volksmärchen*, p. 149 ["The Girl with No Hands"]; *Balkanmärchen*, p. 64 ["The Shepherd and the Three Samovilas (Nymphs)"]; *Märchen aus Iran*, pp. 150ff. ["The Secret of the Bath of Windburg"]; *Nordische Volksmärchen*, I, p. 231 ["The Werewolf"].

17 To the girl looking for her brothers he gives a ball of thread that rolls towards them (*Finnische und Estnische Volksmärchen*, p. 260 ["The Contending Brothers"]). The prince who is searching for the kingdom of heaven is given a boat that goes by itself (*Deutsche Märchen seit Grimm*, pp. 381f. ["The Iron Boots"]). Other gifts are a flute that sets everybody dancing (*Balkanmärchen*, p. 173 ["The Twelve Crumbs"]), or the path-finding ball, the staff of invisibility (*Nordische Volksmärchen*, I, p. 97 ["The Princess with Twelve Pairs of Golden Shoes"]), miraculous dogs (ibid., p. 287 ["The Three Dogs"]), or a book of secret wisdom (*Chinesische Volksmärchen*, p. 258 ["Jang Liang"]).

morning is cleverer than evening." [18] He also sees through the gloomy situation of the hero who has got himself into trouble, or at least can give him such information as will help him on his journey. To this end he makes ready use of animals, particularly birds. To the prince who has gone in search of the kingdom of heaven the old hermit says: "I have lived here for three hundred years, but never yet has anybody asked me about the kingdom of heaven. I cannot tell you myself; but up there, on another floor of the house, live all kinds of birds, and they can surely tell you." [19] The old man knows what roads lead to the goal and points them out to the hero.[20] He warns of dangers to come and supplies the means of meeting them effectively. For instance, he tells the boy who has gone to fetch the silver water that the well is guarded by a lion who has the deceptive trick of sleeping with his eyes open and watching with his eyes shut;[21] or he counsels the youth who is riding to a magic fountain in order to fetch the healing draught for the king, only to draw the water at a trot because of the lurking witches who lasso everybody that comes to the fountain.[22] He charges the princess whose lover has been changed into a werewolf to make a fire and put a cauldron of tar over it. Then she must plunge her beloved white lily into the boiling tar, and when the werewolf comes, she must empty the cauldron over its head, which will release her lover from the spell.[23] Occasionally the old man is a very critical old man, as in the Caucasian tale of the youngest prince who wanted to build a flawless church for his father, so as to inherit the kingdom. This he does, and nobody can discover a single flaw, but then an old man comes along and says, "That's a fine church you've built, to be sure! What a pity the main wall is a bit crooked!" The prince has the church pulled down again

18 *Finnische und estnische Volksmärchen,* loc. cit.

19 *Deutsche Märchen seit Grimm,* p. 382 [op. cit.]. In one Balkan tale (*Balkanmärchen,* p. 65 ["The Shepherd and the Three Samovilas"]) the old man is called the "Czar of all the birds." Here the magpie knows all the answers. Cf. the mysterious "master of the dovecot" in Gustav Meyrink's novel *Der weisse Dominikaner.*

20 *Märchen aus Iran,* p. 152 [op. cit.].

21 *Spanische und Portugiesische Märchen,* p. 158 ["The White Parrot"].

22 Ibid., p. 199 ["Queen Rose, or Little Tom"].

23 *Nordische Volksmärchen,* Vol. I, p. 231f. ["The Werewolf"].

and builds a new one, but here too the old man discovers a flaw, and so on for the third time.[24]

406   The old man thus represents knowledge, reflection, insight, wisdom, cleverness, and intuition on the one hand, and on the other, moral qualities such as goodwill and readiness to help, which make his "spiritual" character sufficiently plain. Since the archetype is an autonomous content of the unconscious, the fairytale, which usually concretizes the archetypes, can cause the old man to appear in a dream in much the same way as happens in modern dreams. In a Balkan tale the old man appears to the hard-pressed hero in a dream and gives him good advice about accomplishing the impossible tasks that have been imposed upon him.[25] His relation to the unconscious is clearly expressed in one Russian fairytale, where he is called the "King of the Forest." As the peasant sat down wearily on a tree stump, a little old man crept out: "all wrinkled he was and a green beard hung down to his knees." "Who are you?" asked the peasant. "I am Och, King of the Forest," said the manikin. The peasant hired out his profligate son to him, "and the King of the Forest departed with the young man, and conducted him to that other world under the earth and brought him to a green hut. . . . In the hut everything was green: the walls were green and the benches, Och's wife was green and the children were green . . . and the little water-women who waited on him were as green as rue." Even the food was green. The King of the Forest is here a vegetation or tree numen who reigns in the woods and, through the nixies, also has connections with water, which clearly shows his relation to the unconscious since the latter is frequently expressed through wood and water symbols.

407   There is equally a connection with the unconscious when the old man appears as a dwarf. The fairytale about the princess who was searching for her lover says: "Night came and the darkness, and still the princess sat in the same place and wept. As she sat there lost in thought, she heard a voice greeting her: 'Good evening, pretty maid! Why are you sitting here so lonely and sad?' She sprang up hastily and felt very confused, and that was no wonder. But when she looked round there was only a tiny little old man standing before her, who nodded his head at her

---

[24] *Kaukasische Märchen*, pp. 35f. ["The False and the True Nightingale"].
[25] *Balkanmärchen*, p. 217 ["The Lubi (She-Devil) and the Fair of the Earth"].

and looked so kind and simple." In a Swiss fairytale, the peasant's son who wants to bring the king's daughter a basket of apples encounters "es chlis isigs Männdli, das frogt-ne, was er do i dem Chratte häig?" (a little iron man who asked what he had there in the basket). In another passage the "Männdli" has "es isigs Chlaidli a" (iron clothes on). By "isig" presumably "eisern" (iron) is meant, which is more probable than "eisig" (icy). In the latter case it would have to be "es Chlaidli vo Is" (clothes of ice).[26] There are indeed little ice men, and little metal men too; in fact, in a modern dream I have even come across a little black iron man who appeared at a critical juncture, like the one in this fairytale of the country bumpkin who wanted to marry the princess.

408   In a modern series of visions in which the figure of the wise old man occurred several times, he was on one occasion of normal size and appeared at the very bottom of a crater surrounded by high rocky walls; on another occasion he was a tiny figure on the top of a mountain, inside a low, stony enclosure. We find the same motif in Goethe's tale of the dwarf princess who lived in a casket.[27] In this connection we might also mention the Anthroparion, the little leaden man of the Zosimos vision,[28] as well as the metallic men who dwell in the mines, the crafty dactyls of antiquity, the homunculi of the alchemists, and the gnomic throng of hobgoblins, brownies, gremlins, etc. How "real" such conceptions are became clear to me on the occasion of a serious mountaineering accident: after the catastrophe two of the climbers had the collective vision, in broad daylight, of a little hooded man who scrambled out of an inaccessible crevasse in the ice face and passed across the glacier, creating a regular panic in the two beholders. I have often encountered motifs which made me think that the unconscious must be the world of the infinitesimally small. Such an idea could be derived rationalistically from the obscure feeling that in all these visions we are dealing with something endopsychic, the inference being that a thing must be exceedingly small in order to fit

---

26 This occurs in the tale of the griffin, No. 84 in the volume of children's fairytales collected by the brothers Grimm (1912), II, pp. 84ff. The text swarms with phonetic mistakes. [The English text (trans. by Margaret Hunt, rev. by James Stern, no. 165) has "hoary."—TRANS.]   27 Goethe, "Die neue Melusine."
28 Cf. "The Visions of Zosimos," par. 87 (III, i, 2–3).

inside the head. I am no friend of any such "rational" con-
jectures, though I would not say that they are all beside the
mark. It seems to me more probable that this liking for dimin-
utives on the one hand and for superlatives—giants, etc.—on the
other is connected with the queer uncertainty of spatial and
temporal relations in the unconscious.[29] Man's sense of proportion, his rational conception of big and small, is distinctly
anthropomorphic, and it loses its validity not only in the realm
of physical phenomena but also in those parts of the collective
unconscious beyond the range of the specifically human. The
atman is "smaller than small and bigger than big," he is "the
size of a thumb" yet he "encompasses the earth on every side
and rules over the ten-finger space." And of the Cabiri Goethe
says: "little in length / mighty in strength." In the same way,
the archetype of the wise old man is quite tiny, almost imperceptible, and yet it possesses a fateful potency, as anyone can
see when he gets down to fundamentals. The archetypes have
this peculiarity in common with the atomic world, which is
demonstrating before our eyes that the more deeply the investigator penetrates into the universe of microphysics the more
devastating are the explosive forces he finds enchained there.
That the greatest effects come from the smallest causes has become patently clear not only in physics but in the field of psychological research as well. How often in the critical moments
of life everything hangs on what appears to be a mere nothing!

409   In certain primitive fairytales, the illuminating quality of
our archetype is expressed by the fact that the old man is identified with the sun. He brings a firebrand with him which he uses
for roasting a pumpkin. After he has eaten, he takes the fire
away again, which causes mankind to steal it from him.[30] In a
North American Indian tale, the old man is a witch-doctor who
owns the fire.[31] Spirit too has a fiery aspect, as we know from
the language of the Old Testament and from the story of the
Pentecostal miracle.

[29] In one Siberian fairytale (*Märchen aus Sibirien*, no. 13 ["The Man Turned to
Stone"]) the old man is a white shape towering up to heaven.
[30] *Indianermärchen aus Südamerika*, p. 285 ["The End of the World and the
Theft of Fire"—Bolivian].
[31] *Indianermärchen aus Nordamerika*, p. 74 [Tales of Manabos: "The Theft of
Fire"].

410   Apart from his cleverness, wisdom, and insight, the old man, as we have already mentioned, is also notable for his moral qualities; what is more, he even tests the moral qualities of others and makes his gifts dependent on this test. There is a particularly instructive example of this in the Estonian fairy-tale of the stepdaughter and the real daughter. The former is an orphan distinguished for her obedience and good behaviour. The story begins with her distaff falling into a well. She jumps in after it, but does not drown, and comes to a magic country where, continuing her quest, she meets a cow, a ram, and an appletree whose wishes she fulfils. She now comes to a wash-house where a dirty old man is sitting who wants her to wash him. The following dialogue develops: "Pretty maid, pretty maid, wash me, do, it is hard for me to be so dirty!" "What shall I heat the stove with?" "Collect wooden pegs and crows' dung and make a fire with that." But she fetches sticks, and asks, "Where shall I get the bath-water?" "Under the barn there stands a white mare. Get her to piss into the tub!" But she takes clean water, and asks, "Where shall I get a bath-switch?" "Cut off the white mare's tail and make a bath-switch of that!" But she makes one out of birch-twigs, and asks, "Where shall I get soap?" "Take a pumice-stone and scrub me with that!" But she fetches soap from the village and with that she washes the old man.

411   As a reward he gives her a bag full of gold and precious stones. The daughter of the house naturally becomes jealous, throws her distaff into the well, where she finds it again in-stantly. Nevertheless she goes on and does everything wrong that the stepdaughter had done right, and is rewarded accord-ingly. The frequency of this motif makes further examples superfluous.

412   The figure of the superior and helpful old man tempts one to connect him somehow or other with God. In the German tale of the soldier and the black princess [32] it is related how the princess, on whom a curse has been laid, creeps out of her iron coffin every night and devours the soldier standing guard over the tomb. One soldier, when his turn came, tried to escape. "That evening he stole away, fled over the fields and mountains,

---

[32] *Deutsche Märchen seit Grimm,* pp. 189ff.

and came to a beautiful meadow. Suddenly a little man stood before him with a long grey beard, but it was none other than the Lord God himself, who could no longer go on looking at all the mischief the devil wrought every night. 'Whither away?' said the little grey man, 'may I come with you?' And because the little old man looked so friendly the soldier told him that he had run away and why he had done so." Good advice follows, as always. In this story the old man is taken for God in the same naïve way that the English alchemist, Sir George Ripley,[33] describes the "old king" as "antiquus dierum"—"the Ancient of Days."

413   Just as all archetypes have a positive, favourable, bright side that points upwards, so also they have one that points downwards, partly negative and unfavourable, partly chthonic, but for the rest merely neutral. To this the spirit archetype is no exception. Even his dwarf form implies a kind of limitation and suggests a naturalistic vegetation-numen sprung from the underworld. In one Balkan tale, the old man is handicapped by the loss of an eye. It has been gouged out by the Vili, a species of winged demon, and the hero is charged with the task of getting them to restore it to him. The old man has therefore lost part of his eyesight—that is, his insight and enlightenment—to the daemonic world of darkness; this handicap is reminiscent of the fate of Osiris, who lost an eye at the sight of a black pig (his wicked brother Set), or again of Wotan, who sacrificed his eye at the spring of Mimir. Characteristically enough, the animal ridden by the old man in our fairytale is a goat, a sign that he himself has a dark side. In a Siberian tale, he appears as a one-legged, one-handed, and one-eyed greybeard who wakens a dead man with an iron staff. In the course of the story the latter, after being brought back to life several times, kills the old man by a mistake, and thus throws away his good fortune. The story is entitled "The One-sided Old Man," and in truth his handicap shows that he consists of one half only. The other half is invisible, but appears in the shape of a murderer who seeks the hero's life. Eventually the hero succeeds in killing his persistent murderer, but in the struggle he also kills the one-sided old man, so that the identity of the two victims is clearly revealed. It is thus possible that the old man is his own opposite, a life-

33 In his "Cantilena" (15 cent.). [Cf. *Mysterium Coniunctionis,* par. 374.]

94

bringer as well as a death-dealer—"ad utrumque peritus" (skilled in both), as is said of Hermes.[34]

414   In these circumstances, whenever the "simple" and "kindly" old man appears, it is advisable for heuristic and other reasons to scrutinize the context with some care. For instance, in the Estonian tale we first mentioned, about the hired boy who lost the cow, there is a suspicion that the helpful old man who happened to be on the spot so opportunely had surreptitiously made away with the cow beforehand in order to give his protégé an excellent reason for taking to flight. This may very well be, for everyday experience shows that it is quite possible for a superior, though subliminal, foreknowledge of fate to contrive some annoying incident for the sole purpose of bullying our Simple Simon of an ego-consciousness into the way he should go, which for sheer stupidity he would never have found by himself. Had our orphan guessed that it was the old man who had whisked off his cow as if by magic, he would have seemed like a spiteful troll or a devil. And indeed the old man has a wicked aspect too, just as the primitive medicine-man is a healer and helper and also the dreaded concocter of poisons. The very word φάρμακον means 'poison' as well as 'antidote,' and poison can in fact be both.

415   The old man, then, has an ambiguous elfin character—witness the extremely instructive figure of Merlin—seeming, in certain of his forms, to be good incarnate and in others an aspect of evil. Then again, he is the wicked magician who, from sheer egoism, does evil for evil's sake. In a Siberian fairytale, he is an evil spirit "on whose head were two lakes with two ducks swimming in them." He feeds on human flesh. The story relates how the hero and his companions go to a feast in the next village, leaving their dogs at home. These, acting on the principle "when the cat's away the mice do play," also arrange a feast, at the climax of which they all hurl themselves on the stores of meat. The men return home and chase out the dogs, who dash off into the wilderness. "Then the Creator spoke to Ememqut [the hero of the tale]: 'Go and look for the dogs with your wife.'" But he gets caught in a terrible snow-storm and has to seek shelter in the hut of the evil spirit. There now follows the

[34] Prudentius, *Contra Symmachum*, I, 94 (trans. by Thomson, I, p. 356). See Hugo Rahner, "Die seelenheilende Blume."

well-known motif of the biter bit. The "Creator" is Ememqut's father, but the father of the Creator is called the "Self-created" because he created himself. Although we are nowhere told that the old man with the two lakes on his head lured the hero and his wife into the hut in order to satisfy his hunger, it may be conjectured that a very peculiar spirit must have got into the dogs to cause them to celebrate a feast like the men and afterwards—contrary to their nature—to run away, so that Ememqut had to go out and look for them; and that the hero was then caught in a snow-storm in order to drive him into the arms of the wicked old man. The fact that the Creator, son of the Self-created, was a party to the advice raises a knotty problem whose solution we had best leave to the Siberian theologians.

416   In a Balkan fairytale the old man gives the childless Czarina a magic apple to eat, from which she becomes pregnant and bears a son, it being stipulated that the old man shall be his godfather. The boy, however, grows up into a horrid little tough who bullies all the children and slaughters the cattle. For ten years he is given no name. Then the old man appears, sticks a knife into his leg, and calls him the "Knife Prince." The boy now wants to set forth on his adventures, which his father, after long hesitation, finally allows him to do. The knife in his leg is of vital importance: if he draws it out himself, he will live; if anybody else does so, he will die. In the end the knife becomes his doom, for an old witch pulls it out when he is asleep. He dies, but is restored to life by the friends he has won.[35] Here the old man is a helper, but also the contriver of a dangerous fate which might just as easily have turned out for the bad. The evil showed itself early and plainly in the boy's villainous character.

417   In another Balkan tale, there is a variant of our motif that is worth mentioning: A king is looking for his sister who has been abducted by a stranger. His wanderings bring him to the hut of an old woman, who warns him against continuing the search. But a tree laden with fruit, ever receding before him, lures him away from the hut. When at last the tree comes to a halt, an old man climbs down from the branches. He regales the king and takes him to a castle, where the sister is living with the old man as his wife. She tells her brother that the old man is a wicked

[35] *Balkanmärchen,* pp. 34ff. ["The Deeds of the Czar's Son and His Two Companions"].

spirit who will kill him. And sure enough, three days after-wards, the king vanishes without trace. His younger brother now takes up the search and kills the wicked spirit in the form of a dragon. A handsome young man is thereby released from the spell and forthwith marries the sister. The old man, appearing at first as a tree-numen, is obviously connected with the sister. He is a murderer. In an interpolated episode, he is accused of enchanting a whole city by turning it to iron, i.e., making it immovable, rigid, and locked up.[36] He also holds the king's sister a captive and will not let her return to her relatives. This amounts to saying that the sister is animus-possessed. The old man is therefore to be regarded as her animus. But the manner in which the king is drawn into this possession, and the way he seeks for his sister, make us think that she has an anima sig-nificance for her brother. The fateful archetype of the old man has accordingly first taken possession of the king's anima— in other words, robbed him of the archetype of life which the anima personifies—and forced him to go in search of the lost charm, the "treasure hard to attain," thus making him the mythical hero, the higher personality who is an expression of the self. Meanwhile, the old man acts the part of the villain and has to be forcibly removed, only to appear at the end as the husband of the sister-anima, or more properly as the bride-groom of the soul, who celebrates the sacred incest that symbol-izes the union of opposites and equals. This bold enantiodromia, a very common occurrence, not only signifies the rejuvenation and transformation of the old man, but hints at a secret inner relation of evil to good and vice versa.

418   So in this story we see the archetype of the old man in the guise of an evil-doer, caught up in all the twists and turns of an individuation process that ends suggestively with the *hieros gamos.* Conversely, in the Russian tale of the Forest King, he starts by being helpful and benevolent, but then refuses to let his hired boy go, so that the main episodes in the story deal with the boy's repeated attempts to escape from the clutches of the magician. Instead of the quest we have flight, which none-theless appears to win the same reward as adventures valiantly sought, for in the end the hero marries the king's daughter. The

36 Ibid., pp. 177ff. ["The Son-in-Law from Abroad"].

97

magician, however, must rest content with the role of the biter bit.

IV. THERIOMORPHIC SPIRIT SYMBOLISM IN FAIRYTALES

419   The description of our archetype would not be complete if we omitted to consider one special form of its manifestation, namely its animal form. This belongs essentially to the theriomorphism of gods and demons and has the same psychological significance. The animal form shows that the contents and functions in question are still in the extrahuman sphere, i.e., on a plane beyond human consciousness, and consequently have a share on the one hand in the daemonically superhuman and on the other in the bestially subhuman. It must be remembered, however, that this division is only true within the sphere of consciousness, where it is a necessary condition of thought. Logic says *tertium non datur*, meaning that we cannot envisage the opposites in their oneness. In other words, while the abolition of an obstinate antinomy can be no more than a postulate for us, this is by no means so for the unconscious, whose contents are without exception paradoxical or antinomial by nature, not excluding the category of being. If anyone unacquainted with the psychology of the unconscious wants to get a working knowledge of these matters, I would recommend a study of Christian mysticism and Indian philosophy, where he will find the clearest elaboration of the antinomies of the unconscious.

420   Although the old man has, up to now, looked and behaved more or less like a human being, his magical powers and his spiritual superiority suggest that, in good and bad alike, he is outside, or above, or below the human level. Neither for the primitive nor for the unconscious does his animal aspect imply any devaluation, for in certain respects the animal is superior to man. It has not yet blundered into consciousness nor pitted a self-willed ego against the power from which it lives; on the contrary, it fulfils the will that actuates it in a well-nigh perfect manner. Were it conscious, it would be morally better than man. There is deep doctrine in the legend of the fall: it is the expression of a dim presentiment that the emancipation of ego-consciousness was a Luciferian deed. Man's whole history con-

sists from the very beginning in a conflict between his feeling of inferiority and his arrogance. Wisdom seeks the middle path and pays for this audacity by a dubious affinity with daemon and beast, and so is open to moral misinterpretation.

421   Again and again in fairytales we encounter the motif of helpful animals. These act like humans, speak a human language, and display a sagacity and a knowledge superior to man's. In these circumstances we can say with some justification that the archetype of the spirit is being expressed through an animal form. A German fairytale [37] relates how a young man, while searching for his lost princess, meets a wolf, who says, "Do not be afraid! But tell me, where is your way leading you?" The young man recounts his story, whereupon the wolf gives him as a magic gift a few of his hairs, with which the young man can summon his help at any time. This intermezzo proceeds exactly like the meeting with the helpful old man. In the same story, the archetype also displays its other, wicked side. In order to make this clear I shall give a summary of the story:

422   While the young man is watching his pigs in the wood, he discovers a large tree, whose branches lose themselves in the clouds. "How would it be," says he to himself, "if you were to look at the world from the top of that great tree?" So he climbs up, all day long he climbs, without even reaching the branches. Evening comes, and he has to pass the night in a fork of the tree. Next day he goes on climbing and by noon has reached the foliage. Only towards evening does he come to a village nestling in the branches. The peasants who live there give him food and shelter for the night. In the morning he climbs still further. Towards noon, he reaches a castle in which a young girl lives. Here he finds that the tree goes no higher. She is a king's daughter, held prisoner by a wicked magician. So the young man stays with the princess, and she allows him to go into all the rooms of the castle: one room alone she forbids him to enter. But curiosity is too strong. He unlocks the door, and there in the room he finds a raven fixed to the wall with three nails. One nail goes through his throat, the two others through the wings. The raven complains of thirst and the young man, moved by pity, gives him water to drink. At each sip a nail falls out,

[37] *Deutsche Märchen seit Grimm,* pp. 1ff. ["The Princess in the Tree"].

and at the third sip the raven is free and flies out at the window. When the princess hears of it she is very frightened and says, "That was the devil who enchanted me! It won't be long now before he fetches me again." And one fine morning she has indeed vanished.

423   The young man now sets out in search of her and, as we have described above, meets the wolf. In the same way he meets a bear and a lion, who also give him some hairs. In addition the lion informs him that the princess is imprisoned nearby in a hunting-lodge. The young man finds the house and the princess, but is told that flight is impossible, because the hunter possesses a three-legged white horse that knows everything and would infallibly warn its master. Despite that, the young man tries to flee away with her, but in vain. The hunter overtakes him but, because he had saved his life as a raven, lets him go and rides off again with the princess. When the hunter has disappeared into the wood, the young man creeps back to the house and persuades the princess to wheedle from the hunter the secret of how he obtained his clever white horse. This she successfully does in the night, and the young man, who has hidden himself under the bed, learns that about an hour's journey from the hunting-lodge there dwells a witch who breeds magic horses. Whoever was able to guard the foals for three days might choose a horse as a reward. In former times, said the hunter, she used to make a gift of twelve lambs into the bargain, in order to satisfy the hunger of the twelve wolves who lived in the woods near the farmstead, and prevent them from attacking; but to him she gave no lambs. So the wolves followed him as he rode away, and while crossing the borders of her domain they succeeded in tearing off one of his horse's hoofs. That was why it had only three legs.

424   Then the young man made haste to seek out the witch and agreed to serve her on condition that she gave him not only a horse of his own choosing but twelve lambs as well. To this she consented. Instantly she commanded the foals to run away, and, to make him sleepy, she gave him brandy. He drinks, falls asleep, and the foals escape. On the first day he catches them with the help of the wolf, on the second day the bear helps him, and on the third the lion. He can now go and choose his reward. The witch's little daughter tells him which horse her mother rides.

This is naturally the best horse, and it too is white. Hardly has he got it out of the stall when the witch pierces the four hoofs and sucks the marrow out of the bones. From this she bakes a cake and gives it to the young man for his journey. The horse grows deathly weak, but the young man feeds it on the cake, whereupon the horse recovers its former strength. He gets out of the woods unscathed after quieting the twelve wolves with the twelve lambs. He then fetches the princess and rides away with her. But the three-legged horse calls out to the hunter, who sets off in pursuit and quickly catches up with them, because the four-legged horse refuses to gallop. As the hunter approaches, the four-legged horse cries out to the three-legged, "Sister, throw him off!" The magician is thrown and trampled to pieces by the two horses. The young man sets the princess on the three-legged horse, and the pair of them ride away to her father's kingdom, where they get married. The four-legged horse begs him to cut off both their heads, for otherwise they would bring disaster upon him. This he does, and the horses are transformed into a handsome prince and a wonderfully beautiful princess, who after a while repair "to their own kingdom." They had been changed into horses by the hunter, long ago.

425   Apart from the theriomorphic spirit symbolism in this tale, it is especially interesting to note that the function of knowing and intuition is represented by a riding-animal. This is as much as to say that the spirit can be somebody's property. The three-legged white horse is thus the property of the demonic hunter, and the four-legged one the property of the witch. Spirit is here partly a function, which like any other object (horse) can change its owner, and partly an autonomous subject (magician as owner of the horse). By obtaining the four-legged horse from the witch, the young man frees a spirit or a thought of some special kind from the grip of the unconscious. Here as elsewhere, the witch stands for a *mater natura* or the original "matriarchal" state of the unconscious, indicating a psychic constitution in which the unconscious is opposed only by a feeble and still-dependent consciousness. The four-legged horse shows itself superior to the three-legged, since it can command the latter. And since the quaternity is a symbol of wholeness and wholeness plays a considerable role in the picture-world of the uncon-

scious,[38] the victory of four-leggedness over three-leggedness is not altogether unexpected. But what is the meaning of the opposition between threeness and fourness, or rather, what does threeness mean as compared with wholeness? In alchemy this problem is known as the axiom of Maria and runs all through alchemical philosophy for more than a thousand years, finally to be taken up again in the Cabiri scene in *Faust*. The earliest literary version of it is to be found in the opening words of Plato's *Timaeus*,[39] of which Goethe gives us a reminder. Among the alchemists we can see clearly how the divine Trinity has its counterpart in a lower, chthonic triad (similar to Dante's three-headed devil). This represents a principle which, by reason of its symbolism, betrays affinities with evil, though it is by no means certain that it expresses nothing but evil. Everything points rather to the fact that evil, or its familiar symbolism, belongs to the family of figures which describe the dark, nocturnal, lower, chthonic element. In this symbolism the lower stands to the higher as a correspondence [40] in reverse; that is to say it is conceived, like the upper, as a triad. Three, being a masculine number, is logically correlated with the wicked hunter, who can be thought of alchemically as the lower triad. Four, a feminine number, is assigned to the old woman. The two horses are miraculous animals that talk and know and thus represent the unconscious spirit, which in one case is subordinated to the wicked magician and in the other to the old witch.

426   Between the three and the four there exists the primary opposition of male and female, but whereas fourness is a symbol of wholeness, threeness is not. The latter, according to alchemy, denotes polarity, since one triad always presupposes another, just as high presupposes low, lightness darkness, good evil. In terms of energy, polarity means a potential, and wherever a

38 With reference to the quaternity I would call attention to my earlier writings, and in particular to *Psychology and Alchemy* and "Psychology and Religion."
39 The oldest representation I know of this problem is that of the four sons of Horus, three of whom are occasionally depicted with the heads of animals, and the other with the head of a man. Chronologically this links up with Ezekiel's vision of the four creatures, which then reappear in the attributes of the four evangelists. Three have animal heads and one a human head (the angel). [Cf. frontispiece to *Psychology and Religion: West and East*.—EDITORS.]
40 According to the dictum in the "Tabula smaragdina," "Quod est inferius, est sicut quod est superius" (That which is below is like that which is above).

potential exists there is the possibility of a current, a flow of events, for the tension of opposites strives for balance. If one imagines the quaternity as a square divided into two halves by a diagonal, one gets two triangles whose apices point in opposite directions. One could therefore say metaphorically that if the wholeness symbolized by the quaternity is divided into equal halves, it produces two opposing triads. This simple reflection shows how three can be derived from four, and in the same way the hunter of the captured princess explains how his horse, from being four-legged, became three-legged, through having one hoof torn off by the twelve wolves. The three-leggedness is due to an accident, therefore, which occurred at the very moment when the horse was leaving the territory of the dark mother. In psychological language we should say that when the unconscious wholeness becomes manifest, i.e., leaves the unconscious and crosses over into the sphere of consciousness, one of the four remains behind, held fast by the *horror vacui* of the unconscious. There thus arises a triad, which as we know—not from the fairytale but from the history of symbolism—constellates a corresponding triad in opposition to it [41]—in other words, a conflict ensues. Here too we could ask with Socrates, "One, two, three—but, my dear Timaeus, of those who yesterday were the banqueters and today are the banquet-givers, where is the fourth?" [42] He has remained in the realm of the dark mother, caught by the wolfish greed of the unconscious, which is unwilling to let anything escape from its magic circle save at the cost of a sacrifice.

427   The hunter or old magician and the witch correspond to the negative parental imagos in the magic world of the unconscious. The hunter first appears in the story as a black raven. He has stolen away the princess and holds her a prisoner. She describes him as "the devil." But it is exceedingly odd that he himself is locked up in the one forbidden room of the castle and fixed to the wall with three nails, as though *crucified*. He is imprisoned, like all jailers, in his own prison, and bound like all who curse. The prison of both is a magic castle at the top of a gigantic tree, presumably the world-tree. The princess belongs to the upper

---

41 Cf. *Psychology and Alchemy*, fig. 54 and par. 539; and, for a more detailed account, "The Spirit Mercurius," par. 271.

42 This unexplained passage has been put down to Plato's "drollery."

region of light near the sun. Sitting there in captivity on the world-tree, she is a kind of *anima mundi* who has got herself into the power of darkness. But this catch does not seem to have done the latter much good either, seeing that the captor is crucified and moreover with three nails. The crucifixion evidently betokens a state of agonizing bondage and suspension, fit punishment for one foolhardy enough to venture like a Prometheus into the orbit of the opposing principle. This was what the raven, who is identical with the hunter, did when he ravished a precious soul from the upper world of light; and so, as a punishment, he is nailed to the wall in that upper world. That this is an inverted reflection of the primordial Christian image should be obvious enough. The Saviour who freed the soul of humanity from the dominion of the prince of this world was nailed to a cross down below on earth, just as the thieving raven is nailed to the wall in the celestial branches of the world-tree for his presumptuous meddling. In our fairytale, the peculiar instrument of the magic spell is the triad of nails. Who it was that made the raven captive is not told in the tale, but it sounds as if a spell had been laid upon him in the triune name.[43]

428   Having climbed up the world-tree and penetrated into the magic castle where he is to rescue the princess, our young hero is permitted to enter all the rooms but one, the very room in which the raven is imprisoned. Just as in paradise there was one tree of which it was forbidden to eat, so here there is one room that is not to be opened, with the natural result that it is entered at once. Nothing excites our interest more than a prohibition. It is the surest way of provoking disobedience. Obviously there is some secret scheme afoot to free not so much the princess as the raven. As soon as the hero catches sight of him, the raven begins to cry piteously and to complain of thirst,[44] and the

43 In *Deutsche Märchen seit Grimm* (I, p. 256 ["The Mary-Child"]) it is said that the "Three-in-One" is in the forbidden room, which seems to me worth noting.
44 Aelian (*De natura animalium*, I, 47) relates that Apollo condemned the ravens to perpetual thirst because a raven sent to fetch water dallied too long. In German folklore it is said that the raven has to suffer from thirst in June or August, the reason given being that he alone did not mourn at the death of Christ, and that he failed to return when Noah sent him forth from the ark. (Köhler, *Kleinere Schriften zur Märchenforschung*, p. 3.) For the raven as an allegory of evil, see the exhaustive account by Hugo Rahner, "Earth Spirit and Divine Spirit in Patristic Theology." On the other hand the raven is closely connected with Apollo

young man, moved by the virtue of compassion, slakes it, not with hyssop and gall, but with quickening water, whereupon the three nails fall out and the raven escapes through the open window. Thus the evil spirit regains his freedom, changes into the hunter, steals the princess for the second time, but this time locks her up in his hunting-lodge on earth. The secret scheme is partially unveiled: the princess must be brought down from the upper world to the world of men, which was evidently not possible without the help of the evil spirit and man's disobedience.

429   But since in the human world, too, the hunter of souls is the princess's master, the hero has to intervene anew, to which end, as we have seen, he filches the four-legged horse from the witch and breaks the three-legged spell of the magician. It was the triad that first transfixed the raven, and the triad also represents the power of the evil spirit. These are the two triads that point in opposite directions.

430   Turning now to quite another field, the realm of psychological experience, we know that three of the four functions of consciousness can become differentiated, i.e., conscious, while the other remains connected with the matrix, the unconscious, and is known as the "inferior" function. It is the Achilles heel of even the most heroic consciousness: somewhere the strong man is weak, the clever man foolish, the good man bad, and the reverse is also true. In our fairytale the triad appears as a mutilated quaternity. If only one leg could be added to the other three, it would make a whole. The enigmatic axiom of Maria runs: ". . . from the third comes the one as the fourth" (ἐκ τοῦ τρίτου τὸ ἓν τέταρτον)—which presumably means, when the third produces the fourth it at once produces unity. The lost component which is in the possession of the wolves belonging to the Great Mother is indeed only a quarter, but, together with the three, it makes a whole which does away with division and conflict.

---

as his sacred animal, and in the Bible too he has a positive significance. See Psalm 147 : 9: "He giveth to the beast his food, and to the young ravens which cry"; Job 38 : 41: "Who provideth for the raven his food? when his young ones cry unto God, they wander for lack of meat." Cf. also Luke 12 : 24. Ravens appear as true "ministering spirits" in I Kings 17 : 6, where they bring Elijah the Tishbite his daily fare.

431   But how is it that a quarter, on the evidence of symbolism, is at the same time a triad? Here the symbolism of our fairytale leaves us in the lurch, and we are obliged to have recourse to the facts of psychology. I have said previously that three functions can become differentiated, and only one remains under the spell of the unconscious. This statement must be defined more closely. It is an empirical fact that only *one* function becomes more or less successfully differentiated, which on that account is known as the superior or main function, and together with extraversion or introversion constitutes the type of conscious attitude. This function has associated with it one or two partially differentiated auxiliary functions which hardly ever attain the same degree of differentiation as the main function, that is, the same degree of applicability by the will. Accordingly they possess a higher degree of spontaneity than the main function, which displays a large measure of reliability and is amenable to our intentions. The fourth, inferior function proves on the other hand to be inaccessible to our will. It appears now as a teasing and distracting imp, now as a *deus ex machina*. But always it comes and goes of its own volition. From this it is clear that even the differentiated functions have only partially freed themselves from the unconscious; for the rest they are still rooted in it and to that extent they operate under its rule. Hence the three "differentiated" functions at the disposal of the ego have three corresponding unconscious components that have not yet broken loose from the unconscious.[45] And just as the three conscious and differentiated parts of these functions are confronted by a fourth, undifferentiated function which acts as a painfully disturbing factor, so also the superior function seems to have its worst enemy in the unconscious. Nor should we omit to mention one final turn of the screw: like the devil who delights in disguising himself as an angel of light, the inferior function secretly and mischievously influences the superior function most of all, just as the latter represses the former most strongly.[46]

432   These unfortunately somewhat abstract formulations are necessary in order to throw some light on the tricky and allusive

[45] Pictured as three princesses, buried neck deep, in *Nordische Volksmärchen*, II, pp. 126ff. ["The Three Princesses in the White Land"].
[46] For the function theory, see *Psychological Types*.

associations in our—save the mark!—"childishly simple" fairy-tale. The two antithetical triads, the one banning and the other representing the power of evil, tally to a hair's breadth with the functional structure of the conscious and unconscious psyche. Being a spontaneous, naïve, and uncontrived product of the psyche, the fairytale cannot very well express anything except what the psyche actually is. It is not only *our* fairytale that depicts these structural psychic relations, but countless other fairytales do the same.[47]

433   Our fairytale reveals with unusual clarity the essentially antithetical nature of the spirit archetype, while on the other hand it shows the bewildering play of antinomies all aiming at the great goal of higher consciousness. The young swineherd who climbs from the animal level up to the top of the giant world-tree and there, in the upper world of light, discovers his captive anima, the high-born princess, symbolizes the ascent of consciousness, rising from almost bestial regions to a lofty perch with a broad outlook, which is a singularly appropriate image for the enlargement of the conscious horizon.[48] Once the masculine consciousness has attained this height, it comes face to face with its feminine counterpart, the anima.[49] She is a personification of the unconscious. The meeting shows how inept it is to designate the latter as the "subconscious": it is not merely "below" consciousness but also above it, so far above it indeed that the hero has to climb up to it with considerable effort. This "upper" unconscious, however, is far from being a "superconscious" in the sense that anyone who reaches it, like our hero, would stand as high above the "subconscious" as above the earth's surface. On the contrary, he makes the disagreeable discovery that his high and mighty anima, the Princess Soul, is bewitched up there and no freer than a bird in a golden cage.

47 I would like to add, for the layman's benefit, that the theory of the psyche's structure was not derived from fairytales and myths, but is grounded on empirical observations made in the field of medico-psychological research and was corroborated only secondarily through the study of comparative symbology, in spheres very far removed from ordinary medical practice.

48 A typical enantiodromia is played out here: as one cannot go any higher along this road, one must now realize the other side of one's being, and climb down again.

49 The young man asks himself, on catching sight of the tree, "How would it be if you were to look at the world from the top of that great tree?"

He may pat himself on the back for having soared up from the flatlands and from almost bestial stupidity, but his soul is in the power of an evil spirit, a sinister father-imago of subterrene nature in the guise of a raven, the celebrated theriomorphic figure of the devil. What use now is his lofty perch and his wide horizon, when his own dear soul is languishing in prison? Worse, she plays the game of the underworld and ostensibly tries to stop the young man from discovering the secret of her imprisonment, by forbidding him to enter that one room. But secretly she leads him to it by the very fact of her veto. It is as though the unconscious had two hands of which one always does the opposite of the other. The princess wants and does not want to be rescued. But the evil spirit too has got himself into a fix, by all accounts: he wanted to filch a fine soul from the shining upper world—which he could easily do as a winged being—but had not bargained on being shut up there himself. Black spirit though he is, he longs for the light. That is his secret justification, just as his being spellbound is a punishment for his transgression. But so long as the evil spirit is caught in the upper world, the princess cannot get down to earth either, and the hero remains lost in paradise. So now he commits the sin of disobedience and thereby enables the robber to escape, thus causing the abduction of the princess for the second time—a whole chain of calamities. In the result, however, the princess comes down to earth and the devilish raven assumes the human shape of the hunter. The other-worldly anima and the evil principle both descend to the human sphere, that is, they dwindle to human proportions and thus become approachable. The three-legged, all-knowing horse represents the hunter's own power: it corresponds to the unconscious components of the differentiated functions.[50] The hunter himself personifies the inferior function, which also manifests itself in the hero as his inquisitiveness and love of adventure. As the story unfolds, he becomes more and more like the hunter: he too obtains his horse from the witch. But, unlike him, the hunter omitted to

---

[50] The "omniscience" of the unconscious components is naturally an exaggeration. Nevertheless they do have at their disposal—or are influenced by—subliminal perceptions and memories of the unconscious, as well as by its instinctive archetypal contents. It is these that give unconscious activities their unexpectedly accurate information.

obtain the twelve lambs in order to feed the wolves, who then injured his horse. He forgot to pay tribute to the chthonic powers because he was nothing but a robber. Through this omission the hero learns that the unconscious lets its creatures go only at the cost of sacrifice.[51] The number 12 is presumably a time symbol, with the subsidiary meaning of the twelve labours (ἄθλα)[52] that have to be performed for the unconscious before one can get free.[53] The hunter looks like a previous unsuccessful attempt of the hero to gain possession of his soul through robbery and violence. But the conquest of the soul is in reality a work of patience, self-sacrifice, and devotion. By gaining possession of the four-legged horse the hero steps right into the shoes of the hunter and carries off the princess as well. The quaternity in our tale proves to be the greater power, for it integrates into its totality that which it still needed in order to become whole.

434   The archetype of the spirit in this, be it said, by no means primitive fairytale is expressed theriomorphically as a system of three functions which is subordinated to a unity, the evil spirit, in the same way that some unnamed authority has crucified the raven with a triad of three nails. The two supraordinate unities correspond in the first case to the inferior function which is the arch-enemy of the main function, namely to the hunter; and in the second case to the main function, namely to the hero. Hunter and hero are ultimately equated with one another, so that the hunter's function is resolved in the hero. As a matter of fact, the hero lies dormant in the hunter from the very beginning, egging him on, with all the unmoral means at his disposal, to carry out the rape of the soul, and then causing him to play her into the hero's hands against the hunter's will. On the surface a furious conflict rages between them, but down below the one goes about the other's business. The knot is unravelled directly the hero succeeds in capturing the quaternity—or in psychological language, when he assimilates the inferior function

51 The hunter has reckoned without his host, as generally happens. Seldom or never do we think of the price exacted by the spirit's activity.
52 Cf. the Heracles cycle.
53 The alchemists stress the long duration of the work and speak of the "longissima via," "diuturnitas immensae meditationis," etc. The number 12 may be connected with the ecclesiastical year, in which the redemptive work of Christ is fulfilled. The lamb-sacrifice probably comes from this source too.

into the ternary system. That puts an end to the conflict at one blow, and the figure of the hunter melts into thin air. After this victory, the hero sets his princess upon the three-legged steed and together they ride away to her father's kingdom. From now on she rules and personifies the realm of spirit that formerly served the wicked hunter. Thus the anima is and remains the representative of that part of the unconscious which can never be assimilated into a humanly attainable whole.

435   *Postscript.* Only after the completion of my manuscript was my attention drawn by a friend to a Russian variant of our story. It bears the title "Maria Morevna." [54] The hero of the story is no swineherd, but Czarevitch Ivan. There is an interesting explanation of the three helpful animals: they correspond to Ivan's three sisters and their husbands, who are really birds. The three sisters represent an unconscious triad of functions related to both the animal and spiritual realms. The bird-men are a species of angel and emphasize the auxiliary nature of the unconscious functions. In the story they intervene at the critical moment when the hero—unlike his German counterpart—gets into the power of the evil spirit and is killed and dismembered (the typical fate of the God-man!).[55] The evil spirit is an old man who is often shown naked and is called Koschei [56] the Deathless. The corresponding witch is the well-known Baba Yaga. The three helpful animals of the German variant are doubled here, appearing first as the bird-men and then as the lion, the strange bird, and the bees. The princess is Queen Maria Morevna, a redoubtable martial leader—Mary the queen of heaven is lauded in the Russian Orthodox hymnal as "leader of hosts"!—who has chained up the evil spirit with twelve chains in the forbidden room in her castle. When Ivan slakes the old devil's thirst he makes off with the queen. The magic riding animals do not in the end turn into human beings. This Russian story has a distinctly more primitive character.

[54] "Daughter of the sea."—Afanas'ev, *Russian Fairy Tales,* pp. 553ff.
[55] The old man puts the dismembered body into a barrel which he throws into the sea. This is reminiscent of the fate of Osiris (head and phallus).
[56] From *kost,* 'bone,' and *pakost, kapost,* 'disgusting, dirty.'

V. SUPPLEMENT

436   The following remarks lay no claim to general interest, being in the main technical. I wanted at first to delete them from this revised version of my essay, but then I changed my mind and appended them in a supplement. The reader who is not specifically interested in psychology can safely skip this section. For, in what follows, I have dealt with the abstruse-looking problem of the three- and four-leggedness of the magic horses, and presented my reflections in such a way as to demonstrate the method I have employed. This piece of psychological reasoning rests firstly on the irrational data of the material, that is, of the fairytale, myth, or dream, and secondly on the conscious realization of the "latent" rational connections which these data have with one another. That such connections exist at all is something of a hypothesis, like that which asserts that dreams have a meaning. The truth of this assumption is not established *a priori:* its usefulness can only be proved by application. It therefore remains to be seen whether its methodical application to irrational material enables one to interpret the latter in a meaningful way. Its application consists in approaching the material as if it had a coherent inner meaning. For this purpose most of the data require a certain amplification, that is, they need to be clarified, generalized, and approximated to a more or less general concept in accordance with Cardan's rule of interpretation. For instance, the three-leggedness, in order to be recognized for what it is, has first to be separated from the horse and then approximated to its specific principle—the principle of threeness. Likewise, the four-leggedness in the fairytale, when raised to the level of a general concept, enters into relationship with the threeness, and as a result we have the enigma mentioned in the *Timaeus,* the problem of three and four. Triads and tetrads represent archetypal structures that play a significant part in all symbolism and are equally important for the investigation of myths and dreams. By raising the irrational datum (three-leggedness and four-leggedness) to the level of a general concept we elicit the universal meaning of this motif and encourage the inquiring mind to tackle the problem seriously. This task involves a series of reflections and deductions of a

111

technical nature which I would not wish to withhold from the psychologically interested reader and especially from the professional, the less so as this labour of the intellect represents a typical unravelling of symbols and is indispensable for an adequate understanding of the products of the unconscious. Only in this way can the nexus of unconscious relationships be made to yield their own meaning, in contrast to those deductive interpretations derived from a preconceived theory, e.g., interpretations based on astronomy, meteorology, mythology, and—last but not least—the sexual theory.

437   The three-legged and four-legged horses are in truth a recondite matter worthy of closer examination. The three and the four remind us not only of the dilemma we have already met in the theory of psychological functions, but also of the axiom of Maria Prophetissa, which plays a considerable role in alchemy. It may therefore be rewarding to examine more closely the meaning of the miraculous horses.

438   The first thing that seems to me worthy of note is that the three-legged horse which is assigned to the princess as her mount is a mare, and is moreover herself a bewitched princess. Threeness is unmistakably connected here with femininity, whereas from the dominating religious standpoint of consciousness it is an exclusively masculine affair, quite apart from the fact that 3, as an uneven number, is masculine in the first place. One could therefore translate threeness as "masculinity" outright, this being all the more significant when one remembers the ancient Egyptian triunity of God, Ka-mutef,[57] and Pharaoh.

439   Three-leggedness, as the attribute of some animal, denotes the unconscious masculinity immanent in a female creature. In a real woman it would correspond to the animus who, like the magic horse, represents "spirit." In the case of the anima, however, threeness does not coincide with any Christian idea of the Trinity but with the "lower triangle," the inferior function triad that constitutes the "shadow." The inferior half of the personality is for the greater part unconscious. It does not denote the whole of the unconscious, but only the personal segment of it. The anima, on the other hand, so far as she is distinguished from the shadow, personifies the collective un-

[57] Ka-mutef means "bull of his mother." See Jacobsohn, "Die dogmatische Stellung des Königs in der Theologie der alten Aegypter," pp. 17, 35, 41ff.

conscious. If threeness is assigned to her as a riding-animal, it means that she "rides" the shadow, is related to it as the *mar*.[58] In that case she possesses the shadow. But if she herself is the horse, then she has lost her dominating position as a personification of the collective unconscious and is "ridden"—possessed —by Princess A, spouse of the hero. As the fairytale rightly says, she has been changed by witchcraft into the three-legged horse (Princess B).

We can sort out this imbroglio more or less as follows:

440   1. Princess A is the anima [59] of the hero. She rides—that is, possesses—the three-legged horse, who is the shadow, the inferior function-triad of her later spouse. To put it more simply: she has taken possession of the inferior half of the hero's personality. She has caught him on his weak side, as so often happens in ordinary life, for where one is weak one needs support and completion. In fact, a woman's place is on the weak side of a man. This is how we would have to formulate the situation if we regarded the hero and Princess A as two ordinary people. But since it is a fairy-story played out mainly in the world of magic, we are probably more correct in interpreting Princess A as the hero's anima. In that case the hero has been wafted out of the profane world through his encounter with the anima, like Merlin by his fairy: as an ordinary man he is like one caught in a marvellous dream, viewing the world through a veil of mist.

441   2. The matter is now considerably complicated by the unexpected fact that the three-legged horse is a mare, an equivalent of Princess A. She (the mare) is Princess B, who in the shape of a horse corresponds to Princess A's shadow (i.e., her inferior function-triad). Princess B, however, differs from Princess A in that, unlike her, she does not ride the horse but is contained in it: she is bewitched and has thus come under the spell of a masculine triad. Therefore, she is possessed by a shadow.

442   3. The question now is, *whose* shadow? It cannot be the shadow of the hero, for this is already taken up by the latter's

---

[58] Cf. *Symbols of Transformation*, pars. 370ff., 421.
[59] The fact that she is no ordinary girl, but is of royal descent and moreover the *electa* of the evil spirit, proves her nonhuman, mythological nature. I must assume that the reader is acquainted with the idea of the anima.

anima. The fairytale gives us the answer: it is the hunter or magician who has bewitched her. As we have seen, the hunter is somehow connected with the hero, since the latter gradually puts himself in his shoes. Hence one could easily arrive at the conjecture that the hunter is at bottom none other than the shadow of the hero. But this supposition is contradicted by the fact that the hunter stands for a formidable power which extends not only to the hero's anima but much further, namely to the royal brother-sister pair of whose existence the hero and his anima have no notion, and who appear very much out of the blue in the story itself. The power that extends beyond the orbit of the individual has a more than individual character and cannot therefore be identified with the shadow, if we conceive and define this as the dark half of the personality. As a supra-individual factor the numen of the hunter is a dominant of the collective unconscious, and its characteristic features— hunter, magician, raven, miraculous horse, crucifixion or suspension high up in the boughs of the world-tree [60]—touch the Germanic psyche very closely. Hence the Christian *Weltanschauung,* when reflected in the ocean of the (Germanic) unconscious, logically takes on the features of Wotan.[61] In the figure of the hunter we meet an *imago dei,* a God-image, for Wotan is also a god of winds and spirits, on which account the Romans fittingly interpreted him as Mercury.

443   4. The Prince and his sister, Princess B, have therefore been seized by a pagan god and changed into horses, i.e., thrust down to the animal level, into the realm of the unconscious. The inference is that in their proper human shape the pair of them

---

[60] "I ween that I hung / on the windy tree,
    Hung there for nights full nine;
With the spear I was wounded, / and offered I was
    To Othin, myself to myself,
On the tree that none / may ever know
    What root beneath it runs."
                    —*Hovamol,* 139 (trans. by H. A. Bellows, p. 60).
[61] Cf. the experience of God as described by Nietzsche in "Ariadne's Lament":
        "I am but thy quarry,
        Cruellest of hunters!
        Thy proudest captive,
        Thou brigand back of the clouds!"
                    —*Gedichte und Sprüche,* pp. 155ff.

once belonged to the sphere of collective consciousness. But who are they?

444   In order to answer this question we must proceed from the fact that these two are an undoubted counterpart of the hero and Princess A. They are connected with the latter also because they serve as their mounts, and in consequence they appear as their lower, animal halves. Because of its almost total unconsciousness, the animal has always symbolized the psychic sphere in man which lies hidden in the darkness of the body's instinctual life. The hero rides the stallion, characterized by the even (feminine) number 4; Princess A rides the mare who has only three legs (3 = a masculine number). These numbers make it clear that the transformation into animals has brought with it a modification of sex character: the stallion has a feminine attribute, the mare a masculine one. Psychology can confirm this development as follows: to the degree that a man is overpowered by the (collective) unconscious there is not only a more unbridled intrusion of the instinctual sphere, but a certain feminine character also makes its appearance, which I have suggested should be called "anima." If, on the other hand, a woman comes under the domination of the unconscious, the darker side of her feminine nature emerges all the more strongly, coupled with markedly masculine traits. These latter are comprised under the term "animus." [62]

445   5. According to the fairytale, however, the animal form of the brother-sister pair is "unreal" and due simply to the magic influence of the pagan hunter-god. If they were nothing but animals, we could rest content with this interpretation. But that would be to pass over in unmerited silence the singular allusion to a modification of sex character. The white horses are no ordinary horses: they are miraculous beasts with supernatural powers. Therefore the human figures out of which the horses were magically conjured must likewise have had something supernatural about them. The fairytale makes no comment here, but if our assumption is correct that the two animal forms correspond to the subhuman components of hero and princess, then it follows that the human forms—Prince and Princess B—must correspond to their superhuman components. The

[62] Cf. Emma Jung, "On the Nature of the Animus."

superhuman quality of the original swineherd is shown by the fact that he becomes a hero, practically a half-god, since he does not stay with his swine but climbs the world-tree, where he is very nearly made its prisoner, like Wotan. Similarly, he could not have become like the hunter if he did not have a certain resemblance to him in the first place. In the same way the imprisonment of Princess A on the top of the world-tree proves her electness, and in so far as she shares the hunter's bed, as stated by the tale, she is actually the bride of God.

446   It is these extraordinary forces of heroism and election, bordering on the superhuman, which involve two quite ordinary humans in a superhuman fate. Accordingly, in the profane world a swineherd becomes a king, and a princess gets an agreeable husband. But since, for fairytales, there is not only a profane but also a magical world, human fate does not have the final word. The fairytale therefore does not omit to point out what happens in the world of magic. There too a prince and princess have got into the power of the evil spirit, who is himself in a tight corner from which he cannot extricate himself without extraneous help. So the human fate that befalls the swineherd and Princess A is paralleled in the world of magic. But in so far as the hunter is a pagan God-image and thus exalted above the world of heroes and paramours of the gods, the parallelism goes beyond the merely magical into a divine and spiritual sphere, where the evil spirit, the Devil himself— or at least *a* devil—is bound by the spell of an equally mighty or even mightier counter-principle indicated by the three nails. This supreme tension of opposites, the mainspring of the whole drama, is obviously the conflict between the upper and lower triads, or, to put it in theological terms, between the Christian God and the devil who has assumed the features of Wotan.[63]

447   6. We must, it seems, start from this highest level if we want to understand the story correctly, for the drama takes its rise from the initial transgression of the evil spirit. The immediate consequence of this is his crucifixion. In that distressing situation he needs outside help, and as it is not forthcoming from above, it can only be summoned from below. A young swine-

[63] As regards the triadic nature of Wotan cf. Ninck, *Wodan und germanischer Schicksalsglaube*, p. 142. His horse is also described as, among other things, three-legged.

herd, possessed with the boyish spirit of adventure, is reckless and inquisitive enough to climb the world-tree. Had he fallen and broken his neck, no doubt everybody would have said, "What evil spirit could have given him the crazy idea of climbing up an enormous tree like that!" Nor would they have been altogether wrong, for that is precisely what the evil spirit was after. The capture of Princess A was a transgression in the profane world, and the bewitching of the—as we may suppose—semidivine brother-sister pair was just such an enormity in the magical world. We do not know, but it is possible, that this heinous crime was committed before the bewitching of Princess A. At any rate, both episodes point to a transgression of the evil spirit in the magical world as well as in the profane.

448   It is assuredly not without a deeper meaning that the rescuer or redeemer should be a swineherd, like the Prodigal Son. He is of lowly origin and has this much in common with the curious conception of the redeemer in alchemy. His first liberating act is to deliver the evil spirit from the divine punishment meted out to him. It is from this act, representing the first stage of the lysis, that the whole dramatic tangle develops.

449   7. The moral of this story is in truth exceedingly odd. The finale satisfies in so far as the swineherd and Princess A are married and become the royal pair. Prince and Princess B likewise celebrate their wedding, but this—in accordance with the archaic prerogative of kings—takes the form of incest, which, though somewhat repellent, must be regarded as more or less habitual in semidivine circles.[64] But what, we may ask, happens to the evil spirit, whose rescue from condign punishment sets the whole thing in motion? The wicked hunter is trampled to pieces by the horses, which presumably does no lasting damage to a spirit. Apparently he vanishes without trace, but only apparently, for he does after all leave a trace behind him, namely a hard-won happiness in both the profane and the magical world. Two halves of the quaternity, represented on one side by the swineherd and Princess A and on the other by

64 The assumption that they are a brother-sister pair is supported by the fact that the stallion addresses the mare as "sister." This may be just a figure of speech; on the other hand sister means sister, whether we take it figuratively or nonfiguratively. Moreover, incest plays a significant part in mythology as well as in alchemy.

Prince and Princess B, have each come together and united: two marriage-pairs now confront one another, parallel but otherwise divided, inasmuch as the one pair belongs to the profane and the other to the magical world. But in spite of this indubitable division, secret psychological connections, as we have seen, exist between them which allow us to derive the one pair from the other.

450　　　Speaking in the spirit of the fairytale, which unfolds its drama from the highest point, one would have to say that the world of half-gods is anterior to the profane world and produces it out of itself, just as the world of half-gods must be thought of as proceeding from the world of gods. Conceived in this way, the swineherd and Princess A are nothing less than earthly simulacra of Prince and Princess B, who in their turn would be the descendants of divine prototypes. Nor should we forget that the horse-breeding witch belongs to the hunter as his female counterpart, rather like an ancient Epona (the Celtic goddess of horses). Unfortunately we are not told how the magical conjuration into horses happened. But it is evident that the witch had a hand in the game because both the horses were raised from her stock and are thus, in a sense, her productions. Hunter and witch form a pair—the reflection, in the nocturnal-chthonic part of the magical world, of a divine parental pair. The latter is easily recognized in the central Christian idea of *sponsus et sponsa,* Christ and his bride, the Church.

451　　　If we wanted to explain the fairytale personalistically, the attempt would founder on the fact that archetypes are not whimsical inventions but autonomous elements of the unconscious psyche which were there before any invention was thought of. They represent the unalterable structure of a psychic world whose "reality" is attested by the determining effects it has upon the conscious mind. Thus, it is a significant psychic reality that the human pair [65] is matched by another pair in the unconscious, the latter pair being only in appearance a reflection of the first. In reality the royal pair invariably comes first, as an *a priori,* so that the human pair has far more the significance of an individual concretization, in space and time, of

[65] Human in so far as the anima is replaced by a human person.

an eternal and primordial image—at least in its mental structure, which is imprinted upon the biological continuum.

452   We could say, then, that the swineherd stands for the "animal" man who has a soul-mate somewhere in the upper world. By her royal birth she betrays her connection with the pre-existent, semidivine pair. Looked at from this angle, the latter stands for everything a man can become if only he climbs high enough up the world-tree.[66] For to the degree that the young swineherd gains possession of the patrician, feminine half of himself, he approximates to the pair of half-gods and lifts himself into the sphere of royalty, which means universal validity. We come across the same theme in Christian Rosencreutz's *Chymical Wedding,* where the king's son must first free his bride from the power of a Moor, to whom she has voluntarily given herself as a concubine. The Moor represents the alchemical *nigredo* in which the arcane substance lies hidden, an idea that forms yet another parallel to our mythologem, or, as we would say in psychological language, another variant of this archetype.

453   As in alchemy, our fairytale describes the unconscious processes that compensate the conscious, Christian situation. It depicts the workings of a spirit who carries our Christian thinking beyond the boundaries set by ecclesiastical concepts, seeking an answer to questions which neither the Middle Ages nor the present day have been able to solve. It is not difficult to see in the image of the second royal pair a correspondence to the ecclesiastical conception of bridegroom and bride, and in that of the hunter and witch a distortion of it, veering towards an atavistic, unconscious Wotanism. The fact that it is a *German* fairytale makes the position particularly interesting, since this same Wotanism was the psychological godfather of National Socialism, a phenomenon which carried the distortion to the lowest pitch before the eyes of the world.[67] On the other hand, the fairytale makes it clear that it is possible for a man to attain totality, to become whole, only with the co-operation of the spirit of darkness, indeed that the latter is actually a *causa*

---

66 The great tree corresponds to the *arbor philosophica* of the alchemists. The meeting between an earthly human being and the anima, swimming down in the shape of a mermaid, is to be found in the so-called "Ripley Scrowle." Cf. *Psychology and Alchemy,* fig. 257.   67 Cf. my "Wotan."

instrumentalis of redemption and individuation. In utter perversion of this goal of spiritual development, to which all nature aspires and which is also prefigured in Christian doctrine, National Socialism destroyed man's moral autonomy and set up the nonsensical totalitarianism of the State. The fairytale tells us how to proceed if we want to overcome the power of darkness: we must turn his own weapons against him, which naturally cannot be done if the magical underworld of the hunter remains unconscious, and if the best men in the nation would rather preach dogmatisms and platitudes than take the human psyche seriously.

VI. CONCLUSION

454   When we consider the spirit in its archetypal form as it appears to us in fairytales and dreams, it presents a picture that differs strangely from the conscious idea of spirit, which is split up into so many meanings. Spirit was originally a spirit in human or animal form, a *daimonion* that came upon man from without. But our material already shows traces of an expansion of consciousness which has gradually begun to occupy that originally unconscious territory and to transform those *daimonia,* at least partially, into voluntary acts. Man conquers not only nature, but spirit also, without realizing what he is doing. To the man of enlightened intellect it seems like the correction of a fallacy when he recognizes that what he took to be spirits is simply the human spirit and ultimately his own spirit. All the superhuman things, whether good or bad, that former ages predicated of the *daimonia,* are reduced to "reasonable" proportions as though they were pure exaggeration, and everything seems to be in the best possible order. But were the unanimous convictions of the past really and truly only exaggerations? If they were not, then the integration of the spirit means nothing less than its demonization, since the superhuman spiritual agencies that were formerly tied up in nature are introjected into human nature, thus endowing it with a power which extends the bounds of the personality *ad infinitum,* in the most perilous way. I put it to the enlightened rationalist: has his rational

reduction led to the beneficial control of matter and spirit? He will point proudly to the advances in physics and medicine, to the freeing of the mind from medieval stupidity and—as a well-meaning Christian—to our deliverance from the fear of demons. But we continue to ask: what have all our other cultural achievements led to? The fearful answer is there before our eyes: man has been delivered from no fear, a hideous nightmare lies upon the world. So far reason has failed lamentably, and the very thing that everybody wanted to avoid rolls on in ghastly progression. Man has achieved a wealth of useful gadgets, but, to offset that, he has torn open the abyss, and what will become of him now—where can he make a halt? After the last World War we hoped for reason: we go on hoping. But already we are fascinated by the possibilities of atomic fission and promise ourselves a Golden Age—the surest guarantee that the abomination of desolation will grow to limitless dimensions. And who or what is it that causes all this? It is none other than that harmless (!), ingenious, inventive, and sweetly reasonable human spirit who unfortunately is abysmally unconscious of the demonism that still clings to him. Worse, this spirit does everything to avoid looking himself in the face, and we all help him like mad. Only, heaven preserve us from psychology—*that* depravity might lead to self-knowledge! Rather let us have wars, for which somebody else is always to blame, nobody seeing that all the world is driven to do just what all the world flees from in terror.

455   It seems to me, frankly, that former ages did not exaggerate, that the spirit has not sloughed off its demonisms, and that mankind, because of its scientific and technological development, has in increasing measure delivered itself over to the danger of possession. True, the archetype of the spirit is capable of working for good as well as for evil, but it depends upon man's free—i.e., conscious—decision whether the good also will be perverted into something satanic. Man's worst sin is unconsciousness, but it is indulged in with the greatest piety even by those who should serve mankind as teachers and examples. When shall we stop taking man for granted in this barbarous manner and in all seriousness seek ways and means to exorcize him, to rescue him from possession and unconsciousness, and

make this the most vital task of civilization? Can we not understand that all the outward tinkerings and improvements do not touch man's inner nature, and that everything ultimately depends upon whether the man who wields the science and the technics is capable of responsibility or not? Christianity has shown us the way, but, as the facts bear witness, it has not penetrated deeply enough below the surface. What depths of despair are still needed to open the eyes of the world's responsible leaders, so that at least they can refrain from leading themselves into temptation?

III

THE PSYCHOLOGY OF THE CHILD
ARCHETYPE

THE PSYCHOLOGY OF THE CHILD ARCHETYPE

I.   INTRODUCTION

259   The author of the companion essay [1] on the mythology of the "child" or the child god has asked me for a psychological commentary on the subject of his investigations. I am glad to accede to his request, although the undertaking seems to me no small venture in view of the great significance of the child motif in mythology. Kerényi himself has enlarged upon the occurrence of this motif in Greece and Rome, with parallels drawn from Indian, Finnish, 'and other sources, thus indicating that the presentation of the theme would allow of yet further extensions. Though a comprehensive description would contribute nothing decisive in principle, it would nevertheless produce an overwhelming impression of the world-wide incidence and frequency of the motif. The customary treatment of mythological motifs so far in separate departments of science, such as philology, ethnology, the history of civilization, and comparative religion, was not exactly a help to us in recognizing their universality; and the psychological problems raised by this universality could easily be shelved by hypotheses of migration. Consequently Adolf Bastian's [2] ideas met with little success in their day. Even then there was sufficient empirical material available to permit far-reaching psychological conclusions, but the necessary premises were lacking. Although the psychological knowledge of that time included myth-formation in its province— witness Wundt's *Völkerpsychologie*—it was not in a position to demonstrate this same process as a living function actually present in the psyche of civilized man, any more than it could understand mythological motifs as structural elements of the psyche. True to its history, when psychology was metaphysics first of

1 Kerényi, "The Primordial Child in Primordial Times."
2 *Der Mensch in der Geschichte* (1860).

125

all, then the study of the senses and their functions, and then of the conscious mind and *its* functions, psychology identified its proper subject with the conscious psyche and its contents and thus completely overlooked the existence of a nonconscious psyche. Although various philosophers, among them Leibniz, Kant, and Schelling, had already pointed very clearly to the problem of the dark side of the psyche, it was a physician who felt impelled, from his scientific and medical experience, to point to the *unconscious* as the essential basis of the psyche. This was C. G. Carus,[3] the authority whom Eduard von Hartmann followed. In recent times it was, once again, medical psychology that approached the problem of the unconscious without philosophical preconceptions. It became clear from many separate investigations that the psychopathology of the neuroses and of many psychoses cannot dispense with the hypothesis of a dark side of the psyche, i.e., the unconscious. It is the same with the psychology of dreams, which is really the *terra intermedia* between normal and pathological psychology. In the dream, as in the products of psychoses, there are numberless interconnections to which one can find parallels only in mythological associations of ideas (or perhaps in certain poetic creations which are often characterized by a borrowing, not always conscious, from myths). Had thorough investigation shown that in the majority of such cases it was simply a matter of forgotten knowledge, the physician would not have gone to the trouble of making extensive researches into individual and collective parallels. But, in point of fact, typical mythologems were observed among individuals to whom all knowledge of this kind was absolutely out of the question, and where indirect derivation from religious ideas that might have been known to them, or from popular figures of speech, was impossible.[4] Such conclusions forced us to assume that we must be dealing with "autochthonous" revivals independent of all tradition, and, consequently, that "myth-forming" structural elements must be present in the unconscious psyche.[5]

3 *Psyche* (1846).
4 A working example in "The Concept of the Collective Unconscious," pars. 105ff., above.
5 Freud, in his *Interpretation of Dreams* (p. 261), paralleled certain aspects of infantile psychology with the Oedipus legend and observed that its "universal

260   These products are never (or at least very seldom) myths with a definite form, but rather mythological components which, because of their typical nature, we can call "motifs," "primordial images," types or—as I have named them—*archetypes*. The child archetype is an excellent example. Today we can hazard the formula that the archetypes appear in myths and fairytales just as they do in dreams and in the products of psychotic fantasy. The medium in which they are embedded is, in the former case, an ordered and for the most part immediately understandable context, but in the latter case a generally unintelligible, irrational, not to say delirious sequence of images which nonetheless does not lack a certain hidden coherence. In the individual, the archetypes appear as involuntary manifestations of unconscious processes whose existence and meaning can only be inferred, whereas the myth deals with traditional forms of incalculable age. They hark back to a prehistoric world whose spiritual preconceptions and general conditions we can still observe today among existing primitives. Myths on this level are as a rule tribal history handed down from generation to generation by word of mouth. Primitive mentality differs from the civilized chiefly in that the conscious mind is far less developed in scope and intensity. Functions such as thinking, willing, etc. are not yet differentiated; they are pre-conscious, and in the case of thinking, for instance, this shows itself in the circumstance that the primitive does not think *consciously*, but that thoughts *appear*. The primitive cannot assert that he thinks; it is rather that "something thinks in him." The spontaneity of the act of thinking does not lie, causally, in his conscious mind, but in his unconscious. Moreover, he is incapable of any conscious effort of will; he must put himself beforehand

validity" was to be explained in terms of the same infantile premise. The real working out of mythological material was then taken up by my pupils (A. Maeder, "Essai d'interprétation de quelques rêves," 1907, and "Die Symbolik in den Legenden, Märchen, Gebräuchen, und Träumen," 1908; F. Riklin, "Über Gefängnispsychosen," 1907, and *Wishfulfilment and Symbolism in Fairy Tales*, orig. 1908); and by K. Abraham, *Dreams and Myths*, orig. 1909. They were succeeded by Otto Rank of the Viennese school (*The Myth of the Birth of the Hero*, orig. 1922). In the *Psychology of the Unconscious* (orig. 1911; revised and expanded as *Symbols of Transformation*), I presented a somewhat more comprehensive examination of psychic and mythological parallels. Cf. also my essay in this volume, "Concerning the Archetypes, with Special Reference to the Anima Concept."

into the "mood of willing," or let himself be put—hence his *rites d'entrée et de sortie.* His consciousness is menaced by an almighty unconscious: hence his fear of magical influences which may cross his path at any moment; and for this reason, too, he is surrounded by unknown forces and must adjust himself to them as best he can. Owing to the chronic twilight state of his consciousness, it is often next to impossible to find out whether he merely dreamed something or whether he really experienced it. The spontaneous manifestation of the unconscious and its archetypes intrudes everywhere into his conscious mind, and the mythical world of his ancestors—for instance, the *alchera* or *bugari* of the Australian aborigines—is a reality equal if not superior to the material world.[6] It is not the world as we know it that speaks out of his unconscious, but the unknown world of the psyche, of which we know that it mirrors our empirical world only in part, and that, for the other part, it moulds this empirical world in accordance with its own psychic assumptions. The archetype does not proceed from physical facts, but describes how the psyche experiences the physical fact, and in so doing the psyche often behaves so autocratically that it denies tangible reality or makes statements that fly in the face of it.

261   The primitive mentality does not *invent* myths, it *experiences* them. Myths are original revelations of the preconscious psyche, involuntary statements about unconscious psychic happenings, and anything but allegories of physical processes.[7] Such allegories would be an idle amusement for an unscientific intellect. Myths, on the contrary, have a vital meaning. Not merely do they represent, they *are* the psychic life of the primitive tribe, which immediately falls to pieces and decays when it loses its mythological heritage, like a man who has lost his soul. A tribe's mythology is its living religion, whose loss is always and everywhere, even among the civilized, a moral catastrophe. But religion is a vital link with psychic processes independent of and beyond consciousness, in the dark hinterland of the psyche. Many of these unconscious processes may be indirectly occasioned by consciousness, but never by conscious choice. Others appear to arise spontaneously, that is to say, from no discernible or demonstrable conscious cause.

6 This fact is well known, and the relevant ethnological literature is too extensive to be mentioned here.   7 Cf. "The Structure of the Psyche," pars. 330ff.

262   Modern psychology treats the products of unconscious fan-
tasy-activity as self-portraits of what is going on in the unconscious, or as statements of the unconscious psyche about itself.
They fall into two categories. First, fantasies (including dreams)
of a personal character, which go back unquestionably to personal experiences, things forgotten or repressed, and can thus be
completely explained by individual anamnesis. Second, fantasies
(including dreams) of an impersonal character, which cannot
be reduced to experiences in the individual's past, and thus cannot be explained as something individually acquired. These
fantasy-images undoubtedly have their closest analogues in
mythological types. We must therefore assume that they correspond to certain *collective* (and not personal) structural elements
of the human psyche in general, and, like the morphological
elements of the human body, are *inherited*. Although tradition
and transmission by migration certainly play a part, there are,
as we have said, very many cases that cannot be accounted for
in this way and drive us to the hypothesis of "autochthonous
revival." These cases are so numerous that we are obliged to assume the existence of a collective psychic substratum. I have
called this the *collective unconscious*.

263   The products of this second category resemble the types of
structures to be met with in myth and fairytale so much that
we must regard them as related. It is therefore wholly within
the realm of possibility that both, the mythological types as well
as the individual types, arise under quite similar conditions. As
already mentioned, the fantasy-products of the second category
(as also those of the first) arise in a state of reduced intensity of
consciousness (in dreams, delirium, reveries, visions, etc.). In all
these states the check put upon unconscious contents by the concentration of the conscious mind ceases, so that the hitherto unconscious material streams, as though from opened side-sluices,
into the field of consciousness. This mode of origination is the
general rule.[8]

264   Reduced intensity of consciousness and absence of concentration and attention, Janet's *abaissement du niveau mental,*
correspond pretty exactly to the primitive state of consciousness

---

[8] Except for certain cases of spontaneous vision, *automatismes téléologiques*
(Flournoy), and the processes in the method of "active imagination" which I have
described [e.g., in "The Transcendent Function" and *Mysterium Coniunctionis*,
pars. 706, 753f.—EDITORS].

in which, we must suppose, myths were originally formed. It is therefore exceedingly probable that the mythological archetypes, too, made their appearance in much the same manner as the manifestations of archetypal structures among individuals today.

265   The methodological principle in accordance with which psychology treats the products of the unconscious is this: Contents of an archetypal character are manifestations of processes in the collective unconscious. Hence they do not refer to anything that is or has been conscious, but to something essentially unconscious. In the last analysis, therefore, it is impossible to say what they refer to. Every interpretation necessarily remains an "as-if." The ultimate core of meaning may be circumscribed, but not described. Even so, the bare circumscription denotes an essential step forward in our knowledge of the pre-conscious structure of the psyche, which was already in existence when there was as yet no unity of personality (even today the primitive is not securely possessed of it) and no consciousness at all. We can also observe this pre-conscious state in early childhood, and as a matter of fact it is the dreams of this early period that not infrequently bring extremely remarkable archetypal contents to light.[9]

266   If, then, we proceed in accordance with the above principle, there is no longer any question whether a myth refers to the sun or the moon, the father or the mother, sexuality or fire or water; all it does is to circumscribe and give an approximate description of an *unconscious core of meaning*. The ultimate meaning of this nucleus was never conscious and never will be. It was, and still is, only interpreted, and every interpretation that comes anywhere near the hidden sense (or, from the point of view of scientific intellect, nonsense, which comes to the same thing) has always, right from the beginning, laid claim not only to absolute truth and validity but to instant reverence and religious devotion. Archetypes were, and still are, living psychic forces that demand to be taken seriously, and they have a strange way of making sure of their effect. Always they were the bringers

[9] The relevant material can be found in the unpublished reports of the seminars I gave at the Federal Polytechnic Institute (ETH) in Zurich in 1936–39, and in Michael Fordham's book *The Life of Childhood*.

of protection and salvation, and their violation has as its consequence the "perils of the soul" known to us from the psychology of primitives. Moreover, they are the unfailing causes of neurotic and even psychotic disorders, behaving exactly like neglected or maltreated physical organs or organic functional systems.

267   An archetypal content expresses itself, first and foremost, in metaphors. If such a content should speak of the sun and identify with it the lion, the king, the hoard of gold guarded by the dragon, or the power that makes for the life and health of man, it is neither the one thing nor the other, but the unknown third thing that finds more or less adequate expression in all these similes, yet—to the perpetual vexation of the intellect—remains unknown and not to be fitted into a formula. For this reason the scientific intellect is always inclined to put on airs of enlightenment in the hope of banishing the spectre once and for all. Whether its endeavours were called euhemerism, or Christian apologetics, or Enlightenment in the narrow sense, or Positivism, there was always a myth hiding behind it, in new and disconcerting garb, which then, following the ancient and venerable pattern, gave itself out as ultimate truth. In reality we can never legitimately cut loose from our archetypal foundations unless we are prepared to pay the price of a neurosis, any more than we can rid ourselves of our body and its organs without committing suicide. If we cannot deny the archetypes or otherwise neutralize them, we are confronted, at every new stage in the differentiation of consciousness to which civilization attains, with the task of finding a new *interpretation* appropriate to this stage, in order to connect the life of the past that still exists in us with the life of the present, which threatens to slip away from it. If this link-up does not take place, a kind of rootless consciousness comes into being no longer oriented to the past, a consciousness which succumbs helplessly to all manner of suggestions and, in practice, is susceptible to psychic epidemics. With the loss of the past, now become "insignificant," devalued, and incapable of revaluation, the saviour is lost too, for the saviour is either the insignificant thing itself or else arises out of it. Over and over again in the "metamorphosis of the gods" he rises up as the prophet or first-born of a new

generation and appears unexpectedly in the unlikeliest places (sprung from a stone, tree, furrow, water, etc.) and in ambiguous form (Tom Thumb, dwarf, child, animal, and so on).

268   This archetype of the "child god" is extremely widespread and intimately bound up with all the other mythological aspects of the child motif. It is hardly necessary to allude to the still living "Christ-child," who, in the legend of Saint Christopher, also has the typical feature of being "smaller than small and bigger than big." In folklore the child motif appears in the guise of the *dwarf* or the *elf* as personifications of the hidden forces of nature. To this sphere also belongs the little metal man of late antiquity, the ἀνθρωπάριον,[10] who, till far into the Middle Ages, on the one hand inhabited the mine-shafts,[11] and on the other represented the alchemical metals,[12] above all Mercurius reborn in perfect form (as the hermaphrodite, *filius sapientiae,* or *infans noster*).[13] Thanks to the religious interpretation of the "child," a fair amount of evidence has come down to us from the Middle Ages showing that the "child" was not merely a traditional figure, but a vision spontaneously experienced (as a so-called "irruption of the unconscious"). I would mention Meister Eckhart's vision of the "naked boy" and the dream of Brother Eustachius.[14] Interesting accounts of these spontaneous experiences are also to be found in English ghost-stories, where we read of the vision of a "Radiant Boy" said to have been seen in a place where there are Roman remains.[15] This apparition was supposed to be of evil omen. It almost looks as though we were dealing with the figure of a *puer aeternus* who had become inauspicious through "metamorphosis," or in other words had shared the fate of the classical and the Germanic gods, who have all become bugbears. The mystical character of the experience is also confirmed in Part II of Goethe's *Faust,* where Faust him-

---

10 Berthelot, *Alchimistes grecs,* III, xxv.

11 Agricola, *De animantibus subterraneis* (1549); Kircher, *Mundus subterraneus* (1678), VIII, 4.

12 Mylius, *Philosophia reformata* (1622).

13 "Allegoria super librum Turbae" in *Artis auriferae,* I (1572), p. 161.

14 *Texte aus der deutschen Mystik des 14. und 15. Jahrhunderts,* ed. Spamer, pp. 143, 150.

15 Ingram, *The Haunted Homes and Family Traditions of Great Britain,* pp. 43ff.

self is transformed into a boy and admitted into the "choir of blessed youths," this being the "larval stage" of Doctor Marianus.[16]

269   In the strange tale called *Das Reich ohne Raum*, by Bruno Goetz, a *puer aeternus* named Fo (= Buddha) appears with whole troops of "unholy" boys of evil significance. (Contemporary parallels are better let alone.) I mention this instance only to demonstrate the enduring vitality of the child archetype.

270   The child motif not infrequently occurs in the field of psychopathology. The "imaginary" child is common among women with mental disorders and is usually interpreted in a Christian sense. Homunculi also appear, as in the famous Schreber case,[17] where they come in swarms and plague the sufferer. But the clearest and most significant manifestation of the child motif in the therapy of neuroses is in the maturation process of personality induced by the analysis of the unconscious, which I have termed the process of *individuation*.[18] Here we are confronted with preconscious processes which, in the form of more or less well-formed fantasies, gradually pass over into the conscious mind, or become conscious as dreams, or, lastly, are made conscious through the method of active imagination.[19] This material is rich in archetypal motifs, among them frequently that of the child. Often the child is formed after the Christian model; more often, though, it develops from earlier, altogether non-Christian levels—that is to say, out of chthonic animals such as crocodiles, dragons, serpents, or monkeys. Sometimes the child appears in the cup of a flower, or out of a golden egg, or as the centre of a mandala. In dreams it often appears as the dreamer's son or daughter or as a boy, youth, or young girl; occasionally it seems to be of exotic origin, Indian or Chinese, with a dusky skin, or, appearing more cosmically, surrounded by stars or with a starry

16 An old alchemical authority variously named Morienes, Morienus, Marianus ("De compositione alchemiae," Manget, *Bibliotheca chemica curiosa*, I, pp. 509ff.). In view of the explicitly alchemical character of *Faust*, Part II, such a connection would not be surprising.

17 Schreber, *Memoirs of My Nervous Illness*.

18 For a general presentation see infra, "Conscious, Unconscious, and Individuation." Special phenomena in the following text, also in *Psychology and Alchemy*, Part II.

19 "The Relations between the Ego and the Unconscious," Part II, ch. 3 [also "The Transcendent Function"—EDITORS].

coronet; or as the king's son or the witch's child with daemonic attributes. Seen as a special instance of "the treasure hard to attain" motif,[20] the child motif is extremely variable and assumes all manner of shapes, such as the jewel, the pearl, the flower, the chalice, the golden egg, the quaternity, the golden ball, and so on. It can be interchanged with these and similar images almost without limit.

II. THE PSYCHOLOGY OF THE CHILD ARCHETYPE

1. *The Archetype as a Link with the Past*

271   As to the *psychology* of our theme I must point out that every statement going beyond the purely phenomenal aspects of an archetype lays itself open to the criticism we have expressed above. Not for a moment dare we succumb to the illusion that an archetype can be finally explained and disposed of. Even the best attempts at explanation are only more or less successful translations into another metaphorical language. (Indeed, language itself is only an image.) The most we can do is to *dream the myth onwards* and give it a modern dress. And whatever explanation or interpretation does to it, we do to our own souls as well, with corresponding results for our own well-being. The archetype—let us never forget this—is a psychic organ present in all of us. A bad explanation means a correspondingly bad attitude to this organ, which may thus be injured. But the ultimate sufferer is the bad interpreter himself. Hence the "explanation" should always be such that the functional significance of the archetype remains unimpaired, so that an adequate and meaningful connection between the conscious mind and the archetypes is assured. For the archetype is an element of our psychic structure and thus a vital and necessary component in our psychic economy. It represents or personifies certain instinctive data of the dark, primitive psyche, the real but invisible roots of consciousness. Of what elementary importance the connection with these roots is, we see from the preoccupation of the primitive mentality with certain "magic" factors, which are nothing less than what we would call archetypes. This original form of

20 *Symbols of Transformation*, index, s.v.

religio ("linking back") is the essence, the working basis of all religious life even today, and always will be, whatever future form this life may take.

272   There is no "rational" substitute for the archetype any more than there is for the cerebellum or the kidneys. We can examine the physical organs anatomically, histologically, and embryologically. This would correspond to an outline of archetypal phenomenology and its presentation in terms of comparative history. But we only arrive at the *meaning* of a physical organ when we begin to ask teleological questions. Hence the query arises: What is the biological purpose of the archetype? Just as physiology answers such a question for the body, so it is the business of psychology to answer it for the archetype.

273   Statements like "The child motif is a vestigial memory of one's own childhood" and similar explanations merely beg the question. But if, giving this proposition a slight twist, we were to say, "The child motif is a picture of certain *forgotten* things in our childhood," we are getting closer to the truth. Since, however, the archetype is always an image belonging to the whole human race and not merely to the individual, we might put it better this way: "The child motif represents the preconscious, childhood aspect of the collective psyche." [21]

274   We shall not go wrong if we take this statement for the time being *historically,* on the analogy of certain psychological experiences which show that certain phases in an individual's life can become autonomous, can personify themselves to the extent

[21] It may not be superfluous to point out that lay prejudice is always inclined to identify the child motif with the concrete experience "child," as though the real child were the cause and pre-condition of the existence of the child motif. In psychological reality, however, the empirical idea "child" is only the means (and not the only one) by which to express a psychic fact that cannot be formulated more exactly. Hence by the same token the mythological idea of the child is emphatically not a copy of the empirical child but a *symbol* clearly recognizable as such: it is a wonder-child, a divine child, begotten, born, and brought up in quite extraordinary circumstances, and not—this is the point—a human child. Its deeds are as miraculous or monstrous as its nature and physical constitution. Only on account of these highly unempirical properties is it necessary to speak of a "child motif" at all. Moreover, the mythological "child" has various forms: now a god, giant, Tom Thumb, animal, etc., and this points to a causality that is anything but rational or concretely human. The same is true of the "father" and "mother" archetypes which, mythologically speaking, are equally irrational symbols.

that they result in a *vision of oneself*—for instance, one sees oneself as a child. Visionary experiences of this kind, whether they occur in dreams or in the waking state, are, as we know, conditional on a dissociation having previously taken place between past and present. Such dissociations come about because of various incompatibilities; for instance, a man's present state may have come into conflict with his childhood state, or he may have violently sundered himself from his original character in the interests of some arbitrary persona[22] more in keeping with his ambitions. He has thus become unchildlike and artificial, and has lost his roots. All this presents a favourable opportunity for an equally vehement confrontation with the primary truth.

275   In view of the fact that men have not yet ceased to make statements about the child god, we may perhaps extend the individual analogy to the life of mankind and say in conclusion that humanity, too, probably always comes into conflict with its childhood conditions, that is, with its original, unconscious, and instinctive state, and that the danger of the kind of conflict which induces the vision of the "child" actually exists. Religious observances, i.e., the retelling and ritual repetition of the mythical event, consequently serve the purpose of bringing the image of childhood, and everything connected with it, again and again before the eyes of the conscious mind so that the link with the original condition may not be broken.

2. *The Function of the Archetype*

276   The child motif represents not only something that existed in the distant past but also something that exists *now;* that is to say, it is not just a vestige but a system functioning in the present whose purpose is to compensate or correct, in a meaningful manner, the inevitable one-sidednesses and extravagances of the conscious mind. It is in the nature of the conscious mind to concentrate on relatively few contents and to raise them to the highest pitch of clarity. A necessary result and precondition is the exclusion of other potential contents of consciousness. The exclusion is bound to bring about a certain one-sidedness of the conscious contents. Since the differentiated consciousness of

22 *Psychological Types,* Def. 48; and *Two Essays on Analytical Psychology,* index, s.v. "persona."

civilized man has been granted an effective instrument for the practical realization of its contents through the dynamics of his will, there is all the more danger, the more he trains his will, of his getting lost in one-sidedness and deviating further and further from the laws and roots of his being. This means, on the one hand, the possibility of human freedom, but on the other it is a source of endless transgressions against one's instincts. Accordingly, primitive man, being closer to his instincts, like the animal, is characterized by fear of novelty and adherence to tradition. To our way of thinking he is painfully backward, whereas we exalt progress. But our progressiveness, though it may result in a great many delightful wish-fulfilments, piles up an equally gigantic Promethean debt which has to be paid off from time to time in the form of hideous catastrophes. For ages man has dreamed of flying, and all we have got for it is saturation bombing! We smile today at the Christian hope of a life beyond the grave, and yet we often fall into chiliasms a hundred times more ridiculous than the notion of a happy Hereafter. Our differentiated consciousness is in continual danger of being up-rooted; hence it needs compensation through the still existing state of childhood.

²77   The symptoms of compensation are described, from the progressive point of view, in scarcely flattering terms. Since, to the superficial eye, it looks like a retarding operation, people speak of inertia, backwardness, scepticism, fault-finding, conservatism, timidity, pettiness, and so on. But inasmuch as man has, in high degree, the capacity for cutting himself off from his own roots, he may also be swept uncritically to catastrophe by his dangerous one-sidedness. The retarding ideal is always more primitive, more natural (in the good sense as in the bad), and more "moral" in that it keeps faith with law and tradition. The progressive ideal is always more abstract, more unnatural, and less "moral" in that it demands disloyalty to tradition. Progress enforced by will is always *convulsive*. Backwardness may be closer to naturalness, but in its turn it is always menaced by painful awakenings. The older view of things realized that progress is only possible *Deo concedente,* thus proving itself conscious of the opposites and repeating the age-old *rites d'entrée et de sortie* on a higher plane. The more differentiated consciousness becomes, the greater the danger of severance from the root-

condition. Complete severance comes when the *Deo concedente* is forgotten. Now it is an axiom of psychology that when a part of the psyche is split off from consciousness it is only *apparently* inactivated; in actual fact it brings about a possession of the personality, with the result that the individual's aims are falsified in the interests of the split-off part. If, then, the childhood state of the collective psyche is repressed to the point of total exclusion, the unconscious content overwhelms the conscious aim and inhibits, falsifies, even destroys its realization. Viable progress only comes from the co-operation of both.

3. *The Futurity of the Archetype*

278   One of the essential features of the child motif is its futurity. The child is potential future. Hence the occurrence of the child motif in the psychology of the individual signifies as a rule an anticipation of future developments, even though at first sight it may seem like a retrospective configuration. Life is a flux, a flowing into the future, and not a stoppage or a backwash. It is therefore not surprising that so many of the mythological saviours are child gods. This agrees exactly with our experience of the psychology of the individual, which shows that the "child" paves the way for a future change of personality. In the individuation process, it anticipates the figure that comes from the synthesis of conscious and unconscious elements in the personality. It is therefore a symbol which unites the opposites; [23] a mediator, bringer of healing, that is, one who makes whole. Because it has this meaning, the child motif is capable of the numerous transformations mentioned above: it can be expressed by roundness, the circle or sphere, or else by the quaternity as another form of wholeness.[24] I have called this wholeness that transcends consciousness the "self." [25] The goal of the individuation process is the synthesis of the self. From another point of view the term "entelechy" might be preferable to "synthesis." There is an empirical reason why "entelechy" is, in certain conditions, more fitting: the symbols

23 *Psychological Types,* ch. V, 3: "The Significance of the Uniting Symbol."
24 *Psychology and Alchemy,* pars. 327ff.; "Psychology and Religion," pars. 108ff.
25 *Two Essays on Analytical Psychology,* pars. 399ff. [Cf. also *Aion* (Part II of this volume), ch. 4.—EDITORS.]

of wholeness frequently occur at the beginning of the individuation process, indeed they can often be observed in the first dreams of early infancy. This observation says much for the *a priori* existence of potential wholeness,[26] and on this account the idea of *entelechy* instantly recommends itself. But in so far as the individuation process occurs, empirically speaking, as a synthesis, it looks, paradoxically enough, as if something already existent were being put together. From this point of view, the term "synthesis" is also applicable.

4. *Unity and Plurality of the Child Motif*

279　In the manifold phenomenology of the "child" we have to distinguish between the *unity* and *plurality* of its respective manifestations. Where, for instance, numerous homunculi, dwarfs, boys, etc., appear, having no individual characteristics at all, there is the probability of a *dissociation*. Such forms are therefore found especially in schizophrenia, which is essentially a fragmentation of personality. The many children then represent the products of its dissolution. But if the plurality occurs in normal people, then it is the representation of an as yet incomplete synthesis of personality. The personality (viz., the "self") is still in the *plural stage*, i.e., an ego may be present, but it cannot experience its wholeness within the framework of its own personality, only within the community of the family, tribe, or nation; it is still in the stage of unconscious identification with the plurality of the group. The Church takes due account of this widespread condition in her doctrine of the *corpus mysticum,* of which the individual is by nature a member.

280　If, however, the child motif appears in the form of a unity, we are dealing with an unconscious and provisionally complete synthesis of the personality, which in practice, like everything unconscious, signifies no more than a possibility.

5. *Child God and Child Hero*

281　Sometimes the "child" looks more like a *child god,* sometimes more like a young *hero.* Common to both types is the

26 *Psychology and Alchemy,* pars. 328ff.

miraculous birth and the adversities of early childhood—abandonment and danger through persecution. The god is by nature wholly supernatural; the hero's nature is human but raised to the limit of the supernatural—he is "semi-divine." While the god, especially in his close affinity with the symbolic animal, personifies the collective unconscious which is not yet integrated into a human being, the hero's supernaturalness includes human nature and thus represents a synthesis of the ("divine," i.e., not yet humanized) unconscious and human consciousness. Consequently he signifies the potential anticipation of an individuation process which is approaching wholeness.

282   For this reason the various "child"-fates may be regarded as illustrating the kind of psychic events that occur in the entelechy or genesis of the "self." The "miraculous birth" tries to depict the way in which this genesis is experienced. Since it is a psychic genesis, everything must happen non-empirically, e.g., by means of a virgin birth, or by miraculous conception, or by birth from unnatural organs. The motifs of "insignificance," exposure, abandonment, danger, etc. try to show how precarious is the psychic possibility of wholeness, that is, the enormous difficulties to be met with in attaining this "highest good." They also signify the powerlessness and helplessness of the life-urge which subjects every growing thing to the law of maximum self-fulfilment, while at the same time the environmental influences place all sorts of insuperable obstacles in the way of individuation. More especially the threat to one's inmost self from dragons and serpents points to the danger of the newly acquired consciousness being swallowed up again by the instinctive psyche, the unconscious. The lower vertebrates have from earliest times been favourite symbols of the collective psychic substratum,[27] which is localized anatomically in the subcortical centres, the cerebellum and the spinal cord. These organs constitute the snake.[28] Snake-dreams usually occur, therefore, when the conscious mind is deviating from its instinctual basis.

283   The motif of "smaller than small yet bigger than big" complements the impotence of the child by means of its equally

[27] Higher vertebrates symbolize mainly affects.
[28] This interpretation of the snake is found as early as Hippolytus, *Elenchos,* IV, 49–51 (Legge trans., I, p. 117). Cf. also Leisegang, *Die Gnosis,* p. 146.

miraculous deeds. This paradox is the essence of the hero and runs through his whole destiny like a red thread. He can cope with the greatest perils, yet, in the end, something quite insignificant is his undoing: Baldur perishes because of the mistletoe, Maui because of the laughter of a little bird, Siegfried because of his one vulnerable spot, Heracles because of his wife's gift, others because of common treachery, and so on.

284   The hero's main feat is to overcome the monster of darkness: it is the long-hoped-for and expected triumph of consciousness over the unconscious. Day and light are synonyms for consciousness, night and dark for the unconscious. The coming of consciousness was probably the most tremendous experience of primeval times, for with it a world came into being whose existence no one had suspected before. "And God said: 'Let there be light!' " is the projection of that immemorial experience of the separation of the conscious from the unconscious. Even among primitives today the possession of a soul is a precarious thing, and the "loss of soul" a typical psychic malady which drives primitive medicine to all sorts of psychotherapeutic measures. Hence the "child" distinguishes itself by deeds which point to the conquest of the dark.

III. THE SPECIAL PHENOMENOLOGY OF THE CHILD ARCHETYPE

1. *The Abandonment of the Child*

285   Abandonment, exposure, danger, etc. are all elaborations of the "child's" insignificant beginnings and of its mysterious and miraculous birth. This statement describes a certain psychic experience of a creative nature, whose object is the emergence of a new and as yet unknown content. In the psychology of the individual there is always, at such moments, an agonizing situation of conflict from which there seems to be no way out—at least for the conscious mind, since as far as this is concerned, *tertium non datur*. But out of this collision of opposites the unconscious psyche always creates a third thing of an irrational nature,[29] which the conscious mind neither expects nor understands. It presents itself in a form that is neither a straight "yes"

[29] *Psychological Types*, Def. 51.

nor a straight "no," and is consequently rejected by both. For the conscious mind knows nothing beyond the opposites and, as a result, has no knowledge of the thing that unites them. Since, however, the solution of the conflict through the union of opposites is of vital importance, and is moreover the very thing that the conscious mind is longing for, some inkling of the creative act, and of the significance of it, nevertheless gets through. From this comes the numinous character of the "child." A meaningful but unknown content always has a secret fascination for the conscious mind. The new configuration is a nascent whole; it is on the way to wholeness, at least in so far as it excels in "wholeness" the conscious mind when torn by opposites and surpasses it in completeness. For this reason all uniting symbols have a redemptive significance.

286   Out of this situation the "child" emerges as a symbolic content, manifestly separated or even isolated from its background (the mother), but sometimes including the mother in its perilous situation, threatened on the one hand by the negative attitude of the conscious mind and on the other by the *horror vacui* of the unconscious, which is quite ready to swallow up all its progeny, since it produces them only in play, and destruction is an inescapable part of its play. Nothing in all the world welcomes this new birth, although it is the most precious fruit of Mother Nature herself, the most pregnant with the future, signifying a higher stage of self-realization. That is why Nature, the world of the instincts, takes the "child" under its wing: it is nourished or protected by animals.

287   "Child" means something evolving towards independence. This it cannot do without detaching itself from its origins: abandonment is therefore a necessary condition, not just a concomitant symptom. The conflict is not to be overcome by the conscious mind remaining caught between the opposites, and for this very reason it needs a symbol to point out the necessity of detaching itself from its origins. Because the symbol of the "child" fascinates and grips the conscious mind, its redemptive effect passes over into consciousness and brings about that separation from the conflict-situation which the conscious mind by itself was unable to achieve. The symbol anticipates a nascent state of consciousness. So long as this is not actually in being, the "child" remains a mythological projection which requires

142

religious repetition and renewal by ritual. The Christ Child, for instance, is a religious necessity only so long as the majority of men are incapable of giving psychological reality to the saying: "Except ye become as little children. . . ." Since all such developments and transitions are extraordinarily difficult and dangerous, it is no wonder that figures of this kind persist for hundreds or even thousands of years. Everything that man should, and yet cannot, be or do—be it in a positive or negative sense—lives on as a mythological figure and anticipation alongside his consciousness, either as a religious projection or—what is still more dangerous—as unconscious contents which then project themselves spontaneously into incongruous objects, e.g., hygienic and other "salvationist" doctrines or practices. All these are so many rationalized substitutes for mythology, and their unnaturalness does more harm than good.

288   The conflict-situation that offers no way out, the sort of situation that produces the "child" as the irrational third, is of course a formula appropriate only to a psychological, that is, modern stage of development. It is not strictly applicable to the psychic life of primitives, if only because primitive man's child-like range of consciousness still excludes a whole world of possible psychic experiences. Seen on the nature-level of the primitive, our modern *moral* conflict is still an *objective* calamity that threatens life itself. Hence not a few child-figures are culture-heroes and thus identified with things that promote culture, e.g., fire,[30] metal, corn, maize, etc. As bringers of light, that is, enlargers of consciousness, they overcome darkness, which is to say that they overcome the earlier unconscious state. Higher consciousness, or knowledge going beyond our present-day consciousness, is equivalent to being *all alone in the world*. This loneliness expresses the conflict between the bearer or symbol of higher consciousness and his surroundings. The conquerors of darkness go far back into primeval times, and, together with many other legends, prove that there once existed a state of *original psychic distress*, namely *unconsciousness*. Hence in all probability the "irrational" fear which primitive man has of the dark even today. I found a form of religion among a tribe living on Mount Elgon that corresponded to

30 Even Christ is of a fiery nature ("he that is near to me is near to the fire"— Origen, *In Jeremiam Homiliae*, XX, 3); likewise the Holy Ghost.

pantheistic optimism. Their optimistic mood was, however, always in abeyance between six o'clock in the evening and six o'clock in the morning, during which time it was replaced by fear, for in the night the dark being Ayik has his dominion— the "Maker of Fear." During the daytime there were no monster snakes anywhere in the vicinity, but at night they were lurking on every path. At night the whole of mythology was let loose.

2. The Invincibility of the Child

289   It is a striking paradox in all child myths that the "child" is on the one hand delivered helpless into the power of terrible enemies and in continual danger of extinction, while on the other he possesses powers far exceeding those of ordinary humanity. This is closely related to the psychological fact that though the child may be "insignificant," unknown, "a mere child," he is also divine. From the conscious standpoint we seem to be dealing with an insignificant content that has no releasing, let alone redeeming, character. The conscious mind is caught in its conflict-situation, and the combatant forces seem so overwhelming that the "child" as an isolated content bears no relation to the conscious factors. It is therefore easily overlooked and falls back into the unconscious. At least, this is what we should have to fear if things turned out according to our conscious expectations. Myth, however, emphasizes that it is not so, but that the "child" is endowed with superior powers and, despite all dangers, will unexpectedly pull through. The "child" is born out of the womb of the unconscious, begotten out of the depths of human nature, or rather out of living Nature herself. It is a personification of vital forces quite outside the limited range of our conscious mind; of ways and possibilities of which our one-sided conscious mind knows nothing; a wholeness which embraces the very depths of Nature. It represents the strongest, the most ineluctable urge in every being, namely the urge to realize itself. It is, as it were, an incarnation of *the inability to do otherwise,* equipped with all the powers of nature and instinct, whereas the conscious mind is always getting caught up in its supposed ability to do otherwise. The urge and compulsion to self-realization is a law of nature and thus of invincible power, even though its effect, at the start, is insignifi-

cant and improbable. Its power is revealed in the miraculous deeds of the child hero, and later in the *athla* ('works') of the bondsman or thrall (of the Heracles type), where, although the hero has outgrown the impotence of the "child," he is still in a menial position. The figure of the thrall generally leads up to the real epiphany of the semi-divine hero. Oddly enough, we have a similar modulation of themes in alchemy—in the synonyms for the *lapis*. As the *materia prima*, it is the *lapis exilis et vilis*. As a substance in process of transmutation, it is *servus rubeus* or *fugitivus;* and finally, in its true apotheosis, it attains the dignity of a *filius sapientiae* or *deus terrenus,* a "light above all lights," a power that contains in itself all the powers of the upper and nether regions. It becomes a *corpus glorificatum* which enjoys everlasting incorruptibility and is therefore a panacea ("bringer of healing").[31] The size and invincibility of the "child" are bound up in Hindu speculation with the nature of the atman, which corresponds to the "smaller than small yet bigger than big" motif. As an individual phenomenon, the self is "smaller than small"; as the equivalent of the cosmos, it is "bigger than big." The self, regarded as the counter-pole of the world, its "absolutely other," is the *sine qua non* of all empirical knowledge and consciousness of subject and object. Only because of this psychic "otherness" is consciousness possible at all. Identity does not make consciousness possible; it is only separation, detachment, and agonizing confrontation through opposition that produce consciousness and insight. Hindu introspection recognized this psychological fact very early and consequently equated the subject of cognition with the subject of ontology in general. In accordance with the predominantly introverted attitude of Indian thinking, the object lost the attribute of absolute reality and, in some systems, became a mere illusion. The Greek-Occidental type of mind could not free itself from the conviction of the world's absolute existence—at the cost, however, of the cosmic significance of the self. Even today Western man finds it hard to see the psychological necessity for a transcendental subject of cognition as the counter-pole of the empirical universe, although the postulate of a world-

31 The material is collected in *Psychology and Alchemy*, Parts II and III. For Mercurius as a servant, see the parable of Eirenaeus Philalethes, *Ripley Reviv'd: or, An Exposition upon Sir George Ripley's Hermetico-Poetical Works* (1678).

confronting self, at least as a *point of reflection,* is a logical necessity. Regardless of philosophy's perpetual attitude of dissent or only half-hearted assent, there is always a compensating tendency in our unconscious psyche to produce a symbol of the self in its cosmic significance. These efforts take on the archetypal forms of the hero myth such as can be observed in almost any individuation process.

290   The phenomenology of the "child's" birth always points back to an original psychological state of non-recognition, i.e., of darkness or twilight, of non-differentiation between subject and object, of unconscious identity of man and the universe. This phase of non-differentiation produces the *golden egg,* which is both man and universe and yet neither, but an irrational third. To the twilight consciousness of primitive man it seems as if the egg came out of the womb of the wide world and were, accordingly, a cosmic, objective, external occurrence. To a differentiated consciousness, on the other hand, it seems evident that this egg is nothing but a symbol thrown up by the psyche or—what is even worse—a fanciful speculation and therefore "nothing but" a primitive phantasm to which no "reality" of any kind attaches. Present-day medical psychology, however, thinks somewhat differently about these "phantasms." It knows only too well what dire disturbances of the bodily functions and what devastating psychic consequences can flow from "mere" fantasies. "Fantasies" are the natural expressions of the life of the unconscious. But since the unconscious is the psyche of all the body's autonomous functional complexes, its "fantasies" have an aetiological significance that is not to be despised. From the psychopathology of the individuation process we know that the formation of symbols is frequently associated with physical disorders of a psychic origin, which in some cases are felt as decidedly "real." In medicine, fantasies are *real things* with which the psychotherapist has to reckon very seriously indeed. He cannot therefore deprive of all justification those primitive phantasms whose content is so real that it is projected upon the external world. In the last analysis the human body, too, is built of the stuff of the world, the very stuff wherein fantasies become visible; indeed, without it they could not be experienced at all. Without this stuff they would be like a sort of abstract

crystalline lattice in a solution where the crystallization process had not yet started.

291   The symbols of the self arise in the depths of the body and they express its materiality every bit as much as the structure of the perceiving consciousness. The symbol is thus a living body, *corpus et anima;* hence the "child" is such an apt formula for the symbol. The uniqueness of the psyche can never enter wholly into reality, it can only be realized approximately, though it still remains the absolute basis of all consciousness. The deeper "layers" of the psyche lose their individual uniqueness as they retreat farther and farther into darkness. "Lower down," that is to say as they approach the autonomous functional systems, they become increasingly collective until they are universalized and extinguished in the body's materiality, i.e., in chemical substances. The body's carbon is simply carbon. Hence "at bottom" the psyche is simply "world." In this sense I hold Kerényi to be absolutely right when he says that in the symbol the *world itself* is speaking. The more archaic and "deeper," that is the more *physiological,* the symbol is, the more collective and universal, the more "material" it is. The more abstract, differentiated, and specific it is, and the more its nature approximates to conscious uniqueness and individuality, the more it sloughs off its universal character. Having finally attained full consciousness, it runs the risk of becoming a mere allegory which nowhere oversteps the bounds of conscious comprehension, and is then exposed to all sorts of attempts at rationalistic and therefore inadequate explanation.

3. *The Hermaphroditism of the Child*

292   It is a remarkable fact that perhaps the majority of cosmogonic gods are of a bisexual nature. The hermaphrodite means nothing less than a union of the strongest and most striking opposites. In the first place this union refers back to a primitive state of mind, a twilight where differences and contrasts were either barely separated or completely merged. With increasing clarity of consciousness, however, the opposites draw more and more distinctly and irreconcilably apart. If, therefore, the hermaphrodite were only a product of primitive non-differentiation, we would have to expect that it would soon be eliminated

with increasing civilization. This is by no means the case; on the contrary, man's imagination has been preoccupied with this idea over and over again on the high and even the highest levels of culture, as we can see from the late Greek and syncretic philosophy of Gnosticism. The hermaphroditic *rebis* has an important part to play in the natural philosophy of the Middle Ages. And in our own day we hear of Christ's androgyny in Catholic mysticism.[32]

293   We can no longer be dealing, then, with the continued existence of a primitive phantasm, or with an original contamination of opposites. Rather, as we can see from medieval writings,[33] the primordial idea has become a *symbol of the creative union of opposites,* a "uniting symbol" in the literal sense. In its functional significance the symbol no longer points back, but forward to a goal not yet reached. Notwithstanding its monstrosity, the hermaphrodite has gradually turned into a subduer of conflicts and a bringer of healing, and it acquired this meaning in relatively early phases of civilization. This vital meaning explains why the image of the hermaphrodite did not fade out in primeval times but, on the contrary, was able to assert itself with increasing profundity of symbolic content for thousands of years. The fact that an idea so utterly archaic could rise to such exalted heights of meaning not only points to the vitality of archetypal ideas, it also demonstrates the rightness of the principle that the archetype, because of its power to unite opposites, mediates between the unconscious substratum and the conscious mind. It throws a bridge between present-day consciousness, always in danger of losing its roots, and the natural, unconscious, instinctive wholeness of primeval times. Through this mediation the uniqueness, peculiarity, and one-sidedness of our present individual consciousness are linked up again with its natural, racial roots. Progress and development are ideals not lightly to be rejected, but they lose all meaning if man only arrives at his new state as a fragment of himself, having left his essential hinterland behind him in the shadow of the unconscious, in a state of primitivity or, indeed, barbarism. The conscious mind, split off from its origins, incapable of

32 Koepgen, *Die Gnosis des Christentums,* pp. 315ff.
33 For the *lapis* as mediator and medium, cf. *Tractatus aureus,* in Manget, *Bibliotheca chemica curiosa,* I, p. 408b, and *Artis auriferae* (1572), p. 641.

realizing the meaning of the new state, then relapses all too easily into a situation far worse than the one from which the innovation was intended to free it—*exempla sunt odiosa!* It was Friedrich Schiller who first had an inkling of this problem; but neither his contemporaries nor his successors were capable of drawing any conclusions. Instead, people incline more than ever to educate *children* and nothing more. I therefore suspect that the *furor paedogogicus* is a god-sent method of by-passing the central problem touched on by Schiller, namely the *education of the educator*. Children are educated by what the grown-up *is* and not by what he *says*. The popular faith in words is a veritable disease of the mind, for a superstition of this sort always leads farther and farther away from man's foundations and seduces people into a disastrous identification of the personality with whatever slogan may be in vogue. Meanwhile everything that has been overcome and left behind by so-called "progress" sinks deeper and deeper into the unconscious, from which there re-emerges in the end the primitive condition of *identity with the mass*. Instead of the expected progress, this condition now becomes reality.

294   As civilization develops, the bisexual primordial being turns into a symbol of the unity of personality, a symbol of the self, where the war of opposites finds peace. In this way the primordial being becomes the distant goal of man's self-development, having been from the very beginning a projection of his unconscious wholeness. Wholeness consists in the union of the conscious and the unconscious personality. Just as every individual derives from masculine and feminine genes, and the sex is determined by the predominance of the corresponding genes, so in the psyche it is only the conscious mind, in a man, that has the masculine sign, while the unconscious is by nature feminine. The reverse is true in the case of a woman. All I have done in my anima theory is to rediscover and reformulate this fact.[34] It had long been known.

295   The idea of the *coniunctio* of male and female, which became almost a technical term in Hermetic philosophy, appears in Gnosticism as the *mysterium iniquitatis,* probably not uninfluenced by the Old Testament "divine marriage" as

[34] *Psychological Types,* Def. 48; and "Relations between the Ego and the Unconscious," pars. 296ff.

performed, for instance, by Hosea.[35] Such things are hinted at not only by certain traditional customs,[36] but by the quotation from the Gospel according to the Egyptians in the second epistle of Clement: "When the two shall be one, the outside as the inside, and the male with the female neither male nor female." [37] Clement of Alexandria introduces this logion with the words: "When ye have trampled on the garment of shame (with thy feet) . . . ," [38] which probably refers to the body; for Clement as well as Cassian (from whom the quotation was taken over), and the pseudo-Clement, too, interpreted the words in a spiritual sense, in contrast to the Gnostics, who would seem to have taken the *coniunctio* all too literally. They took care, however, through the practice of abortion and other restrictions, that the biological meaning of their acts did not swamp the religious significance of the rite. While, in Church mysticism, the primordial image of the *hieros gamos* was sublimated on a lofty plane and only occasionally—as for instance with Mechthild of Magdeburg [39]—approached the physical sphere in emotional intensity, for the rest of the world it remained very much alive and continued to be the object of especial psychic preoccupation. In this respect the symbolical drawings of Opicinus de Canistris [40] afford us an interesting glimpse of the way in which this primordial image was instrumental in uniting opposites, even in a pathological state. On the other hand, in the Hermetic philosophy that throve in the Middle Ages the *coniunctio* was performed wholly in the physical realm in the admittedly abstract theory of the *coniugium solis et lunae,* which despite this drawback gave the creative imagination much occasion for anthropomorphic flights.

296   Such being the state of affairs, it is readily understandable that the primordial image of the hermaphrodite should reappear in modern psychology in the guise of the male-female antithesis, in other words as *male* consciousness and personified *female* unconscious. But the psychological process of bringing things to consciousness has complicated the picture considerably. Whereas the old science was almost exclusively a field in

35 Hosea 1 : 2ff.   36 Cf. Fendt, *Gnostische Mysterien.*
37 James, *The Apocryphal New Testament,* p. 11.
38 Clement, *Stromata,* III, 13, 92, 2.   39 *The Flowing Light of the Godhead.*
40 Salomon, *Opicinus de Canistris.*

which only the man's unconscious could project itself, the new psychology had to acknowledge the existence of an autonomous female psyche as well. Here the case is reversed, and a feminine consciousness confronts a masculine personification of the unconscious, which can no longer be called *anima* but *animus*. This discovery also complicates the problem of the *coniunctio*.

297   Originally this archetype played its part entirely in the field of fertility magic and thus remained for a very long time a purely biological phenomenon with no other purpose than that of fecundation. But even in early antiquity the symbolical meaning of the act seems to have increased. Thus, for example, the physical performance of the *hieros gamos* as a sacred rite not only became a mystery—it faded to a mere conjecture.[41] As we have seen, Gnosticism, too, endeavoured in all seriousness to subordinate the physiological to the metaphysical. Finally, the Church severed the *coniunctio* from the physical realm altogether, and natural philosophy turned it into an abstract *theoria*. These developments meant the gradual transformation of the archetype into a psychological process which, in theory, we can call a combination of conscious and unconscious processes. In practice, however, it is not so simple, because as a rule the feminine unconscious of a man is projected upon a feminine partner, and the masculine unconscious of a woman is projected upon a man. The elucidation of these problems is a special branch of psychology and has no part in a discussion of the mythological hermaphrodite.

4. *The Child as Beginning and End*

298   Faust, after his death, is received as a boy into the "choir of blessed youths." I do not know whether Goethe was referring, with this peculiar idea, to the *cupids* on antique grave-stones. It is not unthinkable. The figure of the *cucullatus* points to the hooded, that is, the *invisible* one, the genius of the departed, who reappears in the child-like frolics of a new life, surrounded by the sea-forms of dolphins and tritons. The sea is the favourite

41 Cf. the diatribe by Bishop Asterius (Foucart, *Mystères of d'Eleusis*, pp. 477ff.). According to Hippolytus' account the hierophant actually made himself impotent by a draught of hemlock. The self-castration of priests in the worship of the Mother Goddess is of similar import.

symbol for the unconscious, the mother of all that lives. Just as the "child" is, in certain circumstances (e.g., in the case of Hermes and the Dactyls), closely related to the phallus, symbol of the begetter, so it comes up again in the sepulchral phallus, symbol of a renewed begetting.

299   The "child" is therefore *renatus in novam infantiam*. It is thus both beginning and end, an initial and a terminal creature. The initial creature existed before man was, and the terminal creature will be when man is not. Psychologically speaking, this means that the "child" symbolizes the pre-conscious and the post-conscious essence of man. His pre-conscious essence is the unconscious state of earliest childhood; his post-conscious essence is an anticipation by analogy of life after death. In this idea the all-embracing nature of psychic wholeness is expressed. Wholeness is never comprised within the compass of the conscious mind—it includes the indefinite and indefinable extent of the unconscious as well. Wholeness, empirically speaking, is therefore of immeasurable extent, older and younger than consciousness and enfolding it in time and space. This is no speculation, but an immediate psychic experience. Not only is the conscious process continually accompanied, it is often guided, helped, or interrupted, by unconscious happenings. The child had a psychic life before it had consciousness. Even the adult still says and does things whose significance he realizes only later, if ever. And yet he said them and did them as if he knew what they meant. Our dreams are continually saying things beyond our conscious comprehension (which is why they are so useful in the therapy of neuroses). We have intimations and intuitions from unknown sources. Fears, moods, plans, and hopes come to us with no visible causation. These concrete experiences are at the bottom of our feeling that we know ourselves very little; at the bottom, too, of the painful conjecture that we might have surprises in store for ourselves.

300   Primitive man is no puzzle to himself. The question "What is man?" is the question that man has always kept until last. Primitive man has so much psyche outside his conscious mind that the experience of something psychic outside him is far more familiar to him than to us. Consciousness hedged about by psychic powers, sustained or threatened or deluded by them, is the age-old experience of mankind. This experience has pro-

jected itself into the archetype of the child, which expresses man's wholeness. The "child" is all that is abandoned and exposed and at the same time divinely powerful; the insignificant, dubious beginning, and the triumphal end. The "eternal child" in man is an indescribable experience, an incongruity, a handicap, and a divine prerogative; an imponderable that determines the ultimate worth or worthlessness of a personality.

IV. CONCLUSION

301   I am aware that a psychological commentary on the child archetype without detailed documentation must remain a mere sketch. But since this is virgin territory for the psychologist, my main endeavour has been to stake out the possible extent of the problems raised by our archetype and to describe, at least cursorily, its different aspects. Clear-cut distinctions and strict formulations are quite impossible in this field, seeing that a kind of fluid interpenetration belongs to the very nature of all archetypes. They can only be roughly circumscribed at best. Their living meaning comes out more from their presentation as a whole than from a single formulation. Every attempt to focus them more sharply is immediately punished by the intangible core of meaning losing its luminosity. No archetype can be reduced to a simple formula. It is a vessel which we can never empty, and never fill. It has a potential existence only, and when it takes shape in matter it is no longer what it was. It persists throughout the ages and requires interpreting ever anew. The archetypes are the imperishable elements of the unconscious, but they change their shape continually.

302   It is a well-nigh hopeless undertaking to tear a single archetype out of the living tissue of the psyche; but despite their interwovenness they do form units of meaning that can be apprehended intuitively. Psychology, as one of the many expressions of psychic life, operates with ideas which in their turn are derived from archetypal structures and thus generate a somewhat more abstract kind of myth. Psychology therefore translates the archaic speech of myth into a modern mythologem—not yet, of course, recognized as such—which constitutes one element of the myth "science." This seemingly hopeless undertaking

is a *living and lived myth,* satisfying to persons of a correspond-ing temperament, indeed beneficial in so far as they have been cut off from their psychic origins by neurotic dissociation.

303   As a matter of experience, we meet the child archetype in spontaneous and in therapeutically induced individuation proc-esses. The first manifestation of the "child" is as a rule a totally unconscious phenomenon. Here the patient identifies himself with his personal infantilism. Then, under the influence of therapy, we get a more or less gradual separation from and objectification of the "child," that is, the identity breaks down and is accompanied by an intensification (sometimes technically induced) of fantasy, with the result that archaic or mythological features become increasingly apparent. Further transformations run true to the hero myth. The theme of "mighty feats" is gen-erally absent, but on the other hand the mythical dangers play all the greater part. At this stage there is usually another identi-fication, this time with the hero, whose role is attractive for a variety of reasons. The identification is often extremely stub-born and dangerous to the psychic equilibrium. If it can be broken down and if consciousness can be reduced to human proportions, the figure of the hero can gradually be differen-tiated into a symbol of the self.

304   In practical reality, however, it is of course not enough for the patient merely to *know about* such developments; what counts is his experience of the various transformations. The initial stage of personal infantilism presents the picture of an "abandoned" or "misunderstood" and unjustly treated child with overweening pretensions. The epiphany of the hero (the second identification) shows itself in a corresponding inflation: the colossal pretension grows into a conviction that one is some-thing extraordinary, or else the impossibility of the pretension ever being fulfilled only proves one's own inferiority, which is favourable to the role of the heroic sufferer (a negative infla-tion). In spite of their contradictoriness, both forms are identi-cal, because conscious megalomania is balanced by unconscious compensatory inferiority and conscious inferiority by uncon-scious megalomania (you never get one without the other). Once the reef of the second identification has been successfully circumnavigated, conscious processes can be cleanly separated from the unconscious, and the latter observed objectively. This

leads to the possibility of an accommodation with the unconscious, and thus to a possible synthesis of the conscious and unconscious elements of knowledge and action. This in turn leads to a shifting of the centre of personality from the ego to the self.[42]

305   In this psychological framework the motifs of abandonment, invincibility, hermaphroditism, and beginning and end take their place as distinct categories of experience and understanding.

[42] A more detailed account of these developments is to be found in "The Relations between the Ego and the Unconscious."

reflecting on feelings as Bursts from Self

ego no longer identifies with complexes

Personality shifts to focus on self

IV

TRANSFORMATION SYMBOLISM
IN THE MASS

1. INTRODUCTION [1]

296   The Mass is a still-living mystery, the origins of which go
back to early Christian times. It is hardly necessary to point out
that it owes its vitality partly to its undoubted psychological
efficacy, and that it is therefore a fit subject for psychological
study. But it should be equally obvious that psychology can only
approach the subject from the phenomenological angle, for the
realities of faith lie outside the realm of psychology.

297   My exposition falls into four parts: in this introduction I
indicate some of the New Testament sources of the Mass, with
notes on its structure and significance. In section 2, I recapitu-
late the sequence of events in the rite. In 3, I cite a parallel
from pagan antiquity to the Christian symbolism of sacrifice and
transformation: the visions of Zosimos. Finally, in 4, I attempt
a psychological discussion of the sacrifice and transformation.

*

298   The oldest account of the sacrament of the Mass is to be
found in I Corinthians 11 : 23ff.:

1 The following account and examination of the principal symbol in the Mass is
not concerned either with the Mass as a whole, or with its liturgy in particular,
but solely with the ritual actions and texts which relate to the transformation
process in the strict sense. In order to give the reader an adequate account of this,
I had to seek professional help. I am especially indebted to the theologian Dr.
Gallus Jud for reading through and correcting the first two sections.

For the tradition which I have received of the Lord and handed down to you is that the Lord Jesus, on the night he was betrayed, took bread, gave thanks, broke it, and said: *This is my body for you; do this in remembrance of me. And after he had supped, he took the chalice also, and said: This chalice is the new testament in my blood.* As often as you drink, do this in remembrance of me. For as often as you eat this bread and drink the chalice, you declare the death of the Lord, until he comes.[2]

²⁹⁹   Similar accounts are to be found in Matthew, Mark, and Luke. In John the corresponding passage speaks of a "supper," [3] but there it is connected with the washing of the disciples' feet. At this supper Christ utters the words which characterize the meaning and substance of the Mass (John 15:1, 4, 5). "I am the true vine." "Abide in me, and I in you." "I am the vine, ye are the branches." The correspondence between the liturgical accounts points to a traditional source outside the Bible. There is no evidence of an actual feast of the Eucharist until after A.D. 150.

³⁰⁰   The Mass is a Eucharistic feast with an elaborately developed liturgy. It has the following structure:

CONSECRATION

OBLATION   COMMUNION

PRELIMINARIES   CONCLUSION

³⁰¹   As this investigation is concerned essentially with the symbol of transformation, I must refrain from discussing the Mass as a whole.

³⁰²   In the sacrifice of the Mass two distinct ideas are blended together: the ideas of *deipnon* and *thysia*. *Thysia* comes from the verb θύειν, 'to sacrifice' or 'to slaughter'; but it also has the mean-

---

[2] [This is a translation of the Karl von Weizsäcker version (1875) used here by the author. Elsewhere the Biblical quotations are taken from the AV and occasionally from the RSV and the DV. Following are the Greek and Latin (Vulgate) versions of the italicized portion of this passage.—TRANS.]

"... τοῦτο μού ἐστιν τὸ σῶμα τὸ ὑπὲρ ὑμῶν. τοῦτο ποιεῖτε εἰς τὴν ἐμὴν ἀνάμνησιν. ὡσαύτως καὶ τὸ ποτήριον μετὰ τὸ δειπνῆσαι λέγων· τοῦτο τὸ ποτήριον ἡ καινὴ διαθήκη ἐστὶν ἐν τῷ ἐμῷ αἵματι."

"... hoc est corpus meum, quod pro vobis tradetur: hoc facite in meam commemorationem. Similiter et calicem, postquam coenavit, dicens: Hic calix novum testamentum est in meo sanguine."   [3] δεῖπνον, 'coena.'

ing of 'blazing' or 'flaring up.' This refers to the leaping sacrificial fire by which the gift offered to the gods was consumed. Originally the food-offering was intended for the nourishment of the gods; the smoke of the burnt sacrifice carried the food up to their heavenly abode. At a later stage the smoke was conceived as a spiritualized form of food-offering; indeed, all through the Christian era up to the Middle Ages, spirit (or *pneuma*) continued to be thought of as a fine, vaporous substance.[4]

303   *Deipnon* means 'meal.' In the first place it is a meal shared by those taking part in the sacrifice, at which the god was believed to be present. It is also a "sacred" meal at which "consecrated" food is eaten, and hence a *sacrifice* (from *sacrificare,* 'to make sacred,' 'to consecrate').

304   The dual meaning of *deipnon* and *thysia* is implicitly contained in the words of the sacrament: "the body which (was given) for you." [5] This may mean either "which was given to you to eat" or, indirectly, "which was given for you to God." The idea of a meal immediately invests the word 'body' with the meaning of σάρξ, 'flesh' (as an edible substance). In Paul, σῶμα and σάρξ are practically identical.[6]

305   Besides the authentic accounts of the institution of the sacrament, we must also consider Hebrews 13:10–15 as a possible source for the Mass:

We have an altar, whereof they have no right to eat which serve the tabernacle. For the bodies of those beasts, whose blood is brought into the sanctuary by the high priest for sin, are burned without the camp. Wherefore Jesus also, that he might sanctify the people with his own blood, suffered without the gate. Let us go forth therefore unto him without the camp, bearing his reproach. For here have we no continuing city, but we seek one to come. By him therefore let us offer the sacrifice of praise to God continually. . . .

306   As a further source we might mention Hebrews 7:17: "Thou art a priest for ever after the order of Melchisedec." [7] The idea

---

4 This of course has nothing to do with the official conception of spirit by the Church.   5 "τὸ σῶμα τὸ ὑπὲρ ὑμῶν."

6 Käsemann, *Leib und Leib Christi,* p. 120.

7 Dr. Jud kindly drew my attention to the equally relevant passage in Malachi 1:10–11: "Who is there even among you that would shut the doors for nought? neither do ye kindle fire on mine altar for nought. . . . And in every place incense shall be offered unto my name, and a pure offering . . ."

of perpetual sacrifice and of an eternal priesthood is an essential component of the Mass. Melchisedec, who according to Hebrews 7 : 3 was "without father, without mother, without descent, having neither beginning of days, nor end of life, but made like unto the Son of God," was believed to be a pre-Christian incarnation of the Logos.

307   The idea of an eternal priesthood and of a sacrifice offered to God "continually" brings us to the true *mysterium fidei,* the transformation of the substances, which is the third aspect of the Mass. The ideas of *deipnon* and *thysia* do not in themselves imply or contain a mystery, although, in the burnt offering which is reduced to smoke and ashes by the fire, there is a primitive allusion to a transformation of substance in the sense of its spiritualization. But this aspect is of no practical importance in the Mass, where it only appears in subsidiary form in the censing, as an incense-offering. The *mysterium,* on the other hand, manifests itself clearly enough in the eternal priest "after the order of Melchisedec" and in the sacrifice which he offers to God "continually." The manifestation of an order outside time involves the idea of a *miracle* which takes place "vere, realiter, substantialiter" at the moment of transubstantiation, for the substances offered are no different from natural objects, and must in fact be definite commodities whose nature is known to everybody, namely pure wheaten bread and wine. Furthermore, the officiating priest is an ordinary human being who, although he bears the indelible mark of the priesthood upon him and is thus empowered to offer sacrifice, is nevertheless not yet in a position to be the instrument of the divine self-sacrifice enacted in the Mass.[8] Nor is the congregation standing behind him yet purged from sin, consecrated, and itself transformed into a sacrificial gift. The ritual of the Mass takes this situation and transforms it step by step until the climax is reached—the Conse-

---

[8] That is to say, not before he has accomplished the preparatory part of the service. In offering these gifts the priest is not the "master" of the sacrifice. "Rather that which causes them to be sacrificed in the first place is sanctifying grace. For that is what their sacrifice means: their sanctification. The man who each time performs the sacred act is the servant of grace, and that is why the gifts and their sacrifice are always pleasing to God. The fact that the servant may be bad does not affect them in any way. The priest is only the servant, and even this he has from grace, not from himself." Joseph Kramp, S.J., *Die Opferanschauungen der römischen Messliturgie,* p. 148.

cration, when Christ himself, as sacrificer and sacrificed, speaks the decisive words through the mouth of the priest. At that moment Christ is present in time and space. Yet his presence is not a reappearance, and therefore the inner meaning of the consecration is not a repetition of an event which occurred once in history, but the revelation of something existing in eternity, a rending of the veil of temporal and spatial limitations which separates the human spirit from the sight of the eternal. This event is necessarily a mystery, because it is beyond the power of man to conceive or describe. In other words, the rite is necessarily and in every one of its parts a *symbol*. Now a symbol is not an arbitrary or intentional sign standing for a known and conceivable fact, but an admittedly anthropomorphic—hence limited and only partly valid—expression for something suprahuman and only partly conceivable. It may be the best expression possible, yet it ranks below the level of the mystery it seeks to describe. The Mass is a symbol in this sense. Here I would like to quote the words of Father Kramp: "It is generally admitted that the sacrifice is a *symbolic* act, by which I mean that the offering of a material gift to God has no purpose in itself, but merely serves as a means to express an idea. And the choice of this means of expression brings a wide range of anthropomorphism into play: man confronts God as he confronts his own kind, almost as if God were a human being. We offer a gift to God as we offer it to a good friend or to an earthly ruler." [9]

308   In so far, then, as the Mass is an anthropomorphic symbol standing for something otherworldly and beyond our power to conceive, its symbolism is a legitimate subject for comparative psychology and analytical research. My psychological explanations are, of course, exclusively concerned with the symbolical expression.

[9] Ibid., p. 17.

2. THE SEQUENCE OF THE TRANSFORMATION RITE

309   The rite of transformation may be said to begin with the Offertory, an antiphon recited during the offering of the sacrificial gifts. Here we encounter the first ritual act relating to the transformation.[1]

I. OBLATION OF THE BREAD

310   The Host is lifted up towards the cross on the altar, and the priest makes the sign of the cross over it with the paten. The bread is thus brought into relation with Christ and his death on the cross; it is marked as a "sacrifice" and thereby becomes sacred. The elevation exalts it into the realm of the spiritual: it is a preliminary act of spiritualization. Justin makes the interesting remark that the presentation of the cleansed lepers in the temple was an image of the Eucharistic bread.[2] This links up with the later alchemical idea of the imperfect or "leprous" substance which is made perfect by the *opus*. (*Quod natura relinquit imperfectum, arte perficitur.*—"What nature leaves imperfect is perfected by the art.")

[1] In the account that follows I have made extensive use of Brinktrine, *Die Heilige Messe in ihrem Werden und Wesen.*

[2] "Τύπος τοῦ ἄρτου τῆς εὐχαριστίας."

II. PREPARATION OF THE CHALICE

311   This is still more solemn than that of the bread, corresponding to the "spiritual" nature of the wine, which is reserved for the priest.[3] Some water is mingled with the wine.

312   The mixing of water with the wine originally referred to the ancient custom of not drinking wine unless mixed with water. A drunkard was therefore called᷐ *akratopotes*, an 'unmixed drinker.' In modern Greek, wine is still called κρασί (mixture). From the custom of the Monophysite Armenians, who did not add any water to the Eucharistic wine (so as to preserve the exclusively divine nature of Christ), it may be inferred that water has a hylical, or physical, significance and represents man's material nature. The mixing of water and wine in the Roman rite would accordingly signify that divinity is mingled with humanity as indivisibly as the wine with the water.[4] St. Cyprian (bishop of Carthage, d. 258) says that the wine refers to Christ, and the water to the congregation as the body of Christ. The significance of the water is explained by an allusion to the Book of Revelation 17:15: "The waters which thou sawest, where the whore sitteth, are peoples, and multitudes, and nations, and tongues." (In alchemy, *meretrix* the whore is a synonym for the *prima materia,* the *corpus imperfectum* which is sunk in darkness, like the man who wanders in darkness, unconscious and unredeemed. This idea is foreshadowed in the Gnostic image of Physis, who with passionate arms draws the Nous down from heaven and wraps him in her dark embrace.) As the water is an imperfect or even leprous substance, it has to be blessed and consecrated before being mixed, so that only a purified body may be joined to the wine of the spirit, just as Christ is to be united only with a pure and sanctified congregation. Thus this part of the rite has the special significance of preparing a perfect body—the glorified body of resurrection.

313   At the time of St. Cyprian the communion was generally celebrated with water.[5] And, still later, St. Ambrose (bishop of

---

[3] That is, in the Roman rite. In the Greek Uniate rites, communion is received in bread *and* wine.

[4] This is the interpretation of Yves, bishop of Chartres (d. 1116).

[5] Cyprian attacks this heretical custom in his letter to Caecilius. Letter 63 to Caecilius, Migne, *P.L.,* vol. 4, cols. 372ff. (trans. by Carey, pp. 181ff.).

Milan, d. 397) says: "In the shadow there was water from the rock, as it were the blood of Christ." [6] The water communion is prefigured in John 7:37–39: "If any man thirst, let him come unto me, and drink. He that believeth on me, as the scripture hath said, out of his belly flow rivers of living water. (But this he spake of the Spirit, which they that believe on him should receive: for the Holy Ghost was not yet given, because that Jesus was not yet glorified.)" And also in John 4:14: "But whosoever drinketh of the water that I shall give him shall never thirst; but the water that I shall give him shall be in him a well of water springing up into everlasting life." The words "as the scripture hath said, out of his belly shall flow rivers of living water" do not occur anywhere in the Old Testament. They must therefore come from a writing which the author of the Johannine gospel obviously regarded as holy, but which is not known to us. It is just possible that they are based on Isaiah 58:11: "And the Lord shall guide thee continually, and satisfy thy soul in drought, and make fat thy bones: and thou shalt be like a watered garden, and like a spring of water, whose waters fail not." Another possibility is Ezekiel 47:1: "Afterward he brought me again unto the door of the house; and, behold, waters issued out from under the threshold of the house eastward . . . and the waters came down from under from the right side of the house, at the south side of the altar." In the Church Order of Hippolytus (d. c. 235) the water chalice is associated with the baptismal font, where the inner man is renewed as well as the body.[7] This interpretation comes very close to the baptismal *krater* of Poimandres [8] and to the Hermetic basin filled with *nous* which God gave to those seeking ἔννοια.[9] Here the water signifies the *pneuma*, i.e., the spirit of prophecy, and also the doctrine which a man receives

---

[6] "In umbra erat aqua de petra quasi sanguis ex Christo." The *umbra*, 'shadow,' refers to the foreshadowing in the Old Testament, in accordance with the saying: "Umbra in lege, imago in evangelio, veritas in coelestibus" (The shadow in the Law, the image in the Gospel, the truth in Heaven). Note that this remark of Ambrose does not refer to the Eucharist but to the water symbolism of early Christianity in general; and the same is true of the passages from John. St. Augustine himself says: "There the rock was Christ; for to us that is Christ which is placed on the altar of God." *Tractatus in Joannem*, XLV, 9 (trans. by Innes).

[7] Connolly, ed., *The So-called Egyptian Church Order and Derived Documents*.

[8] Berthelot, *Collection des anciens alchimistes grecs*, III, li. 8.

[9] *Corpus Hermeticum*, Lib. IV, 4, in *Hermetica*, I, p. 151.

and passes on to others.[10] The same image of the spiritual water occurs in the "Odes of Solomon": [11]

For there went forth a stream, and became a river great and broad; . . . and all the thirsty upon earth were given to drink of it; and thirst was relieved and quenched; for from the Most High the draught was given. Blessed then are the ministers of that draught who are entrusted with that water of His; they have assuaged the dry lips, and the will that had fainted they have raised up; and souls that were near departing they have caught back from death; and limbs that had fallen they straightened and set up; they gave strength for their feebleness and light to their eyes. For everyone knew them in the Lord, and they lived by the water of life for ever.[12]

314   The fact that the Eucharist was also celebrated with water shows that the early Christians were mainly interested in the symbolism of the mysteries and not in the literal observance of the sacrament. (There were several other variants—"galactophagy," for instance—which all bear out this view.)

315   Another, very graphic, interpretation of the wine and water is the reference to John 19:34: "And forthwith came there out blood and water." Deserving of special emphasis is the remark of St. John Chrysostom (patriarch of Constantinople, d. 407), that in drinking the wine Christ drank his own blood. (See Section 3, on Zosimos.)

316   In this section of the Mass we meet the important prayer:

O God, who in creating human nature, didst wonderfully dignify it, and hast still more wonderfully renewed it; grant that, by the mystery of this water and wine, we may be made partakers of his divinity who vouchsafed to become partaker of our humanity, Jesus Christ. . . .[13]

---

10 Strack and Billerbeck, *Kommentar zum Neuen Testament aus Talmud und Midrasch*, II, p. 492.   11 A collection of Gnostic hymns from the 2nd cent.
12 Ode VI in *The Odes of Solomon*, ed. Bernard, p. 55, after the J. Rendel Harris version. Cf. the ὕδωρ θεῖον, the *aqua permanens* of early alchemy, also the treatise of Komarius (Berthelot, IV, xx).
13 "Deus, qui humanae substantiae dignitatem mirabiliter condidisti, et mirabilius reformasti; da nobis per huius aquae et vini mysterium, eius divinitatis esse consortes, qui humanitatis nostrae fieri dignatus est particeps, Jesus Christus . . ." [Here and throughout this essay the English translation is taken from *The Small Missal*, London, 1924.—TRANS.]

III. ELEVATION OF THE CHALICE

317   The lifting up of the chalice in the air prepares the spiritualization (i.e., volatilization) of the wine.[14] This is confirmed by the invocation to the Holy Ghost which immediately follows (*Veni sanctificator*), and it is even more evident in the Mozarabic liturgy, which has "Veni spiritus sanctificator." [15] The invocation serves to infuse the wine with holy spirit, for it is the Holy Ghost who begets, fulfils, and transforms (cf. the "Obumbratio Mariae," Pentecostal fire). After the elevation, the chalice was, in former times, set down to the right of the Host, to correspond with the blood that flowed from the right side of Christ.

IV. CENSING OF THE SUBSTANCES AND THE ALTAR

318   The priest makes the sign of the cross three times over the substances with the thurible, twice from right to left and once from left to right.[16] The counterclockwise movement (from right to left) corresponds psychologically to a circumambulation downwards, in the direction of the unconscious, while the clockwise (left-to-right) movement goes in the direction of consciousness. There is also a complicated censing of the altar.[17]

319   The censing has the significance of an incense offering and is therefore a relic of the original *thysia*. At the same time it signifies a transformation of the sacrificial gifts and of the altar, a spiritualization of all the physical substances subserving the rite. Finally, it is an apotropaic ceremony to drive away any demonic forces that may be present, for it fills the air with the fragrance of the *pneuma* and renders it uninhabitable by evil spirits. The vapour also suggests the sublimated body, the *corpus volatile sive spirituale,* or wraithlike "subtle body." Rising up as a "spiritual" substance, the incense implements and represents the ascent of

---

[14] This is *my* interpretation and not that of the Church, which sees in this only an act of devotion.

[15] "Mozarabic" from Arabic *musta'rib*, 'Arabianized,' with reference to the Visigothic-Spanish form of ritual. [The Latin phrases: "Come, O sanctifying one." "Come, O sanctifying spirit."—EDITORS.]

[16] The circumambulation from left to right is strictly observed in Buddhism.

[17] The censing is only performed at High Mass.

prayer—hence the *Dirigatur, Domine, oratio mea, sicut incensum, in conspectu tuo.*[18]

320   The censing brings the preparatory, spiritualizing rites to an end. The gifts have been sanctified and prepared for the actual transubstantiation. Priest and congregation are likewise purified by the prayers *Accendat in nobis Dominus ignem sui amoris* and *Lavabo inter innocentes,*[19] and are made ready to enter into the mystic union of the sacrificial act which now follows.

V. THE EPICLESIS

321   The *Suscipe, sancta Trinitas,* like the *Orate, fratres,* the *Sanctus,* and the *Te igitur,* is a propitiatory prayer which seeks to insure the acceptance of the sacrifice. Hence the Preface that comes after the Secret is called *Illatio* in the Mozarabic rite (the equivalent of the Greek ἀναφορά), and in the old Gallican liturgy is known as *Immolatio* (in the sense of *oblatio*), with reference to the presentation of the gifts. The words of the *Sanctus,* "Benedictus qui venit in nomine Domini," [20] point to the expected appearance of the Lord which has already been prepared, on the ancient principle that a "naming" has the force of a "summons." After the Canon there follows the "Commemoration of the Living," together with the prayers *Hanc igitur* and *Quam oblationem.* In the Mozarabic Mass these are followed by the Epiclesis (invocation): "Adesto, adesto Jesu, bone Pontifex, in medio nostri: sicut fuisti in medio discipulorum tuorum." [21] This naming likewise has the original force of a summons. It is an intensification of the *Benedictus qui venit,* and it may be, and sometimes was, regarded as the actual manifestation of the Lord, and hence as the culminating point of the Mass.

18 ["Let my prayer, O Lord, ascend like incense in thy sight."]
19 ["May the Lord enkindle in us the fire of his love." / "I will wash my hands among the innocent."]
20 ["Blessed is he that cometh in the name of the Lord."]
21 ["Be present, be present in our midst, O Jesus, great High Priest: as thou wert in the midst of thy disciples."]

VI. THE CONSECRATION

322   This, in the Roman Mass, is the climax, the transubstantiation of the bread and wine into the body and blood of Christ. The formula for the consecration of the bread runs: [22]

> Qui pridie quam pateretur, accepit panem in sanctas ac venerabiles manus suas, et elevatis oculis in caelum ad te Deum, Patrem suum omnipotentem, tibi gratias agens, benedixit, fregit, deditque discipulis suis, dicens: Accipite, et manducate ex hoc omnes. Hoc est enim Corpus meum.

And for the consecration of the chalice:

> Simili modo postquam coenatum est, accipiens et hunc praeclarum Calicem in sanctas ac venerabiles manus suas, item tibi gratias agens, benedixit, deditque discipulis suis, dicens: Accipite, et bibite ex eo omnes. Hic est enim Calix Sanguinis mei, novi et aeterni testamenti: mysterium fidei: qui pro vobis et pro multis effundetur in remissionem peccatorum. Haec quotiescumque feceritis, in mei memoriam facietis.

323   The priest and congregation, as well as the substances and the altar, have now been progressively purified, consecrated, exalted, and spiritualized by means of the prayers and rites which began with the Preliminaries and ended with the Canon, and are thus prepared as a mystical unity for the divine epiphany. Hence the uttering of the words of the consecration signifies Christ himself speaking in the first person, his living presence in the *corpus mysticum* of priest, congregation, bread, wine, and incense, which together form the mystical unity offered for sacrifice. At this moment the eternal character of the one divine sacrifice is made evident: it is experienced at a particular time and a particular place, as if a window or a door had been opened upon that which lies beyond space and time. It is in this sense that we have to understand the words of St. Chrysostom: "And this word once uttered in any church, at any altar, makes perfect the sacrifice from that day to this, and till his Second Coming." It is clear that only by our Lord's presence in his words, and by their virtue, is the imperfect body of the sacrifice made perfect,

[22] According to the edict of the Church these words ought not, on account of their sacredness, to be translated into any profane tongue. Although there are missals that sin against this wise edict, I would prefer the Latin text to stand untranslated.

and not by the preparatory action of the priest. Were this the efficient cause, the rite would be no different from common magic. The priest is only the *causa ministerialis* of the transubstantiation. The real cause is the living presence of Christ which operates spontaneously, as an act of divine grace.

324   Accordingly, John of Damascus (d. 754) says that the words have a consecrating effect no matter by what priest they be spoken, as if Christ were present and uttering them himself. And Duns Scotus (d. 1308) remarks that, in the sacrament of the Last Supper, Christ, by an act of will, offers himself as a sacrifice in every Mass, through the agency of the priest.[23] This tells us plainly enough that the sacrificial act is not performed by the priest, but by Christ himself. The agent of transformation is nothing less than the divine will working through Christ. The Council of Trent declared that in the sacrifice of the Mass "the selfsame Christ is contained and bloodlessly sacrificed," [24] although this is not a repetition of the historical sacrifice but a bloodless renewal of it. As the sacramental words have the power to accomplish the sacrifice, being an expression of God's will, they can be described metaphorically as the sacrificial knife or sword which, guided by his will, consummates the *thysia*. This comparison was first drawn by the Jesuit father Lessius (d. 1623), and has since gained acceptance as an ecclesiastical figure of speech. It is based on Hebrews 4:12: "For the word of God is quick, and powerful, and sharper than any two-edged sword," and perhaps even more on the Book of Revelation 1:16: "And out of his mouth went a sharp two-edged sword." The "mactation theory" first appeared in the sixteenth century. Its originator, Cuesta, bishop of Leon (d. 1560), declared that Christ was slaughtered by the priest. So the sword metaphor followed quite naturally.[25] Nicholas Cabasilas, archbishop of Thessalonica (d.

23 Klug, in *Theologie und Glaube*, XVIII (1926), 335f. Cited by Brinktrine, p. 192.
24 "idem ille Christus continetur et incruente immolatur." Sessio XXII. Denzinger and Bannwart, *Enchiridion Symbolorum*, p. 312.
25 "Missa est sacrificium hac ratione quia Christus aliquo modo moritur et a sacerdote mactatur" (The Mass is a sacrifice for the reason that in it Christ dies after a certain manner, and is slain by the priest). Hauck, *Realenzyklopädie*, XII, p. 693. The question of the *mactatio* had already been raised by Nicholas Cabasilas of Thessalonica: "De divino altaris sacrificio," in Migne, *P.G.*, vol. 150, cols. 363ff. The sword as a sacrificial instrument also occurs in the Zosimos visions (see section 3).

c. 1363), gives a vivid description of the corresponding rite in the Greek Orthodox Church:

> The priest cuts a piece of bread from the loaf, reciting the text: "As a lamb he was led to the slaughter." Laying it on the table he says: "The lamb of God is slain." Then a sign of the cross is imprinted on the bread and a small lance is stabbed into its side, to the text: "And one of the soldiers with a spear pierced his side, and forthwith came there out blood and water." With these words water and wine are mixed in the chalice, which is placed beside the bread.

The δῶρον (gift) also represents the giver; that is to say, Christ is both the sacrificer and the sacrificed.

325   Kramp writes: "Sometimes the *fractio* and sometimes the *elevatio* which precedes the Pater noster was taken as symbolizing the death of Christ, sometimes the sign of the cross at the end of the *Supplices,* and sometimes the *consecratio;* but no one ever thought of taking a symbol like the 'mystical slaughter' as a sacrifice which constitutes the essence of the Mass. So it is not surprising that there is no mention of any 'slaughter' in the liturgy." [26]

VII. THE GREATER ELEVATION

326   The consecrated substances are lifted up and shown to the congregation. The Host in particular represents a beatific vision of heaven, in fulfilment of Psalm 27:8: "Thy face, Lord, will I seek," for in it the Divine Man is present.

VIII. THE POST-CONSECRATION

327   There now follows the significant prayer *Unde et memores,* which I give in full together with the *Supra quae* and *Supplices:*

> Wherefore, O Lord, we thy servants, as also thy holy people, calling to mind the blessed passion of the same Christ thy Son our Lord, his resurrection from hell, and glorious ascension into heaven, offer unto thy most excellent majesty, of thy gifts and grants, a pure Host, a holy Host, an immaculate Host, the holy bread of eternal life, and the chalice of everlasting salvation.

[26] Kramp, p. 56.

Upon which vouchsafe to look down with a propitious and serene countenance, and to accept them, as thou wert graciously pleased to accept the gifts of thy just servant Abel, and the sacrifice of our patriarch Abraham, and that which thy high priest Melchisedec offered to thee, a holy sacrifice, an immaculate Host.

We most humbly beseech thee, almighty God, command these things to be carried by the hands of thy holy angel to thy altar on high, in the sight of thy divine majesty, that as many of us as, by participation at this altar, shall receive the most sacred body and blood of thy Son, may be filled with all heavenly benediction and grace. Through the same Christ, our Lord. Amen.[27]

328   The first prayer shows that in the transformed substances there is an allusion to the resurrection and glorification of our Lord, and the second prayer recalls the sacrifices prefigured in the Old Testament. Abel sacrificed a lamb; Abraham was to sacrifice his son, but a ram was substituted at the last moment. Melchisedec offers no sacrifice, but comes to meet Abraham with bread and wine. This sequence is probably not accidental—it forms a sort of crescendo. Abel is essentially the son, and sacrifices an animal; Abraham is essentially the father—indeed, the "tribal father"—and therefore on a higher level. He does not offer a choice possession merely, but is ready to sacrifice the best and dearest thing he has—his only son. Melchisedec ("teacher of righteousness"), is, according to Hebrews 7:1, king of Salem and "priest of the most high God," El 'Elyon. Philo Byblius mentions a Ἐλιοῦν ὁ ὕψιστος as a Canaanite deity,[28] but he cannot be identical with Yahweh. Abraham nevertheless acknowledges the

27 "Unde et memores, Domine, nos servi tui, sed et plebs tua sancta, eiusdem Christi Filii tui, Domini nostri, tam beatae passionis, nec non et ab inferis resurrectionis, sed et in caelos gloriosae ascensionis: offerimus praeclarae majestati tuae de tuis donis ac datis, hostiam puram, hostiam sanctam, hostiam immaculatam, Panem sanctum vitae aeternae, et Calicem salutis perpetuae.

"Supra quae propitio ac sereno vultu respicere digneris: et accepta habere, sicuti accepta habere dignatus es munera pueri tui justi Abel, et sacrificium Patriarchae nostri Abrahae: et quod tibi obtulit summus sacerdos tuus Melchisedech, sanctum sacrificium, immaculatam hostiam.

"Supplices te rogamus, omnipotens Deus: jube haec perferri per manus sancti Angeli tui in sublime altare tuum, in conspectu divinae majestatis tuae: ut, quotquot ex hac altaris participatione sacrosanctum Filii tui corpus, et sanguinem sumpserimus, omni benedictione caelesti et gratia repleamur. Per eundem Christum, Dominum nostrum. Amen."

28 Eusebius, *Evangelica praeparatio*, I, 10, 11 (Migne, *P.G.*, vol. 21, col. 30).

priesthood of Melchisedec [29] by paying him "a tenth part of all." By virtue of his priesthood, Melchisedec stands above the patriarch, and his feasting of Abraham has the significance of a priestly act. We must therefore attach a symbolical meaning to it, as is in fact suggested by the bread and wine. Consequently the symbolical offering ranks even higher than the sacrifice of a son, which is still the sacrifice of somebody else. Melchisedec's offering is thus a prefiguration of Christ's sacrifice of himself.

329   In the prayer *Supplices te rogamus* we beseech God to bring the gifts "by the hands of thy holy angel to thy altar on high." This singular request derives from the apocryphal *Epistolae Apostolorum,* where there is a legend that Christ, before he became incarnate, bade the archangels take his place at God's altar during his absence.[30] This brings out the idea of the eternal priesthood which links Christ with Melchisedec.

IX. END OF THE CANON

330   Taking up the Host, the priest makes the sign of the cross three times over the chalice, and says: "Through Him, and with Him, and in Him." Then he makes the sign of the cross twice between himself and the chalice. This establishes the identity of Host, chalice, and priest, thus affirming once more the unity of all parts of the sacrifice. The union of Host and chalice signifies the union of the body and blood, i.e., the quickening of the body with a soul, for blood is equivalent to soul. Then follows the *Pater noster.*

X. BREAKING OF THE HOST ("FRACTIO")

331   The prayer "Deliver us, O Lord, we beseech thee, from all evils, past, present, and to come" lays renewed emphasis on the petition made in the preceding *Pater noster:* "but deliver us from evil." The connection between this and the sacrificial death of Christ lies in the descent into hell and the breaking of the

[29] "Sidik" is a Phoenician name for God. Sir Leonard Woolley gives a very interesting explanation of this in his report on the excavations at Ur: *Abraham: Recent Discoveries and Hebrew Origins.*   [30] Kramp, p. 98.

infernal power. The breaking of the bread that now follows is symbolic of Christ's death. The Host is broken in two over the chalice. A small piece, the *particula,* is broken off from the left half and used for the rite of *consignatio* and *commixtio.* In the Byzantine rite the bread is divided into four, the four pieces being marked with letters as follows:

ΙΣ

NI   KA

ΧΣ

This means "'Ιησοῦς Χριστὸς νικᾷ"—'Jesus Christ is victorious.' The peculiar arrangement of the letters obviously represents a quaternity, which as we know always has the character of wholeness. This quaternity, as the letters show, refers to Christ glorified, king of glory and Pantokrator.

332   Still more complicated is the Mozarabic *fractio:* the Host is first broken into two, then the left half into five parts, and the right into four. The five are named *corporatio (incarnatio), nativitas, circumcisio, apparitio,* and *passio;* and the four *mors, resurrectio, gloria, regnum.* The first group refers exclusively to the human life of our Lord, the second to his existence beyond this world. According to the old view, five is the number of the natural ("hylical") man, whose outstretched arms and legs form, with the head, a pentagram. Four, on the other hand, signifies eternity and totality (as shown for instance by the Gnostic name "Barbelo," which is translated as "fourness is God"). This symbol, I would add in passing, seems to indicate that extension in space signifies God's suffering (on the cross) and, on the other hand, his dominion over the universe.

XI. CONSIGNATIO

333   The sign of the cross is made over the chalice with the *particula,* and then the priest drops it into the wine.

XII. COMMIXTIO

334   This is the mingling of bread and wine, as explained by Theodore of Mopsuestia (d. 428?): ". . . he combines them into one, whereby it is made manifest to everybody that although

they are two they are virtually one." [31] The text at this point says: "May this mixture and consecration [*commixtio et consecratio*] of the body and blood of our Lord help us," etc. The word 'consecration' may be an allusion to an original consecration by contact, though that would not clear up the contradiction since a consecration of both substances has already taken place. Attention has therefore been drawn to the old custom of holding over the sacrament from one Mass to another, the Host being dipped in wine and then preserved in softened, or mixed, form. There are numerous rites that end with minglings of this kind. Here I would only mention the consecration by water, or the mixed drink of honey and milk which the neophytes were given after communion in the Church Order of Hippolytus.

335   The *Leonine Sacramentary* (seventh century) interprets the *commixtio* as a mingling of the heavenly and earthly nature of Christ. The later view was that it symbolizes the resurrection, since in it the blood (or soul) of our Lord is reunited with the body lying in the sepulchre. There is a significant reversal here of the original rite of baptism. In baptism, the body is immersed in water for the purpose of transformation; in the *commixtio,* on the other hand, the body, or *particula,* is steeped in wine, symbolizing spirit, and this amounts to a glorification of the body. Hence the justification for regarding the *commixtio* as a symbol of the resurrection.

XIII. CONCLUSION

336   On careful examination we find that the sequence of ritual actions in the Mass contains, sometimes clearly and sometimes by subtle allusions, a representation in condensed form of the life and sufferings of Christ. Certain phases overlap or are so close together that there can be no question of conscious and deliberate condensation. It is more likely that the historical evolution of the Mass gradually led to its becoming a concrete picture of the most important aspects of Christ's life. First of all (in the *Benedictus qui venit* and *Supra quae*) we have an anticipation and prefiguration of his coming. The uttering of the words

[31] Rücker, ed., *Ritus baptismi et missae quam descripsit Theodorus ep. Mopsuestanus.*

of consecration corresponds to the incarnation of the Logos, and also to Christ's passion and sacrificial death, which appears again in the *fractio*. In the *Libera nos* there is an allusion to the descent into hell, while the *consignatio* and *commixtio* hint at resurrection.

337   In so far as the offered gift is the sacrificer himself, in so far as the priest and congregation offer themselves in the sacrificial gift, and in so far as Christ is both sacrificer and sacrificed, there is a mystical unity of all parts of the sacrificial act.[32] The combination of offering and offerer in the single figure of Christ is implicit in the doctrine that just as bread is composed of many grains of wheat, and wine of many grapes, so the mystical body of the Church is made up of a multitude of believers. The mystical body, moreover, includes both sexes, represented by the bread and wine.[33] Thus the two substances—the masculine wine and the feminine bread—also signify the androgynous nature of the mystical Christ.

338   The Mass thus contains, as its essential core, the mystery and miracle of God's transformation taking place in the human sphere, his becoming Man, and his return to his absolute existence in and for himself. Man, too, by his devotion and self-sacrifice as a ministering instrument, is included in the mysterious process. God's offering of himself is a voluntary act of love, but the actual sacrifice was an agonizing and bloody death brought about by men *instrumentaliter et ministerialiter*. (The words *incruente immolatur*—'bloodlessly sacrificed'—refer only to the rite, not to the thing symbolized.) The terrors of death on the cross are an indispensable condition for the transformation. This is in the first place a bringing to life of substances which are in themselves lifeless, and, in the second, a substantial alteration of them, a spiritualization, in accordance with the ancient conception of *pneuma* as a subtle material entity (the *corpus glorificationis*). This idea is expressed in the concrete participation in the body and blood of Christ in the Communion.

[32] This unity is a good example of *participation mystique*, which Lévy-Bruhl stressed as being one of the main characteristics of primitive psychology—a view that has recently been contested by ethnologists in a very short-sighted manner. The idea of unity should not, however, be regarded as "primitive" but rather as showing that *participation mystique* is a characteristic of symbols in general. The symbol always includes the unconscious, hence man too is contained in it. The *numinosity* of the symbol is an expression of this fact.   [33] Kramp, p. 55.

3. PARALLELS TO THE TRANSFORMATION
MYSTERY

I. THE AZTEC "TEOQUALO"

339   Although the Mass itself is a unique phenomenon in the history of comparative religion, its symbolic content would be profoundly alien to man were it not rooted in the human psyche. But if it is so rooted, then we may expect to find similar patterns of symbolism both in the earlier history of mankind and in the world of pagan thought contemporary with it. As the prayer *Supra quae* shows, the liturgy of the Mass contains allusions to the "prefigurations" in the Old Testament, and thus indirectly to ancient sacrificial symbolism in general. It is clear, then, that in Christ's sacrifice and the Communion one of the deepest chords in the human psyche is struck: human sacrifice and ritual anthropophagy. Unfortunately I cannot enter into the wealth of ethnological material in question here, so must content myself with mentioning the ritual slaying of the king to promote the fertility of the land and the prosperity of his people, the renewal and revivification of the gods through human sacrifice, and the totem meal, the purpose of which was to reunite the participants with the life of their ancestors. These hints will suffice to show how the symbols of the Mass penetrate into the deepest layers of the psyche and its history. They are evidently

178

among the most ancient and most central of religious conceptions. Now with regard to these conceptions there is still a widespread prejudice, not only among laymen, but in scientific circles too, that beliefs and customs of this kind must have been "invented" at some time or other, and were then handed down and imitated, so that they would not exist at all in most places unless they had got there in the manner suggested. It is, however, always precarious to draw conclusions from our modern, "civilized" mentality about the primitive state of mind. Primitive consciousness differs from that of the present-day white man in several very important respects. Thus, in primitive societies, "inventing" is very different from what it is with us, where one novelty follows another. With primitives, life goes on in the same way for generations; nothing alters, except perhaps the language. But that does not mean that a new one is "invented." Their language is "alive" and can therefore change, a fact that has been an unpleasant discovery for many lexicographers of primitive languages. Similarly, no one "invents" the picturesque slang spoken in America; it just springs up in inexhaustible abundance from the fertile soil of colloquial speech. Religious rites and their stock of symbols must have developed in much the same way from beginnings now lost to us, and not just in one place only, but in many places at once, and also at different periods. They have grown spontaneously out of the basic conditions of human nature, which are never invented but are everywhere the same.

340 So it is not surprising that we find religious rites which come very close to Christian practices in a field untouched by classical culture. I mean the rites of the Aztecs, and in particular that of the *teoqualo*, 'god-eating,' as recorded by Fray Bernardino de Sahagún, who began his missionary work among the Aztecs in 1529, eight years after the conquest of Mexico. In this rite, a doughlike paste was made out of the crushed and pounded seeds of the prickly poppy (*Argemone mexicana*) and moulded into the figure of the god Huitzilopochtli:

And upon the next day the body of Huitzilopochtli died.
And he who slew him was the priest known as Quetzalcoatl. And that with which he slew him was a dart, pointed with flint, which he shot into his heart.
He died in the presence of Moctezuma and of the keeper of the

god, who verily spoke to Huitzilopochtli—who verily appeared before him, who indeed could make him offerings; and of four masters of the youths, front rank leaders. Before all of them died Huitzilopochtli.

And when he had died, thereupon they broke up his body of . . . dough. His heart was apportioned to Moctezuma.

And as for the rest of his members, which were made, as it were, to be his bones, they were distributed and divided up among all. . . . Each year . . . they ate it. . . . And when they divided up among themselves his body made of . . . dough, it was broken up exceeding small, very fine, as small as seeds. The youths ate it.

And of this which they ate, it was said: "The god is eaten." And of those who ate it, it was said: "They guard the god." [1]

341   The idea of a divine body, its sacrifice in the presence of the high priest to whom the god appears and with whom he speaks, the piercing with the spear, the god's death followed by ritual dismemberment, and the eating (communio) of a small piece of his body, are all parallels which cannot be overlooked and which caused much consternation among the worthy Spanish Fathers at the time.

342   In Mithraism, a religion that sprang up not long before Christianity, we find a special set of sacrificial symbols and, it would seem, a corresponding ritual which unfortunately is known to us only from dumb monuments. There is a transitus, with Mithras carrying the bull; a bull-sacrifice for seasonal fertility; a stereotyped representation of the sacrificial act, flanked on either side by dadophors carrying raised and lowered torches; and a meal at which pieces of bread marked with crosses were laid on the table. Even small bells have been found, and these probably have some connection with the bell which is sounded at Mass. The Mithraic sacrifice is essentially a self-sacrifice, since the bull is a world bull and was originally identical with Mithras himself. This may account for the singularly agonized expression on the face of the tauroktonos,[2] which bears comparison with Guido Reni's Crucifixion. The Mithraic transitus is a motif that corresponds to Christ carrying the cross, just as the

---

[1] Bernardino de Sahagún, General History of the Things of New Spain, Book 3: The Origin of the Gods, trans. by Anderson and Dibble, pp. 5f. (slightly modified).
[2] Cumont, Textes et monuments, I, p. 182. [And cf. Jung, Symbols of Transformation, p. 428 and frontispiece.—EDITORS.]

transformation of the beast of sacrifice corresponds to the resurrection of the Christian God in the form of food and drink. The representations of the sacrificial act, the tauroctony (bull-slaying), recall the crucifixion between two thieves, one of whom is raised up to paradise while the other goes down to hell.

343   These few references to the Mithras cult are but one example of the wealth of parallels offered by the legends and rites of the various Near Eastern gods who die young, are mourned, and rise again. For anyone who knows these religions at all, there can be no doubt as to the basic affinity of the symbolic types and ideas.[3] At the time of primitive Christianity and in the early days of the Church, the pagan world was saturated with conceptions of this kind and with philosophical speculations based upon them, and it was against this background that the thought and visionary ideas of the Gnostic philosophers were unfolded.

II. THE VISION OF ZOSIMOS

344   A characteristic representative of this school of thought was Zosimos of Panopolis, a natural philosopher and alchemist of the third century A.D., whose works have been preserved, though in corrupt state, in the famous alchemical Codex Marcianus, and were published in 1887 by Berthelot in his *Collection des anciens alchimistes grecs*. In various portions of his treatises [4] Zosimos relates a number of dream-visions, all of which appear to go back to one and the same dream.[5] He was clearly a non-Christian Gnostic, and in particular—so one gathers from the famous passage about the *krater* [6]—an adherent of the Poimandres sect, and therefore a follower of Hermes. Although alchemical literature abounds in parables, I would hesitate to class these dream-visions among them. Anyone acquainted with the language of the alchemists will recognize that their parables are mere allegories of ideas that were common knowledge. In the allegorical figures and actions, one can usually see at once

---

3 Cf. Frazer's *The Golden Bough*, Part III: "The Dying God." For the Eucharistic meal of fish, see *Aion*, pars. 174ff., 181ff.

4 *Alchimistes*, III, i, 2, 3; III, v; III, vi.

5 Cf. my paper "The Visions of Zosimos," par. 86, which quotes the relevant passages.   6 *Alchimistes*, III, li, 8. Cf. supra, par. 313.

what substances and what procedures are being referred to under a deliberately theatrical disguise. There is nothing of this kind in the Zosimos visions. Indeed, it comes almost as a surprise to find the alchemical interpretation, namely that the dream and its impressive machinery are simply an illustration of the means for producing the "divine water." Moreover, a parable is a self-contained whole, whereas our vision varies and amplifies a single theme as a dream does. So far as one can assess the nature of these visions at all, I should say that even in the original text the contents of an imaginative meditation have grouped themselves round the kernel of an actual dream and been woven into it. That there really was such a meditation is evident from the fragments of it that accompany the visions in the form of a commentary. As we know, meditations of this kind are often vividly pictorial, as if the dream were being continued on a level nearer to consciousness. In his *Lexicon alchemiae,* Martin Ruland, writing in Frankfort in 1612, defines the meditation that plays such an important part in alchemy as an "internal colloquy with someone else, who is nevertheless not seen, it may be with God, with oneself, or with one's good angel." The latter is a milder and less obnoxious form of the *paredros,* the familiar spirit of ancient alchemy, who was generally a planetary demon conjured up by magic. It can hardly be doubted that real visionary experiences originally lay at the root of these practices, and a vision is in the last resort nothing less than a dream which has broken through into the waking state. We know from numerous witnesses all through the ages that the alchemist, in the course of his imaginative work, was beset by visions of all kinds,[7] and was sometimes even threatened with madness.[8] So the visions of Zosimos are not something unusual or unknown in alchemical experience, though they are perhaps the most important self-revelations ever bequeathed to us by an alchemist.

345   I cannot reproduce here the text of the visions in full, but will give as an example the first vision, in Zosimos' own words:

And while I said this I fell asleep, and I saw a sacrificial priest standing before me, high up on an altar, which was in the shape of a

---

[7] Cf. the examples given in *Psychology and Alchemy,* pars. 347f.
[8] Olympiodorus says this is particularly the effect of lead. Cf. Berthelot, II, iv, 43.

shallow bowl. There were fifteen steps leading up to the altar. And the priest stood there, and I heard a voice from above say to me: "Behold, I have completed the descent down the fifteen steps of darkness and I have completed the ascent up the steps of light. And he who renews me is the priest, casting away the grossness of the body, and by compelling necessity I am sanctified and now stand in perfection as a spirit [*pneuma*]." And I perceived the voice of him who stood upon the altar, and I inquired of him who he was. And he answered me in a fine voice, saying: "I am Ion, priest of the innermost hidden sanctuary, and I submit myself to an unendurable torment. For there came one in haste at early morning, who overpowered me and pierced me through with the sword and cut me in pieces, yet in such a way that the order of my limbs was preserved. And he drew off the scalp of my head with the sword, which he wielded with strength, and he put the bones and the pieces of flesh together and with his own hand burned them in the fire, until I perceived that I was transformed and had become spirit. And that is my unendurable torment." And even as he spoke this, and I held him by force to converse with me, his eyes became as blood. And he spewed out all his own flesh. And I saw how he changed into a manikin [ἀνθρωπάριον, i.e., an homunculus] who had lost a part of himself. And he tore his flesh with his own teeth, and sank into himself.

346   In the course of the visions the Hiereus (priest) appears in various forms. At first he is split into the figures of the Hiereus and the Hierourgon (sacrificer), who is charged with the performance of the sacrifice. But these figures blend into one in so far as both suffer the same fate. The sacrificial priest submits voluntarily to the torture by which he is transformed. But he is also the sacrificer who is sacrificed, since he is pierced through with the sword and ritually dismembered.[9] The *deipnon* consists in his tearing himself to pieces with his own teeth and eating himself; the *thysia,* in his flesh being sacrificially burned on the altar.

347   He is the Hiereus in so far as he rules over the sacrificial rite as a whole, and over the human beings who are transformed during the *thysia.* He calls himself a guardian of spirits. He is also known as the "Brazen Man" and as Xyrourgos, the barber.

9 The dismemberment motif belongs in the wider context of rebirth symbolism. Consequently it plays an important part in the initiation experiences of shamans and medicine men, who are dismembered and then put together again. For details, see Eliade, *Shamanism,* ch. II.

The brazen or leaden man is an allusion to the spirits of the metals, or planetary demons, as protagonists of the sacrificial drama. In all probability they are *paredroi* who were conjured up by magic, as may be deduced from Zosimos' remark that he "held him by force" to converse with him. The planetary demons are none other than the old gods of Olympus who finally expired only in the eighteenth century, as the "souls of the metals"—or rather, assumed a new shape, since it was in this same century that paganism openly arose for the first time (in the French Revolution).

348   Somewhat more curious is the term 'barber,' which we find in other parts of the visions,[10] for there is no mention of cutting the hair or shaving. There is, however, a scalping, which in our context is closely connected with the ancient rites of flaying and their magical significance.[11] I need hardly mention the flaying of Marsyas, who is an unmistakable parallel to the son-lover of Cybele, namely Attis, the dying god who rises again. In one of the old Attic fertility rites an ox was flayed, stuffed, and set up on its feet. Herodotus (IV, 60) reports a number of flaying ceremonies among the Scythians, and especially scalpings. In general, flaying signifies transformation from a worse state to a better, and hence renewal and rebirth. The best examples are to be found in the religion of ancient Mexico.[12] Thus, in order to renew the moon-goddess a young woman was decapitated and skinned, and a youth then put the skin round him to represent the risen goddess. The prototype of this renewal is the snake casting its skin every year, a phenomenon round which primitive fantasy has always played. In our vision the skinning is restricted to the head, and this can probably be explained by the underlying idea of spiritual transformation. Since olden times shaving the head has been associated with consecration,

[10] [Cf. Berthelot, III, i, 3 and v, 1-2; and "The Visions of Zosimos," par. 86.— EDITORS.]

[11] Cf. Frazer's *The Golden Bough*, Part IV: *Adonis, Attis, Osiris*, pp. 242ff. and p. 405, and my *Symbols of Transformation*, pars. 594f. Cf. also Colin Campbell, *The Miraculous Birth of King Amon-Hotep III*, p. 142, concerning the presentation of the dead man, Sen-nezem, before Osiris, Lord of Amentet: "In this scene the god is usually represented enthroned. Before and behind him, hanging from a pole, is the dripping skin of a slain bull that was slaughtered to yield up the soul of Osiris at his reconstruction, with the vase underneath to catch the blood."

[12] Cf. Eduard Seler's account in Hastings, *Encyclopedia*, VIII, pp. 615f.

that is, with spiritual transformation or initiation. The priests of Isis had their heads shaved quite bald, and the tonsure, as we know, is still in use at the present day. This "symptom" of transformation goes back to the old idea that the transformed one becomes like a new-born babe (neophyte, *quasimodogenitus*) with a hairless head. In the myth of the night sea journey, the hero loses all his hair during his incubation in the belly of the monster, because of the terrific heat.[13] The custom of tonsure, which is derived from these primitive ideas, naturally presupposes the presence of a ritual barber.[14] Curiously enough, we come across the barber in that old alchemical "mystery," the *Chymical Wedding* of 1616.[15] There the hero, on entering the mysterious castle, is pounced on by invisible barbers, who give him something very like a tonsure.[16] Here again the initiation and transformation process is accompanied by a shaving.[17]

349   In one variant of these visions there is a dragon who is killed and sacrificed in the same manner as the priest and therefore seems to be identical with him. This makes one think of those far from uncommon medieval pictures, not necessarily alchemical, in which a serpent is shown hanging on the Cross in place of Christ. (*Psychology and Alchemy*, fig. 217. Note the comparison of Christ with the serpent of Moses in John 3: 14.)

350   A notable aspect of the priest is the leaden homunculus, and this is none other than the leaden spirit or planetary demon Saturn. In Zosimos' day Saturn was regarded as a Hebrew god,

13 [*Symbols of Transformation*, pars. 309f.; *Psychology and Alchemy*, par. 490.]
14 Barbers were comparatively well-to-do people in ancient Egypt, and evidently did a flourishing trade. Cf. Erman, *Life in Ancient Egypt*, p. 304: "Barbers, all of whom must . . . have lived in easy circumstances."
15 The real author of the *Chymische Hochzeit* was Johann Valentin Andreae. [It appeared under the pseudonym "Christian Rosencreutz," dated 1459, but actually published at Strasbourg, 1616. Concerning Andreae, cf. "The Psychology of the Transference," par. 407 and n. 18.—EDITORS.]
16 As Andreae must have been a learned alchemist, he might very well have got hold of a copy of the Codex Marcianus and seen the writings of Zosimos. Manuscript copies exist in Gotha, Leipzig, Munich, and Weimar. I know of only one printed edition, published in Italy in the 16th cent., which is very rare.
17 Hence the "shaving of a man" and the "plucking of a fowl," mentioned further on among the magical sacrificial recipes. A similar motif is suggested by the "changing of wigs" at the Egyptian judgment of the dead. Cf. the picture in the tomb of Sennezem (Campbell, p. 143). When the dead man is led before Osiris his wig is black; afterwards (at the sacrifice in the Papyrus of Ani) it is white.

presumably on account of the keeping holy of the Sabbath—Saturday means 'Saturn's Day' [18]—and also on account of the Gnostic parallel with the supreme archon Ialdabaoth ('child of chaos') who, as λεοντοειδής, may be grouped together with Baal, Kronos, and Saturn.[19] The later Arabic designation of Zosimos as al-'Ibrî (the Hebrew) does not of course prove that he himself was a Jew, but it is clear from his writings that he was acquainted with Jewish traditions.[20] The parallel between the Hebrew god and Saturn is of considerable importance as regards the alchemical idea of the transformation of the God of the Old Testament into the God of the New. The alchemists naturally attached great significance to Saturn,[21] for, besides being the outermost planet, the supreme archon (the Harranites named him "Primas"), and the demiurge Ialdabaoth, he was also the *spiritus niger* who lies captive in the darkness of matter, the deity or that part of the deity which has been swallowed up in his own creation. He is the dark god who reverts to his original luminous state in the mystery of alchemical transmutation. As the *Aurora Consurgens* says: "Blessed is he that shall find this science and into whom this prudence of Saturn floweth." [22]

351   The later alchemists were familiar not only with the ritual slaying of a dragon but also with the slaying of a lion, which took the form of his having all four paws cut off. Like the dragon, the lion devours himself, and so is probably only a variant.[23]

---

[18] Plutarch, *Quaestiones convivales*, IV, 5, and Diogenes Laertius, II, §112; Reitzenstein, *Poimandres*, pp. 75f. and 112. In a text named "Ghāya al-hakīm," ascribed to Maslama al-Madjrītī, the following instructions are given when invoking Saturn: "Arrive vêtu à la manière des Juifs, car il est leur patron." Dozy and de Goeje, "Nouveaux documents pour l'étude de la religion des Harraniens," p. 350.

[19] Origen, *Contra Celsum*, VI, 31. Mead, *Pistis Sophia*, ch. 45. Bousset, *Hauptprobleme der Gnosis*, pp. 351ff. Roscher, *Lexikon*, s.v. Kronos, II, col. 1496. The dragon (κρόνος) and Kronos are often confused.

[20] Lippmann, *Entstehung und Ausbreitung der Alchemie*, II, p. 229.

[21] Cf. *Aion*, pars. 128f.

[22] "Beatus homo qui invenerit hanc scientiam et cui affluit providentia Saturni." [Ed. von Franz, pp. 37f.]

[23] See the illustration in Reusner, *Pandora* (1588), and in *Le Songe de Poliphile*, trans. Béroalde de Verville (1600). [*Psych. and Alch.*, fig. 4.] Mostly the pictures show two lions eating one another. The uroboros, too, is often pictured in the form of two dragons engaged in the same process (*Viridarium chymicum*, 1624).

treatise entitled "Isis to Horus," [33] where the angel Amnael brings it to the prophetess in a drinking vessel. As Zosimos was probably an adherent of the Poimandres sect, another thing to be considered here is the *krater* which God filled with *nous* for all those seeking ἔννοια.[34] But *nous* is identical with the alchemical Mercurius. This is quite clear from the Ostanes quotation in Zosimos, which says: "Go to the streams of the Nile and there thou wilt find a stone which hath a spirit. Take and divide it, thrust in thy hand and draw out its heart, for its soul is in its heart." Commenting on this, Zosimos remarks that "having a spirit" is a metaphorical expression for the *exhydrargyrosis,* the expulsion of the quicksilver.[35]

356   During the first centuries after Christ the words *nous* and *pneuma* were used indiscriminately, and the one could easily stand for the other. Moreover the relation of Mercurius to "spirit" is an extremely ancient astrological fact. Like Hermes, Mercurius (or the planetary spirit Mercury) was a god of revelation, who discloses the secret of the art to the adepts. The *Liber quartorum,* which being of Harranite origin cannot be dated later than the tenth century, says of Mercurius: "Ipse enim aperit clausiones operum cum ingenio et intellectu suo" (For he opens with his genius and understanding the locked [insoluble] problems of the work).[36] He is also the "soul of the bodies," the "anima vitalis," [37] and Ruland defines him as "spirit which has become earth." [38] He is a spirit that penetrates into the depths of the material world and transforms it. Like the *nous,* he is symbolized by the serpent. In Michael Maier he points the way to the earthly paradise.[39] Besides being identified with Hermes Trismegistus,[40] he is also called the "mediator" [41] and,

---

[33] Berthelot, *Alchimistes,* I, xiii. [Cf. "The Visions of Zosimos," pars. 97ff.]

[34] Ibid., III, li, 8, and *Hermetica,* ed. Scott, I, p. 151.

[35] Berthelot, *Alchimistes,* III, vi, 5.

[36] Of the later authors I will mention only Johannes Christophorus Steeb, *Coelum sephiroticum* (1679, p. 138): "Omnis intellectus acuminis auctor . . . a coelesti mercurio omnem ingeniorum vim provenire" (The author of all deeper understanding . . . all the power of genius comes from the celestial Mercurius). For the astrological connection see Bouché-Leclercq, *L'Astrologie grecque,* pp. 312, 321–23.   [37] "Aurora consurgens." In Mylius (p. 533) he is a giver of life.

[38] *Lexicon.*   [39] *Symbola,* p. 592.   [40] Ibid., p. 600.

[41] Ripley, *Opera,* Foreword, and in Khunrath's *Chaos.* In Plutarch, Mercurius acts as a kind of world soul.

as the Original Man, the "Hermaphroditic Adam." [42] From numerous passages it is clear that Mercurius is as much a fire as a water, both of which aptly characterize the nature of spirit.[43]

357   Killing with the sword is a recurrent theme in alchemical literature. The "philosophical egg" is divided with the sword, and with it the "King" is transfixed and the dragon or "corpus" dismembered, the latter being represented as the body of a man whose head and limbs are cut off.[44] The lion's paws are likewise cut off with the sword. For the alchemical sword brings about the *solutio* or *separatio* of the elements, thereby restoring the original condition of chaos, so that a new and more perfect body can be produced by a new *impressio formae,* or by a "new imagination." The sword is therefore that which "kills and vivifies," and the same is said of the permanent water or mercurial water. Mercurius is the giver of life as well as the destroyer of the old form. In ecclesiastical symbolism the sword which comes out of the mouth of the Son of Man in the Book of Revelation is, according to Hebrews 4:12, the Logos, the Word of God, and hence Christ himself. This analogy did not escape the notice of the alchemists, who were always struggling to give expression to their fantasies. Mercurius was their mediator and saviour, their *filius macrocosmi* (contrasted with Christ the *filius microcosmi*),[45] the solver and separator. So he too is a sword, for he is a "penetrating spirit" ("more piercing than a two-edged sword"!). Gerhard Dorn, an alchemist of the sixteenth century, says that in our world the sword was changed into Christ our Saviour. He comments as follows:

After a long interval of time the Deus Optimus Maximus immersed himself in the innermost of his secrets, and he decided, out of the compassion of his love as well as for the demands of justice, to take the sword of wrath from the hand of the angel. And having hung the sword on the tree, he substituted for it a golden trident, and thus was the wrath of God changed into love. . . . When peace and

[42] Gerhard Dorn, "Congeries Paracelsicae chemicae," in the *Theatrum chemicum,* I, p. 589.

[43] Cf. "The Spirit Mercurius," pars. 255, 256ff.

[44] Illustration in "Splendor solis," *Aureum vellus* (1598).

[45] Cf. Khunrath, *Chaos,* and *Amphitheatrum sapientiae aeternae* (1604).

justice were united, the water of Grace flowed more abundantly from above, and now it bathes the whole world.[46]

[46] Dorn, "Speculativae philosophiae," in the *Theatrum chemicum*, I, pp. 284ff. The whole passage runs as follows:

"Post primam hominis inobedientiam, Dominus viam hanc amplissimam in callem strictissimam difficilimamque (ut videtis) restrinxit, in cuius ostio collocavit Cherubim angelum, ancipitem gladium manu tenentem, quo quidem arceret omnes ab introitu felicis patriae: hinc deflectentes Adae filii propter peccatum primi sui parentis, in sinistram latam sibimet viam construxerunt, quam evitastis. Longo postea temporis intervallo D. O. M. secreta secretorum suorum introivit, in quibus amore miserente, accusanteque iustitia, conclusit angelo gladium irae suae de manibus eripere, cuius loco tridentem hamum substituit aureum, gladio ad arborem suspenso: & sic mutata est ira Dei in amorem, servata iustitia: quod antequam fieret, fluvius iste non erat, ut iam, in se collectus, sed ante lapsum per totum orbem terrarum roris instar expansus aequaliter: post vero rediit unde processerat tandem, ut pax & iustitia sunt osculatae se, descendit affluentius ab alto manans aqua gratiae, totum nunc mundum alluens. In sinistram partem qui deflectunt, partim suspensum in arbore gladium videntes, eiusque noscentes historiam, quia mundo nimium sunt insiti, praetereunt: nonnulli videntes eius efficaciam perquirere negligunt, alii nec vident, nec vidisse voluissent: hi recta peregrinationem suam ad vallem dirigunt omnes, nisi per hamos resipiscentiae, vel poenitentiae nonnulli retrahantur ad montem Sion. Nostro iam saeculo (quod gratiae est) mutatus est gladius in Christum salvatorem nostrum qui crucis arborem pro peccatis nostris ascendit."

(After man's first disobedience the Lord straitened this wide road into a very narrow and difficult path, as you see. At its entrance he placed an angel of the Cherubim, holding in his hand a double-edged sword with which he was to keep all from entering into Paradise. Turning from thence on account of the sin of their first parents, the sons of Adam built for themselves a broad left-hand path: this you have shunned. After a long interval of time the Deus Optimus Maximus immersed himself in the innermost of his secrets, and he decided, out of the compassion of his love as well as for the demands of justice, to take the sword of wrath from the hand of the angel. And having hung the sword on the tree, he substituted for it a golden trident, and thus was the wrath of God changed into love, and justice remained unimpaired. Previous to this, however, the river was not collected into one as it is now, but before the Fall it was spread equally over the whole world, like dew. But later it returned to the place of its origin. When peace and justice were united, the water of Grace flowed more abundantly from above, and now it bathes the whole world. Some of those who take the left-hand path, on seeing the sword suspended from the tree, and knowing its history, pass it by, because they are too entangled in the affairs of this world; some, on seeing it, do not choose to inquire into its efficacy; others never see it and would not wish to see it. All these continue their pilgrimage into the valley, except for those who are drawn back to Mount Zion by the hook of repentance. Now in our age, which is an age of grace, the sword has become Christ our Saviour, who ascended the tree of the Cross for our sins.) Cf. "The Philosophical Tree," pars. 447ff.

191

358   This passage, which might well have occurred in an author like Rabanus Maurus or Honorius of Autun without doing them discredit, actually occurs in a context which throws light on certain esoteric alchemical doctrines, namely in a colloquy between Animus, Anima, and Corpus. There we are told that it is Sophia, the Sapientia, Scientia, or Philosophia of the alchemists, "de cuius fonte scaturiunt aquae" (from whose fount the waters gush forth). This Wisdom is the *nous* that lies hidden and bound in matter, the "serpens mercurialis" or "humidum radicale" that manifests itself in the "viventis aquae fluvius de montis apice" (stream of living water from the summit of the mountain).[47] That is the water of grace, the "permanent" and "divine" water which "now bathes the whole world." The apparent transformation of the God of the Old Testament into the God of the New is in reality the transformation of the *deus absconditus* (i.e., the *natura abscondita*) into the *medicina catholica* of alchemical wisdom.[48]

359   The divisive and separative function of the sword, which is of such importance in alchemy, is prefigured in the flaming sword of the angel that separated our first parents from paradise. Separation by a sword is a theme that can also be found in the Gnosis of the Ophites: the earthly cosmos is surrounded by a ring of fire which at the same time encloses paradise. But paradise and the ring of fire are separated by the "flaming sword." [49] An important interpretation of this flaming sword is given in Simon Magus: [50] there is an incorruptible essence potentially present in every human being, the divine *pneuma* "which is stationed above and below in the stream of water." Simon says of this *pneuma:* "I and thou, thou before me. I, who am after thee." It is a force "that generates itself, that causes itself to grow; it is its own mother, sister, bride, daughter; its own son, mother, father; a unity, a root of the whole." It is the very

47 Another remark of Dorn's points in the same direction: "The sword was suspended from a tree over the bank of the river" (p. 288).

48 A few pages later Dorn himself remarks: "Scitote, fratres, omnia quae superius dicta sunt et dicentur in posterum, intelligi posse de praeparationibus alchemicis" (Know, brothers, that everything which has been said above and everything which will be said in what follows can also be understood of the alchemical preparations).

49 Leisegang, *Die Gnosis,* pp. 171f.

50 The passage which follows occurs in Hippolytus, *Elenchos,* vi, pp. 4f.

ground of existence, the procreative urge, which is of fiery origin. Fire is related to blood, which "is fashioned warm and ruddy like fire." Blood turns into semen in men, and in women into milk. This "turning" is interpreted as "the flaming sword which turned every way, to keep the way of the tree of life." [51] The operative principle in semen and milk turns into mother and father. The tree of life is guarded by the turning (i.e., transforming) sword, and this is the "seventh power" which begets itself. "For if the flaming sword turned not, then would that fair Tree be destroyed, and perish utterly; but if it turneth into semen and milk, and there be added the Logos and the place of the Lord where the Logos is begotten, he who dwelleth potentially in the semen and milk shall grow to full stature from the littlest spark, and shall increase and become a power boundless and immutable, like to an unchanging Aeon, which suffereth no more change until measureless eternity." [52] It is clear from these remarkable statements of Hippolytus concerning the teachings of Simon Magus that the sword is very much more than an instrument which divides; it is itself the force which "turns" from something infinitesimally small into the infinitely great: from water, fire, and blood it becomes the limitless aeon. What it means is the transformation of the vital spirit in man into the Divine. The natural being becomes the divine *pneuma*, as in the vision of Zosimos. Simon's description of the creative *pneuma*, the true arcane substance, corresponds in every detail to the uroboros or *serpens mercurialis* of the Latinists. It too is its own father, mother, son, daughter, brother, and sister from the earliest beginnings of alchemy right down to the end. [53] It begets and sacrifices itself and is its own instrument of sacrifice, for it is a symbol of the deadly and life-giving water. [54]

360   Simon's ideas also throw a significant light on the above-quoted passage from Dorn, where the sword of wrath is transformed into Christ. Were it not that the philosophoumena of Hippolytus were first discovered in the nineteenth century, on Mount Athos, one might almost suppose that Dorn had made use of them. There are numerous other symbols in alchemy whose origin is so doubtful that one does not know whether to

---

[51] Genesis 3 : 24.   [52] Leisegang, p. 80.
[53] That is why it is called "Hermaphroditus."
[54] One of its symbols is the scorpion, which stings itself to death.

attribute them to tradition, or to a study of the heresiologists, or to spontaneous revival.[55]

361 The sword as the "proper" instrument of sacrifice occurs again in the old treatise entitled "Consilium coniugii de massa solis et lunae." This says: "Both must be killed with their own sword" ("both" referring to Sol and Luna).[56] In the still older "Tractatus Micreris," [57] dating perhaps from the twelfth century, we find the "fiery sword" in a quotation from Ostanes: "The great Astanus [Ostanes] said: Take an egg, pierce it with the fiery sword, and separate its soul from its body." [58] Here the sword is something that divides body and soul, corresponding to the division between heaven and earth, the ring of fire and paradise, or paradise and the first parents. In an equally old treatise, the "Allegoriae sapientum . . . supra librum Turbae," there is even mention of a sacrificial rite: "Take a fowl [*volatile*], cut off its head with the fiery sword, then pluck out its feathers, separate the limbs, and cook over a charcoal fire till it becomes of one colour." [59] Here we have a decapitation with the fiery sword, then a "clipping," or more accurately a "plucking," and finally a "cooking." The cock, which is probably what is meant here, is simply called "volatile," a fowl or winged creature, and this is a common term for spirit, but a spirit still nature-bound and imperfect, and in need of improvement. In another old treatise, with the very similar title "Allegoriae super librum Turbae," [60] we find the following supplementary variants: "Kill the mother [the *prima materia*], tearing off her hands and feet." "Take a viper . . . cut off its head and tail." "Take a cock . . . and pluck it alive." "Take a man, shave him, and drag him over the stone [i.e., dry him on the hot stone] till his body dies." "Take the glass vessel containing bridegroom and bride, throw

---

55 So far I have come across only one alchemical author who admits to having read the *Panarium* of Epiphanius, while declaring at the same time his sincere abhorrence of heresies. The silence of the alchemists in this matter is nothing to wonder at, since the mere proximity to heresy would have put them in danger of their lives. Thus even 90 years after the death of Trithemius of Spanheim, who was supposed to have been the teacher of Paracelsus, the abbot Sigismund of Seon had to compose a moving defence in which he endeavoured to acquit Trithemius of the charge of heresy. Cf. *Trithemius sui-ipsius vindex* (1616).

56 *Ars chemica*, p. 259. Printed in Manget (1702), II.

57 "Micreris" is probably a corruption of "Mercurius."

58 *Theatr. chem.*, V (1622), p. 103.

59 Ibid., p. 68.   60 *Artis auriferae*, I, pp. 139f.

them into the furnace, and roast them for three days, and they will be two in one flesh." "Take the white man from the vessel." [61]

362   One is probably right in assuming that these recipes are instructions for magical sacrifices, not unlike the Greek magic papyri.[62] As an example of the latter I will give the recipe from the Mimaut Papyrus (li. 2ff.): "Take a tomcat and make an Osiris of him [63] [by immersing] his body in water. And when you proceed to suffocate him, talk into his back." Another example from the same papyrus (li. 425): "Take a hoopoe, tear out its heart, pierce it with a reed, then cut it up and throw it into Attic honey."

363   Such sacrifices really were made for the purpose of summoning up the *paredros,* the familiar spirit. That this sort of thing was practised, or at any rate recommended, by the alchemists is clear from the "Liber Platonis quartorum," where it speaks of the "oblationes et sacrificia" offered to the planetary demon. A deeper and more sombre note is struck in the following passage, which I give in the original (and generally very corrupt) text: [64]

Vas . . . oportet esse rotundae figurae: Ut sit artifex huius mutator firmamenti et testae capitis, ut cum sit res, qua indigemus, res simplex, habens partes similes, necesse est ipsius generationem, et in corpore habente similes partibus . . . proiicies ex testa capitis, videlicet capitis elementi hominis et massetur totum cum urina . . .

(The vessel . . . must be round in shape. Thus the artifex must be the transformer of this firmament and of the brain-pan, just as the thing for which we seek is a simple thing having uniform parts. It is therefore necessary that you should generate it in a body [i.e., a vessel] of uniform parts . . . from the brain-pan, that is, from the head of the element Man, and that the whole should be macerated with urine . . .)

364   One asks oneself how literally this recipe is to be taken.[65] The following story from the "Ghāya al-hakīm" is exceedingly enlightening in this connection:

365   The Jacobite patriarch Dionysius I set it on record that in

61 Ibid., pp. 151, 140, 140, 139, 151, 151, resp.

62 *Papyri Graecae Magicae,* trans. and ed. by Karl Preisendanz.

63 ἀποθέωσις = 'sacrifice.'   64 *Theatr. chem.,* V, p. 153.

65 See also pp. 127, 128, 130, and 149 of the same work.

the year 765, a man who was destined for the sacrifice, on beholding the bloody head of his predecessor, was so terrified that
he took flight and lodged a complaint with Abbas, the prefect of
Mesopotamia, against the priests of Harran, who were afterwards severely punished. The story goes on to say that in 830
the Caliph Mamun told the Harranite envoys: "You are without
doubt the people of the head, who were dealt with by my father
Rashid." We learn from the "Ghāya" that a fair-haired man with
dark-blue eyes was lured into a chamber of the temple, where
he was immersed in a great jar filled with sesame oil. Only his
head was left sticking out. There he remained for forty days,
and during this time was fed on nothing but figs soaked in
sesame oil. He was not given a drop of water to drink. As a result of this treatment his body became as soft as wax. The
prisoner was repeatedly fumigated with incense, and magical
formulae were pronounced over him. Eventually his head was
torn off at the neck, the body remaining in the oil. The head
was then placed in a niche on the ashes of burnt olives, and was
packed round with cotton wool. More incense was burned before it, and the head would thereupon predict famines or good
harvests, changes of dynasty, and other future events. Its eyes
could see, though the lids did not move. It also revealed to
people their inmost thoughts, and scientific and technical questions were likewise addressed to it.[66]

366   Even though it is possible that the real head was, in later
times, replaced by a dummy, the whole idea of this ceremony,
particularly when taken in conjunction with the above passage
from the "Liber quartorum," seems to point to an original
human sacrifice. The idea of a mysterious head is, however, considerably older than the school of Harran. As far back as Zosimos
we find the philosophers described as "children of the golden
head," and we also encounter the "round element," which
Zosimos says is the letter omega (Ω). This symbol may well be
interpreted as the head, since the "Liber quartorum" also associates the round vessel with the head. Zosimos, moreover, refers
on several occasions to the "whitest stone, which is in the
head." [67] Probably all these ideas go back to the severed head

66 Dozy and de Goeje, p. 365.
67 "Τὸν πάνυ λευκότατον λίθον τὸν ἐγκέφαλον." Berthelot, *Alchimistes*, III, xxix, 4. Cf.
also I, iii, 1 and III, ii. 1.

of Osiris, which crossed the sea and was therefore associated with the idea of resurrection. The "head of Osiris" also plays an important part in medieval alchemy.

367 In this connection we might mention the legend that was current about Gerbert of Rheims, afterwards Pope Sylvester II (d. 1003). He was believed to have possessed a golden head which spoke to him in oracles. Gerbert was one of the greatest savants of his time, and well known as a transmitter of Arabic science.[68] Can it be that the translation of the "Liber quartorum," which is of Harranite origin, goes back to this author? Unfortunately there is little prospect of our being able to prove this.

368 It has been conjectured that the Harranite oracle head may be connected with the ancient Hebrew teraphim. Rabbinic tradition considers the teraphim to have been originally either the decapitated head or skull of a human being, or else a dummy head.[69] The Jews had teraphim about the house as a sort of lares and penates (who were plural spirits, like the Cabiri). The idea that they were heads goes back to I Samuel 19:13f., which describes how Michal, David's wife, put the teraphim in David's bed in order to deceive the messengers of Saul, who wanted to kill him. "Then Michal took an image and laid it on the bed and put a pillow of goats' hair at its head, and covered it with the clothes (RSV)." The "pillow of goats' hair" is linguistically obscure and has even been interpreted as meaning that the teraphim were goats. But it may also mean something woven or plaited out of goats' hair, like a wig, and this would fit in better with the picture of a man lying in bed. Further evidence for this comes from a legend in a collection of midrashim from the twelfth century, printed in Bin Gorion's *Die Sagen der Juden*. There it is said:

The teraphim were idols, and they were made in the following way. The head of a man, who had to be a first-born, was cut off and the hair plucked out. The head was then sprinkled with salt and anointed with oil. Afterwards a little plaque, of copper or gold, was inscribed with the name of an idol and placed under the tongue of the decapitated head. The head was set up in a room, candles were lit before it, and the people made obeisance. And if any man fell

---

[68] Thorndike, *A History of Magic and Experimental Science*, I, p. 705.
[69] *Jewish Encyclopaedia*, XII, s.v. "Teraphim," pp. 108f.

down before it, the head began to speak, and answered all questions that were addressed to it.[70]

369   This is an obvious parallel to the Harranite ritual with the head. The tearing out of the hair seems significant, since it is an equivalent of scalping or shearing, and is thus a rebirth mystery. It is conceivable that in later times the bald skull was covered with a wig for a rite of renewal, as is also reported from Egypt.

370   It seems probable that this magical procedure is of primitive origin. I am indebted to the South African writer, Laurens van der Post, for the following report from a lecture which he gave in Zurich in 1951:

The tribe in question was an offshoot of the great Swazi nation—a Bantu people. When, some years ago, the old chief died, he was succeeded by his son, a young man of weak character. He soon proved to be so unsatisfactory a chief that his uncles called a meeting of the tribal elders. They decided that something must be done to strengthen their chief, so they consulted the witch doctors. The witch doctors treated him with a medicine which proved ineffective. Another meeting was held and the witch doctors were asked to use the strongest medicine of all on the chief because the situation was becoming desperate. A half brother of the chief, a boy of twelve, was chosen to provide the material for the medicine.

One afternoon a sorcerer went up to the boy, who was tending cattle, and engaged him in conversation. Then, emptying some powder from a horn into his hand, he took a reed and blew the powder into the ears and nostrils of the boy. A witness told me that the lad thereupon began to sway like a drunken person and sank to the ground shivering. He was then taken to the river bed and tied to the roots of a tree. More powder was sprinkled round about, the sorcerer saying: "This person will no longer eat food but only earth and roots."

The boy was kept in the river bed for nine months. Some people say a cage was made and put into the stream, with the boy inside it, for hours on end, so that the water should flow over him and make his skin white. Others reported seeing him crawling about in the river bed on his hands and knees. But all were so frightened that, although there was a mission school only one hundred yards away,

[70] Josef bin Gorion, *Die Sagen der Juden*, p. 325. I am indebted to Dr. Riwkah Schärf for drawing my attention to this passage.

no one except those directly concerned in the ritual would go near him. All are agreed that at the end of nine months this fat, normal, healthy boy was like an animal and quite white-skinned. One woman said, "His eyes were white and the whole of his body was white as white paper."

On the evening that the boy was to be killed a veteran witch doctor was summoned to the chief's kraal and asked to consult the tribal spirits. This he did in the cattle kraal, and after selecting an animal for slaughter he retired to the chief's hut. There the witch doctor was handed parts of the dead boy's body: first the head in a sack, then a thumb and a toe. He cut off the nose and ears and lips, mixed them with medicine, and cooked them over a fire in a broken clay pot. He stuck two spears on either side of the pot. Then those present—twelve in all including the weak chief—leaned over the pot and deeply inhaled the steam. All save the boy's mother dipped their fingers in the pot and licked them. She inhaled but refused to dip her fingers in the pot. The rest of the body the witch doctor mixed into a kind of bread for doctoring the tribe's crops.

371   Although this magical rite is not actually a "head mystery," it has several things in common with the practices previously mentioned. The body is macerated and transformed by long immersion in water. The victim is killed, and the salient portions of the head form the main ingredient of the "strengthening" medicine which was concocted for the chief and his immediate circle. The body is kneaded into a sort of bread, and this is obviously thought of as a strengthening medicine for the tribe's crops as well. The rite is a transformation process, a sort of rebirth after nine months of incubation in the water. Laurens van der Post thinks that the purpose of the "whitening" [71] was to assimilate the mana of the white man, who has the political power. I agree with this view, and would add that painting with white clay often signifies transformation into ancestral spirits, in the same way as the neophytes are made invisible in the Nandi territory, in Kenya, where they walk about in portable, cone-shaped grass huts and demonstrate their invisibility to everyone.

372   Skull worship is widespread among primitives. In Melanesia and Polynesia it is chiefly the skulls of the ancestors that are worshipped, because they establish connections with the spirits

[71] Cf. the alchemical *albedo* and *homo albus*.

or serve as tutelary deities, like the head of Osiris in Egypt. Skulls also play a considerable role as sacred relics. It would lead us too far to go into this primitive skull worship, so I must refer the reader to the literature.[72] I would only like to point out that the cut-off ears, nose, and mouth can represent the head as parts that stand for the whole. There are numerous examples of this. Equally, the head or its parts (brain, etc.) can act as magical food or as a means for increasing the fertility of the land.

373   It is of special significance for the alchemical tradition that the oracle head was also known in Greece. Aelian [73] reports that Cleomenes of Sparta had the head of his friend Archonides preserved in a jar of honey, and that he consulted it as an oracle. The same was said of the head of Orpheus. Onians [74] rightly emphasizes the fact that the ψυχή, whose seat was in the head, corresponds to the modern "unconscious," and that at that stage of development consciousness was identified with θυμός (breath) and φρένες (lungs), and was localized in the chest or heart region. Hence Pindar's expression for the soul—αἰῶνος εἴδωλον (image of Aion)—is extraordinarily apt, for the collective unconscious not only imparts "oracles" but forever represents the microcosm (i.e., the form of a physical man mirroring the Cosmos).

374   There is no evidence to show that any of the parallels we have drawn are historically connected with the Zosimos visions. It seems rather to be a case partly of parallel traditions (transmitted, perhaps, chiefly through the Harran school), and partly of spontaneous fantasies arising from the same archetypal background from which the traditions were derived in the first place. As my examples have shown, the imagery of the Zosimos visions, however strange it may be, is by no means isolated, but is interwoven with older ideas some of which were certainly, and others quite possibly, known to Zosimos, as well as with parallels of uncertain date which continued to mould the speculations of the alchemists for many centuries to come. Religious thought in the early Christian era was not completely cut off from all contact with these conceptions; it was in fact influenced by them, and in turn it fertilized the minds of the natural philosophers during later centuries. Towards the end of the sixteenth century

[72] Hastings, VI, pp. 535f.   [73] *Varia historia,* XII, 8.
[74] Onians, *The Origins of European Thought,* pp. 101ff.

the alchemical *opus* was even represented in the form of a Mass. The author of this tour de force was the Hungarian alchemist, Melchior Cibinensis. I have elaborated this parallel in my book *Psychology and Alchemy*.[75]

375   In the visions of Zosimos, the Hiereus who is transformed into *pneuma* represents the transformative principle at work in nature and the harmony of opposing forces. Chinese philosophy formulated this process as the enantiodromian interplay of Yin and Yang. [76] But the curious personifications and symbols characteristic not only of these visions but of alchemical literature in general show in the plainest possible terms that we are dealing with a psychic process that takes place mainly in the unconscious and therefore can come into consciousness only in the form of a dream or vision. At that time and until very much later no one had any idea of the unconscious; consequently all unconscious contents were projected into the object, or rather were found in nature as apparent objects or properties of matter and were not recognized as purely internal psychic events. There is some evidence that Zosimos was well aware of the spiritual or mystical side of his art, but he believed that what he was concerned with was a spirit that dwelt in natural objects, and not something that came from the human psyche. It remained for modern science to despiritualize nature through its so-called objective knowledge of matter. All anthropomorphic projections were withdrawn from the object one after another, with a twofold result: firstly man's mystical identity with nature [77] was curtailed as never before, and secondly the projections falling back into the human soul caused such a terrific activation of the unconscious that in modern times man was compelled to postulate the existence of an unconscious psyche. The first beginnings of this can be seen in Leibniz and Kant, and then, with mounting intensity, in Schelling, Carus, and von Hartmann, until finally modern psychology discarded the last metaphysical claims of the philosopher-psychologists and restricted the idea of the psyche's existence to the psychological statement, in other

75 Pars. 480–89.
76 The classical example being *The I Ching or Book of Changes*.
77 Mystical or *unconscious* identity occurs in every case of projection, because the content projected upon the extraneous object creates an apparent relationship between it and the subject.

words, to its phenomenology. So far as the dramatic course of the Mass represents the death, sacrifice and resurrection of a god and the inclusion and active participation of the priest and congregation, its phenomenology may legitimately be brought into line with other fundamentally similar, though more primitive, religious customs. This always involves the risk that sensitive people will find it unpleasant when "small things are compared with great." In fairness to the primitive psyche, however, I would like to emphasize that the "holy dread" of civilized man differs but little from the awe of the primitive, and that the God who is present and active in the mystery is a mystery for both. No matter how crass the outward differences, the similarity or equivalence of meaning should not be overlooked.

4. THE PSYCHOLOGY OF THE MASS

I. GENERAL REMARKS ON THE SACRIFICE

376   Whereas I kept to the Church's interpretation when discussing the transformation rite in section 2, in the present section I shall treat this interpretation as a symbol. Such a procedure does not imply any evaluation of the content of religious belief. Scientific criticism must, of course, adhere to the view that when something is held as an opinion, thought to be true, or believed, it does not posit the existence of any real fact other than a psychological one. But that does not mean that a *mere nothing* has been produced. Rather, expression has been given to the psychic reality underlying the statement of the belief or rite as its empirical basis. When psychology "explains" a statement of this kind, it does not, in the first place, deprive the *object* of this statement of any reality—on the contrary, it is granted a psychic reality—and in the second place the intended metaphysical *statement* is not, on that account, turned into an hypostasis, since it was never anything more than a psychic phenomenon. Its specifically "metaphysical" coloration indicates that its object is beyond the reach of human perception and understanding except in its psychic mode of manifestation, and therefore cannot be judged. But every science reaches its end in the unknowable. Yet it would not be a science at all if it

regarded its temporary limitations as definitive and denied the existence of anything outside them. No science can consider its hypotheses to be the final truth.

377   The psychological explanation and the metaphysical statement do not contradict one another any more than, shall we say, the physicist's explanation of matter contradicts the as yet unknown or unknowable nature of matter. The very existence of a belief has in itself the reality of a psychic fact. Just what we posit by the concept "psyche" is simply unknowable, for psychology is in the unfortunate position where the observer and the observed are ultimately identical. Psychology has no Archimedean point outside, since all perception is of a psychic nature and we have only indirect knowledge of what is non-psychic.

378   The ritual event that takes place in the Mass has a dual aspect, human and divine. From the human point of view, gifts are offered to God at the altar, signifying at the same time the self-oblation of the priest and the congregation. The ritual act consecrates both the gifts and the givers. It commemorates and represents the Last Supper which our Lord took with his disciples, the whole Incarnation, Passion, death, and resurrection of Christ. But from the divine point of view this anthropomorphic action is only the outer shell or husk in which what is really happening is not a human action at all but a divine event. For an instant the life of Christ, eternally existent outside time, becomes visible and is unfolded in temporal succession, but in condensed form, in the sacred action: Christ incarnates as a man under the aspect of the offered substances, he suffers, is killed, is laid in the sepulchre, breaks the power of the underworld, and rises again in glory. In the utterance of the words of consecration the Godhead intervenes, Itself acting and truly present, and thus proclaims that the central event in the Mass is Its act of grace, in which the priest has only the significance of a minister. The same applies to the congregation and the offered substances: they are all ministering causes of the sacred event. The presence of the Godhead binds all parts of the sacrificial act into a mystical unity, so that it is God himself who offers himself as a sacrifice in the substances, in the priest, and in the congregation, and who, in the human form of the Son, offers himself as an atonement to the Father.

379   Although this act is an eternal happening taking place within the divinity, man is nevertheless included in it as an essential component, firstly because God clothes himself in our human nature, and secondly because he needs the ministering co-operation of the priest and congregation, and even the material substances of bread and wine which have a special significance for man. Although God the Father is of one nature with God the Son, he appears in time on the one hand as the eternal Father and on the other hand as a man with limited earthly existence. Mankind as a whole is included in God's human nature, which is why man is also included in the sacrificial act. Just as, in the sacrificial act, God is both *agens* and *patiens,* so too is man according to his limited capacity. The *causa efficiens* of the transubstantiation is a spontaneous act of God's grace. Ecclesiastical doctrine insists on this view and even tends to attribute the preparatory action of the priest, indeed the very existence of the rite, to divine prompting,[1] rather than to slothful human nature with its load of original sin. This view is of the utmost importance for a psychological understanding of the Mass. Wherever the magical aspect of a rite tends to prevail, it brings the rite nearer to satisfying the individual ego's blind greed for power, and thus breaks up the mystical body of the Church into separate units. Where, on the other hand, the rite is conceived as the action of God himself, the human participants have only an instrumental or "ministering" significance. The Church's view therefore presupposes the following psychological situation: human consciousness (represented by the priest and congregation) is confronted with an autonomous event which, taking place on a "divine" and "timeless" plane transcending consciousness, is in no way dependent on human action, but which impels man to act by seizing upon him as an instrument and making him the exponent of a "divine" happening. In the ritual action man places himself at the disposal of an autonomous and "eternal" agency operating outside the categories of human consciousness—*si parva licet componere magnis*—in much the same way that a good actor does not merely represent the drama, but allows himself to be overpowered by the genius of the dramatist. The beauty of the ritual action is one of its

[1] John 6:44: "No man can come to me, except the Father which hath sent me draw him."

essential properties, for man has not served God rightly unless he has also served him in beauty. Therefore the rite has no practical utility, for that would be making it serve a purpose—a purely human category. But everything divine is an end-in-itself, perhaps the only legitimate end-in-itself we know. How something eternal can "act" at all is a question we had better not touch, for it is simply unanswerable. Since man, in the action of the Mass, is a tool (though a tool of his own free will), he is not in a position to know anything about the hand which guides him. The hammer cannot discover within itself the power which makes it strike. It is something outside, something autonomous, which seizes and moves him. What happens in the consecration is essentially a miracle, and is meant to be so, for otherwise we should have to consider whether we were not conjuring up God by magic, or else lose ourselves in philosophical wonder how anything eternal can act at all, since action is a process in time with a beginning, a middle, and an end. It is necessary that the transubstantiation should be a cause of wonder and a miracle which man can in no wise comprehend. It is a *mysterium* in the sense of a δρώμενον and δεικνύμενον, a secret that is acted and displayed. The ordinary man is not conscious of anything in himself that would cause him to perform a "mystery." He can only do so if and when *it* seizes upon *him*. This seizure, or rather the sensed or presumed existence of a power outside consciousness which seizes him, is the miracle par excellence, really and truly a miracle when one considers *what* is being represented. What in the world could induce us to represent an absolute impossibility? What is it that for thousands of years has wrung from man the greatest spiritual effort, the loveliest works of art, the profoundest devotion, the most heroic self-sacrifice, and the most exacting service? What else but a miracle? It is a miracle which is not man's to command; for as soon as he tries to work it himself, or as soon as he philosophizes about it and tries to comprehend it intellectually, the bird is flown. A miracle is something that arouses man's wonder precisely because it seems inexplicable. And indeed, from what we know of human nature we could never explain why men are constrained to such statements and to such beliefs. (I am thinking here of the impossible statements made by all religions.) There must be some compelling reason for this, even though it is not to be found in ordinary experience. The very absurdity and impossibility of the state-ments vouches for the existence of this reason. That is the real ground for belief, as was formulated most brilliantly in Ter-tullian's "prorsus credibile, quia ineptum." [2] An improbable opinion has to submit sooner or later to correction. But the statements of religion are the most improbable of all and yet they persist for thousands of years.[3] Their wholly unexpected vitality proves the existence of a sufficient cause which has so far eluded scientific investigation. I can, as a psychologist, only draw attention to this fact and emphasize my belief that there are no facile "nothing but" explanations for psychic phenomena of this kind.

380   The dual aspect of the Mass finds expression not only in the contrast between human and divine action, but also in the dual aspect of God and the God-man, who, although they are by nature a unity, nevertheless represent a duality in the ritual drama. Without this "dichotomy of God," if I may use such a term, the whole act of sacrifice would be inconceivable and would lack actuality. According to the Christian view God has never ceased to be God, not even when he appeared in human form in the temporal order. The Christ of the Johannine gospel declares: "I and my Father are one. He that hath seen me hath seen the Father" (John 10:30, 14:9). And yet on the Cross Christ cries out: "My God, my God, why hast thou forsaken me?" This contradiction must exist if the formula "very God and very man" is psychologically true. And if it is true, then the different sayings of Christ are in no sense a contradiction. Being "very man" means being at an extreme remove and utterly different from God. "De profundis clamavi ad te, Domine"—this cry demonstrates both, the remoteness and the nearness, the outermost darkness and the dazzling spark of the Divine. God in his humanity is presumably so far from himself that he has to seek himself through absolute self-surrender. And where would God's wholeness be if he could not be the "wholly

[2] "Et mortuus est Dei filius, prorsus credibile est, quia ineptum est. Et sepultus resurrexit; certum est, quia impossibile est" (And the Son of God is dead, which is to be believed because it is absurd. And buried He rose again, which is certain because it is impossible). Migne, *P.L.*, vol. 2, col. 751.
[3] The audacity of Tertullian's argument is undeniable, and so is its danger, but that does not detract from its psychological truth.

other"? Accordingly it is with some psychological justification, so it seems to me, that when the Gnostic Nous fell into the power of Physis he assumed the dark chthonic form of the serpent, and the Manichaean "Original Man" in the same situation actually took on the qualities of the Evil One. In Tibetan Buddhism all gods without exception have a peaceful and a wrathful aspect, for they reign over all the realms of being. The dichotomy of God into divinity and humanity and his return to himself in the sacrificial act hold out the comforting doctrine that in man's own darkness there is hidden a light that shall once again return to its source, and that this light actually *wanted* to descend into the darkness in order to deliver the Enchained One who languishes there, and lead him to light everlasting. All this belongs to the stock of pre-Christian ideas, being none other than the doctrine of the "Man of Light," the Anthropos or Original Man, which the sayings of Christ in the gospels assume to be common knowledge. ✕

II. THE PSYCHOLOGICAL MEANING OF SACRIFICE

(a) *The Sacrificial Gifts*

381   Kramp, in his book on the Roman liturgy, makes the following observations about the substances symbolizing the sacrifice:

Now bread and wine are not only the ordinary means of subsistence for a large portion of humanity, they are also to be had all over the earth (which is of the greatest significance as regards the world-wide spread of Christianity). Further, the two together constitute the perfect food of man, who needs both solid and liquid sustenance. Because they can be so regarded as the typical food of man, they are best fitted to serve as a symbol of human life and human personality, a fact which throws significant light on the gift-symbol.[4]

382   It is not immediately apparent why precisely bread and wine should be a "symbol of human life and human personality." This interpretation looks very like a conclusion *a posteriori* from the special meaning which attaches to these substances in the Mass. In that case the meaning would be due to the liturgy and not to the substances themselves, for no one could imagine that

[4] *Die Opferanschauungen,* p. 55.

bread and wine, in themselves, signify human life or human personality. But, in so far as bread and wine are important products of culture, they do express a vital human striving. They represent a definite cultural achievement which is the fruit of attention, patience, industry, devotion, and laborious toil. The words "our daily bread" express man's anxious care for his existence. By producing bread he makes his life secure. But in so far as he "does not live by bread alone," bread is fittingly accompanied by wine, whose cultivation has always demanded a special degree of attention and much painstaking work. Wine, therefore, is equally an expression of cultural achievement. Where wheat and the vine are cultivated, civilized life prevails. But where agriculture and vine-growing do not exist, there is only the uncivilized life of nomads and hunters.

383   So in offering bread and wine man is in the first instance offering up the products of his culture, the best, as it were, that human industry produces. But the "best" can be produced only by the best in man, by his conscientiousness and devotion. Cultural products can therefore easily stand for the psychological conditions of their production, that is, for those human virtues which alone make man capable of civilization.[5]

384   As to the special nature of these substances, bread is undoubtedly a food. There is a popular saying that wine "fortifies," though not in the same sense as food "sustains." It stimulates and "makes glad the heart of man" by virtue of a certain volatile substance which has always been called "spirit." It is thus, unlike innocuous water, an "inspiriting" drink, for a spirit or god dwells within it and produces the ecstasy of intoxication. The wine miracle at Cana was the same as the miracle in the temple of Dionysus, and it is profoundly significant that, on the Damascus Chalice, Christ is enthroned among vine tendrils like Dionysus himself.[6] Bread therefore represents the physical means of subsistence, and wine the spiritual. The offering up of bread and wine is the offering of both the physical and the spiritual fruits of civilization.

5 My reason for saying this is that every symbol has an objective and a subjective—or psychic—origin, so that it can be interpreted on the "objective level" as well as on the "subjective level." This is a consideration of some importance in dream-analysis. Cf. *Psychological Types*, Defs. 38 and 50.

6 Further material in Eisler, *Orpheus—the Fisher*, pp. 280f.

385 But, however sensible he was of the care and labour lavished upon them, man could hardly fail to observe that these cultivated plants grew and flourished according to an inner law of their own, and that there was a power at work in them which he compared to his own life breath or vital spirit. Frazer has called this principle, not unjustly, the "corn spirit." Human initiative and toil are certainly necessary, but even more necessary, in the eyes of primitive man, is the correct and careful performance of the ceremonies which sustain, strengthen, and propitiate the vegetation numen.[7] Grain and wine therefore have something in the nature of a soul, a specific life principle which makes them appropriate symbols not only of man's cultural achievements, but also of the seasonally dying and resurgent god who is their life spirit. Symbols are never simple— only signs and allegories are simple. The symbol always covers a complicated situation which is so far beyond the grasp of language that it cannot be expressed at all in any unambiguous manner.[8] Thus the grain and wine symbols have a fourfold layer of meaning:

1. as agricultural products;

2. as products requiring special processing (bread from grain, wine from grapes);

3. as expressions of psychological achievement (work, industry, patience, devotion, etc.) and of human vitality in general;

4. as manifestations of mana or of the vegetation daemon.

386 From this list it can easily be seen that a symbol is needed to sum up such a complicated physical and psychic situation. The simplest symbolical formula for this is "bread and wine," giving these words the original complex significance which they have always had for tillers of the soil.

(b) The Sacrifice

387 It is clear from the foregoing that the sacrificial gift is symbolic, and that it embraces everything which is expressed by the symbol, namely the physical product, the processed substance, the psychological achievement, and the autonomous, daemonic life principle of cultivated plants. The value of the gift is en-

---

[7] Similarly, in hunting, the *rites d'entrée* are more important than the hunt itself, for on these rites the success of the hunt depends.

[8] Cf. *Psychological Types*, Def. 51.

hanced when it is the best or the first fruits. Since bread and wine are the best that agriculture can offer, they are by the same token man's best endeavour. In addition, bread symbolizes the visible manifestation of the divine numen which dies and rises again, and wine the presence of a pneuma which promises intoxication and ecstasy.[9] The classical world thought of this pneuma as Dionysus, particularly the suffering Dionysus Zagreus, whose divine substance is distributed throughout the whole of nature. In short, what is sacrificed under the forms of bread and wine is nature, man, and God, all combined in the unity of the symbolic gift.

388   The offering of so significant a gift at once raises the question: Does it lie within man's power to offer such a gift at all? Is he psychologically competent to do so? The Church says no, since she maintains that the sacrificing priest is Christ himself. But, since man is included in the gift—included, as we have seen, twice over—the Church also says yes, though with qualifications. On the side of the sacrificer there is an equally complicated, symbolic state of affairs, for the symbol is Christ himself, who is both the sacrificer and the sacrificed. This symbol likewise has several layers of meaning which I shall proceed to sort out in what follows.

389   The act of making a sacrifice consists in the first place in giving something which belongs to me. Everything which belongs to me bears the stamp of "mineness," that is, it has a subtle identity with my ego. This is vividly expressed in certain primitive languages, where the suffix of animation is added to an object—a canoe, for instance—when it belongs to me, but not when it belongs to somebody else. The affinity which all the things bearing the stamp of "mineness" have with my personality is aptly characterized by Lévy-Bruhl [10] as *participation mystique*. It is an irrational, unconscious identity, arising from the fact that anything which comes into contact with me is not only itself, but also a symbol. This symbolization comes about firstly because every human being has unconscious contents, and secondly because every object has an unknown side. Your watch, for instance. Unless you are a watchmaker, you would hardly presume to say that you know how it works. Even if you do, you wouldn't know anything about the molecular structure of the

9 Leisegang, *Der Heilige Geist*, pp. 248ff.   10 *How Natives Think.*

211

steel unless you happened to be a mineralogist or a physicist. And have you ever heard of a scientist who knew how to repair his pocket watch? But where two unknowns come together, it is impossible to distinguish between them. The unknown in man and the unknown in the thing fall together in one. Thus there arises an unconscious identity which sometimes borders on the grotesque. No one is permitted to touch what is "mine," much less use it. One is affronted if "my" things are not treated with sufficient respect. I remember once seeing two Chinese rickshaw boys engaged in furious argument. Just as they were about to come to blows, one of them gave the other's rickshaw a violent kick, thus putting an end to the quarrel. So long as they are unconscious our unconscious contents are always projected, and the projection fixes upon everything "ours," inanimate objects as well as animals and people. And to the extent that "our" possessions are projection carriers, they are *more* than what they are in themselves, and function as such. They have acquired several layers of meaning and are therefore symbolical, though this fact seldom or never reaches consciousness. In reality, our psyche spreads far beyond the confines of the conscious mind, as was apparently known long ago to the old alchemist who said that the soul was for the greater part outside the body.[11]

390   When, therefore, I give away something that is "mine," what I am giving is essentially a symbol, a thing of many meanings; but, owing to my unconsciousness of its symbolic character, it adheres to my ego, because it is part of my personality. Hence there is, explicitly or implicitly, a personal claim bound up with every gift. There is always an unspoken "give that thou mayest receive." Consequently the gift always carries with it a personal intention, for the mere giving of it is not a sacrifice. It only becomes a sacrifice if I give up the implied intention of receiving something in return. If it is to be a true sacrifice, the gift must be given as if it were being destroyed.[12] Only then is it possible

[11] Michael Sendivogius, "Tractatus de sulphure" (16th cent.), in the *Musaeum hermeticum* (1678), p. 617: "[Anima] quae extra corpus multa profundissima imaginatur" ([The soul] which imagines many things of the utmost profundity outside the body).

[12] The parallel to this is total destruction of the sacrificial gift by burning, or by throwing it into water or into a pit.

for the egoistic claim to be given up. Were the bread and wine simply given without any consciousness of an egoistic claim, the fact that it was unconscious would be no excuse, but would on the contrary be sure proof of the existence of a *secret* claim. Because of its egoistic nature, the offering would then inevitably have the character of a magical act of propitiation, with the unavowed purpose and tacit expectation of purchasing the good will of the Deity. That is an ethically worthless simulacrum of sacrifice, and in order to avoid it the giver must at least make himself sufficiently conscious of his identity with the gift to recognize how far he is *giving himself up* in giving the gift. In other words, out of the natural state of identity with what is "mine" there grows the ethical task of sacrificing oneself, or at any rate that part of oneself which is identical with the gift. One ought to realize that when one gives or surrenders oneself there are corresponding claims attached, the more so the less one knows of them. The conscious realization of this alone guarantees that the giving is a real sacrifice. For if I know and admit that I am giving myself, forgoing myself, and do not want to be repaid for it, then I have sacrificed my claim, and thus a part of myself. Consequently, all absolute giving, a giving which is a total loss from the start, is a self-sacrifice. Ordinary giving for which no return is received is felt as a loss; but a sacrifice is meant to be like a loss, so that one may be sure that the egoistic claim no longer exists. Therefore the gift should be given as if it were being destroyed. But since the gift represents myself, I have in that case destroyed myself, given myself away without expectation of return. Yet, looked at in another way, this intentional loss is also a gain, for if you can give yourself it proves that you possess yourself. Nobody can give what he has not got. So anyone who can sacrifice himself and forgo his claim must have had it; in other words, he must have been conscious of the claim. This presupposes an act of considerable self-knowledge, lacking which one remains permanently unconscious of such claims. It is therefore quite logical that the confession of sin should come before the rite of transformation in the Mass. The self-examination is intended to make one conscious of the selfish claim bound up with every gift, so that it may be consciously given up; otherwise the gift is no sacrifice. The sacrifice proves that you possess yourself, for it does not mean just letting yourself be passively taken: it is a conscious and deliberate self-surrender, which proves that you have full control of yourself, that is, of your ego. The ego thus becomes the object of a moral act, for "I" am making a decision on behalf of an authority which is supraordinate to my ego nature. I am, as it were, deciding against my ego and renouncing my claim. The possibility of self-renunciation is an established psychological fact whose philosophical implications I do not propose to discuss. Psychologically, it means that the ego is a relative quantity which can be subsumed under various supraordinate authorities. What are these authorities? They are not to be equated outright with collective moral consciousness, as Freud wanted to do with his superego, but rather with certain psychic conditions which existed in man from the beginning and are not acquired by experience. Behind a man's actions there stands neither public opinion nor the moral code,[13] but the personality of which he is still unconscious. Just as a man still is what he always was, so he already is what he will become. The conscious mind does not embrace the totality of a man, for this totality consists only partly of his conscious contents, and for the other and far greater part, of his unconscious, which is of indefinite extent with no assignable limits. In this totality the conscious mind is contained like a smaller circle within a larger one. Hence it is quite possible for the ego to be made into an object, that is to say, for a more compendious personality to emerge in the course of development and take the ego into its service. Since this growth of personality comes out of the unconscious, which is by definition unlimited, the extent of the personality now gradually realizing itself cannot in practice be limited either. But, unlike the Freudian superego, it is still individual. It is in fact individuality in the highest sense, and therefore theoretically limited, since no individual can possibly display *every* quality. (I have called this process of realization the "individuation process.") So far as the personality is still potential, it can be called transcendent, and

---

[13] If there were really nothing behind him but collective standards of value on the one hand and natural instincts on the other, every breach of morality would be simply a rebellion of instinct. In that case valuable and meaningful innovations would be impossible, for the instincts are the oldest and most conservative element in man and beast alike. Such a view forgets the creative instinct which, although it can behave like an instinct, is seldom found in nature and is confined almost exclusively to *Homo sapiens*.

so far as it is unconscious, it is indistinguishable from all th
things that carry its projections—in other words, the unconsci
personality merges with our environment in accordance with the
above-named *participation mystique*. This fact is of the greatest
practical importance because it renders intelligible the peculiar
symbols through which this projected entity expresses itself in
dreams. By this I mean the symbols of the outside world and the
cosmic symbols. These form the psychological basis for the conception of man as a microcosm, whose fate, as we know, is bound
up with the macrocosm through the astrological components of
his character.

391   The term "self" seemed to me a suitable one for this unconscious substrate, whose actual exponent in consciousness is the
ego. The ego stands to the self as the moved to the mover, or as
object to subject, because the determining factors which radiate
out from the self surround the ego on all sides and are therefore
supraordinate to it. The self, like the unconscious, is an *a priori*
existent out of which the ego evolves. It is, so to speak, an unconscious prefiguration of the ego. It is not I who create myself,
rather I happen to myself. This realization is of fundamental
importance for the psychology of religious phenomena, which
is why Ignatius Loyola started off his *Spiritual Exercises* with
"Homo creatus est" as their "fundamentum." But, fundamental
as it is, it can be only half the psychological truth. If it were the
whole truth it would be tantamount to determinism, for if man
were merely a creature that came into being as a result of something already existing unconsciously, he would have no freedom
and there would be no point in consciousness. Psychology must
reckon with the fact that despite the causal nexus man does
enjoy a feeling of freedom, which is identical with autonomy of
consciousness. However much the ego can be proved to be dependent and preconditioned, it cannot be convinced that it has
no freedom. An absolutely preformed consciousness and a totally
dependent ego would be a pointless farce, since everything
would proceed just as well or even better unconsciously. The
existence of ego consciousness has meaning only if it is free and
autonomous. By stating these facts we have, it is true, established
an antinomy, but we have at the same time given a picture of
things as they are. There are temporal, local, and individual
differences in the degree of dependence and freedom. In reality

both are always present: the supremacy of the self and the hybris of consciousness.

392   This conflict between conscious and unconscious is at least brought nearer to a solution through our becoming aware of it. Such an act of realization is presupposed in the act of self-sacrifice. The ego must make itself conscious of its claim, and the self must cause the ego to renounce it. This can happen in two ways:

393   1. I renounce my claim in consideration of a general moral principle, namely that one must not expect repayment for a gift. In this case the "self" coincides with public opinion and the moral code. It is then identical with Freud's superego and for this reason it is projected into the environment and therefore remains unconscious as an autonomous factor.

394   2. I renounce my claim because I feel impelled to do so for painful inner reasons which are not altogether clear to me. These reasons give me no particular moral satisfaction; on the contrary, I even feel some resistance to them. But I must yield to the power which suppresses my egoistic claim. Here the self is integrated; it is withdrawn from projection and has become perceptible as a determining psychic factor. The objection that in this case the moral code is simply unconscious must be ruled out, because I am perfectly well aware of the moral criticism against which I would have to assert my egoism. Where the ego wish clashes with the moral standard, it is not easy to show that the tendency which suppresses it is individual and not collective. But where it is a case of conflicting loyalties, or we find ourselves in a situation of which the classic example is Hosea's marriage with the harlot, then the ego wish coincides with the collective moral standard, and Hosea would have been bound to accuse Jehovah of immorality. Similarly, the unjust steward would have had to admit his guilt. Jesus took a different view.[14] Experiences of this kind make it clear that the self cannot be equated either with collective morality or with natural instinct, but must be conceived as a determining factor whose nature is individual and unique. The superego is a necessary and unavoidable substitute for the experience of the self.

[14] To the defiler of the Sabbath he said: "Man, if indeed thou knowest what thou doest, thou art blessed; but if thou knowest not, thou art cursed, and a transgressor of the law." James, *The Apocryphal New Testament*, p. 33.

395   These two ways of renouncing one's egoistic claim reveal not only a difference of attitude, but also a difference of situation. In the first case the situation need not affect me personally and directly; in the second, the gift must necessarily be a very personal one which seriously affects the giver and forces him to overcome himself. In the one case it is merely a question, say, of going to Mass; in the other it is more like Abraham's sacrifice of his son or Christ's decision in Gethsemane. The one may be felt very earnestly and experienced with all piety, but the other is the real thing.[15]

396   So long as the self is unconscious, it corresponds to Freud's superego and is a source of perpetual moral conflict. If, however, it is withdrawn from projection and is no longer identical with public opinion, then one is truly one's own yea and nay. The self then functions as a union of opposites and thus constitutes the most immediate experience of the Divine which it is psychologically possible to imagine.[16]

(c) The Sacrificer

397   What I sacrifice is my own selfish claim, and by doing this I give up myself. Every sacrifice is therefore, to a greater or lesser degree, a self-sacrifice. The degree to which it is so depends on the significance of the gift. If it is of great value to me and touches my most personal feelings, I can be sure that in giving up my egoistic claim I shall challenge my ego personality to revolt. I can also be sure that the power which suppresses this claim, and thus suppresses me, must be the self. Hence it is the self that causes me to make the sacrifice; nay more, it compels me to make it.[17] The self is the sacrificer, and I am the sacrificed gift, the human sacrifice. Let us try for a moment to look into Abraham's soul when he was commanded to sacrifice his only son.

15 In order to avoid misunderstandings, I must emphasize that I am speaking only from personal experience, and not of the mysterious reality which the Mass has for the believer.
16 Cf. the "uniting symbol" in *Psychological Types*, Def. 51.
17 In Indian philosophy we find a parallel in Prajapati and Purusha Narayana. Purusha sacrifices himself at the command of Prajapati, but at bottom the two are identical. Cf. the Shatapatha-Brahmana (Sacred Books of the East, XLIV, pp. 172ff.); also the Rig-Veda, X, 90 (trans. by Macnicol, pp. 28–29).

Quite apart from the compassion he felt for his child, would not a father in such a position feel himself as the victim, and feel that he was plunging the knife into his own breast? He would be at the same time the sacrificer and the sacrificed.

398   Now, since the relation of the ego to the self is like that of the son to the father, we can say that when the self calls on us to sacrifice ourselves, it is really carrying out the sacrificial act on itself. We know more or less what this act means to us, but what it means to the self is not so clear. As the self can only be comprehended by us in particular acts, but remains concealed from us as a whole because it is more comprehensive than we are, all we can do is to draw conclusions from the little of the self that we can experience. We have seen that a sacrifice only takes place when we feel the self actually carrying it out on ourselves. We may also venture to surmise that in so far as the self stands to us in the relation of father to son, the self in some sort feels our sacrifice as a sacrifice of itself. From that sacrifice we gain ourselves—our "self"—for we have only what we give. But what does the self gain? We see it entering into manifestation, freeing itself from unconscious projection, and, as it grips us, entering into our lives and so passing from unconsciousness into consciousness, from potentiality into actuality. What it is in the diffuse unconscious state we do not know; we only know that in becoming ourself it has become man.

399   This process of becoming human is represented in dreams and inner images as the putting together of many scattered units, and sometimes as the gradual emergence and clarification of something that was always there.[18] The speculations of alchemy, and also of some Gnostics, revolve round this process. It is

[18] This contradiction is unavoidable because the concept of the self allows only of antinomial statements. The self is by definition an entity more comprehensive than the conscious personality. Consequently the latter cannot pass any comprehensive judgment on the self; any judgment and any statement about it is incomplete and has to be supplemented (but not nullified) by a conditioned negative. If I assert, "The self exists," I must supplement this by saying, "But it seems not to exist." For the sake of completeness I must also invert the proposition and say, "The self does not exist, but yet seems to exist." Actually, this inversion is superfluous in view of the fact that the self is not a philosophical concept like Kant's "thing-in-itself," but an empirical concept of psychology, and can therefore be hypostatized if the above precautions are taken.

likewise expressed in Christian dogma, and more particularly in the transformation mystery of the Mass. The psychology of this process makes it easier to understand why, in the Mass, man appears as both the sacrificer and the sacrificed gift, and why it is not man who is these things, but God who is both: why God becomes the suffering and dying man, and why man, through partaking of the Glorified Body, gains the assurance of resurrection and becomes aware of his participation in Godhead.

400   As I have already suggested, the integration or humanization of the self is initiated from the conscious side by our making ourselves aware of our selfish aims; we examine our motives and try to form as complete and objective a picture as possible of our own nature. It is an act of self-recollection, a gathering together of what is scattered, of all the things in us that have never been properly related, and a coming to terms with oneself with a view to achieving full consciousness. (Unconscious self-sacrifice is merely an accident, not a moral act.) Self-recollection, however, is about the hardest and most repellent thing there is for man, who is predominantly unconscious. Human nature has an invincible dread of becoming more conscious of itself. What nevertheless drives us to it is the self, which demands sacrifice by sacrificing itself to us. Conscious realization or the bringing together of the scattered parts is in one sense an act of the ego's will, but in another sense it is a spontaneous manifestation of the self,[19] which was always there. Individuation appears, on the one hand, as the synthesis of a new unity which previously consisted of scattered particles, and on the other hand, as the revelation of something which existed before the ego and is in fact its father or creator and also its totality. Up to a point we create the self by making ourselves conscious of our unconscious contents, and to that extent it is our son. This is why the alchemists called their incorruptible substance—which means precisely the self—the *filius philosophorum*. But we are forced to make this effort by the unconscious presence of the self, which is all the time urging us to overcome our unconsciousness. From that point of view the self is the father. This accounts for certain alchemical terms, such as Mercurius Senex (Hermes Trismegistus) and Saturnus, who in Gnosticism was regarded as both

19 In so far as it is the self that actuates the ego's self-recollection.

beard and youth, just as Mercurius was in alchemy. These ˌhological connections are seen most clearly in the ancient ˌˌ ˌceptions of the Original Man, the Protanthropos, and the Son of Man. Christ as the Logos is from all eternity, but in his human form he is the "Son of Man." [20] As the Logos, he is the world-creating principle. This corresponds with the relation of the self to consciousness, without which no world could be perceived at all. The Logos is the real *principium individuationis*, because everything proceeds from it, and because everything which is, from crystal to man, exists only in individual form. In the infinite variety and differentiation of the phenomenal world is expressed the essence of the *auctor rerum*. As a correspondence we have, on the one hand, the indefiniteness and unlimited extent of the unconscious self (despite its individuality and uniqueness), its creative relation to individual consciousness, and, on the other hand, the individual human being as a mode of its manifestation. Ancient philosophy paralleled this idea with the legend of the dismembered Dionysus, who, as creator, is the ἀμέριστος (undivided) νοῦς, and, as the creature, the μεμερισμένος (divided) νοῦς.[21] Dionysus is distributed throughout the whole of nature, and just as Zeus once devoured the throbbing heart of the god, so his worshippers tore wild animals to pieces in order to reintegrate his dismembered spirit. The gathering together of the light-substance in Barbelo-Gnosis and in Manichaeism points in the same direction. The psychological equivalent of this is the integration of the self through conscious assimilation of the split-off contents. Self-recollection is a gathering together of the self. It is in this sense that we have to understand the instructions which Monoimos gives to Theophrastus:

Seek him [God] from out thyself, and learn who it is that taketh possession of everything in thee, saying: *my* god, *my* spirit [νοῦς], *my* understanding, *my* soul, *my* body; and learn whence is sorrow and joy, and love and hate, and waking though one would not, and sleeping though one would not, and getting angry though one

---

[20] If I use the unhistorical term "self" for the corresponding processes in the psyche, I do so out of a conscious desire not to trespass on other preserves, but to confine myself exclusively to the field of empirical psychology.

[21] Firmicus Maternus, *De errore profanarum religionum*, 7, 8.

would not, and falling in love though one would not. And if thou shouldst closely investigate these things, thou wilt find Him in thyself, the One and the Many, like to that little point, for it is from thee that he hath his origin.[22]

401   Self-reflection or—what comes to the same thing—the urge to individuation gathers together what is scattered and multifarious, and exalts it to the original form of the One, the Primordial Man. In this way our existence as separate beings, our former ego nature, is abolished, the circle of consciousness is widened, and because the paradoxes have been made conscious the sources of conflict are dried up. This approximation to the self is a kind of repristination or apocatastasis, in so far as the self has an "incorruptible" or "eternal" character on account of its being pre-existent to consciousness.[23] This feeling is expressed in the words from the *benedictio fontis:* "Et quos aut sexus in corpore aut aetas discernit in tempore, omnes in unam pariat gratia mater infantiam" (And may Mother Grace bring forth into one infancy all those whom sex has separated in the body, or age in time).

402   The figure of the divine sacrificer corresponds feature for feature to the empirical modes of manifestation of the archetype that lies at the root of almost all known conceptions of God. This archetype is not merely a static image, but dynamic, full of movement. It is always a drama, whether in heaven, on earth, or in hell.[24]

(d) The Archetype of Sacrifice

403   Comparing the basic ideas of the Mass with the imagery of the Zosimos visions, we find that, despite considerable differences, there is a remarkable degree of similarity. For the sake of clearness I give the similarities and differences in tabular form.

---

22 Hippolytus, *Elenchos*, VIII, 15.
23 And also on account of the fact that the unconscious is only conditionally bound by space and time. The comparative frequency of telepathic phenomena proves that space and time have only a relative validity for the psyche. Evidence for this is furnished by Rhine's experiments. Cf. my "Synchronicity."
24 The word "hell" may strike the reader as odd in this connection. I would, however, recommend him to study the brothel scene in James Joyce's *Ulysses*, or James Hogg's *The Private Memoirs and Confessions of a Justified Sinner.*

Zosimos	*Mass*

SIMILARITIES

1. The chief actors are two priests.	1. There is the priest, and Christ the eternal priest.
2. One priest slays the other.	2. The *Mactatio Christi* takes place as the priest pronounces the words of consecration.
3. Other human beings are sacrificed as well.	3. The congregation itself is a sacrificial gift.
4. The sacrifice is a voluntary self-sacrifice.	4. Christ offers himself freely as a sacrifice.
5. It is a painful death.	5. He suffers in the sacrificial act.
6. The victim is dismembered.	6. Breaking of the Bread.
7. There is a *thysia*.	7. Offering up of incense.
8. The priest eats his own flesh.	8. Christ drinks his own blood (St. Chrysostom).
9. He is transformed into spirit.	9. The substances are transformed into the body and blood of Christ.
10. A shining white figure appears, like the midday sun.	10. The Host is shown as the Beatific Vision ("Quaesivi vultum tuum, Domine") in the greater elevation.
11. Production of the "divine water."	11. The Grace conferred by the Mass; similarity of water chalice and font; water a symbol of grace.

DIFFERENCES

1. The whole sacrificial process is an individual dream vision, a fragment of the unconscious depicting itself in dream consciousness.	1. The Mass is a conscious artifact, the product of many centuries and many minds.
2. The dreamer is only a spectator of the symbolic action.	2. Priest and congregation both participate in the mystery.
3. The action is a bloody and gruesome human sacrifice.	3. Nothing obnoxious; the *mactatio* itself is not mentioned. There is only the bloodless sacrifice of bread and wine (*incruente immolatur!*).

4. The sacrifice is accompanied by a scalping.	4. Nothing comparable.
5. It is also performed on a dragon, and is therefore an animal sacrifice.	5. Symbolic sacrifice of the Lamb.
6. The flesh is roasted.	6. The substances are spiritually transformed.
7. The meaning of the sacrifice is the production of the divine water, used for the transmutation of metals and, mystically, for the birth of the self.	7. The meaning of the Mass is the communion of the living Christ with his flock.
8. What is transformed in the vision is presumably the planetary demon Saturn, the supreme Archon (who is related to the God of the Hebrews). It is the dark, heavy, material principle in man—*hyle*—which is transformed into pneuma.	8. What is transformed in the Mass is God, who as Father begat the Son in human form, suffered and died in that form, and rose up again to his origin.

404   The gross concretism of the vision is so striking that one might easily feel tempted, for aesthetic and other reasons, to drop the comparison with the Mass altogether. If I nevertheless venture to bring out certain analogies, I do so not with the rationalistic intention of devaluing the sacred ceremony by putting it on a level with a piece of pagan nature worship. If I have any aim at all apart from scientific truth, it is to show that the most important mystery of the Catholic Church rests, among other things, on psychic conditions which are deeply rooted in the human soul.

405   The vision, which in all probability has the character of a dream, must be regarded as a spontaneous psychic product that was never consciously intended. Like all dreams, it is a product of nature. The Mass, on the other hand, is a product of man's mind or spirit, and is a definitely conscious proceeding. To use an old but not outmoded nomenclature, we can call the vision *psychic,* and the Mass *pneumatic.* The vision is undifferentiated raw material, while the Mass is a highly differentiated artifact. That is why the one is gruesome and the other beautiful. If the Mass is antique, it is antique in the best sense of the word,

and its liturgy is therefore satisfying to the highest requirements of the present day. In contrast to this, the vision is archaic and primitive, but its symbolism points directly to the fundamental alchemical idea of the incorruptible substance, namely to the self, which is beyond change. The vision is a piece of unalloyed naturalism, banal, grotesque, squalid, horrifying and profound as nature herself. Its meaning is not clear, but it allows itself to be divined with the abysmal uncertainty and ambiguity that pertain to all things nonhuman, suprahuman, and subhuman. The Mass, on the other hand, represents and clearly expresses the Deity itself, and clothes it in the garment of the most beautiful humanity.

406   From all this it is evident that the vision and the Mass are two different things, so different as to be almost incommensurable. But if we could succeed in reconstructing the natural process in the unconscious on which the Mass is psychically based, we should probably obtain a picture which would be rather more commensurable with the vision of Zosimos. According to the view of the Church, the Mass is based on the historical events in the life of Jesus. From this "real" life we can single out certain details that add a few concretistic touches to our picture and thus bring it closer to the vision. For instance, I would mention the scourging, the crowning with thorns, and the clothing in a purple robe, which show Jesus as the archaic sacrificed king. This is further emphasized by the Barabbas episode (the name means "son of the father") which leads to the sacrifice of the king. Then there is the agony of death by crucifixion, a shameful and horrifying spectacle, far indeed from any "incruente immolatur"! The right pleural cavity and probably the right ventricle of the heart were cut open by the spear, so that blood clots and serum flowed out. If we add these details to the process which underlies the Mass, we shall see that they form a striking equivalent to certain archaic and barbarous features of the vision. There are also the fundamental dogmatic ideas to be considered. As is shown by the reference to the sacrifice of Isaac in the prayer *Unde et memores,* the sacrifice has the character not only of a human sacrifice, but the sacrifice of a son— and an *only* son. That is the cruellest and most horrible kind of sacrifice we can imagine, so horrible that, as we know, Abraham

was not required to carry it out.[25] And even if he had carr.
out, a stab in the heart with a knife would have been a quick
relatively painless death for the victim. Even the bloody Az
ceremony of cutting out the heart was a swift death. But th
sacrifice of the son which forms the essential feature of the Mass
began with scourging and mockery, and culminated in six hours
of suspension on a cross to which the victim was nailed hand
and foot—not exactly a quick death, but a slow and exquisite
form of torture. As if that were not enough, crucifixion was regarded as a disgraceful death for slaves, so that the physical
cruelty is balanced by the moral cruelty.

407   Leaving aside for the moment the unity of nature of Father
and Son—which it is possible to do because they are two distinct
Persons who are not to be confused with one another—let us try
to imagine the feelings of a father who saw his son suffering such
a death, knowing that it was he himself who had sent him into
the enemy's country and deliberately exposed him to this danger. Executions of this kind were generally carried out as an act
of revenge or as punishment for a crime, with the idea that both
father and son should suffer. The idea of punishment can be
seen particularly clearly in the crucifixion between two thieves.
The punishment is carried out on God himself, and the model
for this execution is the ritual slaying of the king. The king is
killed when he shows signs of impotence, or when failure of the
crops arouses doubts as to his efficacy. Therefore he is killed in
order to improve the condition of his people, just as God is sacrificed for the salvation of mankind.

408   What is the reason for this "punishment" of God? Despite
the almost blasphemous nature of this question, we must nevertheless ask it in view of the obviously punitive character of the

[25] How Jewish piety reacted to this sacrifice can be seen from the following
Talmudic legend: " 'And I,' cried Abraham, 'swear that I will not go down from
the altar until you have heard me. When you commanded me to sacrifice my son
Isaac you offended against your word, "in Isaac shall your descendants be
named." So if ever my descendants offend against you, and you wish to punish
them, then remember that you too are not without fault, and forgive them.'
'Very well, then,' replied the Lord, 'there behind you is a ram caught in the
thicket with his horns. Offer up that instead of your son Isaac. And if ever your
descendants sin against me, and I sit in judgment over them on New Year's Day,
let them blow the horn of a ram, that I may remember my words, and temper
justice with mercy.' " Fromer and Schnitzer, *Legenden aus dem Talmud*, pp. 34f.

sacrifice. The usual explanation is that Christ was punished for our sins.[26] The dogmatic validity of this answer is not in question here. As I am in no way concerned with the Church's explanation, but only wish to reconstruct the underlying psychic process, we must logically assume the existence of a guilt proportionate to the punishment. If mankind is the guilty party, logic surely demands that mankind should be punished. But if God takes the punishment on himself, he exculpates mankind, and we must then conjecture that it is not mankind that is guilty, but God (which would logically explain why he took the guilt on himself). For reasons that can readily be understood, a satisfactory answer is not to be expected from orthodox Christianity. But such an answer may be found in the Old Testament, in Gnosticism, and in late Catholic speculation. From the Old Testament we know that though Yahweh was a guardian of the law he was not just, and that he suffered from fits of rage which he had every occasion to regret.[27] And from certain Gnostic systems it is clear that the *auctor rerum* was a lower archon who falsely imagined that he had created a perfect world, whereas in fact it was woefully imperfect. On account of his Saturnine disposition this demiurgic archon has affinities with the Jewish Yahweh, who was likewise a world creator. His work was imperfect and did not prosper, but the blame cannot be placed on the creature any more than one can curse the pots for being badly turned out by the potter! This argument led to the Marcionite Reformation and to purging the New Testament of elements derived from the Old. Even as late as the seventeenth century the learned Jesuit, Nicolas Caussin, declared that the unicorn was a fitting symbol for the God of the Old Testament, because in his wrath he reduced the world to confusion like an angry rhinoceros (unicorn), until, overcome by the love of a pure virgin, he was changed in her lap into a God of Love.[28]

[26] Isaiah 53:5: "But he was wounded for our transgressions, he was bruised for our iniquities: the chastisement of our peace was upon him; and with his stripes we are healed."　　[27] See "Answer to Job," in this volume.

[28] Caussin, *De symbolica Aegyptiorum sapientia. Polyhistor symbolicus, Electorum symbolorum, et Parabolarum historicarum stromata* (1618), p. 401. Cf. also Philippus Picinelli, *Mondo Simbolico*, p. 299: "Of a truth God, terrible beyond measure, appeared before the world peaceful and wholly tamed after dwelling in the womb of the most blessed Virgin. St. Bonaventura said that Christ was tamed and pacified by the most kindly Mary, so that he should not punish the sinner with eternal death."

409   In these explanations we find the natural logic we missed
the answer of the Church. God's guilt consisted in the fact th
as creator of the world and king of his creatures, he was inadequate and therefore had to submit to the ritual slaying. For
primitive man the concrete king was perfectly suited to this
purpose, but not for a higher level of civilization with a more
spiritual conception of God. Earlier ages could still dethrone
their gods by destroying their images or putting them in chains.
At a higher level, however, one god could be dethroned only by
another god, and when monotheism developed, God could only
transform himself.

410   The fact that the transformative process takes the form of a
"punishment"—Zosimos uses this very word (κόλασις)—may be
due to a kind of rationalization or a need to offer some explanation of its cruelty. Such a need only arises at a higher level of
consciousness with developed feeling, which then seeks an adequate reason for the revolting and incomprehensible cruelty of
the procedure. (A modern parallel would be the experience of
dismemberment in shamanistic initiations.) The readiest conjecture at this level is that some guilt or sin is being punished.
In this way the transformation process acquires a moral function
that can scarcely be conceived as underlying the original event.
It seems more likely that a higher and later level of consciousness found itself confronted with an experience for which no
sensible reasons or explanations had ever been given, but which
it tried to make intelligible by weaving into it a moral aetiology.
It is not difficult to see that dismemberment originally served
the purpose of reconstituting the neophyte as a new and more
effective human being. Initiation even has the aspect of a healing.[29] In the light of these facts, moral interpretation in terms
of punishment seems beside the mark and arouses the suspicion
that dismemberment has still not been properly understood. A
moral interpretation is inadequate because it fails to understand
the contradiction at the heart of its explanation, namely that
guilt should be avoided if one doesn't want to be punished. But,
for the neophyte, it would be a real sin if he shrank from the
torture of initiation. The torture inflicted on him is *not* a punishment but the indispensable means of leading him towards
his destiny. Also, these ceremonies often take place at so young
an age that a guilt of corresponding proportions is quite out of
29 Eliade, *Shamanism,* esp. chs. II and VII.

the question. For this reason, the moralistic view of suffering as punishment seems to me not only inadequate but misleading. It is obviously a primitive attempt to give a psychological explanation of an age-old archetypal idea that had never before been the object of reflection. Such ideas and rituals, far from ever having been invented, simply happened and were acted long before they were thought. I have seen primitives practising rites of which none of them had the remotest idea what they meant, and in Europe we still find customs whose meaning has always been unconscious. First attempts at explanation usually turn out to be somewhat clumsy.

411   The aspect of torture, then, is correlated with a detached and observing consciousness that has not yet understood the real meaning of dismemberment. What is performed concretely on the sacrificial animal, and what the shaman believes to be actually happening to himself, appears on a higher level, in the vision of Zosimos, as a psychic process in which a product of the unconscious, an homunculus, is cut up and transformed. By all the rules of dream-interpretation, this is an aspect of the observing subject himself; that is to say, Zosimos sees himself as an homunculus, or rather the unconscious represents him as such, as an incomplete, stunted, dwarfish creature who is made of some heavy material (lead or bronze) and thus signifies the "hylical man." Such a one is dark, and sunk in materiality. He is essentially unconscious and therefore in need of transformation and enlightenment. For this purpose his body must be taken apart and dissolved into its constituents, a process known in alchemy as the *divisio, separatio* and *solutio,* and in later treatises as *discrimination* and *self-knowledge.*[30] This psychological process is admittedly painful and for many people a positive torture. But, as always, every step forward along the path of individuation is achieved only at the cost of suffering.

412   In the case of Zosimos there is of course no real consciousness of the transformative process, as is abundantly clear from his own interpretation of the vision: he thought the dream imagery was showing him the "production of the waters." We can see from this that he was still exteriorizing the transformation and did not feel it in any way as an alteration of his own psyche.

[30] Particularly in Gerhard Dorn, "Speculativae philosophiae," *Theatrum chemicum,* I (1602), pp. 276f.

413 A similar state of affairs prevails in Christian psychology whenever the rites and dogmas are taken as merely external factors and are not experienced as inner events. But, just as the *imitatio Christi* in general, and the Mass in particular, endeavour to include the believer in the process of transformation, the Mass actually representing him as a sacrificial gift parallel with Christ, so a better understanding of Christianity raises it as high above the sphere of "mind" as the rite of the Mass is above the archaic level of the Zosimos vision. The Mass tries to effect a *participation mystique*—or identity—of priest and congregation with Christ, so that on the one hand the soul is assimilated to Christ and on the other hand the Christ-figure is recollected in the soul. It is a transformation of God and man alike, since the Mass is, at least by implication, a repetition of the whole drama of Incarnation.

III. THE MASS AND THE INDIVIDUATION PROCESS

414 Looked at from the psychological standpoint, Christ, as the Original Man (Son of Man, second Adam, τέλειος ἄνθρωπος), represents a totality which surpasses and includes the ordinary man, and which corresponds to the total personality that transcends consciousness.[31] We have called this personality the "self." Just as, on the more archaic level of the Zosimos vision, the homunculus is transformed into pneuma and exalted, so the mystery of the Eucharist transforms the soul of the empirical man, who is only a part of himself, into his totality, symbolically expressed by Christ. In this sense, therefore, we can speak of the Mass as the *rite of the individuation process.*

415 Reflections of this kind can be found very early on in the old Christian writings, as for instance in the Acts of John, one of the most important of the apocryphal texts that have come down to us.[32] That part of the text with which we are concerned here begins with a description of a mystical "round dance" which Christ instituted before his crucifixion. He told his disciples to hold hands and form a ring, while he himself stood

31 Cf. my *Aion*, Ch. V.
32 *The Apocryphal New Testament.* The Acts of John were probably written during the first half of the 2nd cent.

in the centre. As they moved round in a circle, Christ sang a song of praise, from which I would single out the following characteristic verses: [33]

> I will be saved and I will save, Amen.
> I will be loosed and I will loose,[34] Amen.
> I will be wounded and I will wound, Amen.
> I will be begotten and I will beget, Amen.
> I will eat and I will be eaten, Amen.
> . . .
> I will be thought, being wholly spirit, Amen.
> I will be washed and I will wash, Amen.
> Grace paces the round. I will blow the pipe. Dance
>   the round all, Amen.
> . . .
> The Eight [ogdoad] sings praises with us, Amen.
> The Twelve paces the round aloft, Amen.
> To each and all it is given to dance, Amen.
> Who joins not the dance mistakes the event, Amen.
> . . .
> I will be united and I will unite, Amen.
> . . .
> A lamp am I to you that perceive me, Amen.
> A mirror am I to you that know me, Amen.
> A door am I to you that knock on me, Amen.
> A way am I to you the wayfarer.

Now as you respond to my dancing, behold yourself in me who speaks . . .

As you dance, ponder what I do, for yours is this human suffering which I will to suffer. For you would be powerless to understand your suffering had I not been sent to you as the Logos by the Father. . . . If you had understood suffering, you would have non-suffering. Learn to suffer, and you shall understand how not to suffer. . . . Understand the Word of Wisdom in me.[35]

416   I would like to interrupt the text here, as we have come to a natural break, and introduce a few psychological remarks. They will help us to understand some further passages that still have

---

33 Ibid., pp. 253f., modified.

34 [Or: I will be freed and I will free.—TRANS.]

35 Trans. based on James, pp. 253f., and that of Ralph Manheim from the German of Max Pulver, "Jesus' Round Dance and Crucifixion according to the Acts of St. John," in *The Mysteries*, pp. 179f.

to be discussed. Although our text is obviously based on New Testament models, what strikes us most of all is its antithetical and paradoxical style, which has very little in common with the spirit of the Gospels. This feature only appears in a veiled way in the canonical writings, for instance in the parable of the unjust steward (Luke 16), in the Lord's Prayer ("Lead us not into temptation"), in Matthew 10:16 ("Be wise as serpents"), John 10:34 ("Ye are gods"), in the logion of the Codex Bezae to Luke 6:4,[36] in the apocryphal saying "Whoso is near unto me is near unto the fire," and so on. Echoes of the antithetical style can also be found in Matthew 10:26: ". . . . for nothing is covered that will not be revealed, or hidden that will not be known."

417   Paradox is a characteristic of the Gnostic writings. It does more justice to the *unknowable* than clarity can do, for uniformity of meaning robs the mystery of its darkness and sets it up as something that is *known*. That is a usurpation, and it leads the human intellect into hybris by pretending that it, the intellect, has got hold of the transcendent mystery by a cognitive act and has "grasped" it. The paradox therefore reflects a higher level of intellect and, by not forcibly representing the unknowable as known, gives a more faithful picture of the real state of affairs.

418   These antithetical predications show the amount of *reflection* that has gone into the hymn: it formulates the figure of our Lord in a series of paradoxes, as God and man, sacrificer and sacrificed. The latter formulation is important because the hymn was sung just before Jesus was arrested, that is, at about the moment when the synoptic gospels speak of the Last Supper and John—among other things—of the parable of the vine. John, significantly enough, does not mention the Last Supper, and in the Acts of John its place is taken by the "round dance." But the round table, like the round dance, stands for synthesis and union. In the Last Supper this takes the form of participation in the body and blood of Christ, i.e., there is an ingestion and assimilation of the Lord, and in the round dance there is a circular circumambulation round the Lord as the central point. Despite the outward difference of the symbols, they have a common meaning: Christ is taken into the midst of the disciples. But, although the two rites have this common basic meaning,

36 See James, p. 33.

the outward difference between them should not be overlooked. The classical Eucharistic feast follows the synoptic gospels, whereas the one in the Acts of John follows the Johannine pattern. One could almost say that it expresses, in a form borrowed from some pagan mystery feast, a more immediate relationship of the congregation to Christ, after the manner of the Johannine parable: "I am the vine, ye are the branches. He that abideth in me, and I in him, the same bringeth forth much fruit" (John 15:5). This close relationship is represented by the circle and central point: the two parts are indispensable to each other and equivalent. Since olden times the circle with a centre has been a symbol for the Deity, illustrating the wholeness of God incarnate: the single point in the centre and the series of points constituting the circumference. Ritual circumambulation often bases itself quite consciously on the cosmic picture of the starry heavens revolving, on the "dance of the stars," an idea that is still preserved in the comparison of the twelve disciples with the zodiacal constellations, as also in the depictions of the zodiac that are sometimes found in churches, in front of the altar or on the roof of the nave. Some such picture may well have been at the back of the medieval ball-game of pelota that was played in church by the bishop and his clergy.

419   At all events, the aim and effect of the solemn round dance is to impress upon the mind the image of the circle and the centre and the relation of each point along the periphery to that centre.[37] Psychologically this arrangement is equivalent to a mandala and is thus a symbol of the self,[38] the point of reference not only of the individual ego but of all those who are of like mind or who are bound together by fate. The self is not an ego but a supraordinate totality embracing the conscious and the unconscious. But since the latter has no assignable limits and

---

[37] Another idea of the kind is that every human being is a ray of sunlight. This image occurs in the Spanish poet Jorge Guillén, *Cantico: Fe de Vida*, pp. 24–25 ("Más allá," VI):

> Where could I stray to, where?
> This point is my centre . . .
>
> With this earth and this ocean
> To rise to the infinite:
> One ray more of the sun.   (Trans. by J. M. Cohen.)

[38] Cf. *Aion*, Ch. IV.

in its deeper layers is of a collective nature, it cannot be distinguished from that of another individual. As a result, it continually creates that ubiquitous *participation mystique* which is the unity of many, the *one* man in all men. This psychological fact forms the basis for the archetype of the ἄνθρωπος, the Son of Man, the *homo maximus*, the *vir unus*, purusha, etc.[39] Because the unconscious, in fact and by definition, cannot be discriminated as such, the most we can hope to do is to infer its nature from the empirical material. Certain unconscious contents are undoubtedly personal and individual and cannot be attributed to any other individual. But, besides these, there are numerous others that can be observed in almost identical form in many different individuals in no way connected with one another. These experiences suggest that the unconscious has a collective aspect. It is therefore difficult to understand how people today can still doubt the existence of a collective unconscious. After all, nobody would dream of regarding the instincts or human morphology as personal acquisitions or personal caprices. The unconscious is the universal mediator among men. It is in a sense the all-embracing One, or the one psychic substratum common to all. The alchemists knew it as their Mercurius and they called him the mediator in analogy to Christ.[40] Ecclesiastical doctrine says the same thing about Christ, and so, particularly, does our hymn. Its antithetical statements could, however, be interpreted as referring just as well to Mercurius, if not better.

420   For instance, in the first verse, "I will be saved," it is not clear how far the Lord is able to say such a thing of himself, since he is the saviour (σωτήρ) par excellence. Mercurius, on the other hand, the helpful arcane substance of the alchemists, is the world-soul imprisoned in matter and, like the Original Man who fell into the embrace of Physis, is in need of salvation through the labours of the artifex. Mercurius is set free ("loosed") and redeemed; as *aqua permanens* he is also the

[39] The universality of this figure may explain why its epiphanies take so many different forms. For instance, it is related in the Acts of John (James, p. 251) that Drusiana saw the Lord once "in the likeness of John" and another time "in that of a youth." The disciple James saw him as a child, but John as an adult. John saw him first as "a small man and uncomely," and then again as one reaching to heaven (p. 251). Sometimes his body felt "material and solid," but sometimes "the substance was immaterial and as if it existed not at all" (p. 252).
[40] "The Spirit Mercurius," pt. 2, ch. 9.

classical solvent. "I will be wounded, and I will wound" is
clearer: it refers to the wound in Christ's side and to the divisive
sword. But Mercurius too, as the arcane substance, is divided or
pierced through with the sword (*separatio* and *penetratio*), and
wounds himself with the sword or *telum passionis,* the dart of
love. The reference to Christ is less clear in the words "I will be
begotten, and I will beget." The first statement refers essentially to him in so far as the Son was begotten by the Holy Ghost
and not created, but the "begetting" is generally held to be the
property of the Holy Ghost and not of Christ as such. It
certainly remains a moot point whether Mercurius as the world-
soul was begotten or created, but he is unquestionably "vivifying," and in his ithyphallic form as Hermes Kyllenios he is
actually the symbol of generation. "Eating" as compared with
"being eaten" is not exactly characteristic of Christ, but rather
of the devouring dragon, the corrosive Mercurius, who, as the
uroboros, also eats himself, like Zosimos's homunculus.

421   "I will be thought," if evangelical at all, is an exclusively
Johannine, post-apostolic speculation concerning the nature of
the Logos. Hermes was very early considered to be Nous and
Logos, and Hermes Trismegistus was actually the Nous of revelation. Mercurius, until well into the seventeenth century, was
thought of as the *veritas* hidden in the human body, i.e., in
matter, and this truth had to be known by meditation, or by
cogitatio, reflection. Meditation is an idea that does not occur
at all in the New Testament.[41] The *cogitatio* which might possibly correspond to it usually has a negative character and appears as the wicked *cogitatio cordis* of Genesis 6:5 (and 8:21):
"Cuncta cogitatio cordis intenta ad malum" (DV: ". . . all the
thought of their heart was bent upon evil at all times"; AV:
". . . every imagination of the thoughts of his heart . . ."). In
I Peter 4:1 ἔννοια is given as "cogitatio" (DV: ". . . arm yourselves with the same intent"; AV: "same mind"; RSV: "same
thought"). "Cogitare" has a more positive meaning in II Corinthians 10:7, where it really means to "bethink oneself," "remember by reflection": "hoc cogitet iterum apud se" ("τοῦτο
λογιζέσθω πάλιν ἐφ' ἑαυτοῦ"; DV: "let him reflect within himself";

41 "Haec meditare" (ταῦτα μελέτα) in I Tim. 4:15 has more the meaning of
'see to' or 'attend to' these things. [Both DV and AV have "meditate on these
things," but RSV has "practise these duties."—Trans.]

AV: "let him of himself think this again"; RSV: "let him remind himself"). But this positive thinking in us is of God (II Cor. 3:5: "non quod sufficientes simus cogitare aliquid a nobis, quasi ex nobis"; "οὐχ ὅτι ἀφ' ἑαυτῶν ἱκανοί ἐσμεν λογίσασθαί τι ὡς ἐξ ἑαυτῶν, ἀλλ' ἡ ἱκανότης ἡμῶν ἐκ τοῦ θεοῦ"; DV: "Not that we are sufficient of ourselves to think anything, as from ourselves, but our sufficiency is from God"). The only place where *cogitatio* has the character of a meditation culminating in enlightenment is Acts 10:19: "Petro autem cogitante de visione, dixit Spiritus ei" ("Τοῦ δὲ Πέτρου διενθυμουμένου περὶ τοῦ ὁράματος εἶπεν τὸ πνεῦμα αὐτῷ"; DV: "But while Peter was pondering over the vision, the spirit said to him . . .").

422   Thinking, in the first centuries of our era, was more the concern of the Gnostics than of the Church, for which reason the great Gnostics, such as Basilides and Valentinus, seem almost like Christian theologians with a bent for philosophy. With John's doctrine of the Logos, Christ came to be regarded simultaneously as the Nous and the object of human thought; the Greek text says literally: "Νοηθῆναι θέλω νοῦς ὢν ὅλος" [42] (I will be thought, being wholly spirit). Similarly, the Acts of Peter say of Christ: "Thou art perceived of the spirit only." [43]

423   The "washing" refers to the *purificatio,* or to baptism, and equally to the washing of the dead body. The latter idea lingered on into the eighteenth century, as the alchemical washing of the "black corpse," an *opus mulierum.* The object to be washed was the black *prima materia:* it, the washing material *(sapo sapientum!),* and the washer were—all three of them—the selfsame Mercurius in different guises. But whereas in alchemy the *nigredo* and sin were identical concepts (since both needed washing), in Christian Gnosticism there are only a few hints of Christ's possible identity with the darkness. The λούσασθαι ("I will be washed") in our text is one of them.

424   The "ogdoad," being a double quaternity, belongs to the symbolism of the mandala. It obviously represents the archetype of the round dance in the "supra-celestial place," since it sings in harmony. The same applies to the number Twelve, the zodiacal archetype of the twelve disciples, a cosmic idea that still

42 Lipsius and Bonnet, eds., *Acta Apostolorum Apocrypha,* I, p. 197.
43 James, p. 335

235

in Dante's *Paradiso*, where the saints form shining con-
ions.

nyone who does not join in the dance, who does not make
ircumambulation of the centre (Christ and Anthropos), is
smitten with blindness and sees nothing. What is described here
as an outward event is really a symbol for the inward turning
towards the centre in each of the disciples, towards the archetype
of man, towards the self—for the dance can hardly be understood as an historical event. It should be understood, rather, as
a sort of paraphrase of the Eucharist, an amplifying symbol that
renders the mystery more assimilable to consciousness, and it
must therefore be interpreted as a psychic phenomenon. It is
an act of conscious realization on a higher level, establishing a
connection between the consciousness of the individual and the
supraordinate symbol of totality.

426   The "Acts of Peter" says of Christ:

Thou art unto me father, thou my mother, thou my brother, thou
my friend, thou my bondsman, thou my steward. Thou art All and
All is in thee; thou Art, and there is naught else that is save thee
only.

Unto him therefore do ye also, brethren, flee, and if ye learn that
in him alone ye exist, ye shall obtain those things whereof he saith
unto you: "Which neither eye hath seen nor ear heard, neither have
they entered into the heart of man." [44]

427   The words "I will be united" must be understood in this
sense, as meaning that subjective consciousness is united with an
objective centre, thus producing the unity of God and man
represented by Christ. The self is brought into actuality through
the concentration of the many upon the centre, and the self
wants this concentration. It is the subject and the object of the
process. Therefore it is a "lamp" to those who "perceive" it.
Its light is invisible if it is not perceived; it might just as well
not exist. It is as dependent on being perceived as the act of
perception is on light. This brings out once again the paradoxical subject-object nature of the unknowable. Christ, or the self,
is a "mirror": on the one hand it reflects the subjective consciousness of the disciple, making it visible to him, and on the
other hand it "knows" Christ, that is to say it does not merely

[44] James, p. 335.

reflect the empirical man, it also shows him as a (transcendental) whole. And, just as a "door" opens to one who "knocks" on it, or a "way" opens out to the wayfarer who seeks it, so, when you relate to your own (transcendental) centre, you initiate a process of conscious development which leads to oneness and wholeness. You no longer see yourself as an isolated point on the periphery, but as the One in the centre. Only subjective consciousness is isolated; when it relates to its centre it is integrated into wholeness. Whoever joins in the dance sees himself in the reflecting centre, and his suffering is the suffering which the One who stands in the centre "wills to suffer." The paradoxical identity and difference of ego and self could hardly be formulated more trenchantly.

428   As the text says, you would not be able to understand what you suffer unless there were that Archimedean point outside, the objective standpoint of the self, from which the ego can be seen as a phenomenon. Without the objectivation of the self the ego would remain caught in hopeless subjectivity and would only gyrate round itself. But if you can see and understand your suffering without being subjectively involved, then, because of your altered standpoint, you also understand "how not to suffer," for you have reached a place beyond all involvements ("you have me as a bed, rest upon me"). This is an unexpectedly psychological formulation of the Christian idea of overcoming the world, though with a Docetist twist to it: "Who I am, you shall know when I depart. What now I am seen to be, I am not." [45] These statements are clarified by a vision in which John sees the Lord "standing in the midst of the cave and illuminating it." He says to John:

429   John, for the multitude below in Jerusalem I am being crucified and pierced with lances and staves, and vinegar and gall are given me to drink. But to you I speak, and what I say, hear: I put it into your mind to go up on this mountain, that you might hear those things which a disciple must learn from his master and a man from his God. And with these words he showed me a cross of light, and about the cross a great multitude that had no form [μίαν μορφὴν μὴ ἔχοντα], and in the cross there was one form and one appearance. And above [ἐπάνω] the cross I saw the Lord himself, and he had no outward shape [σχῆμα], but only a voice, and a voice not

45 Ibid., p. 254.

such as we knew, but one sweet and kind and truly [that] of [a] God, which spoke to me: John, one man must hear this from me, for I require one that shall hear. For your sakes this cross of light was named by me now Logos, now Nous, now Jesus, now Christ, now Door, now Way, now Bread, now Seed [σπόρος], now Resurrection, now Son, now Father, now Pneuma, now Life, now Truth, now Faith [πίστις], now Grace. So is it called for men; but in itself and in its essence, as spoken of to you, it is the Boundary of all things, and the composing of things unstable,[46] and the harmony of wisdom, and the wisdom that is in harmony. For there are [places] of the right and of the left, Powers, Authorities, Archons, Daemons, Workings, Threatenings, Wraths, Devils, Satan, and the Nether Root whence proceeded the nature of whatever comes to be. And so it is this cross which joined all things together through the Word, and which separated the things that are from those that are below, and which caused all things to flow forth from the One.

But this is not the cross of wood which you will see when you go down from here; neither am I he that is on the cross, whom now you do not see, but only hear his voice. I passed for that which I am not, for I am not what I was to many others. But what they will say of me is vile and not worthy of me. Since, then, the place of rest is neither seen nor named, how much less will they see and name me, their Lord!

Now the formless multitude about the cross is of the lower nature. And if those whom you see in the cross have not one form, then not all the parts of him who descended have yet been recollected. But when the nature of man has been taken up and a generation of men that obey my voice draws near to me, he that now hears me shall be united with them and shall no longer be what he now is, but shall stand above them, as I do now. For so long as you call not yourself mine, I am not what I was. But if you understand me, you shall be in your understanding as I am, and I shall be what I was when I have you with me. For this you are through me. . . .

Behold, what you are, I have shown you. But what I am, I alone know, and no man else. Therefore let me have what is mine, but behold what is thine through me. And behold me truly, not as I have said I am, but as you, being akin to me, know me.[47]

430   Our text throws some doubt on the traditional view of Docetism. Though it is perfectly clear from the texts that Christ only seemed to have a body, which only seemed to suffer, this

46 Ἀνάγγη βιάβα uncertain.

47 Based on James, pp. 254ff., and the author's modified version of Hennecke, ed., *Neutestamentliche Apokryphen*, pp. 186ff.

is Docetism at its grossest. The Acts of John are more subtle, and the argument used is almost epistemological: the historical facts are real enough, but they reveal no more than is intelligible to the senses of the ordinary man. Yet even for the knower of divine secrets the act of crucifixion is a mystery, a symbol that expresses a parallel psychic event in the beholder. In the language of Plato it is an event which occurs in a "supra-celestial place," i.e., on a "mountain" and in a "cave" where a cross of light is set up, its many synonyms signifying that it has many aspects and many meanings. It expresses the unknowable nature of the "Lord," the supraordinate personality and τέλειος ἄνθρωπος, and since it is a quaternity, a whole divided into four parts, it is the classic symbol of the self.

431   Understood in this sense, the Docetism of the Acts of John appears more as a completion of the historical event than a devaluation of it. It is not surprising that the common people should have failed to appreciate its subtlety, though it is plain enough from a psychological point of view. On the other hand, the educated public of those days were by no means unfamiliar with the parallelism of earthly and metaphysical happenings, only it was not clear to them that their visionary symbols were not necessarily metaphysical realities but were perceptions of intrapsychic or subliminal processes that I have called "phenomena of assimilation." The contemplation of Christ's sacrificial death in its traditional form and cosmic significance constellated analogous psychic processes which in their turn gave rise to a wealth of symbols, as I have shown elsewhere.[48] This is, quite obviously, what has happened here, and it took the form of a visible split between the historical event down below on earth, as perceived by the senses, and its ideal, visionary reflection on high, the cross appearing on the one hand as a wooden instrument of torture and on the other as a glorious symbol. Evidently the centre of gravity has shifted to the ideal event, with the result that the psychic process is involuntarily given the greater importance. Although the emphasis on the pneuma detracts from the meaning of the concrete event in a rather one-sided and debatable way, it cannot be dismissed as superfluous, since a concrete event by itself can never create meaning, but is largely dependent for this on the manner in which it is understood.

48 Cf. *Aion.*

Interpretation is necessary before the meaning of a thing can be grasped. The naked facts by themselves "mean" nothing. So one cannot assert that the Gnostic attempts at interpretation were entirely lacking in merit, even though it went far beyond the framework of early Christian tradition. One could even venture to assert that it was already implicit in that tradition, since the cross and the crucified are practically synonymous in the language of the New Testament.[49]

432   The text shows the cross as the antithesis of the formless multitude: it is, or it has, "form" and its meaning is that of a central point defined by the crossing of two straight lines. It is identical with the Kyrios (Lord) and the Logos, with Jesus and with Christ. How John could "see" the Lord above the cross, when the Lord is described as having no "outward shape," must remain a mystery. He only hears an explanatory voice, and this may indicate that the cross of light is only a visualization of the unknowable, whose voice can be heard apart from the cross. This seems to be confirmed by the remark that the cross was named Logos and so on "for your sakes."

433   The cross signifies order as opposed to the disorderly chaos of the formless multitude. It is, in fact, one of the prime symbols of order, as I have shown elsewhere. In the domain of psychological processes it functions as an organizing centre, and in states of psychic disorder [50] caused by an invasion of unconscious contents it appears as a mandala divided into four. No doubt this was a frequent phenomenon in early Christian times, and not only in Gnostic circles.[51] Gnostic introspection could hardly fail, therefore, to perceive the numinosity of this archetype and be duly impressed by it. For the Gnostics the cross had exactly the same function that the atman or Self has always had for the East. This realization is one of the central experiences of Gnosticism.

---

[49] The quaternity, earlier hinted at in the vision of Ezekiel, is patently manifest in the pre-Christian Book of Enoch. (Cf. "Answer to Job," below, pars. 662ff.) In the Apocalypse of Sophonias [Zephaniah], Christ appears surrounded by a garland of doves (Stern, "Die koptische Apokalypse des Sophonias," p. 124). Cf. also the mosaic of St. Felix at Nola, showing a cross surrounded by doves. There is another in San Clemente, Rome (Wickhoff, "Das Apsismosaik in der Basilica des H. Felix zu Nola," pp. 158ff.; and Rossi, *Musaici Cristiani delle Chiese di Roma anteriori al secolo XV*, pl. XXIX).
[50] Symbolized by the formless multitude.
[51] Cf. "speaking with tongues" and glossolalia.

434   The definition of the cross or centre as διορισμός, the "boundary" of all things, is exceedingly original, for it suggests that the limits of the universe are not to be found in a nonexistent periphery but in its centre. There alone lies the possibility of transcending this world. All instability culminates in that which is unchanging and quiescent, and in the self all disharmonies are resolved in the "harmony of wisdom."

435   As the centre symbolizes the idea of totality and finality, it is quite appropriate that the text should suddenly start speaking of the dichotomy of the universe, polarized into right and left, brightness and darkness, heaven and the "nether root," the *omnium genetrix*. This is a clear reminder that everything is contained in the centre and that, as a result, the Lord (i.e., the cross) unites and composes all things and is therefore "nirdvanda," free from the opposites, in conformity with Eastern ideas and also with the psychology of this archetypal symbol. The Gnostic Christ-figure and the cross are counterparts of the typical mandalas spontaneously produced by the unconscious. They are *natural symbols* and they differ fundamentally from the dogmatic figure of Christ, in whom all trace of darkness is expressly lacking.

436   In this connection mention should be made of Peter's valedictory words, which he spoke during his martyrdom (he was crucified upside down, at his own request):

O name of the cross, hidden mystery! O grace ineffable that is pronounced in the name of the cross! O nature of man, that cannot be separated from God! O love unspeakable and indivisible, that cannot be shown forth by unclean lips! I grasp thee now, I that am at the end of my earthly course. I will declare thee as thou art, I will not keep silent the mystery of the cross which was once shut and hidden from my soul. You that hope in Christ, let not the cross be for you that which appears; for it is another thing, and different from that which appears, this suffering which is in accordance with Christ's. And now above all, because you that can hear are able to hear it of me, who am at the last and farewell hour of my life, hearken: separate your souls from everything that is of the senses, from everything that appears to be but in truth is not. Lock your eyes, close your ears, shun those happenings which are seen! Then you shall perceive that which was done to Christ, and the whole mystery of your salvation. . . .

Learn the mystery of all nature and the beginning of all things, as it was. For the first man, of whose race I bear the likeness, fell head downwards, and showed forth a manner of birth such as had not existed till then, for it was dead, having no motion. And being pulled downwards, and having also cast his origin upon the earth, he established the whole disposition of things; for, being hanged up in the manner appointed, he showed forth the things of the right as those of the left, and the things of the left as those of the right, and changed about all the marks of their nature, so that things that were not fair were perceived to be fair, and those that were in truth evil were perceived to be good. Wherefore the Lord says in a mystery: "Except ye make the things of the right as those of the left, and those of the left as those of the right, and those that are above as those below, and those that are behind as those that are before, ye shall not have knowledge of the kingdom."

This understanding have I brought you, and the figure in which you now see me hanging is the representation of that first man who came to birth.

437   In this passage, too, the symbolical interpretation of the cross is coupled with the problem of opposites, first in the unusual idea that the creation of the first man caused everything to be turned upside down, and then in the attempt to unite the opposites by identifying them with one another. A further point of significance is that Peter, crucified head downwards, is identical not only with the first created man, but with the cross:

For what else is Christ but the word, the sound of God? So the word is this upright beam on which I am crucified; and the sound is the beam which crosses it, the nature of man; but the nail which holds the centre of the crossbeam to the upright is man's conversion and repentance (μετάνοια).[52]

438   In the light of these passages it can hardly be said that the author of the Acts of John—presumably a Gnostic—has drawn the necessary conclusions from his premises or that their full implications have become clear to him. On the contrary, one gets the impression that the light has swallowed up everything dark. Just as the enlightening vision appears high above the actual scene of crucifixion, so, for John, the enlightened one stands high above the formless multitude. The text says: "Therefore care not for the many, and despise those that are outside

[52] Based on James, pp. 334f.

the mystery!" [53] This overweening attitude arises from an inflation caused by the fact that the enlightened John has identified with his own light and confused his ego with the self. Therefore he feels superior to the darkness in him. He forgets that light only has a meaning when it illuminates something dark and that his enlightenment is no good to him unless it helps him to recognize his own darkness. If the powers of the left are as real as those of the right, then their union can only produce a third thing that shares the nature of both. Opposites unite in a new energy potential: the "third" that arises out of their union is a figure "free from the opposites," beyond all moral categories. This conclusion would have been too advanced for the Gnostics. Recognizing the danger of Gnostic irrealism, the Church, more practical in these matters, has always insisted on the concretism of the historical events despite the fact that the original New Testament texts predict the ultimate deification of man in a manner strangely reminiscent of the words of the serpent in the Garden of Eden: "Ye shall be as gods." [54] Nevertheless, there was some justification for postponing the elevation of man's status until after death, as this avoided the danger of Gnostic inflation.[55]

439   Had the Gnostic not identified with the self, he would have been bou. ¹ to see how much darkness was in him—a realization that comes more naturally to modern man but causes him no less difficulties. Indeed, he is far more likely to assume that he himself is wholly of the devil than to believe that God could ever indulge in paradoxical statements. For all the ill consequences of his fatal inflation, the Gnostic did, however, gain an insight into religion, or into the psychology of religion, from which we can still learn a thing or two today. He looked deep into the background of Christianity and hence into its future developments. This he could do because his intimate connection with pagan Gnosis made him an "assimilator" that helped to integrate the Christian message into the spirit of the times.

440   The extraordinary number of synonyms piled on top of one another in an attempt to define the cross have their analogy in the Naassene and Peratic symbols of Hippolytus, all pointing to

53 Ibid., p. 255.   54 Genesis 3 : 5.
55 The possibility of inflation was brought very close indeed by Christ's words: "Ye are gods" (John 10 : 34).

this one centre. It is the ἓν τὸ πᾶν of alchemy, which is on the one hand the heart and governing principle of the macrocosm, and on the other hand its reflection in a point, in a microcosm such as man has always been thought to be. He is of the same essence as the universe, and his own mid-point is its centre. This inner experience, shared by Gnostics, alchemists, and mystics alike, has to do with the nature of the unconscious—one could even say that it *is* the experience of the unconscious; for the unconscious, though its objective existence and its influence on consciousness cannot be doubted, is in itself undifferentiable and therefore unknowable. Hypothetical germs of differentiation may be conjectured to exist in it, but their existence cannot be proved, because everything appears to be in a state of mutual contamination. The unconscious gives the impression of multiplicity and unity at once. However overwhelmed we may be by the vast quantity of things differentiated in space and time, we know from the world of the senses that the validity of its laws extends to immense distances. We therefore believe that it is one and the same universe throughout, in its smallest part as in its greatest. On the other hand the intellect always tries to discern differences, because it cannot discriminate without them. Consequently the unity of the cosmos remains, for it, a somewhat nebulous postulate which it doesn't rightly know what to do with. But as soon as introspection starts penetrating into the psychic background it comes up against the unconscious, which, unlike consciousness, shows only the barest traces of any definite contents, surprising the investigator at every turn with a confusing medley of relationships, parallels, contaminations, and identifications. Although he is forced, for epistemological reasons, to postulate an indefinite number of distinct and separate archetypes, yet he is constantly overcome by doubt as to how far they are really distinguishable from one another. They overlap to such a degree and have such a capacity for combination that all attempts to isolate them conceptually must appear hopeless. In addition the unconscious, in sharpest contrast to consciousness and its contents, has a tendency to personify itself in a uniform way, just as if it possessed only one shape or one voice. Because of this peculiarity, the unconscious conveys an experience of unity, to which are due all those qualities enumerated by the Gnostics and alchemists, and a lot more besides.

441   As can plainly be seen from Gnosticism and other spiritual movements of the kind, people are naïvely inclined to take all the manifestations of the unconscious at their face value and to believe that in them the essence of the world itself, the ultimate truth, has been unveiled. This assumption does not seem to me quite as unwarranted as it may look at first sight, because the spontaneous utterances of the unconscious do after all reveal a psyche which is not identical with consciousness and which is, at times, greatly at variance with it. These utterances occur as a natural psychic activity that can neither be learnt nor controlled by the will. The manifestation of the unconscious is therefore a revelation of the unknown in man. We have only to disregard the dependence of dream language on environment and substitute "eagle" for "aeroplane," "dragon" for "automobile" or "train," "snake-bite" for "injection," and so forth, in order to arrive at the more universal and more fundamental language of mythology. This gives us access to the primordial images that underlie all thinking and have a considerable influence even on our scientific ideas.[56]

442   In these archetypal forms, something, presumably, is expressing itself that must in some way be connected with the mysterious operation of a natural psyche—in other words, with a cosmic factor of the first order. To save the honour of the objective psyche, which the contemporary hypertrophy of consciousness has done so much to depreciate, I must again emphasize that without the psyche we could not establish the existence of any world at all, let alone know it. But, judging by all we do know, it is certain that the original psyche possesses no consciousness of itself. This only comes in the course of development, a development that falls mostly within the historical epoch.[57] Even today we know of primitive tribes whose level of consciousness is not so far removed from the darkness of the primordial psyche, and numerous vestiges of this state can still be found among civilized people. It is even probable, in view of its potentialities for further differentiation, that our modern consciousness is still on a relatively low level. Nevertheless, its development so

56 Cf. Pauli, "The Influence of Archetypal Ideas on Kepler's Scientific Theories."
57 Cf. the remarkable account of developing consciousness in an ancient Egyptian text, translated, with commentary, by Jacobsohn, entitled "Das Gespräch eines Lebensmüden mit seinem Ba."

far has made it emancipated enough to forget its dependence on the unconscious psyche. It is not a little proud of this emancipation, but it overlooks the fact that although it has apparently got rid of the unconscious it has become the victim of its own verbal concepts. The devil is cast out with Beelzebub. Our dependence on words is so strong that a philosophical brand of "existentialism" had to restore the balance by pointing to a reality that exists in spite of words—at considerable risk, however, of concepts such as "existence," "existential," etc. turning into more words which delude us into thinking that we have caught a reality. One can be—and is—just as dependent on words as on the unconscious. Man's advance towards the Logos was a great achievement, but he must pay for it with loss of instinct and loss of reality to the degree that he remains in primitive dependence on mere words. Because words are substitutes for things, which of course they cannot be in reality, they take on intensified forms, become eccentric, outlandish, stupendous, swell up into what schizophrenic patients call "power words." A primitive word-magic develops, and one is inordinately impressed by it because anything out of the ordinary is felt to be especially profound and significant. Gnosticism in particular affords some very instructive examples of this. Neologisms tend not only to hypostatize themselves to an amazing degree, but actually to replace the reality they were originally intended to express.

443   This rupture of the link with the unconscious and our submission to the tyranny of words have one great disadvantage: the conscious mind becomes more and more the victim of its own discriminating activity, the picture we have of the world gets broken down into countless particulars, and the original feeling of unity, which was integrally connected with the unity of the unconscious psyche, is lost. This feeling of unity, in the form of the correspondence theory and the sympathy of all things, dominated philosophy until well into the seventeenth century and is now, after a long period of oblivion, looming up again on the scientific horizon, thanks to the discoveries made by the psychology of the unconscious and by parapsychology. The manner in which the unconscious forcibly obtrudes upon the conscious by means of neurotic disturbances is not only

reminiscent of contemporary political and social conditions but even appears as an accompanying phenomenon. In both cases there is an analogous dissociation: in the one case a splitting of the world's consciousness by an "iron curtain," and in the other a splitting of the individual personality. This dissociation extends throughout the entire world, so that a psychological split runs through vast numbers of individuals who, in their totality, call forth the corresponding mass phenomena. In the West it was chiefly the mass factor, and in the East technology, that undermined the old hierarchies. The cause of this development lay principally in the economic and psychological uprootedness of the industrial masses, which in turn was caused by the rapid technological advance. But technology, it is obvious, is based on a specifically rationalistic differentiation of consciousness which tends to repress all irrational psychic factors. Hence there arises, in the individual and nation alike, an unconscious counterposition which in time grows strong enough to burst out into open conflict.

444   The same situation in reverse was played out on a smaller scale and on a spiritual plane during the first centuries of our era, when the spiritual disorientation of the Roman world was compensated by the irruption of Christianity. Naturally, in order to survive, Christianity had to defend itself not only against its enemies but also against the excessive pretensions of some of its adherents, including those of the Gnostics. Increasingly it had to rationalize its doctrines in order to stem the flood of irrationality. This led, over the centuries, to that strange marriage of the originally irrational Christian message with human reason, which is so characteristic of the Western mentality. But to the degree that reason gradually gained the upper hand, the intellect asserted itself and demanded autonomy. And just as the intellect subjugated the psyche, so also it subjugated Nature and begat on her an age of scientific technology that left less and less room for the natural and irrational man. Thus the foundations were laid for an inner opposition which today threatens the world with chaos. To make the reversal complete, all the powers of the underworld now hide behind reason and intellect, and under the mask of rationalistic ideology a stubborn faith seeks to impose itself by fire and sword, vying with the darkest aspects

247

:h militant. By a strange enantiodromia,[58] the Chris-
of the West has become the defender of the irrational,
spite of having fathered rationalism and intellectual-
s not succumbed to them so far as to give up its belief
ın the ⸱⸱ghts of man, and especially the freedom of the individual. But this freedom guarantees a recognition of the
irrational principle, despite the lurking danger of chaotic individualism. By appealing to the eternal rights of man, faith
binds itself inalienably to a higher order, not only on account
of the historical fact that Christ has proved to be an ordering
factor for many hundreds of years, but also because the self
effectively compensates chaotic conditions no matter by what
name it is known: for the self is the Anthropos above and beyond this world, and in him is contained the freedom and
dignity of the individual man. From this point of view, dispar-
agement and vilification of Gnosticism are an anachronism. Its
obviously psychological symbolism could serve many people
today as a bridge to a more living appreciation of Christian
tradition.

445   These historical changes have to be borne in mind if we
wish to understand the Gnostic figure of Christ, because the sayings in the Acts of John concerning the nature of the Lord only
become intelligible when we interpret them as expressing an
experience of the original unity as contrasted with the formless
multiplicity of conscious contents. This Gnostic Christ, of whom
we hear hints even in the Gospel according to St. John, symbolizes man's original unity and exalts it as the saving goal of his
development. By "composing the unstable," by bringing order
into chaos, by resolving disharmonies and centring upon the
mid-point, thus setting a "boundary" to the multitude and
focusing attention upon the cross, consciousness is reunited with
the unconscious, the unconscious man is made one with his
centre, which is also the centre of the universe, and in this wise
the goal of man's salvation and exaltation is reached.

446   Right as this intuition may be, it is also exceedingly dangerous, for it presupposes a coherent ego-consciousness capable of
resisting the temptation to identify with the self. Such an ego-
consciousness seems to be comparatively rare, as history shows;

58 [Cf. *Psychological Types*, Def. 18, and *Two Essays on Analytical Psychology*,
par. 111.—EDITORS.]

usually the ego identifies with the inner Christ, and the danger is increased by an *imitatio Christi* falsely understood. The result is inflation, of which our text affords eloquent proof. In order to exorcise this danger, the Church has not made too much of the "Christ within," but has made all it possibly could of the Christ whom we "have seen, heard, and touched with hands," in other words, with the historical event "below in Jerusalem." This is a wise attitude, which takes realistic account of the primitiveness of man's consciousness, then as now. For the less mindful it is of the unconscious, the greater becomes the danger of its identification with the latter, and the greater, therefore, the danger of inflation, which, as we have experienced to our cost, can seize upon whole nations like a psychic epidemic. If Christ is to be "real" for this relatively primitive consciousness, then he can be so only as an historical figure and a metaphysical entity, but not as a psychic centre in all too perilous proximity to a human ego. The Gnostic development, supported by scriptural authority, pushed so far ahead that Christ was clearly recognized as an inner, psychic fact. This also entailed the relativity of the Christ-figure, as expressively formulated in our text: "For so long as you call not yourself mine, I am not what I was. . . . I shall be what I was when I have you with me." From this it follows unmistakably that although Christ was whole once upon a time, that is, before time and consciousness began, he either lost this wholeness or gave it away to mankind [59] and can only get it back again through man's integration. His wholeness depends on man: "You shall be in your understanding as I am"—this ineluctable conclusion shows the danger very clearly. The ego is dissolved in the self; unbeknown to itself, and with all its inadequacy and darkness, it has become a god and deems itself superior to its unenlightened fellows. It has identified with its own conception of the "higher man," quite regardless of the fact that this figure consists of "Places of the right and left, Authorities, Archons, Daemons" etc., and the devil himself. A figure like this is simply not to be comprehended, an awesome

[59] This view may be implicit in the *kenosis* passage (Philippians 2:5f.): "Have this mind in you which was also in Christ Jesus, who though he was by nature God, did not consider being equal to God a thing to be clung to, but emptied himself [ἐκένωσεν, *exinanivit*], taking the nature of a slave and being made like unto man" (DV).

mystery with which one had better not identify if one has any
sense. It is sufficient to know that such a mystery exists and that
somewhere man can feel its presence, but he should take care
not to confuse his ego with it. On the contrary, the confrontation with his own darkness should not only warn him against
identification but should inspire him with salutary terror on
beholding just what he is capable of becoming. He cannot conquer the tremendous polarity of his nature on his own resources;
he can only do so through the terrifying experience of a psychic
process that is independent of him, that works *him* rather than
he *it*.

447   If such a process exists at all, then it is something that can
be experienced. My own personal experience, going back over
several decades and garnered from many individuals, and the
experience of many other doctors and psychologists, not to mention the statements—terminologically different, but essentially
the same—of all the great religions,[60] all confirm the existence
of a compensatory ordering factor which is independent of the
ego and whose nature transcends consciousness. The existence
of such a factor is no more miraculous, in itself, than the orderli-
ness of radium decay, or the attunement of a virus to the anatomy and physiology of human beings,[61] or the symbiosis of
plants and animals. What is miraculous in the extreme is that
man can have conscious, reflective knowledge of these hidden
processes, while animals, plants, and inorganic bodies seemingly
lack it. Presumably it would also be an ecstatic experience for a
radium atom to know that the time of its decay is exactly determined, or for the butterfly to recognize that the flower has
made all the necessary provisions for its propagation.

448   The numinous experience of the individuation process is,
on the archaic level, the prerogative of shamans and medicine
men; later, of the physician, prophet, and priest; and finally, at
the civilized stage, of philosophy and religion. The shaman's
experience of sickness, torture, death, and regeneration implies,
at a higher level, the idea of being made whole through sacrifice, of being changed by transubstantiation and exalted to the

---

[60] Including shamanism, whose widespread phenomenology anticipates the alchemist's individuation symbolism on an archaic level. For a comprehensive account
see Eliade, *Shamanism*.
[61] Cf. Portmann, "Die Bedeutung der Bilder in der lebendigen Energiewandlung."

pneumatic man—in a word, of apotheosis. The Mass is the summation and quintessence of a development which began many thousands of years ago and, with the progressive broadening and deepening of consciousness, gradually made the isolated experience of specifically gifted individuals the common property of a larger group. The underlying psychic process remained, of course, hidden from view and was dramatized in the form of suitable "mysteries" and "sacraments," these being reinforced by religious teachings, exercises, meditations, and acts of sacrifice which plunge the celebrant so deeply into the sphere of the mystery that he is able to become conscious of his intimate connection with the mythic happenings. Thus, in ancient Egypt, we see how the experience of "Osirification," [62] originally the prerogative of the Pharaohs, gradually passed to the aristocracy and finally, towards the end of the Old Kingdom, to the single individual as well. Similarly, the mystery religions of the Greeks, originally esoteric and not talked about, broadened out into collective experience, and at the time of the Caesars it was considered a regular sport for Roman tourists to get themselves initiated into foreign mysteries. Christianity, after some hesitation, went a step further and made celebration of the mysteries a public institution, for, as we know, it was especially concerned to introduce as many people as possible to the experience of the mystery. So, sooner or later, the individual could not fail to become conscious of his own transformation and of the necessary psychological conditions for this, such as confession and repentance of sin. The ground was prepared for the realization that, in the mystery of transubstantiation, it was not so much a question of magical influence as of psychological processes—a realization for which the alchemists had already paved the way by putting their *opus operatum* at least on a level with the ecclesiastical mystery, and even attributing to it a cosmic significance since, by its means, the divine world-soul could be liberated from imprisonment in matter. As I think I have shown, the "philosophical" side of alchemy is nothing less than a symbolic anticipation of certain psychological insights, and these—to judge by the example of Gerhard Dorn—were pretty far advanced by the end of the sixteenth century. [63] Only our in-

62 Cf. Neumann, *The Origins and History of Consciousness*, pp. 220ff.
63 *Aion*, pp. 162ff.

tellectualized age could have been so deluded as to see in alchemy nothing but an abortive attempt at chemistry, and in the
interpretative methods of modern psychology a mere "psycholo-
gizing," i.e., annihilation, of the mystery. Just as the alchemists
knew that the production of their stone was a miracle that could
only happen "Deo concedente," so the modern psychologist is
aware that he can produce no more than a description, couched
in scientific symbols, of a psychic process whose real nature
transcends consciousness just as much as does the mystery of life
or of matter. At no point has he explained the mystery itself,
thereby causing it to fade. He has merely, in accordance with
the spirit of Christian tradition, brought it a little nearer to
individual consciousness, using the empirical material to set
forth the individuation process and show it as an actual and
experienceable fact. To treat a metaphysical statement as a
psychic process is not to say that it is "merely psychic," as my
critics assert—in the fond belief that the word "psychic" postulates something known. It does not seem to have occurred to
people that when we say "psyche" we are alluding to the densest
darkness it is possible to imagine. The ethics of the researcher
require him to admit where his knowledge comes to an end.
This end is the beginning of true wisdom.

V

FOREWORD TO THE *I CHING*

FOREWORD TO THE "I CHING" [1]

964   Since I am not a Sinologue, a foreword to the Book of Changes from my hand must be a testimonial of my individual experience with this great and singular book. It also affords me a welcome opportunity to pay tribute again to the memory of my late friend, Richard Wilhelm. He himself was profoundly aware of the cultural significance of his translation of the *I Ching*, a version unrivalled in the West.

965   If the meaning of the Book of Changes were easy to grasp, the work would need no foreword. But this is far from being the case, for there is so much that is obscure about it that Western scholars have tended to dispose of it as a collection of "magic spells," either too abstruse to be intelligible or of no value whatsoever. Legge's translation of the *I Ching*, up to now the only version available in English, has done little to make the work accessible to Western minds.[2] Wilhelm, however, has made

1 [Grateful acknowledgment is made here to Cary F. Baynes for permission to use, with a few minor changes, her translation of this Foreword, which Professor Jung wrote specially for the English edition of the *I Ching or Book of Changes*, translated by Mrs. Baynes from the German translation of Richard Wilhelm (New York and London, 1950); 2nd edn. in 1 vol., 1961; 3rd edn. in small format, 1967. References are to the 3rd edn.—TRANS.]

2 Legge makes the following comment on the explanatory text for the individual lines: "According to our notions, a framer of emblems should be a good deal of a poet, but those of the *Yi* only make us think of a dryasdust. Out of more than three hundred and fifty, the greater number are only grotesque" (*The Yi King*,

every effort to open the way to an understanding of the symbolism of the text. He was in a position to do this because he himself was taught the philosophy and the use of the *I Ching* by the venerable sage Lao Nai-hsüan; moreover, he had over a period of many years put the peculiar technique of the oracle into practice. His grasp of the living meaning of the text gives his version of the *I Ching* a depth of perspective that an exclusively academic knowledge of Chinese philosophy could never provide.

966   I am greatly indebted to Wilhelm for the light he has thrown upon the complicated problem of the *I Ching,* and for insight into its practical application. For more than thirty years I have interested myself in this oracle technique, for it seemed to me of uncommon significance as a method of exploring the unconscious. I was already fairly familiar with the *I Ching* when I first met Wilhelm in the early nineteen twenties; he confirmed then what I already knew, and taught me many things more.

967   I do not know Chinese and have never been in China. I can assure my reader that it is not altogether easy to find the right approach to this monument of Chinese thought, which departs so completely from our ways of thinking. In order to understand what such a book is all about, it is imperative to cast off certain of our Western prejudices. It is a curious fact that such a gifted and intelligent people as the Chinese has never developed what we call science. Our science, however, is based upon the principle of causality, and causality is considered to be an axiomatic truth. But a great change in our standpoint is setting in. What Kant's *Critique of Pure Reason* failed to do is being accomplished by modern physics. The axioms of causality are being shaken to their foundations: we know now that what we term natural laws are merely statistical truths and thus must necessarily allow for exceptions. We have not sufficiently taken into account as yet that we need the laboratory with its incisive restrictions in order to demonstrate the invariable validity of natural law. If we leave things to nature, we see a very different

p. 22). Of the "lessons" of the hexagrams, the same author says: "But why, it may be asked, why should they be conveyed to us by such an array of lineal figures, and in such a farrago of emblematic representations" (p. 25). However, we are nowhere told that Legge ever bothered to put the method to a practical test.

picture: every process is partially or totally interfered with by chance, so much so that under natural circumstances a course of events absolutely conforming to specific laws is almost an exception.

968 The Chinese mind, as I see it at work in the *I Ching*, seems to be exclusively preoccupied with the chance aspect of events. What we call coincidence seems to be the chief concern of this peculiar mind, and what we worship as causality passes almost unnoticed. We must admit that there is something to be said for the immense importance of chance. An incalculable amount of human effort is directed to combatting and restricting the nuisance or danger that chance represents. Theoretical considerations of cause and effect often look pale and dusty in comparison with the practical results of chance. It is all very well to say that the crystal of quartz is a hexagonal prism. The statement is quite true in so far as an ideal crystal is envisaged. But in nature one finds no two crystals exactly alike, although all are unmistakably hexagonal. The actual form, however, seems to appeal more to the Chinese sage than the ideal one. The jumble of natural laws constituting empirical reality holds more significance for him than a causal explanation of events that, in addition, must usually be separated from one another in order to be properly dealt with.

969 The manner in which the *I Ching* tends to look upon reality seems to disfavour our causal procedures. The moment under actual observation appears to the ancient Chinese view more of a chance hit than a clearly defined result of concurrent causal chains. The matter of interest seems to be the configuration formed by chance events at the moment of observation, and not at all the hypothetical reasons that seemingly account for the coincidence. While the Western mind carefully sifts, weighs, selects, classifies, isolates, the Chinese picture of the moment encompasses everything down to the minutest nonsensical detail, because all of the ingredients make up the observed moment.

970 Thus it happens that when one throws the three coins, or counts through the forty-nine yarrow-stalks, these chance details enter into the picture of the moment of observation and form a part of it—a part that is insignificant to us, yet most meaningful to the Chinese mind. With us it would be a banal and almost meaningless statement (at least on the face of it) to say that

257

whatever happens in a given moment has inevitably the quality peculiar to that moment. This is not an abstract argument but a very practical one. There are certain connoisseurs who can tell you merely from the appearance, taste, and behaviour of a wine the site of its vineyard and the year of its origin. There are antiquarians who with almost uncanny accuracy will name the time and place of origin and the maker of an *objet d'art* or piece of furniture on merely looking at it. And there are even astrologers who can tell you, without any previous knowledge of your nativity, what the position of sun and moon was and what zodiacal sign rose above the horizon at the moment of your birth. In the face of such facts, it must be admitted that moments can leave long-lasting traces.

971   In other words, whoever invented the *I Ching* was convinced that the hexagram worked out in a certain moment coincided with the latter in quality no less than in time. To him the hexagram was the exponent of the moment in which it was cast —even more so than the hours of the clock or the divisions of the calendar could be—inasmuch as the hexagram was understood to be an indicator of the essential situation prevailing at the moment of its origin.

972   This assumption involves a certain curious principle which I have termed synchronicity,[3] a concept that formulates a point of view diametrically opposed to that of causality. Since the latter is a merely statistical truth and not absolute, it is a sort of working hypothesis of how events evolve one out of another, whereas synchronicity takes the coincidence of events in space and time as meaning something more than mere chance, namely, a peculiar interdependence of objective events among themselves as well as with the subjective (psychic) states of the observer or observers.

973   The ancient Chinese mind contemplates the cosmos in a way comparable to that of the modern physicist, who cannot deny that his model of the world is a decidedly psychophysical structure. The microphysical event includes the observer just as much as the reality underlying the *I Ching* comprises subjective, i.e., psychic conditions in the totality of the momentary

[3] [Cf. Jung's "Synchronicity: An Acausal Connecting Principle." In that work (pp. 450–53) he is concerned with the synchronistic aspects of the *I Ching*.— EDITORS.]

situation. Just as causality describes the sequence of events, so synchronicity to the Chinese mind deals with the coincidence of events. The causal point of view tells us a dramatic story about how *D* came into existence: it took its origin from *C*, which existed before *D*, and *C* in its turn had a father, *B*, etc. The synchronistic view on the other hand tries to produce an equally meaningful picture of coincidence. How does it happen that *A'*, *B'*, *C'*, *D'*, etc., appear all at the same moment and in the same place? It happens in the first place because the physical events *A'* and *B'* are of the same quality as the psychic events *C'* and *D'*, and further because all are the exponents of one and the same momentary situation. The situation is assumed to represent a legible or understandable picture.

974   Now the sixty-four hexagrams of the *I Ching* are the instrument by which the meaning of sixty-four different yet typical situations can be determined. These interpretations are equivalent to causal explanations. Causal connection can be determined statistically and can be subjected to experiment. Inasmuch as situations are unique and cannot be repeated, experimenting with synchronicity seems to be impossible under ordinary conditions.[4] In the *I Ching*, the only criterion of the validity of synchronicity is the observer's opinion that the text of the hexagram amounts to a true rendering of his psychic condition. It is assumed that the fall of the coins or the result of the division of the bundle of yarrow-stalks is what it necessarily must be in a given "situation," inasmuch as anything happening at that moment belongs to it as an indispensable part of the picture. If a handful of matches is thrown to the floor, they form the pattern characteristic of that moment. But such an obvious truth as this reveals its meaningful nature only if it is possible to read the pattern and to verify its interpretation, partly by the observer's knowledge of the subjective and objective situation, partly by the character of subsequent events. It is obviously not a procedure that appeals to a critical mind used to experimental verification of facts or to factual evidence. But for someone who likes to look at the world at the angle from which ancient China saw it, the *I Ching* may have some attraction.

975   My argument as outlined above has of course never entered

4 Cf. J. B. Rhine, *The Reach of the Mind.*

a Chinese mind. On the contrary, according to the old tradition, it is "spiritual agencies," acting in a mysterious way, that make the yarrow-stalks give a meaningful answer.[5] These powers form, as it were, the living soul of the book. As the latter is thus a sort of animated being, the tradition assumes that one can put questions to the *I Ching* and expect to receive intelligent answers. Thus it occurred to me that it might interest the uninitiated reader to see the *I Ching* at work. For this purpose I made an experiment strictly in accordance with the Chinese conception: I personified the book in a sense, asking its judgment about its present situation, i.e., my intention to introduce it to the English-speaking public.

976   Although this procedure is well within the premises of Taoist philosophy, it appears exceedingly odd to us. However, not even the strangeness of insane delusions or of primitive superstition has ever shocked me. I have always tried to remain unbiased and curious—*rerum novarum cupidus*. Why not venture a dialogue with an ancient book that purports to be animated? There can be no harm in it, and the reader may watch a psychological procedure that has been carried out time and again throughout the millennia of Chinese civilization, representing to a Confucius or a Lao-tzu both a supreme expression of spiritual authority and a philosophical enigma. I made use of the coin method, and the answer obtained was hexagram 50, Ting, THE CAULDRON.[6]

977   In accordance with the way my question was phrased, the text of the hexagram must be regarded as though the *I Ching* itself were the speaking person. Thus it describes itself as a cauldron, that is, as a ritual vessel containing cooked food. Here the food is to be understood as spiritual nourishment. Wilhelm says about this:

> The *ting*, as a utensil pertaining to a refined civilization, suggests the fostering and nourishing of able men, which redounded to the benefit of the state. . . . Here we see civilization as it reaches its culmination in religion. The *ting* serves in offering sacrifice to God. . . . The supreme revelation of God appears in prophets and holy men. To venerate them is true veneration of God. The will of God, as revealed through them, should be accepted in humility.

5 They are *shên*, that is, 'spirit-like.' "Heaven produced the 'spirit-like things'" (Legge, p. 41).   6 [Cf. the *I Ching*, pp. 193ff.—EDITORS.]

978 Keeping to our hypothesis, we must conclude that the *I Ching* is here testifying concerning itself.

979 When any of the lines of a given hexagram have the value of six or nine, it means that they are specially emphasized and hence important in the interpretation.[7] In my hexagram the "spiritual agencies" have given the emphasis of a nine to the lines in the second and in the third place. The text says:

> Nine in the second place means:
>
> There is food in the *ting*.
> My comrades are envious,
> But they cannot harm me.
> Good fortune.

980 Thus the *I Ching* says of itself: "I contain (spiritual) nourishment." Since a share in something great always arouses envy, the chorus of the envious [8] is part of the picture. The envious want to rob the *I Ching* of its great possession, that is, they seek to rob it of meaning, or to destroy its meaning. But their enmity is in vain. Its richness of meaning is assured; that is, it is convinced of its positive achievements, which no one can take away. The text continues:

> Nine in the third place means:
>
> The handle of the *ting* is altered.
> One is impeded in his way of life.
> The fat of the pheasant is not eaten.
> Once rain falls, remorse is spent.
> Good fortune comes in the end.

981 The handle [German *Griff*] is the part by which the *ting* can be grasped [*gegriffen*]. Thus it signifies the concept [9] [*Begriff*] one has of the *I Ching* (the *ting*). In the course of time this concept has apparently changed, so that today we can no longer grasp [*begreifen*] the *I Ching*. Thus "one is impeded in

---

[7] See the explanation of the method, ibid., pp. 721ff.

[8] For example, the *invidi* ('the envious') are a constantly recurring image in the old Latin books on alchemy, especially in the *Turba philosophorum* (11th or 12th cent.).

[9] From the Latin *concipere*, 'to take together,' e.g., in a vessel: *concipere* derives from *capere*, 'to take,' 'to grasp.'

his way of life." We are no longer supported by the wise counsel and deep insight of the oracle; therefore we no longer find our way through the mazes of fate and the obscurities of our own natures. The fat of the pheasant, that is, the best and richest part of a good dish, is no longer eaten. But when the thirsty earth finally receives rain again, that is, when this state of want has been overcome, "remorse," that is, sorrow over the loss of wisdom, is ended, and then comes the longed-for opportunity. Wilhelm comments: "This describes a man who, in a highly evolved civilization, finds himself in a place where no one notices or recognizes him. This is a severe block to his effectiveness." The *I Ching* is complaining, as it were, that its excellent qualities go unrecognized and hence lie fallow. It comforts itself with the hope that it is about to regain recognition.

982   The answer given in these two salient lines to the question I put to the *I Ching* requires no particular subtlety for its interpretation, no artifices, and no unusual knowledge. Anyone with a little common sense can understand the meaning of the answer; it is the answer of one who has a good opinion of himself, but whose value is neither generally recognized nor even widely known. The answering subject has an interesting notion of itself: it looks upon itself as a vessel in which sacrificial offerings are brought to the gods, ritual food for their nourishment. It conceives of itself as a cult utensil serving to provide spiritual nourishment for the unconscious elements or forces ("spiritual agencies") that have been projected as gods—in other words, to give these forces the attention they need in order to play their part in the life of the individual. Indeed, this is the original meaning of the word *religio*—a careful observation and taking account of (from *relegere* [10]) the numinous.

983   The method of the *I Ching* does indeed take into account the hidden individual quality in things and men, and in one's own unconscious self as well. I questioned the *I Ching* as one questions a person whom one is about to introduce to friends: one asks whether or not it will be agreeable to him. In answer the *I Ching* tells me of its religious significance, of the fact that at present it is unknown and misjudged, of its hope of

10 This is the classical etymology. The derivation of *religio* from *religare*, 'reconnect,' 'link back,' originated with the Church Fathers.

being restored to a place of honour—this last obviously with a sidelong glance at my as yet unwritten foreword,[11] and above all at the English translation. This seems a perfectly understandable reaction, such as one could expect also from a person in a similar situation.

984   But how has this reaction come about? Simply because I threw three small coins into the air and let them fall, roll, and come to rest, heads up or tails up as the case might be. This peculiar fact—that a reaction that makes sense arises out of a technique which at the outset seemingly excludes all sense—is the great achievement of the *I Ching*. The instance I have just given is not unique; meaningful answers are the rule. Western sinologues and distinguished Chinese scholars have been at pains to inform me that the *I Ching* is a collection of obsolete "magic spells." In the course of these conversations my informant has sometimes admitted having consulted the oracle through a fortune teller, usually a Taoist priest. This could be "only nonsense" of course. But oddly enough, the answer received apparently coincided with the questioner's psychological blind spot remarkably well.

985   I agree with Western thinking that any number of answers to my question were possible, and I certainly cannot assert that another answer would not have been equally significant. However, the answer received was the first and only one; we know nothing of other possible answers. It pleased and satisfied me. To ask the same question a second time would have been tactless and so I did not do it: "the master speaks but once." The heavy-handed pedagogic approach that attempts to fit irrational phenomena into a preconceived rational pattern is anathema to me. Indeed, such things as this answer should remain as they were when they first emerged to view, for only then do we know what nature does when left to herself undisturbed by the meddlesomeness of man. One ought not to go to dead bodies to study life. Moreover, a repetition of the experiment is impossible, for the simple reason that the original situation cannot be reconstructed. Therefore in each instance there is only a first and single answer.

986   To return to the hexagram itself. There is nothing strange in the fact that all of Ting, THE CAULDRON, amplifies the themes

11 I made this experiment before I actually wrote the foreword.

announced by the two salient lines.[12] The first line of the hexagram says:

> A *ting* with legs upturned
> Furthers removal of stagnating stuff.
> One takes a concubine for the sake of her son.
> No blame.

987   A *ting* that is turned upside down is not in use. Hence the *I Ching* is like an unused cauldron. Turning it over serves to remove stagnating matter, as the line says. Just as a man takes a concubine when his wife has no son, so the *I Ching* is called upon when one sees no other way out. Despite the quasi-legal status of the concubine in China, she is in reality only a somewhat awkward makeshift; so likewise the magic procedure of the oracle is an expedient that may be utilized for a higher purpose. There is no blame, although it is an exceptional recourse.

988   The second and third lines have already been discussed. The fourth line says:

> The legs of the *ting* are broken.
> The prince's meal is spilled
> And his person is soiled.
> Misfortune.

989   Here the *ting* has been put to use, but evidently in a very clumsy manner, that is, the oracle has been abused or misinterpreted. In this way the divine food is lost, and one puts oneself to shame. Legge translates as follows: "Its subject will be made to blush for shame." Abuse of a cult utensil such as the *ting* (i.e., the *I Ching*) is a gross profanation. The *I Ching* is evidently insisting here on its dignity as a ritual vessel and protesting against being profanely used.

990   The fifth line says:

> The *ting* has yellow handles, golden carrying rings.
> Perseverance furthers.

---

[12] The Chinese interpret only the changing lines in the hexagram obtained by use of the oracle. I have found all the lines of the hexagram to be relevant in most cases.

991   The *I Ching* has, it seems, met with a new, correct (yellow) understanding, that is, a new concept [*Begriff*] by which it can be grasped. This concept is valuable (golden). There is indeed a new edition in English, making the book more accessible to the Western world than before.

992   The sixth line says:

> The *ting* has rings of jade.
> Great good fortune.
> Nothing that would not act to further.

993   Jade is distinguished for its beauty and soft sheen. If the carrying rings are of jade, the whole vessel is enhanced in beauty, honour, and value. The *I Ching* expresses itself here as being not only well satisfied but indeed very optimistic. One can only await further events and in the meantime remain content with the pleasant conclusion that the *I Ching* approves of the new edition.

994   I have shown in this example as objectively as I can how the oracle proceeds in a given case. Of course the procedure varies somewhat according to the way the question is put. If for instance a person finds himself in a confusing situation, he may himself appear in the oracle as the speaker. Or, if the question concerns a relationship with another person, that person may appear as the speaker. However, the identity of the speaker does not depend entirely on the manner in which the question is phrased, inasmuch as our relations with our fellow beings are not always determined by the latter. Very often our relations depend almost exclusively on our own attitudes, though we may be quite unaware of this fact. Hence, if an individual is unconscious of his role in a relationship, there may be a surprise in store for him; contrary to expectation, he himself may appear as the chief agent, as is sometimes unmistakably indicated by the text. It may also happen that we take a situation too seriously and consider it extremely important, whereas the answer we get on consulting the *I Ching* draws attention to some unsuspected other aspect implicit in the question.

995   Such instances might at first lead one to think that the oracle is fallacious. Confucius is said to have received only one inappropriate answer, i.e., hexagram 22, GRACE—a thoroughly aesthetic hexagram. This is reminiscent of the advice given to

Socrates by his daemon—"You ought to make more music"—whereupon Socrates took to playing the flute. Confucius and Socrates compete for first place as far as rationality and a pedagogic attitude to life are concerned; but it is unlikely that either of them occupied himself with "lending grace to the beard on his chin," as the second line of this hexagram advises. Unfortunately, reason and pedagogy often lack charm and grace, and so the oracle may not have been wrong after all.

996   To come back once more to our hexagram. Though the *I Ching* not only seems to be satisfied with its new edition, but even expresses emphatic optimism, this still does not foretell anything about the effect it will have on the public it is intended to reach. Since we have in our hexagram two *yang* lines stressed by the numerical value nine, we are in a position to find out what sort of prognosis the *I Ching* makes for itself. Lines designated by a six or a nine have, according to the ancient conception, an inner tension so great as to cause them to change into their opposites, that is, *yang* into *yin,* and vice versa. Through this change we obtain in the present instance hexagram 35, Chin, PROGRESS.

997   The subject of this hexagram is someone who meets with all sorts of vicissitudes of fortune in his climb upward, and the text describes how he should behave. The *I Ching* is in this same situation: it rises like the sun and declares itself, but it is rebuffed and finds no confidence—it is "progressing, but in sorrow." However, "one obtains great happiness from one's ancestress." Psychology can help us to elucidate this obscure passage. In dreams and fairy tales the grandmother, or ancestress, often represents the unconscious, because the latter in a man contains the feminine component of the psyche. If the *I Ching* is not accepted by the conscious, at least the unconscious meets it halfway, for the *I Ching* is more closely connected with the unconscious than with the rational attitude of consciousness. Since the unconscious is often represented in dreams by a feminine figure, this may be the explanation here. The feminine person might be the translator, who has given the book her maternal care, and this might easily appear to the *I Ching* a "great happiness." It anticipates general understanding, but is afraid of misuse—"Progress like a hamster." But it is mindful of the admonition, "Take not gain and loss to heart." It remains

free of "partisan motives." It does not thrust itself on anyone.

998   The *I Ching* therefore faces its future on the American book market calmly and expresses itself here just about as any reasonable person would in regard to the fate of so controversial a work. This prediction is so very reasonable and full of common sense that it would be hard to think of a more fitting answer.

999   All this happened before I had written the foregoing paragraphs. When I reached this point, I wished to know the attitude of the *I Ching* to the new situation. The state of things had been altered by what I had written, inasmuch as I myself had now entered upon the scene, and I therefore expected to hear something referring to my own action. I must confess that I had not been feeling too happy in the course of writing this foreword, for, as a person with a sense of responsibility toward science, I am not in the habit of asserting something I cannot prove or at least present as acceptable to reason. It is a dubious task indeed to try to introduce a collection of archaic "magic spells" to a critical modern public with the idea of making them more or less acceptable. I have undertaken it because I myself think that there is more to the ancient Chinese way of thinking than meets the eye. But it is embarrassing to me that I must appeal to the good will and imagination of the reader, instead of giving him conclusive proofs and scientifically watertight explanations. Unfortunately I am only too well aware of the arguments that can be brought against this age-old oracle technique. We are not even certain that the ship that is to carry us over the unknown seas has not sprung a leak somewhere. May not the old text be corrupt? Is Wilhelm's translation accurate? Are we not self-deluded in our explanations?

1000   The *I Ching* insists upon self-knowledge throughout. The method by which this is to be achieved is open to every kind of misuse, and is therefore not for the frivolous-minded and immature; nor is it for intellectualists and rationalists. It is appropriate only for thoughtful and reflective people who like to think about what they do and what happens to them—a predilection not to be confused with the morbid brooding of the hypochondriac. As I have indicated above, I have no answer to the multitude of problems that arise when we seek to harmonize the oracle of the *I Ching* with our accepted scientific canons. But needless to say, nothing "occult" is to be inferred. My position

267

in these matters is pragmatic, and the great disciplines that have taught me the practical usefulness of this viewpoint are psychotherapy and medical psychology. Probably in no other field do we have to reckon with so many unknown quantities, and nowhere else do we become more accustomed to adopting methods that work even though for a long time we may not know why they work. Unexpected cures may arise from questionable therapies and unexpected failures from allegedly reliable methods. In the exploration of the unconscious we come upon very strange things, from which a rationalist turns away with horror, claiming afterward that he did not see anything. The irrational fulness of life has taught me never to discard anything, even when it goes against all our theories (so short-lived at best) or otherwise admits of no immediate explanation. It is of course disquieting, and one is not certain whether the compass is pointing true or not; but security, certitude, and peace do not lead to discoveries. It is the same with this Chinese mode of divination. Clearly the method aims at self-knowledge, though at all times it has also been put to superstitious use.

1001   I of course am thoroughly convinced of the value of self-knowledge, but is there any use in recommending such insight, when the wisest of men throughout the ages have preached the need of it without success? Even to the most biased eye it is obvious that this book represents one long admonition to careful scrutiny of one's own character, attitude, and motives. This attitude appeals to me and has induced me to undertake the foreword. Only once before have I expressed myself in regard to the problem of the *I Ching:* this was in a memorial address in tribute to Richard Wilhelm.[13] For the rest I have maintained a discreet silence. It is by no means easy to feel one's way into such a remote and mysterious mentality as that underlying the *I Ching.* One cannot easily disregard such great minds as Confucius and Lao-tzu, if one is at all able to appreciate the quality of the thoughts they represent; much less can one overlook the fact that the *I Ching* was their main source of inspiration. I know that previously I would not have dared to express myself

13 [Cf. Wilhelm and Jung, *The Secret of the Golden Flower* (1931), in which this address appears as an appendix. The book did not appear in English until a year after Wilhelm's death.—C. F. B.]

[For the address, see vol. 15 of the *Coll. Works.*—EDITORS.]

so explicitly about so uncertain a matter. I can take this risk because I am now in my eighth decade, and the changing opinions of men scarcely impress me any more; the thoughts of the old masters are of greater value to me than the philosophical prejudices of the Western mind.

1002   I do not like to burden my reader with these personal considerations; but, as already indicated, one's own personality is very often implicated in the answer of the oracle. Indeed, in formulating my question I even invited the oracle to comment directly on my action. The answer was hexagram 29, K'an, THE ABYSMAL. Special emphasis is given to the third place by the fact that the line is designated by a six. This line says:

> Forward and backward, abyss on abyss.
> In danger like this, pause at first and wait,
> Otherwise you will fall into a pit in the abyss.
> Do not act in this way.

1003   Formerly I would have accepted unconditionally the advice, "Do not act in this way," and would have refused to give my opinion of the *I Ching,* for the sole reason that I had none. But now the counsel may serve as an example of the way in which the *I Ching* functions. It is a fact that if one begins to think about it, the problems of the *I Ching* do represent "abyss on abyss," and unavoidably one must "pause at first and wait" in the midst of the dangers of limitless and uncritical speculation; otherwise one really will lose one's way in the darkness. Could there be a more uncomfortable position intellectually than that of floating in the thin air of unproven possibilities, not knowing whether what one sees is truth or illusion? This is the dreamlike atmosphere of the *I Ching,* and in it one has nothing to rely upon except one's own so fallible subjective judgment. I cannot but admit that this line represents very appropriately the feelings with which I wrote the foregoing passages. Equally fitting is the comforting beginning of this hexagram—"If you are sincere, you have success in your heart"—for it indicates that the decisive thing here is not the outer danger but the subjective condition, that is, whether one believes oneself to be "sincere" or not.

1004   The hexagram compares the dynamic action in this situation to the behaviour of flowing water, which is not afraid of any dangerous place but plunges over cliffs and fills up the pits that lie in its course (K'an also stands for water). This is the way in which the "superior man" acts and "carries on the business of teaching."

1005   K'an is definitely one of the less agreeable hexagrams. It describes a situation in which the subject seems in grave danger of being caught in all sorts of pitfalls. I have found that K'an often turned up with patients who were too much under the sway of the unconscious (water) and hence threatened with the possible occurrence of psychotic phenomena. If one were superstitious, one would be inclined to assume that some such meaning attaches intrinsically to this hexagram. But just as, in interpreting a dream, one must follow the dream-text with the utmost exactitude, so in consulting the oracle one must keep in mind the form of the question put, for this sets a definite limit to the interpretation of the answer. When I consulted the oracle the first time, I was thinking above all of the meaning for the *I Ching* of the foreword I had still to write. I thus put the book in the foreground and made it, so to speak, the acting subject. But in my second question, it is I who am the acting subject. So it would be illogical to take the *I Ching* as the subject in this case too, and, in addition, the interpretation would become unintelligible. But if I am the subject, the interpretation is meaningful to me, because it expresses the undeniable feeling of uncertainty and risk present in my mind. If one ventures upon such uncertain ground, it is easy to come dangerously under the influence of the unconscious without knowing it.

1006   The first line of the hexagram notes the presence of the danger: "In the abyss one falls into a pit." The second line does the same, then adds the counsel: "One should strive to attain small things only." I apparently anticipated this advice by limiting myself in this foreword to a demonstration of how the *I Ching* functions in the Chinese mind, and by renouncing the more ambitious project of writing a psychological commentary on the whole book.

1007   The simplification of my task is expressed in the fourth line, which says:

> A jug of wine, a bowl of rice with it;
> Earthen vessels
> Simply handed in through the window.
> There is certainly no blame in this.

1008   Wilhelm makes the following comment here:

> Although as a rule it is customary for an official to present certain introductory gifts and recommendations before he is appointed, here everything is simplified to the utmost. The gifts are insignificant, there is no one to sponsor him, he introduces himself; yet all this need not be humiliating if only there is the honest intention of mutual help in danger.

1009   The fifth line continues the theme of limitation. If one studies the nature of water, one sees that it fills a pit only to the rim and then flows on. It does not stay caught there:

> The abyss is not filled to overflowing,
> It is filled only to the rim.

1010   But if, tempted by the danger, and just because of the uncertainty, one were to insist on forcing conviction by special efforts, such as elaborate commentaries and the like, one would only be bogged down in the difficulty, which the top line describes very accurately as a tied-up and caged-in condition. Indeed, the last line often shows the consequences that result when one does not take the meaning of the hexagram to heart.

1011   In our hexagram we have a six in the third place. This *yin* line of mounting tension changes into a *yang* line and thus produces a new hexagram showing a new possibility or tendency. We now have hexagram 48, Ching, THE WELL. The water hole no longer means danger, however, but rather something beneficial, a well:

> Thus the superior man encourages the people at
>   their work,
> And exhorts them to help one another.

1012   The image of people helping one another would seem to refer to the reconstruction of the well, for it is broken down and full of mud. Not even animals drink from it. There are fishes living in it, and one can catch these, but the well is not used for drinking, that is, for human needs. This description is reminiscent of the overturned and unused *ting* that is to receive a new handle. Moreover, like the *ting*, "the well is cleaned, but no one drinks from it":

271

> This is my heart's sorrow,
> For one might draw from it.

1013   The dangerous water-hole or abyss pointed to the *I Ching*, and so does the well, but the latter has a positive meaning: it contains the waters of life. It should be restored to use. But one has no concept [*Begriff*] of it, no utensil with which to carry the water; the jug is broken and leaks. The *ting* needs new handles and carrying rings by which to grasp it, and so also the well must be newly lined, for it contains "a clear, cold spring from which one can drink." One may draw water from it, because "it is dependable."

1014   It is clear that in this prognosis the speaking subject is once more the *I Ching*, representing itself as a spring of living water. The previous hexagram described in detail the danger confronting the person who accidentally falls into the pit within the abyss. He must work his way out of it, in order to discover that it is an old, ruined well, buried in mud, but capable of being restored to use again.

1015   I submitted two questions to the method of chance represented by the coin oracle, the second question being put after I had written my analysis of the answer to the first. The first question was directed, as it were, to the *I Ching*: what had it to say about my intention to write a foreword? The second question concerned my own action, or rather the situation in which I was the acting subject who had discussed the first hexagram. To the first question the *I Ching* replied by comparing itself to a cauldron, a ritual vessel in need of renovation, a vessel that was finding only doubtful favour with the public. To the second question the reply was that I had fallen into a difficulty, for the *I Ching* represented a deep and dangerous water-hole in which one might easily be bogged down. However, the water-hole proved to be an old well that needed only to be renovated in order to be put to useful purposes once more.

1016   These four hexagrams are in the main consistent as regards theme (vessel, pit, well); and as regards intellectual content, they seem to be meaningful. Had a human being made such replies, I should, as a psychiatrist, have had to pronounce him of sound mind, at least on the basis of the material presented.

Indeed, I should not have been able to discover anything delirious, idiotic, or schizophrenic in the four answers. In view of the *I Ching's* extreme age and its Chinese origin, I cannot consider its archaic, symbolic, and flowery language abnormal. On the contrary, I should have had to congratulate this hypothetical person on the extent of his insight into my unexpressed state of doubt. On the other hand, any person of clever and versatile mind can turn the whole thing around and show how I have projected my subjective contents into the symbolism of the hexagrams. Such a critique, though catastrophic from the standpoint of Western rationality, does no harm to the function of the *I Ching*. On the contrary, the Chinese sage would smilingly tell me: "Don't you see how useful the *I Ching* is in making you project your hitherto unrealized thoughts into its abstruse symbolism? You could have written your foreword without ever realizing what an avalanche of misunderstanding might be released by it."

1017 The Chinese standpoint does not concern itself with the attitude one takes toward the performance of the oracle. It is only we who are puzzled, because we trip time and again over our prejudice, viz., the notion of causality. The ancient wisdom of the East lays stress upon the fact that the intelligent individual realizes his own thoughts, but not in the least upon the way in which he does it. The less one thinks about the theory of the *I Ching*, the more soundly one sleeps.

1018 It would seem to me that on the basis of this example an unprejudiced reader should now be in a position to form at least a tentative judgment on the operation of the *I Ching*.[14] More cannot be expected from a simple introduction. If by means of this demonstration I have succeeded in elucidating the psychological phenomenology of the *I Ching*, I shall have carried out my purpose. As to the thousands of questions, doubts, and criticisms that this singular book stirs up—I cannot answer these. The *I Ching* does not offer itself with proofs and results; it does not vaunt itself, nor is it easy to approach. Like a part of nature, it waits until it is discovered. It offers neither facts nor power, but for lovers of self-knowledge, of wisdom—if there be such—it

14 The reader will find it helpful to look up all four of these hexagrams in the [Baynes-Wilhelm] text and to read them together with the relevant commentaries.

seems to be the right book. To one person its spirit appears as clear as day; to another, shadowy as twilight; to a third, dark as night. He who is not pleased by it does not have to use it, and he who is against it is not obliged to find it true. Let it go forth into the world for the benefit of those who can discern its meaning.

VI

TWO CHAPTERS FROM
SYNCHRONICITY

3. FORERUNNERS OF THE IDEA OF SYNCHRONICITY

916   The causality principle asserts that the connection between cause and effect is a necessary one. The synchronicity principle asserts that the terms of a meaningful coincidence are connected by *simultaneity* and *meaning*. So if we assume that the ESP experiments and numerous other observations are established facts, we must conclude that besides the connection between cause and effect there is another factor in nature which expresses itself in the arrangement of events and appears to us as meaning. Although meaning is an anthropomorphic interpretation it nevertheless forms the indispensable criterion of synchronicity. What that factor which appears to us as "meaning" may be in itself we have no possibility of knowing. As an hypothesis, how-ever, it is not quite so impossible as may appear at first sight. We must remember that the rationalistic attitude of the West is not the only possible one and is not all-embracing, but is in many ways a prejudice and a bias that ought perhaps to be corrected. The very much older civilization of the Chinese has always thought differently from us in this respect, and we have to go back to Heraclitus if we want to find something similar in our civilization, at least where philosophy is concerned. Only in astrology, alchemy, and the mantic procedures do we find no differences of principle between our attitude and the Chinese. That is why alchemy developed along parallel lines in East and

West and why in both spheres it strove towards the same goal with more or less identical ideas.[1]

917 In Chinese philosophy one of the oldest and most central ideas is that of Tao, which the Jesuits translated as "God." But that is correct only for the Western way of thinking. Other translations, such as "Providence" and the like, are mere make-shifts. Richard Wilhelm brilliantly interprets it as "meaning." [2] The concept of Tao pervades the whole philosophical thought of China. Causality occupies this paramount position with us, but it acquired its importance only in the course of the last two centuries, thanks to the levelling influence of the statistical method on the one hand and the unparalleled success of the natural sciences on the other, which brought the metaphysical view of the world into disrepute.

918 Lao-tzu gives the following description of Tao in his cele-brated *Tao Teh Ching:* [3]

> There is something formless yet complete
> That existed before heaven and earth.
> How still! how empty!
> Dependent on nothing, unchanging,
> All pervading, unfailing.
> One may think of it as the mother of all things under heaven.
> I do not know its name,
> But I call it "Meaning."
> If I had to give it a name, I should call it "The Great."
> [Ch. XXV.]

919 Tao "covers the ten thousand things like a garment but does not claim to be master over them"(Ch. XXXIV). Lao-tzu de-scribes it as "Nothing," [4] by which he means, says Wilhelm, only its "contrast with the world of reality." Lao-tzu describes its nature as follows:

[1] Cf. *Psychology and Alchemy*, par. 453, and "The Spirit Mercurius," par. 273. Also the doctrine of *chên-yên* in Wei Po-yang ["Phil. Tree," pars. 432ff., and *Mysterium*, pars. 490, 711n] and in Chuang-tzu.

[2] Jung, "Commentary on *The Secret of the Golden Flower,*" par. 28, and Wilhelm, *Chinesische Lebensweisheit.*

[3] [Quotations from Arthur Waley's *The Way and Its Power,* with occasional slight changes to fit Wilhelm's reading.—TRANS.]

[4] Tao is the contingent, which Andreas Speiser defines as "pure nothing" ("Über die Freiheit").

We put thirty spokes together and call it a wheel;
But it is on the space where there is nothing that the utility of
the wheel depends.
We turn clay to make a vessel;
But it is on the space where there is nothing that the utility of
the vessel depends.
We pierce doors and windows to make a house;
And it is on these spaces where there is nothing that the utility of
the house depends.
Therefore just as we take advantage of what is, we should rec-
ognize the utility of what is not. [Ch. XI.]

920   "Nothing" is evidently "meaning" or "purpose," and it is
only called Nothing because it does not appear in the world of
the senses, but is only its organizer.[5] Lao-tzu says:

Because the eye gazes but can catch no glimpse of it,
It is called elusive.
Because the ear listens but cannot hear it,
It is called the rarefied.
Because the hand feels for it but cannot find it,
It is called the infinitesimal. . . .
These are called the shapeless shapes,
Forms without form,
Vague semblances.
Go towards them, and you can see no front;
Go after them, and you see no rear. [Ch. XIV.]

921   Wilhelm describes it as "a borderline conception lying at the
extreme edge of the world of appearances." In it, the opposites
"cancel out in non-discrimination," but are still potentially
present. "These seeds," he continues, "point to something that
corresponds firstly to *the visible,* i.e., something in the nature
of an image; secondly to *the audible,* i.e., something in the
nature of words; thirdly to *extension in space,* i.e., something
with a form. But these three things are not clearly distinguished
and definable, they are a non-spatial and non-temporal unity,
having no above and below or front and back." As the *Tao Teh
Ching* says:

5 Wilhelm, *Chinesische Lebensweisheit,* p. 15: "The relation between meaning
(Tao) and reality cannot be conceived under the category of cause and effect."

Incommensurable, impalpable,
Yet latent in it are forms;
Impalpable, incommensurable,
Yet within it are entities.
Shadowy it is and dim. [Ch. XXI.]

922   Reality, thinks Wilhelm, is conceptually knowable because
according to the Chinese view there is in all things a latent
"rationality." [6] This is the basic idea underlying meaningful
coincidence: it is possible because both sides have the same
meaning. Where meaning prevails, order results:

Tao is eternal, but has no name;
The Uncarved Block, though seemingly of small account,
Is greater than anything under heaven.
If the kings and barons would but possess themselves of it,
The ten thousand creatures would flock to do them homage;
Heaven and earth would conspire
To send Sweet Dew;
Without law or compulsion men would dwell in harmony.
[Ch. XXXII.]

Tao never does;
Yet through it all things are done. [Ch. XXXVII.]

Heaven's net is wide;
Coarse are the meshes, yet nothing slips through. [Ch. LXXIII.]

923   Chuang-tzu (a contemporary of Plato's) says of the psychological premises on which Tao is based: "The state in which
ego and non-ego are no longer opposed is called the pivot of
Tao." [7] It sounds almost like a criticism of our scientific view of
the world when he remarks that "Tao is obscured when you
fix your eye on little segments of existence only," [8] or "Limitations are not originally grounded in the meaning of life. Originally words had no fixed meanings. Differences only arose
through looking at things subjectively." [9] The sages of old, says
Chuang-tzu, "took as their starting-point a state when the
existence of things had not yet begun. That is indeed the ex-

6 Ibid., p. 19.
7 *Das wahre Buch vom südlichen Blütenland*, trans. by R. Wilhelm, II, 3.
8 Ibid., II, 3.   9 II, 7.

treme limit beyond which you cannot go. The next assumption was that though things existed they had not yet begun to be separated. The next, that though things were separated in a sense, affirmation and negation had not yet begun. When affirmation and negation came into being, Tao faded. After Tao faded, then came one-sided attachments." [10] "Outward hearing should not penetrate further than the ear; the intellect should not seek to lead a separate existence, thus the soul can become empty and absorb the whole world. It is Tao that fills this emptiness." If you have insight, says Chuang-tzu, "you use your inner eye, your inner ear, to pierce to the heart of things, and have no need of intellectual knowledge." [11] This is obviously an allusion to the absolute knowledge of the unconscious, and to the presence in the microcosm of macrocosmic events.

924   This Taoistic view is typical of Chinese thinking. It is, whenever possible, *a thinking in terms of the whole,* a point also brought out by Marcel Granet,[12] the eminent authority on Chinese psychology. This peculiarity can be seen in ordinary conversation with the Chinese: what seems to us a perfectly straightforward, precise question about some detail evokes from the Chinese thinker an unexpectedly elaborate answer, as though one had asked him for a blade of grass and got a whole meadow in return. With us details are important for their own sakes; for the Oriental mind they always complete a total picture. In this totality, as in primitive or in our own medieval, pre-scientific psychology (still very much alive!), are included things which seem to be connected with one another only "by chance," by a coincidence whose meaningfulness appears altogether arbitrary. This is where the theory of *correspondentia* [13] comes in, which was propounded by the natural philosophers of the Middle Ages, and particularly the classical idea of the *sympathy of all things.*[14] Hippocrates says:

10 II, 5.   11 IV, 1.

12 *La Pensée chinoise;* also Lily Abegg, *The Mind of East Asia.* The latter gives an excellent account of the synchronistic mentality of the Chinese.

13 Professor W. Pauli kindly calls my attention to the fact that Niels Bohr used "correspondence" as a mediating term between the representation of the discontinuum (particle) and the continuum (wave). Originally (1913–18) he called it the "principle of correspondence," but later (1927) it was formulated as the "argument of correspondence."   14 "συμπάθεια τῶν ὅλων."

There is one common flow, one common breathing, all things are in sympathy. The whole organism and each one of its parts are working in conjunction for the same purpose . . . the great principle extends to the extremest part, and from the extremest part it returns to the great principle, to the one nature, being and not-being.[15]

The universal principle is found even in the smallest particle, which therefore corresponds to the whole.

925   In this connection there is an interesting idea in Philo (25 B.C.–A.D. 42):

God, being minded to unite in intimate and loving fellowship the beginning and end of created things, made heaven the beginning and man the end, the one the most perfect of imperishable objects of sense, the other the noblest of things earthborn and perishable, being, in very truth, a miniature heaven. He bears about within himself, like holy images, endowments of nature that correspond to the constellations. . . . For since the corruptible and the incorruptible are by nature contrary the one to the other, God assigned the fairest of each sort to the beginning and the end, heaven (as I have said) to the beginning, and man to the end.[16]

926   Here the great principle [17] or beginning, heaven, is infused into man the microcosm, who reflects the star-like natures and thus, as the smallest part and end of the work of Creation, contains the whole.

927   According to Theophrastus (371–288 B.C.) the suprasensuous and the sensuous are joined by a bond of community. This bond cannot be mathematics, so must presumably be God.[18] Similarly in Plotinus the individual souls born of the one World Soul are related to one another by sympathy or antipathy, regardless of distance.[19] Similar views are to be found in Pico della Mirandola:

---

15 *De alimento*, a tract ascribed to Hippocrates. (Trans. by John Precope in *Hippocrates on Diet and Hygiene*, p. 174, modified.) "Σύρροια μία, συμπνοία μία, πάντα συμπαθέα κατὰ μὲν οὐλομελίην πάντα κατὰ μέρος δὲ τὰ ἐν ἑκάστῳ μέρει μερέα πρὸς τὸ ἔργον . . . ἀρχὴ μεγάλη ἐς ἔσχατον μέρος ἀφικνέεται, ἐξ ἐσχάτου μέρεος εἰς ἀρχὴν μεγάλην ἀφικνέεται, μία φύσις εἶναι καὶ μὴ εἶναι."

16 *De opificio mundi*, 82 (trans. by F. H. Colson and G. H. Whitaker, I, p. 67).

17 "ἀρχὴ μεγάλη"

18 Eduard Zeller, *Die Philosophie der Griechen*, II, part ii, p. 654.

19 *Enneads*, IV, 3, 8 and 4, 32 (in A. C. H. Drews, *Plotin und der Untergang der antiken Weltanschauung*, p. 179).

Firstly there is the unity in things whereby each thing is at one with itself, consists of itself, and coheres with itself. Secondly there is the unity whereby one creature is united with the others and all parts of the world constitute one world. The third and most important (unity) is that whereby the whole universe is one with its Creator, as an army with its commander.[20]

By this threefold unity Pico means a simple unity which, like the Trinity, has three aspects; "a unity distinguished by a three-fold character, yet in such a way as not to depart from the simplicity of unity." [21] For him the world is *one* being, a visible God, in which everything is naturally arranged from the very beginning like the parts of a living organism. The world appears as the *corpus mysticum* of God, just as the Church is the *corpus mysticum* of Christ, or as a well-disciplined army can be called a sword in the hand of the commander. The view that all things are arranged according to God's will is one that leaves little room for causality. Just as in a living body the different parts work in harmony and are meaningfully adjusted to one another, so events in the world stand in a meaningful relationship which cannot be derived from any immanent causality. The reason for this is that in either case the behaviour of the parts depends on a central control which is supraordinate to them.

928   In his treatise *De hominis dignitate* Pico says: "The Father implanted in man at birth seeds of all kinds and the germs of original life." [22] Just as God is the "copula" of the world, so, within the created world, is man. "Let us make man in our image, who is not a fourth world or anything like a new nature, but is rather the fusion and synthesis of three worlds (the supra-celestial, the celestial, and the sublunary)." [23] In body and spirit

20 *Heptaplus*, VI, prooem., in *Opera omnia*, pp. 40f. ("Est enim primum ea in rebus unitas, qua unumquodque sibi est unum sibique constat atque cohaeret. Est ea secundo, per quam altera alteri creatura unitur, et per quam demum omnes mundi partes unus sunt mundus. Tertia atque omnium principalissima est, qua totum universum cum suo opifice quasi exercitus cum suo duce est unum.")
21 "unitas ita ternario distincta, ut ab unitatis simplicitate non discedat."
22 *Opera omnia*, p. 315. ("Nascenti homini omnifaria semina et origenae vitae germina indidit pater.")
23 *Heptaplus*, V, vi, in ibid., p. 38. ("Faciamus hominem ad imaginem nostram, qui non tam quartus est mundus, quasi nova aliqua natura, quam trium (mundus supercoelestis, coelestis, sublunaris) complexus et colligatio."

man is "the little God of the world," the microcosm.[24] Like God, therefore, man is a centre of events, and all things revolve about him.[25] This thought, so utterly strange to the modern mind, dominated man's picture of the world until a few generations ago, when natural science proved man's subordination to nature and his extreme dependence on causes. The idea of a correlation between events and meaning (now assigned exclusively to man) was banished to such a remote and benighted region that the intellect lost track of it altogether. Schopenhauer remembered it somewhat belatedly after it had formed one of the chief items in Leibniz's scientific explanations.

929   By virtue of his microcosmic nature man is a son of the firmament or macrocosm. "I am a star travelling together with you," the initiate confesses in the Mithraic liturgy.[26] In alchemy the microcosmos has the same significance as the *rotundum*, a favourite symbol since the time of Zosimos of Panopolis, which was also known as the Monad.

930   The idea that the inner and outer man together form the whole, the οὐλομελίη of Hippocrates, a microcosm or smallest part wherein the "great principle" is undividedly present, also characterizes the thought of Agrippa von Nettesheim. He says:

It is the unanimous consent of all Platonists, that as in the archetypal World, all things are in all; so also in this corporeal world, all things are in all, albeit in different ways, according to the receptive nature of each. Thus the Elements are not only in these inferiour bodies, but also in the Heavens, in Stars, in Divels, in Angels, and lastly in God, the maker, and archetype of all things.[27]

24 "God . . . placed man in the centre [of the world] after his image and the similitude of forms" ("Deus . . . hominem in medio [mundi] statuit ad imaginem suam et similitudinem formarum").

25 Pico's doctrine is a typical example of the medieval correspondence theory. A good account of cosmological and astrological correspondence is to be found in Alfons Rosenberg, *Zeichen am Himmel: Das Weltbild der Astrologie*.

26 Albrecht Dieterich, *Eine Mithrasliturgie*, p. 9.

27 Henricus Cornelius Agrippa von Nettesheim, *De occulta philosophia Libri tres*, I, viii, p. 12. Trans. by "J. F." as *Three Books of Occult Philosophy* (1651 edn.), p. 20; republished under the editorship of W. F. Whitehead, p. 55. [Quotations from the J. F. translation have been slightly modified.—TRANS.] ("Est Platonicorum omnium unanimis sententia quemadmodum in archetypo mundo omnia sunt in omnibus, ita etiam in hoc corporeo mundo, omnia in omnibus esse, modis tamen diversis, pro natura videlicet suscipientium: sic et elementa non solum sunt in istis inferioribus, sed in coelis, in stellis, in daemonibus, in angelis, in ipso denique omnium opifice et archetypo.")

The ancients had said: "All things are full of gods." [28] These gods were "divine powers which are diffused in things." [29] Zoroaster had called them "divine allurements," [30] and Synesius "symbolic inticements." [31] This latter interpretation comes very close indeed to the idea of archetypal projections in modern psychology, although from the time of Synesius until quite recently there was no epistemological criticism, let alone the newest form of it, namely psychological criticism. Agrippa shares with the Platonists the view that "there is in the lower beings a certain virtue through which they agree in large measure with the higher," and that as a result the animals are connected with the "divine bodies" (i.e., the stars) and exert an influence on them.[32] Here he quotes Virgil: "I for my part do not believe that they [the rooks] are endowed with divine spirit or with a foreknowledge of things greater than the oracle." [33]

931   Agrippa is thus suggesting that there is an inborn "knowledge" or "perception" in living organisms, an idea which recurs in our own day in Hans Driesch.[34] Whether we like it or not, we find ourselves in this embarrassing position as soon as we begin seriously to reflect on the teleological processes in biology or to investigate the compensatory function of the unconscious, not to speak of trying to explain the phenomenon of synchronicity. Final causes, twist them how we will, postulate a *foreknowledge of some kind*. It is certainly not a knowledge that could be connected with the ego, and hence not a conscious knowledge as we know it, but rather a self-subsistent "unconscious" knowledge which I would prefer to call "absolute knowledge." It is not cognition but, as Leibniz so excellently calls it,

---

28 "Omna plena diis esse."   29 "virtutes divinae in rebus diffusae"
30 "divinae illices"
31 "symbolicae illecebrae." [In J. F. original edn., p. 32; Whitehead edn., p. 69.— TRANS.] Agrippa is basing himself here on the Marsilio Ficino translation (*Auctores Platonici*, II, v⁰). In Synesius (*Opuscula*, ed. by Nicolaus Terzaghi, p. 148), the text of Περὶ ἐνυπνίων III B has τὸ θελγόμενον, from θέλγειν, "to excite, charm, enchant."
32 *De occulta philosophia*, I, iv, p. 69. (J. F. edn., p. 117; Whitehead edn., p. 169.) Similarly in Paracelsus.
33 "Haud equidem credo, quia sit divinius illis
   Ingenium aut rerum fato prudentia maior."
                        —*Georgics*, I, 415f.
34 *Die "Seele" als elementarer Naturfaktor*, pp. 80, 82.

a "perceiving" which consists—or to be more cautious, seems to consist—of images, of subjectless "simulacra." These postulated images are presumably the same as my archetypes, which can be shown to be formal factors in spontaneous fantasy products. Expressed in modern language, the microcosm which contains "the images of all creation" would be the collective unconscious.[35] By the *spiritus mundi*, the *ligamentum animae et corporis*, the *quinta essentia*,[36] which he shares with the alchemists, Agrippa probably means what we would call the unconscious. The spirit that "penetrates all things," or shapes all things, is the World Soul: "The soul of the world therefore is a certain only thing, filling all things, bestowing all things, binding, and knitting together all things, that it might make one frame of the world. . . ." [37] Those things in which this spirit is particularly powerful therefore have a tendency to "beget their like," [38] in other words, to produce correspondences or meaningful coincidences.[39] Agrippa gives a long list of these correspondences, based on the numbers 1 to 12.[40] A similar but more alchemical table of correspondences can be found in a treatise of Aegidius de Vadis.[41] Of these I would only mention the *scala unitatis*, because it is especially interesting from the point of

[35] Cf. supra, "On the Nature of the Psyche," pars. 392f.

[36] Agrippa says of this (op. cit., I, xiv, p. 29; J. F. edn., p. 33; Whitehead edn., p. 70): "That which we call the quintessence: because it is not from the four Elements, but a certain fifth thing, having its being above, and besides them." ("Quoddam quintum super illa [elementa] aut praeter illa subsistens.")

[37] II, lvii, p. 203 (J. F. edn., p. 331): "Est itaque anima mundi, vita quaedam unica omnia replens, omnia perfundens, omnia colligens et connectens, ut unam reddat totius mundi machinam. . . ."

[38] Ibid.: ". . . potentius perfectiusque agunt, tum etiam promptius generant sibi simile."

[39] The zoologist A. C. Hardy reaches similar conclusions: "Perhaps our ideas on evolution may be altered if something akin to telepathy—unconscious no doubt—were found to be a factor in moulding the patterns of behaviour among members of a species. If there was such a non-conscious group-behaviour plan, distributed between, and linking, the individuals of the race, we might find ourselves coming back to something like those ideas of subconscious racial memory of Samuel Butler, but on a group rather than an individual basis." "The Scientific Evidence for Extra-Sensory Perception," in *Discovery*, X, 328, quoted by Soal, q.v.

[40] Op. cit., II, iv–xiv.

[41] "Dialogus inter naturam et filium philosophiae." *Theatrum chemicum*, II (1602), p. 123.

view of the history of symbols: "Yod [the first letter of the tetragrammaton, the divine˅ name]—anima mundi—sol—lapis philosophorum—cor—Lucifer." [42] I must content myself with saying that this is an attempt to set up a hierarchy of archetypes, and that tendencies in this direction can be shown to exist in the unconscious.[43]

932　　Agrippa was an older contemporary of Theophrastus Paracelsus and is known to have had a considerable influence on him.[44] So it is not surprising if the thinking of Paracelsus proves to be steeped in the idea of correspondence. He says:

> If a man will be a philosopher without going astray, he must lay the foundations of his philosophy by making heaven and earth a microcosm, and not be wrong by a hair's breadth. Therefore he who will lay the foundations of medicine must also guard against the slightest error, and must make from the microcosm the revolution of heaven and earth, so that the philosopher does not find anything in heaven and earth which he does not also find in man, and the physician does not find anything in man which heaven and earth do not have. And these two differ only in outward form, and yet the form on both sides is understood as pertaining to one thing.[45]

The *Paragranum* [46] has some pointed psychological remarks to make about physicians:

> For this reason, [we assume] not four, but one arcanum, which is, however, four-square, like a tower facing the four winds. And as little as a tower may lack a corner, so little may the physician lack one of the parts. . . . At the same [time he] knows how the world is symbolized [by] an egg in its shell, and how a chick with all its substance lies hidden within it. Thus everything in the world and in man must lie hidden in the physician. And just as the hens, by their brooding, transform the world prefigured in the shell into a chick, so Alchemy brings to maturity the philosophical arcana lying in the

---

42 Cited in Agrippa, op. cit., II, iv, p. 104 (J. F. edn., p. 176).

43 Cf. Aniela Jaffé, "Bilder und Symbole aus E. T. A. Hoffmann's Märchen 'Der goldene Topf,' " and Marie-Louise von Franz, "Die Passio Perpetuae."

44 Cf. *Alchemical Studies*, index, s.v. "Agrippa."

45 *Das Buch Paragranum*, ed. by Franz Strunz, pp. 35f. Much the same in *Labyrinthus medicorum*, in the *Sämtliche Werke*, ed. Sudhoff, XI, pp. 204ff.

46 Strunz edn., p. 34.

physician. . . . Herein lies the error of those who do not under-stand the physician aright.[47]

What this means for alchemy I have shown in some detail in my *Psychology and Alchemy.*

933   Johannes Kepler thought in much the same way. He says in his *Tertius interveniens* (1610): [48]

> This [viz., a geometrical principle underlying the physical world] is also, according to the doctrine of Aristotle, the strongest tie that links the lower world to the heavens and unifies it therewith so that all its forms are governed from on high; for in this lower world, that is to say the globe of the earth, there is inherent a spiritual nature, capable of *Geometria,* which *ex instinctu creatoris, sine ratio-cinatione* comes to life and stimulates itself into a use of its forces through the geometrical and harmonious combination of the heav-enly rays of light. Whether all plants and animals as well as the globe of the earth have this faculty in themselves I cannot say. But it is not an unbelievable thing. . . . For, in all these things [e.g., in the fact that flowers have a definite colour, form, and number of petals] there is at work the *instinctus divinus, rationis particeps,* and not at all man's own intelligence. That man, too, through his soul and its lower faculties, has a like affinity to the heavens as has the soil of the earth can be tested and proven in many ways.[49]

934   Concerning the astrological "Character," i.e., astrological synchronicity, Kepler says:

> This *Character* is received, not into the body, which is much too inappropriate for this, but into the soul's own nature, which behaves like a point (for which reason it can also be transformed into the point of the *confluxus radiorum*). This [nature of the soul] not only partakes of their reason (on account of which we human beings are called reasonable above other living creatures) but also has another, innate reason [enabling it] to apprehend instantaneously, without long learning, the *Geometriam* in the *radiis* as well as in the *vocibus,* that is to say, in *Musica.*[50]

---

[47] Similar ideas in Jakob Böhme, *The Signature of All Things,* trans. by John Ellistone, p. 10: "Man has indeed the forms of all the three worlds in him, for he is a complete image of God, or of the Being of all beings. . . ." (*Signatura rerum,* I, 7.)

[48] *Opera omnia,* ed. by C. Frisch, I, pp. 605ff.

[49] Ibid., No. 64.   [50] No. 65.

Thirdly, another marvellous thing is that the nature which receives this *Characterem* also induces a certain correspondence *in constellationibus coelestibus* in its relatives. When a mother is great with child and the natural time of delivery is near, nature selects for the birth a day and hour which correspond, on account of the heavens [scil., from an astrological point of view], to the nativity of the mother's brother or father, and this *non qualitative, sed astronomice et quantitative.*[51]

Fourthly, so well does each nature know not only its *charaçterem coelestem* but also the celestial *configurationes* and courses of every day that, whenever a planet moves *de praesenti* into its *characteris ascendentem* or *loca praecipua,* especially into the *Natalitia,*[52] it responds to this and is affected and stimulated thereby in various ways.[53]

935   Kepler supposes that the secret of the marvellous correspondence is to be found in the *earth,* because the earth is animated by an *anima telluris,* for whose existence he adduces a number of proofs. Among these are: the constant temperature below the surface of the earth; the peculiar power of the earth-soul to produce metals, minerals, and fossils, namely the *facultas formatrix,* which is similar to that of the womb and can bring forth in the bowels of the earth shapes that are otherwise found only outside —ships, fishes, kings, popes, monks, soldiers, etc.;[54] further the practice of geometry, for it produces the five geometrical bodies and the six-cornered figures in crystals. The *anima telluris* has all this from an original impulse, independent of the reflection and ratiocination of man.[55]

936   The seat of astrological synchronicity is not in the planets but in the earth;[56] not in matter, but in the *anima telluris.*

[51] No. 67.

[52] ["in die Natalitia" = "into those [positions presiding] at birth," if "in die" is construed as German. The *Gesammelte Werke,* ed. by M. Caspar and F. Hammer, IV, p. 211, has "in die Natalitio" = "in the day of birth," the words "in die" being construed as Latin.—TRANS.]   [53] No. 68.

[54] See the dreams mentioned below.

[55] Kepler, *Opera,* ed. by Frisch, V, p. 254; cf. also II, pp. 270f. and VI, pp. 178f. ". . . formatrix facultas est in visceribus terrae, quae feminae praegnantis more occursantes foris res humanas veluti eas videret, in fissibilibus lapidibus exprimit, ut militum, monachorum, pontificum, regum et quidquid in ore hominum est. . . ."

[56] ". . . quod scl. principatus causae in terra sedeat, non in planetis ipsis." Ibid., II, p. 642.

Therefore every kind of natural or living power in bodies has a certain "divine similitude." [57]

*

937   Such was the intellectual background when Gottfried Wilhelm von Leibniz (1646–1716) appeared with his idea of *pre-established harmony*, that is, an absolute synchronism of psychic and physical events. This theory finally petered out in the concept of "psychophysical parallelism." Leibniz's pre-established harmony and the above-mentioned idea of Schopenhauer's, that the unity of the primal cause produces a simultaneity and inter-relationship of events not in themselves causally connected, are at bottom only a repetition of the old peripatetic view, with a modern deterministic colouring in the case of Schopenhauer and a partial replacement of causality by an antecedent order in the case of Leibniz. For him God is the creator of order. He compares soul and body to two synchronized clocks [58] and uses

[57] ". . . ut omne genus naturalium vel animalium facultatum in corporibus Dei quandam gerat similitudinem." Ibid. I am indebted to Dr. Liliane Frey-Rohn and Dr. Marie-Louise von Franz for this reference to Kepler.

[58] G. W. Leibniz, "Second Explanation of the System of the Communication between Substances" (*The Philosophical Works of Leibniz*, trans. by. G. M. Duncan, pp. 90–91): "From the beginning God has made each of these two substances of such a nature that merely by following its own peculiar laws, received with its being, it nevertheless accords with the other, just as if there were a mutual influence or as if God always put his hand thereto in addition to his general co-operation."

As Professor Pauli has kindly pointed out, it is possible that Leibniz took his idea of the synchronized clocks from the Flemish philosopher Arnold Geulincx (1625–99). In his *Metaphysica vera*, Part III, there is a note to "Octava scientia" (p. 195), which says (p. 296): ". . . horologium voluntatis nostrae quadret cum horologio motus in corpore" (the clock of our will is synchronized with the clock of our physical movement). Another note (p. 297) explains: "Voluntas nostra nullum habet influxum, causalitatem, determinationem aut efficaciam quamcunque in motum . . . cum cogitationes nostras bene excutimus, nullam apud nos invenimus ideam seu notionem determinationis. . . . Restat igitur Deus solus primus motor et solus motor, quia et ita motum ordinat atque disponit et ita simul voluntati nostrae licet libere moderatur, ut eodem temporis momento conspiret et voluntas nostra ad projiciendum v.g. pedes inter ambulandum, et simul ipsa illa pedum projectio seu ambulatio." (Our will has no influence, no causative or determinative power, and no effect of any kind on our movement. . . . If we examine our thoughts carefully, we find in ourselves no idea or concept of determination. . . . There remains, therefore, only God as the prime the same simile to express the relations of the monads or entelechies with one another. Although the monads cannot influence one another directly because, as he says, they "have no windows" [59] (relative abolition of causality!), they are so constituted that they are always in accord without having knowledge of one another. He conceives each monad to be a "little world" or "active indivisible mirror." [60] Not only is man a microcosm enclosing the whole in himself, but every entelechy or monad is in effect such a microcosm. Each "simple substance" has connections "which express all the others." It is "a perpetual living mirror of the universe." [61] He calls the monads of living organisms "souls": "the soul follows its own laws, and the body its own likewise, and they accord by virtue of the harmony pre-established among all substances, since they are all representations of one and the same universe." [62] This clearly expresses the idea that man is a microcosm. "Souls in general," says Leibniz, "are the living mirrors or images of the universe of created things." He distinguishes between minds on the one hand, which are "images of the Divinity . . . capable of knowing the system of the universe, and of imitating something of it by architectonic patterns, each mind being as it were a little

---

mover and only mover, because he arranges and orders movement and freely co-ordinates it with our will, so that our will wishes simultaneously to throw the feet forward into walking, and simultaneously the forward movement and the walking take place.) A note to "Nona scientia" adds (p. 298): "Mens nostra . . . penitus independens est ab illo (scl. corpore) . . . omnia quae de corpore scimus jam praevie quasi ante nostram cognitionem esse in corpore. Ut illa quodam modo nos in corpore legamus, non vero inscribamus, quod Deo proprium est." (Our mind . . . is totally independent of the body . . . everything we know about the body is already in the body, before our thought. So that we can, as it were, read ourselves in our body, but not imprint ourselves on it. Only God can do that.) This idea anticipates Leibniz' clock comparison.

59 *Monadology*, § 7: "Monads have no windows, by which anything could come in or go out. . . . Thus neither substance nor accident can enter a monad from without."

60 Rejoinder to the remarks in Bayle's Dictionary, from the *Kleinere philosophische Schriften*, XI, p. 105.

61 *Monadology*, § 56 (Morris edn., p. 12): "Now this connection or adaptation of all created things with each, and of each with all the rest, means that each simple substance has relations which express all the others, and that consequently it is a perpetual living mirror of the universe."   62 Ibid., § 78 (p. 17).

divinity in its own department," [63] and bodies on the other hand, which "act according to the laws of efficient causes by motions," while the souls act "according to the laws of final causes by appetitions, ends, and means." [64] In the monad or soul alterations take place whose cause is the "appetition." [65] "The passing state, which involves and represents a plurality within the unity or simple substance, is nothing other than what is called perception," says Leibniz.[66] Perception is the "inner state of the monad representing external things," and it must be distinguished from conscious apperception. "For perception is unconscious." [67] Herein lay the great mistake of the Cartesians, "that they took no account of perceptions which are not apperceived." [68] The perceptive faculty of the monad corresponds to the *knowledge,* and its appetitive faculty to the *will,* that is in God.[69]

938   It is clear from these quotations that besides the causal connection Leibniz postulates a complete pre-established parallelism of events both inside and outside the monad. The synchronicity principle thus becomes the absolute rule in all cases where an inner event occurs simultaneously with an outside one. As against this, however, it must be borne in mind that the synchronistic phenomena which can be verified empirically, far from constituting a rule, are so exceptional that most people doubt their existence. They certainly occur much more frequently in reality than one thinks or can prove, but we still do not know whether they occur so frequently and so regularly in any field of experience that we could speak of them as conforming to law.[70] We only know that there must be an under-

---

[63] § 83 (p. 18); cf. *Theodicy,* § 147 (trans. by E. M. Huggard, pp. 215f.).

[64] *Monadology,* § 79 (Morris edn., p. 17).   [65] Ibid., § 15 (p. 5).

[66] § 14 (pp. 4f.).

[67] *Principles of Nature and of Grace, Founded on Reason,* § 4 (Morris edn., p. 22).

[68] *Monadology,* § 14 (p. 5). Cf. also Dr. Marie-Louise von Franz's paper on the dream of Descartes in *Zeitlose Dokumente der Seele.*

[69] *Monadology,* § 48 (p. 11); *Theodicy,* § 149.

[70] I must again stress the possibility that the relation between body and soul may yet be understood as a synchronistic one. Should this conjecture ever be proved, my present view that synchronicity is a relatively rare phenomenon would have to be corrected. Cf. C. A. Meier's observations in *Zeitgemässe Probleme der Traumforschung,* p. 22.

lying principle which might possibly explain all such (related) phenomena.

939   The primitive as well as the classical and medieval views of nature postulate the existence of some such principle alongside causality. Even in Leibniz, causality is neither the only view nor the predominant one. Then, in the course of the eighteenth century, it became the exclusive principle of natural science. With the rise of the physical sciences in the nineteenth century the correspondence theory vanished completely from the surface, and the magical world of earlier ages seemed to have disappeared once and for all until, towards the end of the century, the founders of the Society for Psychical Research indirectly opened up the whole question again through their investigation of telepathic phenomena.

940   The medieval attitude of mind I have described above underlies all the magical and mantic procedures which have played an important part in man's life since the remotest times. The medieval mind would regard Rhine's laboratory-arranged experiments as magical performances, whose effect for this reason would not seem so very astonishing. It was interpreted as a "transmission of energy," which is still commonly the case today, although, as I have said, it is not possible to form any empirically verifiable conception of the transmitting medium.

941   I need hardly point out that for the primitive mind synchronicity is a self-evident fact; consequently at this stage there is no such thing as chance. No accident, no illness, no death is ever fortuitous or attributable to "natural" causes. Everything is somehow due to magical influence. The crocodile that catches a man while he is bathing has been sent by a magician; illness is caused by some spirit or other; the snake that was seen by the grave of somebody's mother is obviously her soul; etc. On the primitive level, of course, synchronicity does not appear as an idea by itself, but as "magical" causality. This is an early form of our classical idea of causality, while the development of Chinese philosophy produced from the significance of the magical the "concept" of Tao, of meaningful coincidence, but no causality-based science.

942   Synchronicity postulates a meaning which is *a priori* in relation to human consciousness and apparently exists outside

man.[71] Such an assumption is found above all in the philosophy of Plato, which takes for granted the existence of transcendental images or models of empirical things, the εἴδη (forms, species), whose reflections (εἴδωλα) we see in the phenomenal world. This assumption not only presented no difficulty to earlier centuries but was on the contrary perfectly self-evident. The idea of an *a priori* meaning may also be found in the older mathematics, as in the mathematician Jacobi's paraphrase of Schiller's poem "Archimedes and His Pupil." He praises the calculation of the orbit of Uranus and closes with the lines:

> What you behold in the cosmos is only the light of God's glory;
> In the Olympian host Number eternally reigns.

943   The great mathematician Gauss is the putative author of the saying: "God arithmetizes." [72]

944   The idea of synchronicity and of a self-subsistent meaning, which forms the basis of classical Chinese thinking and of the naïve views of the Middle Ages, seems to us an archaic assumption that ought at all costs to be avoided. Though the West has done everything possible to discard this antiquated hypothesis, it has not quite succeeded. Certain mantic procedures seem to have died out, but astrology, which in our own day has attained an eminence never known before, remains very much alive. Nor has the determinism of a scientific epoch been able to extinguish altogether the persuasive power of the synchronicity principle. For in the last resort it is not so much a question of superstition as of a truth which remained hidden for so long only because it had less to do with the physical side of events than with their psychic aspects. It was modern psychology and parapsychology which proved that causality does not explain a certain class of

---

[71] In view of the possibility that synchronicity is not only a psychophysical phenomenon but might also occur without the participation of the human psyche, I should like to point out that in this case we should have to speak not of *meaning* but of equivalence or conformity.

[72] "ὁ θεὸς ἀριθμητίζει." But in a letter of 1830 Gauss says: "We must in all humility admit that if number is *merely* a product of our mind, space has a reality outside our mind." (Leopold Kronecker, *Über den Zahlenbegriff*, in his *Werke*, III, p. 252.) Hermann Weyl likewise takes number as a product of reason. ("Wissenschaft als symbolische Konstruktion des Menschen," p. 375). Markus Fierz, on the other hand, inclines more to the Platonic idea. ("Zur physikalischen Erkenntnis," p. 434.)

events and that in this case we have to consider a formal factor, namely synchronicity, as a principle of explanation.

945   For those who are interested in psychology I should like to mention here that the peculiar idea of a self-subsistent meaning is suggested in dreams. Once when this idea was being discussed in my circle somebody remarked: "The geometrical square does not occur in nature except in crystals." A lady who had been present had the following dream that night: *In the garden there was a large sandpit in which layers of rubbish had been deposited. In one of these layers she discovered thin, slaty plates of green serpentine. One of them had black squares on it, arranged concentrically. The black was not painted on, but was ingrained in the stone, like the markings in an agate. Similar marks were found on two or three other plates, which Mr. A (a slight acquaintance) then took away from her.*[73] Another dream-motif of the same kind is the following: *The dreamer was in a wild mountain region where he found contiguous layers of triassic rock. He loosened the slabs and discovered to his boundless astonishment that they had human heads on them in low relief.* This dream was repeated several times at long intervals.[74] Another time the dreamer *was travelling through the Siberian tundra and found an animal he had long been looking for. It was a more than lifesize cock, made of what looked like thin, colourless glass. But it was alive and had just sprung by chance from a microscopic unicellular organism which had the power to turn into all sorts of animals (not otherwise found in the tundra) or even into objects of human use, of whatever size. The next moment each of these chance forms vanished without trace.* Here is another dream of the same type: *The dreamer was walking in a wooded mountain region. At the top of a steep slope he came to a ridge of rock honeycombed with holes, and there he found a little brown man of the same colour as the iron oxide with which the rock was coated.*[75] *The little man was busily*

---

73 According to the rules of dream interpretation this Mr. A would represent the animus, who, as a personification of the unconscious, takes back the designs because the conscious mind has no use for them and regards them only as *lusus naturae*.

74 The recurrence of the dream expresses the persistent attempt of the unconscious to bring the dream content before the conscious mind.

75 An Anthroparion or "metallic man."

engaged in hollowing out a cave, at the back of which a cluster of columns could be seen in the living rock. On the top of each column was a dark brown human head with large eyes, carved with great care out of some very hard stone, like lignite. The little man freed this formation from the amorphous conglomerate surrounding it. The dreamer could hardly believe his eyes at first, but then had to admit that the columns were continued far back into the living rock and must therefore have come into existence without the help of man. He reflected that the rock was at least half a million years old and that the artefact could not possibly have been made by human hands.[76]

946   These dreams seem to point to the presence of a formal factor in nature. They describe not just a *lusus naturae,* but the meaningful coincidence of an absolutely natural product with a human idea apparently independent of it. This is what the dreams are obviously saying,[77] and what they are trying to bring nearer to consciousness through repetition.

[76] Cf. Kepler's ideas quoted above.

[77] Those who find the dreams unintelligible will probably suspect them of harbouring quite a different meaning which is more in accord with their preconceived opinions. One can indulge in wishful thinking about dreams just as one can about anything else. For my part I prefer to keep as close to the dream statement as possible, and to try to formulate it in accordance with its manifest meaning. If it proves impossible to relate this meaning to the conscious situation of the dreamer, then I frankly admit that I do not understand the dream, but I take good care not to juggle it into line with some preconceived theory.

4. CONCLUSION

947   I do not regard these statements as in any way a final proof
of my views, but simply as a conclusion from empirical premises
which I would like to submit to the consideration of my reader.
From the material before us I can derive no other hypothesis
that would adequately explain the facts (including the ESP
experiments). I am only too conscious that synchronicity is a
highly abstract and "irrepresentable" quantity. It ascribes to
the moving body a certain psychoid property which, like space,
time, and causality, forms a criterion of its behaviour. We must
completely give up the idea of the psyche's being somehow
connected with the brain, and remember instead the "meaningful" or "intelligent" behaviour of the lower organisms, which
are without a brain. Here we find ourselves much closer to the
formal factor which, as I have said, has nothing to do with
brain activity.

948   If that is so, then we must ask ourselves whether the relation
of soul and body can be considered from this angle, that is to
say whether the co-ordination of psychic and physical processes
in a living organism can be understood as a synchronistic phenomenon rather than as a causal relation. Both Geulincx and
Leibniz regarded the co-ordination of the psychic and the physical as an act of God, of some principle standing outside empirical nature. The assumption of a causal relation between psyche

and physis leads on the other hand to conclusions which it is difficult to square with experience: either there are physical processes which cause psychic happenings, or there is a pre-existent psyche which organizes matter. In the first case it is hard to see how chemical processes can ever produce psychic processes, and in the second case one wonders how an immaterial psyche could ever set matter in motion. It is not necessary to think of Leibniz's pre-established harmony or anything of that kind, which would have to be absolute and would manifest itself in a universal correspondence and sympathy, rather like the meaningful coincidence of time-points lying on the same degree of latitude in Schopenhauer. The synchronicity principle possesses properties that may help to clear up the body-soul problem. Above all it is the fact of causeless order, or rather, of meaningful orderedness, that may throw light on psychophysical parallelism. The "absolute knowledge" which is characteristic of synchronistic phenomena, a knowledge not mediated by the sense organs, supports the hypothesis of a self-subsistent meaning, or even expresses its existence. Such a form of existence can only be transcendental, since, as the knowledge of future or spatially distant events shows, it is contained in a psychically relative space and time, that is to say in an irrepresentable space-time continuum.

949   It may be worth our while to examine more closely, from this point of view, certain experiences which seem to indicate the existence of psychic processes in what are commonly held to be unconscious states. Here I am thinking chiefly of the remarkable observations made during deep syncopes resulting from acute brain injuries. Contrary to all expectations, a severe head injury is not always followed by a corresponding loss of consciousness. To the observer, the wounded man seems apathetic, "in a trance," and not conscious of anything. Subjectively, however, consciousness is by no means extinguished. Sensory communication with the outside world is in a large measure restricted, but is not always completely cut off, although the noise of battle, for instance, may suddenly give way to a "solemn" silence. In this state there is sometimes a very distinct and impressive sensation or hallucination of levitation, the wounded man seeming to rise into the air in the same position he was in at the moment he was wounded. If he was wounded standing up, he rises in a

standing position, if lying down, he rises in a lying position, if sitting, he rises in a sitting position. Occasionally his surroundings seem to rise with him—for instance the whole bunker in which he finds himself at the moment. The height of the levitation may be anything from eighteen inches to several yards. All feeling of weight is lost. In a few cases the wounded think they are making swimming movements with their arms. If there is any perception of their surroundings at all, it seems to be mostly imaginary, i.e., composed of memory images. During levitation the mood is predominantly euphoric. " 'Buoyant, solemn, heavenly, serene, relaxed, blissful, expectant, exciting' are the words used to describe it. . . . There are various kinds of 'ascension experiences.' " [1] Jantz and Beringer rightly point out that the wounded can be roused from their syncope by remarkably small stimuli, for instance if they are addressed by name or touched, whereas the most terrific bombardment has no effect.

950   Much the same thing can be observed in deep comas resulting from other causes. I would like to give an example from my own medical experience. A woman patient, whose reliability and truthfulness I have no reason to doubt, told me that her first birth was very difficult. After thirty hours of fruitless labour the doctor considered that a forceps delivery was indicated. This was carried out under light narcosis. She was badly torn and suffered great loss of blood. When the doctor, her mother, and her husband had gone, and everything was cleared up, the nurse wanted to eat, and the patient saw her turn round at the door and ask, "Do you want anything before I go to supper?" She tried to answer, but couldn't. She had the feeling that she was sinking through the bed into a bottomless void. She saw the nurse hurry to the bedside and seize her hand in order to take her pulse. From the way she moved her fingers to and fro the patient thought it must be almost imperceptible. Yet she herself felt quite all right, and was slightly amused at the nurse's alarm. She was not in the least frightened. That was the last she could remember for a long time. The next thing she was aware of was that, without feeling her body and its position, she was *looking down* from a point in the ceiling and could see everything going on in the room below her: she saw herself lying in the bed,

1 Hubert Jantz and Kurt Beringer, "Das Syndrom des Schwebeerlebnisses unmittelbar nach Kopfverletzungen," 202.

deadly pale, with closed eyes. Beside her stood the nurse. The doctor paced up and down the room excitedly, and it seemed to her that he had lost his head and didn't know what to do. Her relatives crowded to the door. Her mother and her husband came in and looked at her with frightened faces. She told herself it was too stupid of them to think she was going to die, for she would certainly come round again. All this time she knew that behind her was a glorious, park-like landscape shining in the brightest colours, and in particular an emerald green meadow with short grass, which sloped gently upwards beyond a wrought-iron gate leading into the park. It was spring, and little gay flowers such as she had never seen before were scattered about in the grass. The whole demesne sparkled in the sunlight, and all the colours were of an indescribable splendour. The sloping meadow was flanked on both sides by dark green trees. It gave her the impression of a clearing in the forest, never yet trodden by the foot of man. "I knew that this was the entrance to another world, and that if I turned round to gaze at the picture directly, I should feel tempted to go in at the gate, and thus step out of life." She did not actually *see* this landscape, as her back was turned to it, but she *knew* it was there. She felt there was nothing to stop her from entering in through the gate. She only knew that she would turn back to her body and would not die. That was why she found the agitation of the doctor and the distress of her relatives stupid and out of place.

951   The next thing that happened was that she awoke from her coma and saw the nurse bending over her in bed. She was told that she had been unconscious for about half an hour. The next day, some fifteen hours later, when she felt a little stronger, she made a remark to the nurse about the incompetent and "hysterical" behaviour of the doctor during her coma. The nurse energetically denied this criticism in the belief that the patient had been completely unconscious at the time and could therefore have known nothing of the scene. Only when she described in full detail what had happened during the coma was the nurse obliged to admit that the patient had perceived the events exactly as they happened in reality.

952   One might conjecture that this was simply a psychogenic twilight state in which a split-off part of consciousness still continued to function. The patient, however, had never been hys-

terical and had suffered a genuine heart collapse followed by syncope due to cerebral anaemia, as all the outward and evidently alarming symptoms indicated. She really was in a coma and ought to have had a complete psychic black-out and been altogether incapable of clear observation and sound judgment. The remarkable thing was that it was not an immediate perception of the situation through indirect or unconscious observation, but she saw the whole situation from *above,* as though "her eyes were in the ceiling," as she put it.

953   Indeed, it is not easy to explain how such unusually intense psychic processes can take place, and be remembered, in a state of severe collapse, and how the patient could observe actual events in concrete detail with closed eyes. One would expect such obvious cerebral anaemia to militate against or prevent the occurrence of highly complex psychic processes of that kind.

954   Sir Auckland Geddes presented a very similar case before the Royal Society of Medicine on February 26, 1927, though here the ESP went very much further. During a state of collapse the patient noted the splitting off of an integral consciousness from his bodily consciousness, the latter gradually resolving itself into its organ components. The other consciousness possessed verifiable ESP.[2]

955   These experiences seem to show that in swoon states, where by all human standards there is every guarantee that conscious activity and sense perception are suspended, consciousness, reproducible ideas, acts of judgment, and perceptions can still continue to exist. The accompanying feeling of levitation, alteration of the angle of vision, and extinction of hearing and of coenaesthetic perceptions indicate a shift in the localization of consciousness, a sort of separation from the body, or from the cerebral cortex or cerebrum which is conjectured to be the seat of conscious phenomena. If we are correct in this assumption, then we must ask ourselves whether there is some other nervous substrate in us, apart from the cerebrum, that can think and perceive, or whether the psychic processes that go on in us during loss of consciousness are synchronistic phenomena, i.e., events which have no causal connection with organic processes. This last possibility cannot be rejected out of hand in view of

2 Cf. G. N. M. Tyrrell's report in *The Personality of Man,* pp. 197f. There is another case of this kind on pp. 199f.

the existence of ESP, i.e., of perceptions independent of space and time which cannot be explained as processes in the biological substrate. Where sense perceptions are impossible from the start, it can hardly be a question of anything but synchronicity. But where there are spatial and temporal conditions which would make perception and apperception possible in principle, and only the activity of consciousness, or the cortical function, is extinguished, and where, as in our example, a conscious phenomenon like perception and judgment nevertheless occurs, then the question of a nervous substrate might well be considered. It is well nigh axiomatic that conscious processes are tied to the cerebrum, and that the lower centres contain nothing but chains of reflexes which in themselves are unconscious. This is particularly true of the sympathetic system. Hence the insects, which have no cerebrospinal nervous system at all, but only a double chain of ganglia, are regarded as reflex automata.

956   This view has recently been challenged by the researches which von Frisch, of Graz, made into the life of bees. It turns out that bees not only tell their comrades, by means of a peculiar sort of dance, that they have found a feeding-place, but that they also indicate its direction and distance, thus enabling the beginners to fly to it directly.[3] This kind of message is no different in principle from information conveyed by a human being. In the latter case we would certainly regard such behaviour as a conscious and intentional act and can hardly imagine how anyone could prove in a court of law that it had taken place unconsciously. We could, at a pinch, admit on the basis of psychiatric experiences that objective information can in exceptional cases be communicated in a twilight state, but would expressly deny that communications of this kind are normally unconscious. Nevertheless it would be possible to suppose that in bees the process is unconscious. But that would not help to solve the problem, because we are still faced with the fact that the ganglionic system apparently achieves exactly the same result as our cerebral cortex. Nor is there any proof that bees are unconscious.

957   Thus we are driven to the conclusion that a nervous substrate like the sympathetic system, which is absolutely different

3 Karl von Frisch, *The Dancing Bees,* trans. by Dora Ilse, pp. 112ff.

from the cerebrospinal system in point of origin and function, can evidently produce thoughts and perceptions just as easily as the latter. What then are we to think of the sympathetic system in vertebrates? Can it also produce or transmit specifically psychic processes? Von Frisch's observations prove the existence of transcerebral thought and perception. One must bear this possibility in mind if we want to account for the existence of some form of consciousness during an unconscious coma. During a coma the sympathetic system is not paralysed and could therefore be considered as a possible carrier of psychic functions. If that is so, then one must ask whether the normal state of unconsciousness in sleep, and the potentially conscious dreams it contains, can be regarded in the same light—whether, in other words, dreams are produced not so much by the activity of the sleeping cortex, as by the unsleeping sympathetic system, and are therefore of a transcerebral nature.

958   Outside the realm of psychophysical parallelism, which we cannot at present pretend to understand, synchronicity is not a phenomenon whose regularity it is at all easy to demonstrate. One is as much impressed by the disharmony of things as one is surprised by their occasional harmony. In contrast to the idea of a pre-established harmony, the synchronistic factor merely stipulates the existence of an intellectually necessary principle which could be added as a fourth to the recognized triad of space, time, and causality. These factors are necessary but not absolute—most psychic contents are non-spatial, time and causality are psychically relative—and in the same way the synchronistic factor proves to be only conditionally valid. But unlike causality, which reigns despotically over the whole picture of the macrophysical world and whose universal rule is shattered only in certain lower orders of magnitude, synchronicity is a phenomenon that seems to be primarily connected with psychic conditions, that is to say with processes in the unconscious. Synchronistic phenomena are found to occur—experimentally— with some degree of regularity and frequency in the intuitive, "magical" procedures, where they are subjectively convincing but are extremely difficult to verify objectively and cannot be statistically evaluated (at least at present).

959   On the organic level it might be possible to regard biological morphogenesis in the light of the synchronistic factor. Professor

A. M. Dalcq (of Brussels) understands form, despite its tie with matter, as a "continuity that is supraordinate to the living organism." [4] Sir James Jeans reckons radioactive decay among the causeless events which, as we have seen, include synchronicity. He says: "Radioactive break-up appeared to be an effect without a cause, and suggested that the ultimate laws of nature were not even causal." [5] This highly paradoxical formula, coming from the pen of a physicist, is typical of the intellectual dilemma with which radioactive decay confronts us. It, or rather the phenomenon of "half-life," appears as an instance of acausal orderedness—a conception which also includes synchronicity and to which I shall revert below.

960   Synchronicity is not a philosophical view but an empirical concept which postulates an intellectually necessary principle. This cannot be called either materialism or metaphysics. No serious investigator would assert that the nature of what is observed to exist, and of that which observes, namely the psyche, are known and recognized quantities. If the latest conclusions of science are coming nearer and nearer to a unitary idea of being, characterized by space and time on the one hand and by causality and synchronicity on the other, that has nothing to do with materialism. Rather it seems to show that there is some possibility of getting rid of the incommensurability between the observed and the observer. The result, in that case, would be a unity of being which would have to be expressed in terms of a new conceptual language—a "neutral language," as W. Pauli once called it.

961   Space, time, and causality, the triad of classical physics, would then be supplemented by the synchronicity factor and become a tetrad, a *quaternio* which makes possible a whole judgment:

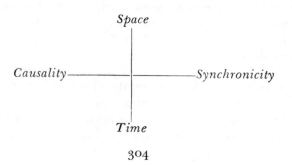

962   Here synchronicity is to the three other principles as the one-
dimensionality of time [6] is to the three-dimensionality of space,
or as the recalcitrant "Fourth" in the *Timaeus,* which, Plato
says, can only be added "by force" to the other three.[7] Just as the
introduction of time as the fourth dimension in modern physics
postulates an irrepresentable space-time continuum, so the idea
of synchronicity with its inherent quality of meaning produces
a picture of the world so irrepresentable as to be completely
baffling.[8] The advantage, however, of adding this concept is
that it makes possible a view which includes the psychoid factor
in our description and knowledge of nature—that is, an *a priori*
meaning or "equivalence." The problem that runs like a red
thread through the speculations of alchemists for fifteen hundred
years thus repeats and solves itself, the so-called axiom of Maria
the Jewess (or Copt): "Out of the Third comes the One as the
Fourth." [9] This cryptic observation confirms what I said above,
that in principle new points of view are not as a rule discovered
in territory that is already known, but in out-of-the-way places
that may even be avoided because of their bad name. The old
dream of the alchemists, the transmutation of chemical elements, this much-derided idea, has become a reality in our own
day, and its symbolism, which was no less an object of ridicule,
has turned out to be a veritable gold-mine for the psychology
of the unconscious. Their dilemma of three and four, which
began with the story that serves as a setting for the *Timaeus* and
extends all the way to the Cabiri scene in *Faust,* Part II, is
recognized by a sixteenth-century alchemist, Gerhard Dorn, as
the decision between the Christian Trinity and the *serpens
quadricornutus,* the four-horned serpent who is the Devil. As
though in anticipation of things to come he anathematizes the
pagan quaternity which was ordinarily so beloved of the alche-

4 "La Morphogénèse dans la cadre de la biologie générale." Cf. above, the similar
conclusion reached by the zoologist A. C. Hardy.

5 *Physics and Philosophy,* p. 127; cf. also p. 151.

6 I am not counting P. A. M. Dirac's multi-dimensionality of time.

7 Cf. my "Psychological Approach to the Dogma of the Trinity," pars. 186ff., 280,
290.

8 Sir James Jeans (*Physics and Philosophy,* p. 215) thinks it possible "that the
springs of events in this substratum include our own mental activities, so that
the future course of events may depend in part on these mental activities." The
causalism of this argument does not seem to me altogether tenable.

9 "ἐκ τοῦ τρίτου τὸ ἓν τέταρτον." Cf. *Psychology and Alchemy,* par. 26.

mists, on the ground that it arose from the binarius (the number 2) and is thus something material, feminine, and devilish.[10] Dr. von Franz has demonstrated this emergence of trinitarian thinking in the *Parable* of Bernard of Treviso, in Khunrath's *Amphitheatrum,* in Michael Maier, and in the anonymous author of the *Aquarium sapientum.*[11] W. Pauli calls attention to the polemical writings of Kepler and of Robert Fludd, in which Fludd's correspondence theory was the loser and had to make room for Kepler's theory of three principles.[12] The decision in favour of the triad, which in certain respects ran counter to the alchemical tradition, was followed by a scientific epoch that knew nothing of correspondence and clung with passionate insistence to a triadic view of the world—a continuation of the trinitarian type of thinking—which described and explained everything in terms of space, time, and causality.

963   The revolution brought about by the discovery of radioactivity has considerably modified the classical views of physics. So great is the change of standpoint that we have to revise the classical schema I made use of above. As I was able, thanks to the friendly interest which Professor Pauli evinced in my work, to discuss these questions of principle with a professional physicist who could at the same time appreciate my psychological arguments, I am in a position to put forward a suggestion that takes modern physics into account. Pauli suggested replacing the opposition of space and time in the classical schema by (conservation of) energy and the space-time continuum. This suggestion led me to a closer definition of the other pair of opposites—causality and synchronicity—with a view to establishing some kind of connection between these two heterogeneous concepts. We finally agreed on the following *quaternio:*

Indestructible Energy

Constant Connection *through Effect* *(Causality)*	*Inconstant Connection* *through Contingence,* *Equivalence, or "Meaning"* *(Synchronicity)*

Space-Time Continuum

[10] "De tenebris contra naturam," in *Theatrum chemicum,* I (1602), pp. 518ff.
[11] Marie-Louise von Franz, "Die Parabel von der Fontina des Grafen von Tarvis."
[12] See Pauli's contribution in *The Interpretation of Nature and the Psyche.*

964   This schema satisfies on the one hand the postulates of modern physics, and on the other hand those of psychology. The psychological point of view needs clarifying. A causalistic explanation of synchronicity seems out of the question for the reasons given above. It consists essentially of "chance" equivalences. Their *tertium comparationis* rests on the psychoid factors I call archetypes. These are *indefinite,* that is to say they can be known and determined only approximately. Although associated with causal processes, or "carried" by them, they continually go beyond their frame of reference, an infringement to which I would give the name "transgressivity," because the archetypes are not found exclusively in the psychic sphere, but can occur just as much in circumstances that are not psychic (equivalence of an outward physical process with a psychic one). Archetypal equivalences are *contingent* to causal determination, that is to say there exist between them and the causal processes no relations that conform to law. They seem, therefore, to represent a special instance of randomness or chance, or of that "random state" which "runs through time in a way that fully conforms to law," as Andreas Speiser says.[13] It is an initial state which is "not governed by mechanistic law" but is the precondition of law, the chance substrate on which law is based. If we consider synchronicity or the archetypes as the contingent, then the latter takes on the specific aspect of a modality that has the functional significance of a world-constituting factor. The archetype represents *psychic probability,* portraying ordinary instinctual events in the form of *types.* It is a special psychic instance of probability in general, which "is made up of the laws of chance and lays down rules for nature just as the laws of mechanics do." [14] We must agree with Speiser that although in the realm of pure intellect the contingent is "a formless substance," it reveals itself to psychic introspection—so far as inward perception can grasp it at all—as an image, or rather a type which underlies not only the psychic equivalences but, remarkably enough, the psychophysical equivalences too.

965   It is difficult to divest conceptual language of its causalistic colouring. Thus the word "underlying," despite its causalistic connotation, does not refer to anything causal, but simply to an

13 *Über die Freiheit,* 4f.   14 Ibid., p. 6.

existing quality, an irreducible contingency which is "Just-So." The meaningful coincidence or equivalence of a psychic and a physical state that have no causal relationship to one another means, in general terms, that it is a modality without a cause, an "acausal orderedness." The question now arises whether our definition of synchronicity with reference to the equivalence of psychic and physical processes is capable of expansion, or rather, requires expansion. This requirement seems to force itself on us when we consider the above, wider conception of synchronicity as an "acausal orderedness." Into this category come all "acts of creation," *a priori* factors such as the properties of natural numbers, the discontinuities of modern physics, etc. Consequently we would have to include constant and experimentally reproducible phenomena within the scope of our expanded concept, though this does not seem to accord with the nature of the phenomena included in synchronicity narrowly understood. The latter are mostly individual cases which cannot be repeated experimentally. This is not of course altogether true, as Rhine's experiments show and numerous other experiences with clairvoyant individuals. These facts prove that even in individual cases which have no common denominator and rank as "curiosities" there are certain regularities and therefore constant factors, from which we must conclude that our narrower conception of synchronicity is probably too narrow and really needs expanding. I incline in fact to the view that synchronicity in the narrow sense is only a particular instance of general acausal orderedness—that, namely, of the equivalence of psychic and physical processes where the observer is in the fortunate position of being able to recognize the *tertium comparationis*. But as soon as he perceives the archetypal background he is tempted to trace the mutual assimilation of independent psychic and physical processes back to a (causal) effect of the archetype, and thus to overlook the fact that they are merely contingent. This danger is avoided if one regards synchronicity as a special instance of general acausal orderedness. In this way we also avoid multiplying our principles of explanation illegitimately, for the archetype *is* the introspectively recognizable form of *a priori* psychic orderedness. If an external synchronistic process now associates itself with it, it falls into the same basic pattern—in other words, it too is "ordered." This form of orderedness differs from that of the properties of natural numbers or the discontinuities of physics in that the latter have existed from eternity and occur regularly, whereas the forms of psychic orderedness are *acts of creation in time.* That, incidentally, is precisely why I have stressed the element of time as being characteristic of these phenomena and called them *synchronistic.*

966   The modern discovery of discontinuity (e.g., the orderedness of energy quanta, of radium decay, etc.) has put an end to the sovereign rule of causality and thus to the triad of principles. The territory lost by the latter belonged earlier to the sphere of correspondence and sympathy, concepts which reached their greatest development in Leibniz's idea of pre-established harmony. Schopenhauer knew far too little about the empirical foundations of correspondence to realize how hopeless his causalistic attempt at explanation was. Today, thanks to the ESP experiments, we have a great deal of empirical material at our disposal. We can form some conception of its reliability when we learn from G. E. Hutchinson [15] that the ESP experiments conducted by S. G. Soal and K. M. Goldney have a probability of 1 : 10^{35}, this being equivalent to the number of molecules in 250,000 tons of water. There are relatively few experiments in the field of the natural sciences whose results come anywhere near so high a degree of certainty. The exaggerated scepticism in regard to ESP is really without a shred of justification. The main reason for it is simply the ignorance which nowadays, unfortunately, seems to be the inevitable accompaniment of specialism and screens off the necessarily limited horizon of specialist studies from all higher and wider points of view in the most undesirable way. How often have we not found that the so-called "superstitions" contain a core of truth that is well worth knowing! It may well be that the originally magical significance of the word "wish," which is still preserved in "wishing-rod" (divining rod, or magic wand) and expresses not just wishing in the sense of desire but a magical action,[16] and

15 S. G. Soal, "Science and Telepathy," p. 6.
16 Jacob Grimm, *Teutonic Mythology,* trans. by J. S. Stallybrass, I, p. 137. Wish-objects are magic implements forged by dwarfs, such as Odin's spear Gungnir, Thor's hammer Mjollnir, and Freya's sword (II, p. 870). Wishing is "gotes kraft" (divine power). "Got hât an sie den wunsch geleit und der wünschelruoten hort"

the traditional belief in the efficacy of prayer, are both based on the experience of concomitant synchronistic phenomena.

967 Synchronicity is no more baffling or mysterious than the discontinuities of physics. It is only the ingrained belief in the sovereign power of causality that creates intellectual difficulties and makes it appear unthinkable that causeless events exist or could ever occur. But if they do, then we must regard them as *creative acts*, as the continuous creation [17] of a pattern that exists from all eternity, repeats itself sporadically, and is not derivable from any known antecedents. We must of course guard against thinking of every event whose cause is unknown as "causeless." This, as I have already stressed, is admissible only when a cause is not even thinkable. But thinkability is itself an idea that needs the most rigorous criticism. Had the atom [18] corresponded to the original philosophical conception of it, its fissionability would be unthinkable. But once it proves to be a measurable quantitity, its non-fissionability becomes unthinkable. Meaningful coincidences are thinkable as pure chance. But the more they multiply and the greater and more exact the

---

(God has bestowed the wish on her and the treasure of [*or:* found by] the wishing-rod). "Beschoenen mit wunsches gewalte" (to make beautiful with the power of the wish) (IV, p. 1329). "Wish" = Sanskrit *manoratha,* literally, "car of the mind" or of the psyche, i.e., wish, desire, fancy. (A. A. Macdonell, *A Practical Sanskrit Dictionary,* s.v.)

[17] Continuous creation is to be thought of not only as a series of successive acts of creation, but also as the eternal presence of the *one* creative act, in the sense that God "was always the Father and always generated the Son" (Origen, *De principiis,* I, 2, 3), or that he is the "eternal Creator of minds" (Augustine, *Confessions,* XI, 31, trans. F. J. Sheed, p. 232). God is contained in his own creation, "nor does he stand in need of his own works, as if he had place in them where he might abide; but endures in his own eternity, where he abides and creates whatever pleases him, both in heaven and earth" (Augustine, on Ps. 113 : 14, in *Expositions on the Book of Psalms*). What happens successively in time is simultaneous in the mind of God: "An immutable order binds mutable things into a pattern, and in this order things which are not simultaneous in time exist simultaneously outside time" (Prosper of Aquitaine, *Sententiae ex Augustino delibatae,* XLI [Migne, *P.L.,* LI, col. 433]). "Temporal succession is without time in the eternal wisdom of God" (LVII [Migne, col. 455]). Before the Creation there was no time—time only began with created things: "Rather did time arise from the created than the created from time" (CCLXXX [Migne, col. 468]). "There was no time before time, but time was created together with the world" (Anon., *De triplici habitaculo,* VI [Migne, *P.L.,* XL, col. 995]).

[18] [From ἄτομος, 'indivisible, that cannot be cut.'—Trans.]

correspondence is, the more their probability sinks and their unthinkability increases, until they can no longer be regarded as pure chance but, for lack of a causal explanation, have to be thought of as meaningful arrangements. As I have already said, however, their "inexplicability" is not due to the fact that the cause is unknown, but to the fact that a cause is not even thinkable in intellectual terms. This is necessarily the case when space and time lose their meaning or have become relative, for under those circumstances a causality which presupposes space and time for its continuance can no longer be said to exist and becomes altogether unthinkable.

968   For these reasons it seems to me necessary to introduce, alongside space, time, and causality, a category which not only enables us to understand synchronistic phenomena as a special class of natural events, but also takes the contingent partly as a universal factor existing from all eternity, and partly as the sum of countless individual acts of creation occurring in time.

VII

PSYCHOLOGICAL COMMENTARY ON
THE TIBETAN BOOK OF THE DEAD

PSYCHOLOGICAL COMMENTARY ON
"THE TIBETAN BOOK OF THE DEAD" [1]

831   Before embarking upon the psychological commentary, I should like to say a few words about the text itself. The Tibetan Book of the Dead, or the *Bardo Thödol*, is a book of instructions for the dead and dying. Like the Egyptian Book of the Dead, it is meant to be a guide for the dead man during the period of his *Bardo* existence, symbolically described as an intermediate state of forty-nine days' duration between death and rebirth. The text falls into three parts. The first part, called *Chikhai Bardo*, describes the psychic happenings at the moment of death. The second part, or *Chönyid Bardo*, deals with the dream-state which supervenes immediately after death, and with what are called "karmic illusions." The third part, or *Sidpa Bardo*, concerns the onset of the birth-instinct and of prenatal

---

1 [Originally published as "Psychologischer Kommentar zum Bardo Thödol" (preceded by an "Einführung," partially translated in the first two pars. here), in *Das Tibetanische Totenbuch*, translated into German by Louise Göpfert-March (Zurich, 1935). As ultimately revised for the 5th (revised and expanded) Swiss edition (1953), the commentary was translated by R. F. C. Hull for publication in the 3rd (revised and expanded) English edition (the original) of *The Tibetan Book of the Dead, or The After-Death Experience on the "Bardo" Plane*, according to Lama Kazi Dawa-Samdup's English rendering, edited by W. Y. Evans-Wentz, with foreword by Sir John Woodroffe (London and New York, 1957). With only minor alterations, it is the translation presented here.—EDITORS.]

events. It is characteristic that supreme insight and illumination, and hence the greatest possibility of attaining liberation, are vouchsafed during the actual process of dying. Soon afterward, the "illusions" begin which lead eventually to reincarnation, the illuminative lights growing ever fainter and more multifarious, and the visions more and more terrifying. This descent illustrates the estrangement of consciousness from the liberating truth as it approaches nearer and nearer to physical rebirth. The purpose of the instruction is to fix the attention of the dead man, at each successive stage of delusion and entanglement, on the ever-present possibility of liberation, and to explain to him the nature of his visions. The text of the *Bardo Thödol* is recited by the lama in the presence of the corpse.

832   I do not think I could better discharge my debt of thanks to the two previous translators of the *Bardo Thödol*, the late Lama Kazi Dawa-Samdup and Dr. Evans-Wentz, than by attempting, with the aid of a psychological commentary, to make the magnificent world of ideas and the problems contained in this treatise a little more intelligible to the Western mind. I am sure that all who read this book with open eyes, and who allow it to impress itself upon them without prejudice, will reap a rich reward.

*

833   The *Bardo Thödol*, fitly named by its editor, Dr. W. Y. Evans-Wentz, "The Tibetan Book of the Dead," caused a considerable stir in English-speaking countries at the time of its first appearance in 1927. It belongs to that class of writings which are not only of interest to specialists in Mahayana Buddhism, but which also, because of their deep humanity and their still deeper insight into the secrets of the human psyche, make an especial appeal to the layman who is seeking to broaden his knowledge of life. For years, ever since it was first published, the *Bardo Thödol* has been my constant companion, and to it I owe not only many stimulating ideas and discoveries, but also many fundamental insights. Unlike the Egyptian Book of the Dead, which always prompts one to say too much or too little, the *Bardo Thödol* offers one an intelligible philosophy addressed to human beings rather than to gods or primitive savages. Its philosophy contains the quintessence of Buddhist psychological criticism; and, as such, one can truly say that it is of an unex-

ampled sublimity. Not only the "wrathful" but also tḥ
ful" deities are conceived as samsaric projections of thє
psyche, an idea that seems all too obvious to the enligḥ.
European, because it reminds him of his own banal simpliflɕɑ
tions. But though the European can easily explain away these
deities as projections, he would be quite incapable of positing
them at the same time as real. The *Bardo Thödol* can do that,
because, in certain of its most essential metaphysical premises,
it has the enlightened as well as the unenlightened European at
a disadvantage. The ever-present, unspoken assumption of the
Bardo Thödol is the antinomian character of all metaphysical
assertions, and also the idea of the qualitative difference of the
various levels of consciousness and of the metaphysical realities
conditioned by them. The background of this unusual book is
not the niggardly European "either-or," but a magnificently
affirmative "both-and." This statement may appear objection-
able to the Western philosopher, for the West loves clarity and
unambiguity; consequently, one philosopher clings to the position, "God is," while another clings equally fervently to the
negation, "God is not." What would these hostile brethren make
of an assertion like the following [p. 96]:

Recognizing the voidness of thine own intellect to be Buddhahood,
and knowing it at the same time to be thine own consciousness, thou
shalt abide in the state of the divine mind of the Buddha.

834   Such an assertion is, I fear, as unwelcome to our Western
philosophy as it is to our theology. The *Bardo Thödol* is in the
highest degree psychological in its outlook; but, with us, philosophy and theology are still in the medieval, pre-psychological
stage where only the assertions are listened to, explained, de-
fended, criticized and disputed, while the authority that makes
them has, by general consent, been deposed as outside the scope
of discussion.

835   Metaphysical assertions, however, are *statements of the
psyche,* and are therefore psychological. To the Western mind,
which compensates its well-known feelings of resentment by a
slavish regard for "rational" explanations, this obvious truth
seems all too obvious, or else it is seen as an inadmissible negation of metaphysical "truth." Whenever the Westerner hears
the word "psychological," it always sounds to him like *"only*

psychological." For him the "soul" is something pitifully small, unworthy, personal, subjective, and a lot more besides. He therefore prefers to use the word "mind" instead, though he likes to pretend at the same time that a statement which may in fact be very subjective indeed is made by the "mind," naturally by the "Universal Mind," or even—at a pinch—by the "Absolute" itself. This rather ridiculous presumption is probably a compensation for the regrettable smallness of the soul. It almost seems as if Anatole France had uttered a truth which were valid for the whole Western world when, in his *Penguin Island,* Cathérine d'Alexandrie offers this advice to God: "Donnez-leur une âme, mais une petite!"

836   It is the psyche which, by the divine creative power inherent in it, makes the metaphysical assertion; it posits the distinctions between metaphysical entities. Not only is it the condition of all metaphysical reality, it *is* that reality.

837   With this great psychological truth the *Bardo Thödol* opens. The book is not a ceremonial of burial, but a set of instructions for the dead, a guide through the changing phenomena of the *Bardo* realm, that state of existence which continues for forty-nine days after death until the next incarnation. If we disregard for the moment the supratemporality of the soul—which the East accepts as a self-evident fact—we, as readers of the *Bardo Thödol,* shall be able to put ourselves without difficulty in the position of the dead man, and shall consider attentively the teaching set forth in the opening section, which is outlined in the quotation above. At this point, the following words are spoken, not presumptuously, but in a courteous manner [pp. 95f.]:

O nobly born (so and so), listen. Now thou art experiencing the Radiance of the Clear Light of Pure Reality. Recognize it. O nobly-born, thy present intellect, in real nature void, not formed into anything as regards characteristics or colour, naturally void, is the very Reality, the All-Good.

Thine own intellect, which is now voidness, yet not to be regarded as of the voidness of nothingness, but as being the intellect itself, unobstructed, shining, thrilling, and blissful, is the very consciousness, the All-good Buddha.

838   This realization is the *Dharmakāya* state of perfect enlightenment; or, as we should express it in our own language, the

318

creative ground of all metaphysical assertion is consciousness, as
the invisible, intangible manifestation of the soul. The "Voidness" is the state transcendent over all assertion and all predica-
tion. The fulness of its discriminative manifestations still lies
latent in the soul.

839   The text continues:

> Thine own consciousness, shining, void, and inseparable from the
> Great Body of Radiance, hath no birth, nor death, and is the Im-
> mutable Light—Buddha Amitābha.

840   The soul is assuredly not small, but the radiant Godhead itself. The West finds this statement either very dangerous, if not
downright blasphemous, or else accepts it unthinkingly and
then suffers from a theosophical inflation. Somehow we always
have a wrong attitude to these things. But if we can master ourselves far enough to refrain from our chief error of always wanting to *do* something with things and put them to practical use,
we may perhaps succeed in learning an important lesson from
these teachings, or at least in appreciating the greatness of the
Bardo Thödol, which vouchsafes to the dead man the ultimate
and highest truth, that even the gods are the radiance and reflection of our own souls. No sun is thereby eclipsed for the Oriental as it would be for the Christian, who would feel robbed
of his God; on the contrary, his soul is the light of the Godhead,
and the Godhead is the soul. The East can sustain this paradox
better than the unfortunate Angelus Silesius, who even today
would be psychologically far in advance of his time.

841   It is highly sensible of the *Bardo Thödol* to make clear to
the dead man the primacy of the psyche, for that is the one thing
which life does not make clear to us. We are so hemmed in by
things which jostle and oppress that we never get a chance, in
the midst of all these "given" things, to wonder by whom they
are "given." It is from this world of "given" things that the dead
man liberates himself; and the purpose of the instruction is to
help him towards this liberation. We, if we put ourselves in his
place, shall derive no lesser reward from it, since we learn from
the very first paragraphs that the "giver" of all "given" things
dwells within us. This is a truth which in the face of all evidence, in the greatest things as in the smallest, is never known,
although it is often so very necessary, indeed vital, for us to

know it. Such knowledge, to be sure, is suitable only for contemplatives who are minded to understand the purpose of existence, for those who are Gnostics by temperament and therefore believe in a saviour who, like the saviour of the Mandaeans, is called "knowledge of life" (Manda d'Hayye). Perhaps it is not granted to many of us to see the world as something "given." A great reversal of standpoint, calling for much sacrifice, is needed before we can see the world as "given" by the very nature of the psyche. It is so much more straightforward, more dramatic, impressive, and therefore more convincing, to see all the things that happen to me than to observe how I make them happen. Indeed, the animal nature of man makes him resist seeing himself as the maker of his circumstances. That is why attempts of this kind were always the object of secret initiations, culminating as a rule in a figurative death which symbolized the total character of this reversal. And, in point of fact, the instruction given in the *Bardo Thödol* serves to recall to the dead man the experiences of his initiation and the teachings of his guru, for the instruction is, at bottom, nothing less than an initiation of the dead into the *Bardo* life, just as the initiation of the living was a preparation for the Beyond. Such was the case, at least, with all the mystery cults in ancient civilizations from the time of the Egyptian and Eleusinian mysteries. In the initiation of the living, however, this "Beyond" is not a world beyond death, but a reversal of the mind's intentions and outlook, a psychological "Beyond" or, in Christian terms, a "redemption" from the trammels of the world and of sin. Redemption is a separation and deliverance from an earlier condition of darkness and unconsciousness, and leads to a condition of illumination and releasedness, to victory and transcendence over everything "given."

842   Thus far the *Bardo Thödol* is, as Dr. Evans-Wentz also feels, an initiation process whose purpose it is to restore to the soul the divinity it lost at birth. Now it is a characteristic of Oriental religious literature that the teaching invariably begins with the most important item, with the ultimate and highest principles which, with us, would come last—as for instance in Apuleius, where Lucius is worshipped as Helios only right at the end. Accordingly, in the *Bardo Thödol,* the initiation is a series of diminishing climaxes ending with rebirth in the womb. The

only "initiation process" that is still alive and practised today in the West is the analysis of the unconscious as used by doctors for therapeutic purposes. This penetration into the ground-layers of consciousness is a kind of rational maieutics in the Socratic sense, a bringing forth of psychic contents that are still germinal, subliminal, and as yet unborn. Originally, this therapy took the form of Freudian psychoanalysis and was mainly concerned with sexual fantasies. This is the realm that corresponds to the last and lowest region of the *Bardo*, known as the *Sidpa Bardo*, where the dead man, unable to profit by the teachings of the *Chikhai* and *Chönyid Bardo*, begins to fall a prey to sexual fantasies and is attracted by the vision of mating couples. Eventually he is caught by a womb and born into the earthly world again. Meanwhile, as one might expect, the Oedipus complex starts functioning. If his karma destines him to be reborn as a man, he will fall in love with his mother-to-be and will find his father hateful and disgusting. Conversely, the future daughter will be highly attracted by her father-to-be and repelled by her mother. The European passes through this specifically Freudian domain when his unconscious contents are brought to light under analysis, but he goes in the reverse direction. He journeys back through the world of infantile-sexual fantasy to the womb. It has even been suggested in psychoanalytical circles that the trauma par excellence is the birth-experience itself—nay more, psychoanalysts even claim to have probed back to memories of intra-uterine origin. Here Western reason reaches its limit, unfortunately. I say "unfortunately," because one rather wishes that Freudian psychoanalysis could have happily pursued these so-called intra-uterine experiences still further back. Had it succeeded in this bold undertaking, it would surely have come out beyond the *Sidpa Bardo* and penetrated from behind into the lower reaches of the *Chönyid Bardo*. It is true that, with the equipment of our existing biological ideas, such a venture would not have been crowned with success; it would have needed a wholly different kind of philosophical preparation from that based on current scientific assumptions. But, had the journey back been consistently pursued, it would undoubtedly have led to the postulate of a pre-uterine existence, a true *Bardo* life, if only it had been possible to find at least some trace of an experiencing subject. As it was, the psychoanalysts never got beyond purely conjectural traces of intra-uterine experiences, and even the famous "birth trauma" has remained such an obvious truism that it can no longer explain anything, any more than can the hypothesis that life is a disease with a bad prognosis because its outcome is always fatal.

843   Freudian psychoanalysis, in all essential aspects, never went beyond the experiences of the *Sidpa Bardo;* that is, it was unable to extricate itself from sexual fantasies and similar "incompatible" tendencies which cause anxiety and other affective states. Nevertheless, Freud's theory is the first attempt made by the West to investigate, as if from below, from the animal sphere of instinct, the psychic territory that corresponds in Tantric Lamaism to the *Sidpa Bardo.* A very justifiable fear of metaphysics prevented Freud from penetrating into the sphere of the "occult." In addition to this, the *Sidpa* state, if we are to accept the psychology of the *Sidpa Bardo,* is characterized by the fierce wind of karma, which whirls the dead man along until he comes to the "womb-door." In other words, the *Sidpa* state permits of no going back, because it is sealed off against the *Chönyid* state by an intense striving downwards, towards the animal sphere of instinct and physical rebirth. That is to say, anyone who penetrates into the unconscious with purely biological assumptions will become stuck in the instinctual sphere and be unable to advance beyond it, for he will be pulled back again and again into physical existence. It is therefore not possible for Freudian theory to reach anything except an essentially negative valuation of the unconscious. It is a "nothing but." At the same time, it must be admitted that this view of the psyche is typically Western, only it is expressed more blatantly, more plainly, and more ruthlessly than others would have dared to express it, though at bottom they think no differently. As to what "mind" means in this connection, we can only cherish the hope that it will carry conviction. But, as even Max Scheler [2] noted with regret, the power of this "mind" is, to say the least of it, doubtful.

844   I think, then, we can state it as a fact that with the aid of psychoanalysis the rationalizing mind of the West has pushed forward into what one might call the neuroticism of the *Sidpa*

[2] [German philosopher and sociologist (1874–1928) working mainly in the field of values.—EDITORS.]

state, and has there been brought to an inevitable standstill by the uncritical assumption that everything psychological is subjective and personal. Even so, this advance has been a great gain, inasmuch as it has enabled us to take one more step behind our conscious lives. This knowledge also gives us a hint of how we ought to read the *Bardo Thödol*—that is, backwards. If, with the help of our Western science, we have to some extent succeeded in understanding the psychological character of the *Sidpa Bardo*, our next task is to see if we can make anything of the preceding *Chönyid Bardo*.

845   The *Chönyid* state is one of karmic illusion—that is to say, illusions which result from the psychic residua of previous existences. According to the Eastern view, karma implies a sort of psychic theory of heredity based on the hypothesis of reincarnation, which in the last resort is an hypothesis of the supratemporality of the soul. Neither our scientific knowledge nor our reason can keep in step with this idea. There are too many if's and but's. Above all, we know desperately little about the possibilities of continued existence of the individual soul after death, so little that we cannot even conceive how anyone could prove anything at all in this respect. Moreover, we know only too well, on epistemological grounds, that such a proof would be just as impossible as the proof of God. Hence we may cautiously accept the idea of karma only if we understand it as *psychic heredity* in the very widest sense of the word. Psychic heredity does exist—that is to say, there is inheritance of psychic characteristics such as predisposition to disease, traits of character, special gifts, and so forth. It does no violence to the psychic nature of these complex facts if natural science reduces them to what appear to be physical aspects (nuclear structures in cells, and so on). They are essential phenomena of life which express themselves, in the main, psychically, just as there are other inherited characteristics which express themselves, in the main, physiologically, on the physical level. Among these inherited psychic factors there is a special class which is not confined either to family or to race. These are the universal dispositions of the mind, and they are to be understood as analogous to Plato's forms (*eidola*), in accordance with which the mind organizes its contents. One could also describe these forms as *categories* analogous to the logical categories which are

always and everywhere present as the basic postulates of reason. Only, in the case of our "forms," we are not dealing with categories of reason but with categories of the *imagination*. As the products of imagination are always in essence visual, their forms must, from the outset, have the character of images and moreover of *typical* images, which is why, following St. Augustine, I call them "archetypes." Comparative religion and mythology are rich mines of archetypes, and so is the psychology of dreams and psychoses. The astonishing parallelism between these images and the ideas they serve to express has frequently given rise to the wildest migration theories, although it would have been far more natural to think of the remarkable similarity of the human psyche at all times and in all places. Archetypal fantasy-forms are, in fact, reproduced spontaneously anytime and anywhere, without there being any conceivable trace of direct transmission. The original structural components of the psyche are of no less surprising a uniformity than are those of the visible body. The archetypes are, so to speak, organs of the pre-rational psyche. They are eternally inherited forms and ideas which have at first no specific content. Their specific content only appears in the course of the individual's life, when personal experience is taken up in precisely these forms. If the archetypes were not pre-existent in identical form everywhere, how could one explain the fact, postulated at almost every turn by the *Bardo Thödol,* that the dead do not know that they are dead, and that this assertion is to be met with just as often in the dreary, half-baked literature of European and American Spiritualism? Although we find the same assertion in Swedenborg, knowledge of his writings can hardly be sufficiently widespread for this little bit of information to have been picked up by every small-town medium. And a connection between Swedenborg and the *Bardo Thödol* is completely unthinkable. It is a primordial, universal idea that the dead simply continue their earthly existence and do not know that they are disembodied spirits—an archetypal idea which enters into immediate, visible manifestation whenever anyone sees a ghost. It is significant, too, that ghosts all over the world have certain features in common. I am naturally aware of the unverifiable spiritualistic hypothesis, though I have no wish to make it my own. I must content myself with the hypothesis of an omnipresent, but differentiated, psychic structure which is inherited and which necessarily gives a certain form and direction to all experience. For, just as the organs of the body are not mere lumps of indifferent, passive matter, but are dynamic, functional complexes which assert themselves with imperious urgency, so also the archetypes, as organs of the psyche, are dynamic, instinctual complexes which determine psychic life to an extraordinary degree. That is why I also call them *dominants* of the unconscious. The layer of unconscious psyche which is made up of these universal dynamic forms I have termed the *collective unconscious.*

846   So far as I know, there is no inheritance of individual prenatal, or pre-uterine, memories, but there are undoubtedly inherited archetypes which are, however, devoid of content, because, to begin with, they contain no personal experiences. They only emerge into consciousness when personal experiences have rendered them visible. As we have seen, *Sidpa* psychology consists in wanting to live and to be born. (The *Sidpa Bardo* is the "*Bardo* of Seeking Rebirth.") Such a state, therefore, precludes any experience of transubjective psychic realities, unless the dead man refuses categorically to be born back again into the world of consciousness. According to the teachings of the *Bardo Thödol,* it is still possible for him, in each of the *Bardo* states, to reach the *Dharmakāya* by transcending the four-faced Mount Meru, provided that he does not yield to his desire to follow the "dim lights." This is as much as to say that the individual must desperately resist the dictates of reason, as we understand it, and give up the supremacy of egohood, regarded by reason as sacrosanct. What this means in practice is complete capitulation to the objective powers of the psyche, with all that this entails; a kind of figurative death, corresponding to the Judgment of the Dead in the *Sidpa Bardo.* It means the end of all conscious, rational, morally responsible conduct of life, and a voluntary surrender to what the *Bardo Thödol* calls "karmic illusion." Karmic illusion springs from belief in a visionary world of an extremely irrational nature, which neither accords with nor derives from our rational judgments but is the exclusive product of uninhibited imagination. It is sheer dream or "fantasy," and every well-meaning person will instantly caution us against it; nor indeed can one

see at first sight what is the difference between fantasies of this kind and the phantasmagoria of a lunatic. Very often only a slight *abaissement du niveau mental* is needed to unleash this world of illusion. The terror and darkness of this moment are reflected in the experiences described in the opening sections of the *Sidpa Bardo*. But the contents of the *Chönyid Bardo* reveal the archetypes, the karmic images which appear first in their terrifying form. The *Chönyid* state is equivalent to a deliberately induced psychosis.

847   One often hears and reads about the dangers of yoga, particularly of the ill-reputed *kundalini* yoga. The deliberately induced psychotic state, which in certain unstable individuals might easily lead to a real psychosis, is a danger that needs to be taken very seriously indeed. These things really are dangerous and ought not to be meddled with in our typically Western way. It is a meddling with fate, which strikes at the very roots of human existence and can let loose a flood of sufferings of which no sane person ever dreamed. These sufferings correspond to the hellish torments of the *Chönyid* state, described in the text as follows:

Then the Lord of Death will place round thy neck a rope and drag thee along; he will cut off thy head, tear out thy heart, pull out thy intestines, lick up thy brain, drink thy blood, eat thy flesh, and gnaw thy bones; but thou wilt be incapable of dying. Even when thy body is hacked to pieces, it will revive again. The repeated hacking will cause intense pain and torture.[3]

848   These tortures aptly describe the real nature of the danger: it is a disintegration of the wholeness of the *Bardo* body, which is a kind of "subtle body" constituting the visible envelope of the psychic self in the after-death state. The psychological equivalent of this dismemberment is psychic dissociation. In its deleterious form it would be schizophrenia (split mind). This most common of all mental illnesses consists essentially in a marked *abaissement du niveau mental* which abolishes the normal checks imposed by the conscious mind and thus gives unlimited scope to the play of the unconscious "dominants."

849   The transition, then, from the *Sidpa* state to the *Chönyid*

3 [Actually from the *Sidpa Bardo* section (p. 166), but similar torments figure in the "Wrathful Deities" section (pp. 131ff.) of the *Chönyid Bardo.*—EDITORS.]

state is a dangerous reversal of the aims and intentions of the conscious mind. It is a sacrifice of the ego's stability and a surrender to the extreme uncertainty of what must seem like a chaotic riot of phantasmal forms. When Freud coined the phrase that the ego was "the true seat of anxiety," he was giving voice to a very true and profound intuition. Fear of self-sacrifice lurks deep in every ego, and this fear is often only the precariously controlled demand of the unconscious forces to burst out in full strength. No one who strives for selfhood (individuation) is spared this dangerous passage, for that which is feared also belongs to the wholeness of the self—the sub-human, or supra-human, world of psychic "dominants" from which the ego originally emancipated itself with enormous effort, and then only partially, for the sake of a more or less illusory freedom. This liberation is certainly a very necessary and very heroic undertaking, but it represents nothing final: it is merely the creation of a *subject*, who, in order to find fulfilment, has still to be confronted by an *object*. This, at first sight, would appear to be the world, which is swelled out with projections for that very purpose. Here we seek and find our difficulties, here we seek and find our enemy, here we seek and find what is dear and precious to us; and it is comforting to know that all evil and all good is to be found out there, in the visible object, where it can be conquered, punished, destroyed, or enjoyed. But nature herself does not allow this paradisal state of innocence to continue for ever. There are, and always have been, those who cannot help but see that the world and its experiences are in the nature of a symbol, and that it really reflects something that lies hidden in the subject himself, in his own transubjective reality. It is from this profound intuition, according to lamaist doctrine, that the *Chönyid* state derives its true meaning, which is why the *Chönyid Bardo* is entitled "The *Bardo* of the Experiencing of Reality."

850   The reality experienced in the *Chönyid* state is, as the last section [pp. 143ff.] of this *Bardo* teaches, the reality of thought. The "thought-forms" appear as realities, fantasy takes on real form, and the terrifying dream evoked by karma and played out by the unconscious "dominants" begins. The first to appear (if we read the text backwards) is the all-destroying God of Death, the epitome of all terrors; he is followed by the

twenty-eight "power-holding" and sinister goddesses and the fifty-eight "blood-drinking" goddesses. In spite of their demonic aspect, which appears as a confusing chaos of terrifying attributes and monstrosities, a certain order is already discernible. We find that there are companies of gods and goddesses who are arranged according to the four directions and are distinguished by typical mystic colours. It gradually becomes clearer that all these deities are organized into mandalas, or circles, containing a cross of the four colours. The colours are co-ordinated with the four aspects of wisdom:

(1) White = the light-path of the mirror-like wisdom;
(2) Yellow = the light-path of the wisdom of equality;
(3) Red = the light-path of the discriminative wisdom;
(4) Green = the light-path of the all-performing wisdom.

851 On a higher level of insight, the dead man knows that the real thought-forms all emanate from himself, and that the four light-paths of wisdom which appear before him are the radiations of his own psychic faculties. This takes us straight to the psychology of the lamaistic mandala, which I have already discussed in the book I brought out with the late Richard Wilhelm, *The Secret of the Golden Flower.*

852 Continuing our ascent backwards through the region of the *Chönyid Bardo,* we come finally to the vision of the Four Great Ones: the green Amogha-Siddhi, the red Amitābha, the yellow Ratna-Sambhava, and the white Vajra-Sattva. The ascent ends with the effulgent blue light of the *Dharmadhātu,* the Buddha-body, which glows in the midst of the mandala from the heart of Vairochana.

853 With this final vision the karmic illusions cease; consciousness, weaned away from all form and from all attachment to objects, returns to the timeless, inchoate state of the *Dharma-kāya.* Thus (reading backwards) the *Chikhai* state, which appeared at the moment of death, is reached.

854 I think these few hints will suffice to give the attentive reader some idea of the psychology of the *Bardo Thödol.* The book describes a way of initiation in reverse, which, unlike the eschatological expectations of Christianity, prepares the soul for a descent into physical being. The thoroughly intellectualistic and rationalistic worldly-mindedness of the European makes it advisable for us to reverse the sequence of the *Bardo Thödol* and

to regard it as an account of Eastern initiation experiences, though one is perfectly free, if one chooses, to substitute Christian symbols for the gods of the *Chönyid Bardo*. At any rate, the sequence of events as I have described it offers a close parallel to the phenomenology of the European unconscious when it is undergoing an "initiation process," that is to say, when it is being analysed. The transformation of the unconscious that occurs under analysis makes it the natural analogue of the religious initiation ceremonies, which do, however, differ in principle from the natural process in that they anticipate the natural course of development and substitute for the spontaneous production of symbols a deliberately selected set of symbols prescribed by tradition. We can see this in the *Exercitia* of Ignatius Loyola, or in the yoga meditations of the Buddhists and Tantrists.

855   The reversal of the order of the chapters, which I have suggested here as an aid to understanding, in no way accords with the original intention of the *Bardo Thödol*. Nor is the psychological use we make of it anything but a secondary intention, though one that is possibly sanctioned by lamaist custom. The real purpose of this singular book is the attempt, which must seem very strange to the educated European of the twentieth century, to enlighten the dead on their journey through the regions of the *Bardo*. The Catholic Church is the only place in the world of the white man where any provision is made for the souls of the departed. Inside the Protestant camp, with its world-affirming optimism, we only find a few mediumistic "rescue circles," whose main concern is to make the dead aware of the fact that they *are* dead.[4] But, generally speaking, we have nothing in the West that is in any way comparable to the *Bardo Thödol*, except for certain secret writings which are inaccessible to the wider public and to the ordinary scientist. According to tradition, the *Bardo Thödol*, too, seems to have been included among the "hidden" books, as Dr. Evans-Wentz makes clear in his Introduction. As such, it forms a special chapter in the magical "cure of the soul" which extends even beyond death. This cult of the dead is rationally based on the belief in the supra-temporality of the soul, but its irrational basis is to be found in the psychological need of the living to do something for the de-

4 Information on this spiritualistic activity will be found in Lord Dowding's writings: *Many Mansions* (1943), *Lychgate* (1945), *God's Magic* (1946).

parted. This is an elementary need which forces itself upon even the most "enlightened" individuals when faced by the death of relatives and friends. That is why, enlightenment or no enlightenment, we still have all manner of ceremonies for the dead. If Lenin had to submit to being embalmed and put on show in a sumptuous mausoleum like an Egyptian pharaoh, we may be quite sure it was not because his followers believed in the resurrection of the body. Apart, however, from the Masses said for the soul in the Catholic Church, the provisions we make for the dead are rudimentary and on the lowest level, not because we cannot convince ourselves of the soul's immortality, but because we have rationalized the above-mentioned psychological need out of existence. We behave as if we did not have this need, and because we cannot believe in a life after death we prefer to do nothing about it. Simpler-minded people follow their own feelings, and, as in Italy, build themselves funeral monuments of gruesome beauty. The Catholic Masses for the soul are on a level considerably above this, because they are expressly intended for the psychic welfare of the deceased and are not a mere gratification of lachrymose sentiments. But the highest application of spiritual effort on behalf of the departed is surely to be found in the instructions of the *Bardo Thödol.* They are so detailed and thoroughly adapted to the apparent changes in the dead man's condition that every serious-minded reader must ask himself whether these wise old lamas might not, after all, have caught a glimpse of the fourth dimension and twitched the veil from the greatest of life's secrets.

856   Even if the truth should prove to be a disappointment, one almost feels tempted to concede at least some measure of reality to the vision of life in the *Bardo.* At any rate, it is unexpectedly original, if nothing else, to find the after-death state, of which our religious imagination has formed the most grandiose conceptions, painted in lurid colours as a terrifying dream-state of a progressively degenerative character.[5] The supreme vision comes not at the end of the *Bardo,* but right at the beginning, at the moment of death; what happens afterward is an ever-deepening descent into illusion and obscuration, down to the ultimate degradation of new physical birth. The spiritual

[5] A similar view in Aldous Huxley, *Time Must Have a Stop* (1945).

climax is reached at the moment when life ends. Human life, therefore, is the vehicle of the highest perfection it is possible to attain; it alone generates the karma that makes it possible for the dead man to abide in the perpetual light of the Voidness without clinging to any object, and thus to rest on the hub of the wheel of rebirth, freed from all illusion of genesis and decay. Life in the *Bardo* brings no eternal rewards or punishments, but merely a descent into a new life which shall bear the individual nearer to his final goal. But this eschatological goal is what he himself brings to birth as the last and highest fruit of the labours and aspirations of earthly existence. This view is not only lofty, it is manly and heroic.

857   The degenerative character of *Bardo* life is corroborated by the spiritualistic literature of the West, which again and again gives one a sickening impression of the utter inanity and banality of communications from the "spirit world." The scientific mind does not hesitate to explain these reports as emanations from the unconscious of the mediums and of those taking part in the séance, and even to extend this explanation to the description of the Hereafter given in the Tibetan Book of the Dead. And it is an undeniable fact that the whole book is created out of the archetypal contents of the unconscious. Behind these there lie—and in this our Western reason is quite right— no physical or metaphysical realities, but "merely" the reality of psychic facts, the data of psychic experience. Now whether a thing is "given" subjectively or objectively, the fact remains that it *is*. The *Bardo Thödol* says no more than this, for its five Dhyāni-Buddhas are themselves no more than psychic data. That is just what the dead man has to recognize, if it has not already become clear to him during life that his own psychic self and the giver of all data are one and the same. The world of gods and spirits is truly "nothing but" the collective unconscious inside me. To turn this sentence round so that it reads "The collective unconscious is the world of gods and spirits outside me," no intellectual acrobatics are needed, but a whole human lifetime, perhaps even many lifetimes of increasing completeness. Notice that I do not say "of increasing perfection," because those who are "perfect" make another kind of discovery altogether.

858   The *Bardo Thödol* began by being a "closed" book, and so it has remained, no matter what kind of commentaries may be written upon it. For it is a book that will only open itself to spiritual understanding, and this is a capacity which no man is born with, but which he can only acquire through special training and special experience. It is good that such to all intents and purposes "useless" books exist. They are meant for those "queer folk" who no longer set much store by the uses, aims, and meaning of present-day "civilization."

VIII

COMMENTARY ON
THE SECRET OF
THE GOLDEN FLOWER

1. DIFFICULTIES ENCOUNTERED BY A EUROPEAN IN TRYING TO UNDERSTAND THE EAST

1   A thorough Westerner in feeling, I cannot but be profoundly impressed by the strangeness of this Chinese text. It is true that some knowledge of Eastern religions and philosophies helps my intellect and my intuition to understand these things up to a point, just as I can understand the paradoxes of primitive beliefs in terms of "ethnology" or "comparative religion." This is of course the Western way of hiding one's heart under the cloak of so-called scientific understanding. We do it partly because the *misérable vanité des savants* fears and rejects with horror any sign of living sympathy, and partly because sympathetic understanding might transform contact with an alien spirit into an experience that has to be taken seriously. Our so-called scientific objectivity would have reserved this text for the philological acumen of sinologists, and would have guarded it jealously from any other interpretation. But Richard Wilhelm penetrated too deeply into the secret and mysterious vitality of Chinese wisdom to allow such a pearl of intuitive insight to disappear into the pigeon-holes of specialists. I am greatly honoured that his choice of a psychological commentator has fallen upon me.

2   This, however, involves the risk that this precious example of more-than-specialist insight will be swallowed by still another specialism. Nevertheless, anyone who belittles the merits of Western science is undermining the foundations of the Western mind. Science is not indeed a perfect instrument, but it is a superb and invaluable tool that works harm only when it is taken as an end in itself. Science must serve; it errs when it usurps the throne. It must be ready to serve all its branches, for each, because of its insufficiency, has need of support from the others. Science is the tool of the Western mind, and with it one can open more doors than with bare hands. It is part and parcel of

335

our understanding, and it obscures our insight only when it claims that the understanding it conveys is the only kind there is. The East teaches us another, broader, more profound, and higher understanding—understanding through life. We know this only by hearsay, as a shadowy sentiment expressing a vague religiosity, and we are fond of putting "Oriental wisdom" in quotation marks and banishing it to the dim region of faith and superstition. But that is wholly to misunderstand the realism of the East. Texts of this kind do not consist of the sentimental, overwrought mystical intuitions of pathological cranks and recluses, but are based on the practical insights of highly evolved Chinese minds, which we have not the slightest justification for undervaluing.

3   This assertion may seem bold, perhaps, and is likely to cause a good deal of head-shaking. Nor is that surprising, considering how little people know about the material. Its strangeness is indeed so arresting that our puzzlement as to how and where the Chinese world of thought might be joined to ours is quite understandable. The usual mistake of Western man when faced with this problem of grasping the ideas of the East is like that of the student in *Faust*. Misled by the devil, he contemptuously turns his back on science and, carried away by Eastern occultism, takes over yoga practices word for word and becomes a pitiable imitator. (Theosophy is our best example of this.) Thus he abandons the one sure foundation of the Western mind and loses himself in a mist of words and ideas that could never have originated in European brains and can never be profitably grafted upon them.

4   An ancient adept has said: "If the wrong man uses the right means, the right means work in the wrong way." [1] This Chinese saying, unfortunately only too true, stands in sharp contrast to our belief in the "right" method irrespective of the man who applies it. In reality, everything depends on the man and little or nothing on the method. The method is merely the path, the direction taken by a man; the way he acts is the true expression of his nature. If it ceases to be this, the method is nothing more than an affectation, something artificially pieced on, rootless and sapless, serving only the illegitimate goal of self-deception. It becomes a means of fooling oneself and of evading what may

1 [*The Secret of the Golden Flower* (1962 edn.), p. 63.]

perhaps be the implacable law of one's being. This is far removed from the earthiness and self-reliance of Chinese thought. It is a denial of one's own nature, a self-betrayal to strange and unclean gods, a cowardly trick for the purpose of feigning mental superiority, everything in fact that is profoundly contrary to the spirit of the Chinese "method." For these insights spring from a way of life that is complete, genuine, and true to itself; from that ancient, cultural life of China which grew logically and organically from the deepest instincts, and which, for us, is forever inaccessible and impossible to imitate.

5   Western imitation is a tragic misunderstanding of the psychology of the East, every bit as sterile as the modern escapades to New Mexico, the blissful South Sea islands, and central Africa, where "the primitive life" is played at in deadly earnest while Western man secretly evades his menacing duties, his *Hic Rhodus hic salta*. It is not for us to imitate what is foreign to our organism or to play the missionary; our task is to build up our Western civilization, which sickens with a thousand ills. This has to be done on the spot, and by the European just as he is, with all his Western ordinariness, his marriage problems, his neuroses, his social and political delusions, and his whole philosophical disorientation.

6   We should do well to confess at once that, fundamentally, we do not understand the utter unworldliness of a text like this— that actually we do not want to understand it. Have we, perhaps, a dim suspicion that a mental attitude which can direct the glance inward to that extent is detached from the world only because these people have so completely fulfilled the instinctive demands of their natures that there is nothing to prevent them from glimpsing the invisible essence of things? Can it be that the precondition for such a vision is liberation from the ambitions and passions that bind us to the visible world, and does not this liberation come from the sensible fulfilment of instinctive demands rather than from the premature and fear-ridden repression of them? Are our eyes opened to the spirit only when the laws of the earth are obeyed? Anyone who knows the history of Chinese culture and has carefully studied the *I Ching*, that book of wisdom which for thousands of years has permeated all Chinese thought, will not lightly wave these doubts aside. He will be aware that the views set forth in our text are nothing extraor-

337

dinary to the Chinese, but are actually inescapable psychological conclusions.

7   For a long time the spirit, and the sufferings of the spirit, were positive values and the things most worth striving for in our peculiar Christian culture. Only in the course of the nineteenth century, when spirit began to degenerate into intellect, did a reaction set in against the unbearable dominance of intellectualism, and this led to the unpardonable mistake of confusing intellect with spirit and blaming the latter for the misdeeds of the former. The intellect does indeed do harm to the soul when it dares to possess itself of the heritage of the spirit. It is in no way fitted to do this, for spirit is something higher than intellect since it embraces the latter and includes the feelings as well. It is a guiding principle of life that strives towards superhuman, shining heights. Opposed to this *yang* principle is the dark, feminine, earthbound *yin,* whose emotionality and instinctuality reach back into the depths of time and down into the labyrinth of the physiological continuum. No doubt these are purely intuitive ideas, but one can hardly dispense with them if one is trying to understand the nature of the human psyche. The Chinese could not do without them because, as the history of Chinese philosophy shows, they never strayed so far from the central psychic facts as to lose themselves in a one-sided over-development and over-valuation of a single psychic function. They never failed to acknowledge the paradoxicality and polarity of all life. The opposites always balanced one another—a sign of high culture. One-sidedness, though it lends momentum, is a mark of barbarism. The reaction that is now beginning in the West against the intellect in favour of feeling, or in favour of intuition, seems to me a sign of cultural advance, a widening of consciousness beyond the narrow confines of a tyrannical intellect.

8   I have no wish to depreciate the tremendous differentiation of the Western intellect; compared with it the Eastern intellect must be described as childish. (Naturally this has nothing to do with intelligence.) If we should succeed in elevating another, and possibly even a third psychic function to the dignified position accorded to the intellect, then the West might expect to surpass the East by a very great margin. Therefore it is sad indeed when the European departs from his own nature and

imitates the East or "affects" it in any way. The possibilities open to him would be so much greater if he would remain true to himself and evolve out of his own nature all that the East has brought forth in the course of the millennia.

9   In general, and looked at from the incurably externalistic standpoint of the intellect, it would seem as if the things the East values so highly were not worth striving for. Certainly the intellect alone cannot comprehend the practical importance Eastern ideas might have for us, and that is why it can classify them as philosophical and ethnological curiosities and nothing more. The lack of comprehension goes so far that even learned sinologists have not understood the practical use of the *I Ching*, and consider the book to be no more than a collection of abstruse magic spells.

2. MODERN PSYCHOLOGY OFFERS A POSSIBILITY OF UNDERSTANDING

10 Observations made in my practical work have opened out to me a quite new and unexpected approach to Eastern wisdom. In saying this I should like to emphasize that I did not have any knowledge, however inadequate, of Chinese philosophy as a starting point. On the contrary, when I began my career as a psychiatrist and psychotherapist, I was completely ignorant of Chinese philosophy, and only later did my professional experience show me that in my technique I had been unconsciously following that secret way which for centuries had been the preoccupation of the best minds of the East. This could be taken for a subjective fancy—which was one reason for my previous reluctance to publish anything on the subject—but Richard Wilhelm, that great interpreter of the soul of China, enthusiastically confirmed the parallel and thus gave me the courage to write about a Chinese text that belongs entirely to the mysterious shadowland of the Eastern mind. At the same time—and this is the extraordinary thing—its content forms a living parallel to what takes place in the psychic development of my patients, none of whom is Chinese.

11 In order to make this strange fact more intelligible to the reader, it must be pointed out that just as the human body shows a common anatomy over and above all racial differences, so, too, the human psyche possesses a common substratum transcending all differences in culture and consciousness. I have called this substratum the collective unconscious. This unconscious psyche, common to all mankind, does not consist merely of contents capable of becoming conscious, but of latent predispositions towards identical reactions. The collective unconscious is simply the psychic expression of the identity of brain structure irrespective of all racial differences. This explains the analogy, sometimes even identity, between the various myth motifs and

symbols, and the possibility of human communication in general. The various lines of psychic development start from one common stock whose roots reach back into the most distant past. This also accounts for the psychological parallelisms with animals.

12   In purely psychological terms this means that mankind has common instincts of ideation and action. All conscious ideation and action have developed on the basis of these unconscious archetypal patterns and always remain dependent on them. This is especially the case when consciousness has not attained any high degree of clarity, when in all its functions it is more dependent on the instincts than on the conscious will, more governed by affect than by rational judgment. This ensures a primitive state of psychic health, but it immediately becomes lack of adaptation when circumstances arise that call for a higher moral effort. Instincts suffice only for a nature that remains more or less constant. An individual who is guided more by the unconscious than by conscious choice therefore tends towards marked psychic conservatism. This is the reason why the primitive does not change in the course of thousands of years, and also why he fears anything strange and unusual. It might easily lead to maladaptation, and thus to the greatest psychic dangers—to a kind of neurosis, in fact. A higher and wider consciousness resulting from the assimilation of the unfamiliar tends, on the other hand, towards autonomy, and rebels against the old gods who are nothing other than those mighty, primordial images that hitherto have held our consciousness in thrall.

13   The stronger and more independent our consciousness becomes, and with it the conscious will, the more the unconscious is thrust into the background, and the easier it is for the evolving consciousness to emancipate itself from the unconscious, archetypal pattern. Gaining in freedom, it bursts the bonds of mere instinctuality and finally reaches a condition of instinctual atrophy. This uprooted consciousness can no longer appeal to the authority of the primordial images; it has Promethean freedom, but it also suffers from godless hybris. It soars above the earth and above mankind, but the danger of its sudden collapse is there, not of course in the case of every individual, but for the weaker members of the community, who then, again like Prometheus, are chained to the Caucasus of the unconscious. The

Chinese would say in the words of the *I Ching:* When
has reached its greatest strength, the dark power of *yin* is
within its depths, for night begins at midday when *yang*
breaks up and begins to change into *yin.*

14   The doctor is in a position to see this cycle of changes translated literally into life. He sees, for instance, a successful busi-
nessman attaining all his desires regardless of death and the
devil, and then, having retired at the height of his success, speed-
ily falling into a neurosis, which turns him into a querulous old
woman, fastens him to his bed, and finally destroys him. The
picture is complete even to the change from masculine to feminine. An exact parallel to this is the story of Nebuchadnezzar in
the Book of Daniel, and Caesarean madness in general. Similar
cases of one-sided exaggeration of the conscious standpoint, and
the resultant *yin*-reaction from the unconscious, form no small
part of the psychiatrist's clientele in our time, which so overval-
ues the conscious will as to believe that "where there's a will
there's a way." Not that I wish to detract in the least from the
high moral value of the will. Consciousness and the will may
well continue to be considered the highest cultural achievements of humanity. But of what use is a morality that destroys
the man? To bring the will and the capacity to achieve it into
harmony seems to me to require more than morality. Morality *à
tout prix* can be a sign of barbarism—more often wisdom is better. But perhaps I look at this with the eyes of a physician who
has to mend the ills following in the wake of one-sided cultural
achievements.

15   Be that as it may, the fact remains that a consciousness
heightened by an inevitable one-sidedness gets so far out of
touch with the primordial images that a breakdown ensues.
Long before the actual catastrophe, the signs of error announce
themselves in atrophy of instinct, nervousness, disorientation,
entanglement in impossible situations and problems. Medical
investigation then discovers an unconscious that is in full revolt
against the conscious values, and that therefore cannot possibly
be assimilated to consciousness, while the reverse is altogether
out of the question. We are confronted with an apparently irreconcilable conflict before which human reason stands helpless,
with nothing to offer except sham solutions or dubious com-
promises. If these evasions are rejected, we are faced with the

question as to what has become of the much needed un personality, and with the necessity of seeking it. At t begins the path travelled by the East since the begin things. Quite obviously, the Chinese were able to foll path because they never succeeded in forcing the oppos ᴗ in man's nature so far apart that all conscious connection between them was lost. The Chinese owe this all-inclusive consciousness to the fact that, as in the case of the primitive mentality, the yea and the nay have remained in their original proximity. Nonetheless, it was impossible not to feel the clash of opposites, so they sought a way of life in which they would be what the Indians call *nirdvandva,* free of opposites.

16   Our text is concerned with this way, and the same problem comes up with my patients also. There could be no greater mistake than for a Westerner to take up the direct practice of Chinese yoga, for that would merely strengthen his will and consciousness against the unconscious and bring about the very effect to be avoided. The neurosis would then simply be intensified. It cannot be emphasized enough that we are not Orientals, and that we have an entirely different point of departure in these matters. It would also be a great mistake to suppose that this is the path every neurotic must travel, or that it is the solution at every stage of the neurotic problem. It is appropriate only in those cases where consciousness has reached an abnormal degree of development and has diverged too far from the unconscious. This is the *sine qua non* of the process. Nothing would be more wrong than to open this way to neurotics who are ill on account of an excessive predominance of the unconscious. For the same reason, this way of development has scarcely any meaning before the middle of life (normally between the ages of thirty-five and forty), and if entered upon too soon can be decidedly injurious.

17   As I have said, the essential reason which prompted me to look for a new way was the fact that the fundamental problem of the patient seemed to me insoluble unless violence was done to one or the other side of his nature. I had always worked with the temperamental conviction that at bottom there are no insoluble problems, and experience justified me in so far as I have often seen patients simply outgrow a problem that had destroyed others. This "outgrowing," as I formerly called it, proved on

further investigation to be a new level of consciousness. Some higher or wider interest appeared on the patient's horizon, and through this broadening of his outlook the insoluble problem lost its urgency. It was not solved logically in its own terms, but faded out when confronted with a new and stronger life urge. It was not repressed and made unconscious, but merely appeared in a different light, and so really did become different. What, on a lower level, had led to the wildest conflicts and to panicky outbursts of emotion, from the higher level of personality now looked like a storm in the valley seen from the mountain top. This does not mean that the storm is robbed of its reality, but instead of being in it one is above it. But since, in a psychic sense, we are both valley and mountain, it might seem a vain illusion to deem oneself beyond what is human. One certainly does feel the affect and is shaken and tormented by it, yet at the same time one is aware of a higher consciousness looking on which prevents one from becoming identical with the affect, a consciousness which regards the affect as an object, and can say, "I *know* that I suffer." What our text says of indolence, "Indolence of which a man is conscious, and indolence of which he is unconscious, are a thousand miles apart," [1] holds true in the highest degree of affect.

18   Now and then it happened in my practice that a patient grew beyond himself because of unknown potentialities, and this became an experience of prime importance to me. In the meantime, I had learned that all the greatest and most important problems of life are fundamentally insoluble. They must be so, for they express the necessary polarity inherent in every self-regulating system. They can never be solved, but only outgrown. I therefore asked myself whether this outgrowing, this possibility of further psychic development, was not the normal thing, and whether getting stuck in a conflict was pathological. Everyone must possess that higher level, at least in embryonic form, and must under favourable circumstances be able to develop this potentiality. When I examined the course of development in patients who quietly, and as if unconsciously, outgrew themselves, I saw that their fates had something in common. The new thing came to them from obscure possibilities either outside or inside themselves; they accepted it and grew with its

1 [*The Golden Flower* (1962 edn.), p. 42.]

help. It seemed to me typical that some took the new thing from outside themselves, others from inside; or rather, that it grew into some persons from without, and into others from within. But the new thing never came exclusively either from within or from without. If it came from outside, it became a profound inner experience; if it came from inside, it became an outer happening. In no case was it conjured into existence intentionally or by conscious willing, but rather seemed to be borne along on the stream of time.

19   We are so greatly tempted to turn everything into a purpose and a method that I deliberately express myself in very abstract terms in order to avoid prejudicing the reader in one way or the other. The new thing must not be pigeon-holed under any heading, for then it becomes a recipe to be used mechanically, and it would again be a case of the "right means in the hands of the wrong man." I have been deeply impressed by the fact that the new thing prepared by fate seldom or never comes up to conscious expectations. And still more remarkable, though the new thing goes against deeply rooted instincts as we have known them, it is a strangely appropriate expression of the total personality, an expression which one could not imagine in a more complete form.

20   What did these people do in order to bring about the development that set them free? As far as I could see they did nothing (*wu wei*[2]) but let things happen. As Master Lü-tsu teaches in our text, the light circulates according to its own law if one does not give up one's ordinary occupation. The art of letting things happen, action through non-action, letting go of oneself as taught by Meister Eckhart, became for me the key that opens the door to the way. We must be able to let things happen in the psyche. For us, this is an art of which most people know nothing. Consciousness is forever interfering, helping, correcting, and negating, never leaving the psychic processes to grow in peace. It would be simple enough, if only simplicity were not the most difficult of all things. To begin with, the task consists solely in observing objectively how a fragment of fantasy develops. Nothing could be simpler, and yet right here the difficulties begin. Apparently one has no fantasy fragments—or yes, there's one, but it is too stupid! Dozens of good reasons are brought against

2 [The Taoist idea of action through non-action.—C.F.B.]

it. One cannot concentrate on it—it is too boring—what would come of it anyway—it is "nothing but" this or that, and so on. The conscious mind raises innumerable objections, in fact it often seems bent on blotting out the spontaneous fantasy activity in spite of real insight and in spite of the firm determination to allow the psychic process to go forward without interference. Occasionally there is a veritable cramp of consciousness.

21   If one is successful in overcoming the initial difficulties, criticism is still likely to start in afterwards in the attempt to interpret the fantasy, to classify it, to aestheticize it, or to devalue it. The temptation to do this is almost irresistible. After it has been faithfully observed, free rein can be given to the impatience of the conscious mind; in fact it must be given, or obstructive resistances will develop. But each time the fantasy material is to be produced, the activity of consciousness must be switched off again.

22   In most cases the results of these efforts are not very encouraging at first. Usually they consist of tenuous webs of fantasy that give no clear indication of their origin or their goal. Also, the way of getting at the fantasies varies with individuals. For many people, it is easiest to write them down; others visualize them, and others again draw or paint them with or without visualization. If there is a high degree of conscious cramp, often only the hands are capable of fantasy; they model or draw figures that are sometimes quite foreign to the conscious mind.

23   These exercises must be continued until the cramp in the conscious mind is relaxed, in other words, until one can let things happen, which is the next goal of the exercise. In this way a new attitude is created, an attitude that accepts the irrational and the incomprehensible simply because it is happening. This attitude would be poison for a person who is already overwhelmed by the things that happen to him, but it is of the greatest value for one who selects, from among the things that happen, only those that are acceptable to his conscious judgment, and is gradually drawn out of the stream of life into a stagnant backwater.

24   At this point, the way travelled by the two types mentioned earlier seems to divide. Both have learned to accept what comes to them. (As Master Lü-tsu teaches: "When occupations come to us, we must accept them; when things come to us, we must un-

derstand them from the ground up." [3]) One man will now take chiefly what comes to him from outside, and the other what comes from inside. Moreover, the law of life demands that what they take from outside and inside will be the very things that were always excluded before. This reversal of one's nature brings an enlargement, a heightening and enrichment of the personality, if the previous values are retained alongside the change—provided that these values are not mere illusions. If they are not held fast, the individual will swing too far to the other side, slipping from fitness into unfitness, from adaptedness into unadaptedness, and even from rationality into insanity. The way is not without danger. Everything good is costly, and the development of personality is one of the most costly of all things. It is a matter of saying yea to oneself, of taking oneself as the most serious of tasks, of being conscious of everything one does, and keeping it constantly before one's eyes in all its dubious aspects—truly a task that taxes us to the utmost.

25   A Chinese can always fall back on the authority of his whole civilization. If he starts on the long way, he is doing what is recognized as being the best thing he could possibly do. But the Westerner who wishes to set out on this way, if he is really serious about it, has all authority against him—intellectual, moral, and religious. That is why it is infinitely easier for him to imitate the Chinese way and leave the troublesome European behind him, or else to seek the way back to the medievalism of the Christian Church and barricade himself behind the wall separating true Christians from the poor heathen and other ethnographic curiosities encamped outside. Aesthetic or intellectual flirtations with life and fate come to an abrupt halt here: the step to higher consciousness leaves us without a rearguard and without shelter. The individual must devote himself to the way with all his energy, for it is only by means of his integrity that he can go further, and his integrity alone can guarantee that his way will not turn out to be an absurd misadventure.

26   Whether his fate comes to him from without or from within, the experiences and happenings on the way remain the same. Therefore I need say nothing about the manifold outer and inner events, the endless variety of which I could never exhaust in any case. Nor would this be relevant to the text under discus-

3 [*The Golden Flower* (1962 edn.), p. 51.]

sion. On the other hand, there is much to be said about the psychic states that accompany the process of development. These states are expressed symbolically in our text, and in the very same symbols that for many years have been familiar to me from my practice.

3. THE FUNDAMENTAL CONCEPTS

A. TAO

27   The great difficulty in interpreting this and similar texts[1] for the European is that the author always starts from the central point, from the point we would call the goal, the highest and ultimate insight he has attained. Thus our Chinese author begins with ideas that demand such a comprehensive understanding that a person of discriminating mind has the feeling he would be guilty of ridiculous pretension, or even of talking utter nonsense, if he should embark on an intellectual discourse on the subtle psychic experiences of the greatest minds of the East. Our text, for example, begins: "That which exists through itself is called the Way." The *Hui Ming Ching* begins with the words: "The subtlest secret of the Tao is human nature and life."

28   It is characteristic of the Western mind that it has no word for Tao. The Chinese character is made up of the sign for "head" and the sign for "going." Wilhelm translates Tao by *Sinn* (Meaning). Others translate it as "way," "providence," or even as "God," as the Jesuits do. This illustrates our difficulty. "Head" can be taken as consciousness,[2] and "going" as travelling a way, and the idea would then be: to go consciously, or the conscious way. This is borne out by the fact that the "light of heaven" which "dwells between the eyes" as the "heart of heaven" is used synonymously with Tao. Human nature and life are contained in the "light of heaven" and, according to the *Hui Ming Ching,* are the most important secrets of the Tao. "Light" is the symbolical equivalent of consciousness, and the nature of consciousness is expressed by analogies with light. The *Hui Ming Ching* is introduced with the verses:

1 Cf. the *Hui Ming Ching* (Book of Consciousness and Life) in *The Secret of the Golden Flower* (1962 edn.), pp. 69ff.
2 The head is also the "seat of heavenly light."

If thou wouldst complete the diamond body with no outflowing,
Diligently heat the roots of consciousness[3] and life.
Kindle light in the blessed country ever close at hand,
And there hidden, let thy true self always dwell.

29   These verses contain a sort of alchemical instruction as to the method or way of producing the "diamond body," which is also mentioned in our text. "Heating" is necessary; that is, there must be an intensification of consciousness in order that light may be kindled in the dwelling place of the true self. Not only consciousness, but life itself must be intensified: the union of these two produces conscious life. According to the *Hui Ming Ching*, the ancient sages knew how to bridge the gap between consciousness and life because they cultivated both. In this way the *sheli*, the immortal body, is "melted out" and the "great Tao is completed." [4]

30   If we take the Tao to be the method or conscious way by which to unite what is separated, we have probably come close to the psychological meaning of the concept. At all events, the separation of consciousness and life cannot very well be understood as anything else than what I described earlier as an aberration or uprooting of consciousness. There can be no doubt, either, that the realization of the opposite hidden in the unconscious—the process of "reversal"—signifies reunion with the unconscious laws of our being, and the purpose of this reunion is the attainment of conscious life or, expressed in Chinese terms, the realization of the Tao.

B. THE CIRCULAR MOVEMENT AND THE CENTRE

31   As I have pointed out, the union of opposites[5] on a higher level of consciousness is not a rational thing, nor is it a matter of will; it is a process of psychic development that expresses itself in symbols. Historically, this process has always been represented in symbols, and today the development of personality is still depicted in symbolic form. I discovered this fact in the following way. The spontaneous fantasy products I discussed earlier

3 In the *Hui Ming Ching*, "human nature" (*hsing*) and "consciousness" (*hui*) are used interchangeably.
4 *The Golden Flower* (1962 edn.), p. 70.
5 Cf. *Psychological Types*, ch. V.

become more profound and gradually concentrate into abstract structures that apparently represent "principles" in the sense of Gnostic *archai*. When the fantasies take the form chiefly of thoughts, intuitive formulations of dimly felt laws or principles emerge, which at first tend to be dramatized or personified. (We shall come back to these again later.) If the fantasies are drawn, symbols appear that are chiefly of the *mandala*[6] type. *Mandala* means "circle," more especially a magic circle. Mandalas are found not only throughout the East but also among us. The early Middle Ages are especially rich in Christian mandalas; most of them show Christ in the centre, with the four evangelists, or their symbols, at the cardinal points. This conception must be a very ancient one, because Horus and his four sons were represented in the same way by the Egyptians.[7] It is known that Horus with his four sons has close connections with Christ and the four evangelists. An unmistakable and very interesting mandala can be found in Jakob Böhme's book *XL Questions concerning the Soule*.[8] It is clear that this mandala represents a psychocosmic system strongly coloured by Christian ideas. Böhme calls it the "Philosophical Eye" [9] or the "Mirror of Wisdom," by which is obviously meant a *summa* of secret knowledge. Most mandalas take the form of a flower, cross, or wheel, and show a distinct tendency towards a quaternary structure reminiscent of the Pythagorean *tetraktys,* the basic number. Mandalas of this sort also occur as sand paintings in the religious ceremonies of the Pueblo and Navaho Indians.[10] But the most beautiful mandalas are, of course, those of the East, especially the ones found in Tibetan Buddhism, which also contain the symbols mentioned in our text. Mandala drawings are often produced by the mentally ill, among them persons who certainly

6 [For a fuller discussion of the *mandala*, see "A Study in the Process of Individuation" and "Concerning Mandala Symbolism" in *The Archetypes and the Collective Unconscious*. For examples of European mandalas, see below, after p. 56.—EDITORS.]

7 Cf. Wallis Budge, *The Gods of the Egyptians*.

8 [The mandala is reproduced in "A Study in the Process of Individuation," p. 297.]

9 Cf. the Chinese concept of the heavenly light between the eyes.

10 Matthews, "The Mountain Chant: A Navajo Ceremony" (1887), and Stevenson, "Ceremonial of Hasjelti Dailjis" (1891).

did not have the least idea of any of the connections we have discussed.[11]

32   Among my patients I have come across cases of women who did not draw mandalas but danced them instead. In India there is a special name for this: *mandala nrithya,* the mandala dance. The dance figures express the same meanings as the drawings. My patients can say very little about the meaning of the symbols but are fascinated by them and find that they somehow express and have an effect on their subjective psychic state.

33   Our text promises to "reveal the secret of the Golden Flower of the great *One."* The golden flower is the light, and the light of heaven is the Tao. The golden flower is a mandala symbol I have often met with in the material brought me by my patients. It is drawn either seen from above as a regular geometric pattern, or in profile as a blossom growing from a plant. The plant is frequently a structure in brilliant fiery colours growing out of a bed of darkness, and carrying the blossom of light at the top, a symbol recalling the Christmas tree. Such drawings also suggest the origin of the golden flower, for according to the *Hui Ming Ching* the "germinal vesicle" is the "dragon castle at the bottom of the sea." [12] Other synonyms are the "yellow castle," the "heavenly heart," the "terrace of living," the "square inch field of the square foot house," the "purple hall of the city of jade," the "dark pass," the "space of former heaven." [13] It is also called the "boundary region of the snow mountains," the "primordial pass," the "kingdom of greatest joy," the "boundless country," the "altar upon which consciousness and life are made." "If a dying man does not know this germinal vesicle," says the *Hui Ming Ching,* "he will not find the unity of consciousness and life in a thousand births, nor in ten thousand aeons." [14]

34   The beginning, where everything is still one, and which therefore appears as the highest goal, lies at the bottom of the sea, in the darkness of the unconscious. In the germinal vesicle, consciousness and life (or human nature and life, *hsing-ming*) are still a "unity, inseparably mixed like the sparks in the

11 The mandala of a somnambulist is reproduced in *Psychiatric Studies,* p. 40.
12 *The Golden Flower* (1962 edn.), p. 70.
13 [Ibid., p. 22.]
14 [Ibid., p. 70.]

refining furnace." "Within the germinal vesicle is the fire of the ruler." "All the sages began their work at the germinal vesicle." [15] Note the fire analogies. I know a series of European mandala drawings in which something like a plant seed surrounded by membranes is shown floating in the water. Then, from the depths below, fire penetrates the seed and makes it grow, causing a great golden flower to unfold from the germinal vesicle.

35 This symbolism refers to a quasi-alchemical process of refining and ennobling. Darkness gives birth to light; out of the "lead of the water region" grows the noble gold; what is unconscious becomes conscious in the form of a living process of growth. (Indian Kundalini yoga offers a perfect analogy.[16]) In this way the union of consciousness and life takes place.

36 When my patients produce these mandala pictures, it is naturally not the result of suggestion; similar pictures were being made long before I knew their meaning or their connection with the practices of the East, which, at that time, were wholly unknown to me. The pictures arise quite spontaneously, and from two sources. One source is the unconscious, which spontaneously produces fantasies of this kind; the other is life, which, if lived with utter devotion, brings an intuition of the self, of one's own individual being. When the self finds expression in such drawings, the unconscious reacts by enforcing an attitude of devotion to life. For in complete agreement with the Eastern view, the mandala is not only a means of expression but also produces an effect. It reacts upon its maker. Age-old magical effects lie hidden in this symbol, for it is derived from the "protective circle" or "charmed circle," whose magic has been preserved in countless folk customs.[17] It has the obvious purpose of drawing a *sulcus primigenius*, a magical furrow around the centre, the temple or *temenos* (sacred precinct), of the innermost personality, in order to prevent an "outflowing" or to guard by apotropaic means against distracting influences from outside. Magical practices are nothing but projections of psychic events, which then exert a counter-influence on the psyche and put a

15 [Ibid., p. 71.]
16 Cf. Avalon, *The Serpent Power.*
17 Cf. the excellent collection in Knuchel, *Die Umwandlung in Kult, Magie und Rechtsbrauch.*

kind of spell upon the personality. Through the ritual action, attention and interest are led back to the inner, sacred precinct, which is the source and goal of the psyche and contains the unity of life and consciousness. The unity once possessed has been lost, and must now be found again.

37 The unity of the two, life and consciousness, is the Tao, whose symbol would be the central white light, also mentioned in the *Bardo Thödol*.[18] This light dwells in the "square inch" or in the "face," that is, between the eyes. It is a visualization of the "creative point," of that which has intensity without extension, in conjunction with the "field of the square inch," the symbol for that which has extension. The two together make the Tao. Human nature (*hsing*) and consciousness (*hui*) are expressed in light symbolism, and therefore have the quality of intensity, while life (*ming*) would coincide with extensity. The one is *yang*-like, the other *yin*-like. The afore-mentioned mandala of a somnambulist girl, aged fifteen and a half, whom I had under observation some thirty years ago, shows in its centre a spring of "Primary Force," or life energy without extension, whose emanations clash with a contrary spatial principle—in complete analogy with the basic idea of our Chinese text.

38 The "enclosure," or *circumambulatio*, is expressed in our text by the idea of "circulation." The circulation is not merely movement in a circle, but means, on the one hand, the marking off of the sacred precinct and, on the other, fixation and concentration. The sun-wheel begins to turn; the sun is activated and begins its course—in other words, the Tao begins to work and takes the lead. Action is reversed into non-action; everything peripheral is subordinated to the command of the centre. Therefore it is said: "Movement is only another name for mastery." Psychologically, this circulation would be the "movement in a circle around oneself," so that all sides of the personality become involved. "The poles of light and darkness are made to rotate," that is, there is an alternation of day and night.

39 The circular movement thus has the moral significance of activating the light and dark forces of human nature, and together with them all psychological opposites of whatever kind they may be. It is nothing less than self-knowledge by means of self-

18 Evans-Wentz, *The Tibetan Book of the Dead.*

brooding (Sanskrit *tapas*). A similar archetypal concept of a perfect being is that of the Platonic man, round on all sides and uniting within himself the two sexes.

40   One of the best modern parallels is the description which Edward Maitland, the biographer of Anna Kingsford,[19] gave of his central experience. He had discovered that when reflecting on an idea, related ideas became visible, so to speak, in a long series apparently reaching back to their source, which to him was the divine spirit. By concentrating on this series, he tried to penetrate to their origin. He writes:

I was absolutely without knowledge or expectation when I yielded to the impulse to make the attempt. I simply experimented on a faculty . . . being seated at my writing-table the while in order to record the results as they came, and resolved to retain my hold on my outer and circumferential consciousness, no matter how far towards my inner and central consciousness I might go. For I knew not whether I should be able to regain the former if I once quitted my hold of it, or to recollect the facts of the experience. At length I achieved my object, though only by a strong effort, the tension occasioned by the endeavour to keep both extremes of the consciousness in view at once being very great.

Once well started on my quest, I found myself traversing a succession of spheres or belts . . . the impression produced being that of mounting a vast ladder stretching from the circumference towards the centre of a system, which was at once my own system, the solar system, the universal system, the three systems being at once diverse and identical. . . . Presently, by a supreme, and what I felt must be a final effort . . . I succeeded in polarizing the whole of the convergent rays of my consciousness into the desired focus. And at the same instant, as if through the sudden ignition of the rays thus fused into a unity, I found myself confronted with a glory of unspeakable whiteness and brightness, and of a lustre so intense as well-nigh to beat me back. . . . But though feeling that I had to explore further, I resolved to make assurance doubly sure by piercing if I could the almost blinding lustre, and seeing what it enshrined. With a great effort I succeeded, and the glance revealed to me that which I had felt must be there. . . . It was the dual form of the Son . . . the unmanifest made manifest, the unformulate formulate, the unindividuate individuate, God as the Lord, proving through His duality that God is Substance as well as Force, Love

[19] *Anna Kingsford, Her Life, Letters, Diary, and Work*, pp. 129f. I am indebted for this reference to my colleague, Dr. Beatrice Hinkle, New York.

as well as Will, Feminine as well as Masculine, Mother as well as Father.

41   He found that God is two in one, like man. Besides this he noticed something that our text also emphasizes, namely "suspension of breathing." He says ordinary breathing stopped and was replaced by an internal respiration, "as if by breathing of a distinct personality within and other than the physical organism." He took this being to be the "entelechy" of Aristotle and the "inner Christ" of the apostle Paul, the "spiritual and substantial individuality engendered within the physical and phenomenal personality, and representing, therefore, the rebirth of man on a plane transcending the material."

42   This genuine[20] experience contains all the essential symbols of our text. The phenomenon itself, the vision of light, is an experience common to many mystics, and one that is undoubtedly of the greatest significance, because at all times and places it proves to be something unconditioned and absolute, a combination of supreme power and profound meaning. Hildegard of Bingen, an outstanding personality quite apart from her mysticism, writes in much the same way about her central vision:

> Since my childhood I have always seen a light in my soul, but not with the outer eyes, nor through the thoughts of my heart; neither do the five outer senses take part in this vision. . . . The light I perceive is not of a local kind, but is much brighter than the cloud which supports the sun. I cannot distinguish height, breadth, or length in it. . . . What I see or learn in such a vision stays long in my memory. I see, hear, and know in the same moment. . . . I cannot recognize any sort of form in this light, although I sometimes see in it another light that is known to me as the living light. . . . While I am enjoying the spectacle of this light, all sadness and sorrow vanish from my memory.[21]

43   I myself know a few individuals who have had personal experience of this phenomenon. So far as I have been able to understand it, it seems to have to do with an acute state of consciousness, as intense as it is abstract, a "detached" consciousness

20 Such experiences are genuine, but their genuineness does not prove that all the conclusions or convictions forming their content are necessarily sound. Even in cases of lunacy one comes across perfectly valid psychic experiences. [Author's note added in the first (1931) English edition.]
21 [*Acta S. Hildegardis,* in Migne, *P.L.,* vol. 197, col. 18.]

(see infra, pars. 64ff.), which, as Hildegard implies, brings into awareness areas of psychic happenings ordinarily covered in darkness. The fact that the general bodily sensations disappear during the experience suggests that their specific energy has been withdrawn and has apparently gone towards heightening the clarity of consciousness. As a rule, the phenomenon is spontaneous, coming and going on its own initiative. Its effect is astonishing in that it almost always brings about a solution of psychic complications and frees the inner personality from emotional and intellectual entanglements, thus creating a unity of being which is universally felt as "liberation."

44   Such a symbolic unity cannot be attained by the conscious will because consciousness is always partisan. Its opponent is the collective unconscious, which does not understand the language of the conscious mind. Therefore it is necessary to have the magic of the symbol which contains those primitive analogies that speak to the unconscious. The unconscious can be reached and expressed only by symbols, and for this reason the process of individuation can never do without the symbol. The symbol is the primitive exponent of the unconscious, but at the same time an idea that corresponds to the highest intuitions of the conscious mind.

45   The oldest mandala drawing known to me is a palaeolithic "sun-wheel," recently discovered in Rhodesia. It, too, is based on the quaternary principle. Things reaching so far back into human history naturally touch upon the deepest layers of the unconscious, and can have a powerful effect on it even when our conscious language proves itself to be quite impotent. Such things cannot be thought up but must grow again from the forgotten depths if they are to express the supreme insights of consciousness and the loftiest intuitions of the spirit, and in this way fuse the uniqueness of present-day consciousness with the age-old past of life.

4. PHENOMENA OF THE WAY

A. THE DISINTEGRATION OF CONSCIOUSNESS

46   The meeting between the narrowly delimited, but intensely clear, individual consciousness and the vast expanse of the collective unconscious is dangerous, because the unconscious has a decidedly disintegrating effect on consciousness. According to the *Hui Ming Ching*, this effect belongs to the peculiar phenomena of Chinese yoga. It says: "Every separate thought takes shape and becomes visible in colour and form. The total spiritual power unfolds its traces. . . ."[1] The relevant illustration in the text [stage 4] shows a sage sunk in contemplation, his head surrounded by tongues of fire, out of which five human figures emerge; these five again split up into twenty-five smaller figures.[2] This would be a schizophrenic process if it were to become a permanent state. Therefore the *Hui Ming Ching*, as though warning the adept, continues: "The shapes formed by the spirit-fire are only empty colours and forms. The light of human nature (*hsing*) shines back on the primordial, the true."

47   So we can understand why the figure of the protecting circle was seized upon. It is intended to prevent the "outflowing" and to protect the unity of consciousness from being burst asunder by the unconscious. The text seeks to mitigate the disintegrating effect of the unconscious by describing the thought-figures as "empty colours and forms," thus depotentiating them as much as possible. This idea runs through the whole of Buddhism (especially the Mahayana form) and, in the instructions to the dead in *The Tibetan Book of the Dead*, it is even pushed to the point of explaining the favourable as well as the unfavourable gods as illusions still to be overcome. It is certainly not within the com-

---

[1] *The Golden Flower* (1962 edn.), pp. 76f. [For elucidation of the four pictures from the *Hui Ming Ching* reproduced here, see ibid., pp. 75–77.—EDITORS.]
[2] These are recollections of earlier incarnations that arise during contemplation.

Stage 1: Gathering the light

Pages 30–33:
Four stages of meditation,
with inspirational texts,
from the *Hui Ming Ching*

359

嬰兒現形圖

Stage 2: Origin of a new being in the place of power

端拱冥心圖

未到彼岸不能無法
既至彼岸又焉用法
頂中常放白毫光
癡人猶待問菩薩

道照於外
宅神於內
冥心至趣
而與吉會

元君端拱坐玄都
三疊胎仙舞八風
燮化純陽天地合
長生固此次工夫

無心於事
無事於心
超出萬幻
塊然一香

Stage 3: Separation of the spirit-body for independent existence

361

Stage 4: The centre in the midst of conditions

petence of the psychologist to establish the metaphysical truth or untruth of this idea; he must be content to determine so far as possible its psychic effect. He need not bother himself whether the shape in question is a transcendental illusion or not, since faith, not science, has to decide this point. In any case we are moving on ground that for a long time has seemed to be outside the domain of science and was looked upon as wholly illusory. But there is no scientific justification for such an assumption; the substantiality of these things is not a scientific problem since it lies beyond the range of human perception and judgment and thus beyond any possibility of proof. The psychologist is concerned not with the substantiality of these complexes but with psychic experience. Without a doubt they are psychic contents that can be experienced, and their autonomy is equally indubitable. They are fragmentary psychic systems that either appear spontaneously in ecstatic states and evoke powerful impressions and effects, or else, in mental disturbances, become fixed in the form of delusions and hallucinations and consequently destroy the unity of the personality.

48   Psychiatrists are always ready to believe in toxins and the like, and even to explain schizophrenia in these terms, putting next to no emphasis on the psychic contents as such. On the other hand, in psychogenic disturbances (hysteria, obsessional neurosis, etc.), where toxic effects and cell degeneration are out of the question, split-off complexes are to be found similar to those occurring in somnambulistic states. Freud would like to explain these spontaneous split-offs as due to unconscious repression of sexuality, but this explanation is by no means valid in all cases, because contents that the conscious mind cannot assimilate can emerge just as spontaneously out of the unconscious, and in these cases the repression theory is inadequate. Moreover, their autonomy can be observed in daily life, in affects that obstinately obtrude themselves against our will and, in spite of the most strenuous efforts to repress them, overwhelm the ego and force it under their control. No wonder the primitive sees in these moods a state of possession or sets them down to a loss of soul. Our colloquial speech reflects the same thing when we say: "I don't know what has got into him today," "he is possessed of the devil," "he is beside himself," etc. Even legal practice recognizes a degree of diminished responsibility in a state of affect.

Autonomous psychic contents are thus quite common experiences for us. Such contents have a disintegrating effect upon consciousness.

49   But besides the ordinary, familiar affects there are subtler, more complex emotional states that can no longer be described as affects pure and simple but are fragmentary psychic systems. The more complicated they are, the more they have the character of personalities. As constituents of the psychic personality, they necessarily have the character of "persons." Such fragmentary systems are to be found especially in mental diseases, in cases of psychogenic splitting of the personality (double personality), and of course in mediumistic phenomena. They are also encountered in the phenomenology of religion. Many of the earlier gods developed from "persons" into personified ideas, and finally into abstract ideas. Activated unconscious contents always appear at first as projections upon the outside world, but in the course of mental development they are gradually assimilated by consciousness and reshaped into conscious ideas that then forfeit their originally autonomous and personal character. As we know, some of the old gods have become, via astrology, nothing more than descriptive attributes (martial, jovial, saturnine, erotic, logical, lunatic, and so on).

50   The instructions of *The Tibetan Book of the Dead* in particular help us to see how great is the danger that consciousness will be disintegrated by these figures. Again and again the dead are instructed not to take these shapes for truth, not to confuse their murky appearance with the pure white light of *Dharmakaya* (the divine body of truth). That is to say, they are not to project the *one* light of highest consciousness into concretized figures and dissolve it into a plurality of autonomous fragmentary systems. If there were no danger of this, and if these systems did not represent menacingly autonomous and disintegrative tendencies, such urgent instructions would not be necessary. Allowing for the simpler, polytheistic attitude of the Eastern mind, these instructions would be almost the equivalent of warning a Christian not to let himself be blinded by the illusion of a personal God, let alone by the Trinity and the host of angels and saints.

51   If tendencies towards dissociation were not inherent in the human psyche, fragmentary psychic systems would never have

been split off; in other words, neither spirits nor gods would ever have come into existence. That is also the reason why our time has become so utterly godless and profane: we lack all knowledge of the unconscious psyche and pursue the cult of consciousness to the exclusion of all else. Our true religion is a monotheism of consciousness, a possession by it, coupled with a fanatical denial of the existence of fragmentary autonomous systems. But we differ from the Buddhist yoga doctrines in that we even deny that these systems are experienceable. This entails a great psychic danger, because the autonomous systems then behave like any other repressed contents: they necessarily induce wrong attitudes since the repressed material reappears in consciousness in a spurious form. This is strikingly evident in every case of neurosis and also holds true for the collective psychic phenomena. Our time has committed a fatal error; we believe we can criticize the facts of religion intellectually. Like Laplace, we think God is a hypothesis that can be subjected to intellectual treatment, to be affirmed or denied. We completely forget that the reason mankind believes in the "daemon" has nothing whatever to do with external factors, but is simply due to a naïve awareness of the tremendous inner effect of autonomous fragmentary systems. This effect is not abolished by criticizing it—or rather, the name we have given it—or by describing the name as false. The effect is collectively present all the time; the autonomous systems are always at work, for the fundamental structure of the unconscious is not affected by the deviations of our ephemeral consciousness.

52 If we deny the existence of the autonomous systems, imagining that we have got rid of them by a mere critique of the name, then the effect which they still continue to exert can no longer be understood, nor can they be assimilated to consciousness. They become an inexplicable source of disturbance which we finally assume must exist somewhere outside ourselves. The resultant projection creates a dangerous situation in that the disturbing effects are now attributed to a wicked will outside ourselves, which is naturally not to be found anywhere but with our neighbour *de l'autre côté de la rivière*. This leads to collective delusions, "incidents," revolutions, war—in a word, to destructive mass psychoses.

53 Insanity is possession by an unconscious content that, as

such, is not assimilated to consciousness, nor can it be assimilated since the very existence of such contents is denied. This attitude is equivalent to saying: "We no longer have any fear of God and believe that everything is to be judged by human standards." This hybris or narrowness of consciousness is always the shortest way to the insane asylum. I recommend the excellent account of this problem in H. G. Wells's novel *Christina Alberta's Father,* and Schreber's *Memoirs of My Nervous Illness.*

54   It must stir a sympathetic chord in the enlightened European when it is said in the *Hui Ming Ching* that the "shapes formed by the spirit-fire are only empty colours and forms." That sounds thoroughly European and seems to suit our reason to a T. We think we can congratulate ourselves on having already reached such a pinnacle of clarity, imagining that we have left all these phantasmal gods far behind. But what we have left behind are only verbal spectres, not the psychic facts that were responsible for the birth of the gods. We are still as much possessed by autonomous psychic contents as if they were Olympians. Today they are called phobias, obsessions, and so forth; in a word, neurotic symptoms. The gods have become diseases; Zeus no longer rules Olympus but rather the solar plexus, and produces curious specimens for the doctor's consulting room, or disorders the brains of politicians and journalists who unwittingly let loose psychic epidemics on the world.

55   So it is better for Western man if he does not know too much about the secret insights of the Oriental sages to begin with, for, as I have said, it would be a case of the "right means in the hands of the wrong man." Instead of allowing himself to be convinced once more that the daemon is an illusion, he ought to experience once more the reality of this illusion. He should learn to acknowledge these psychic forces anew, and not wait until his moods, nervous states, and delusions make it clear in the most painful way that he is not the only master in his house. His dissociative tendencies are actual psychic personalities possessing a differential reality. They are "real" when they are not recognized as real and consequently projected; they are relatively real when they are brought into relationship with consciousness (in religious terms, when a cult exists); but they are unreal to the extent that consciousness detaches itself from its contents. This last stage, however, is reached only when life has been lived so

366

exhaustively and with such devotion that no obligations remain unfulfilled, when no desires that cannot safely be sacrificed stand in the way of inner detachment from the world. It is futile to lie to ourselves about this. Wherever we are still attached, we are still possessed; and when we are possessed, there is one stronger than us who possesses us. ("Verily I say unto thee, thou shalt by no means come out thence, until thou hast paid the uttermost farthing.") It is not a matter of indifference whether one calls something a "mania" or a "god." To serve a mania is detestable and undignified, but to serve a god is full of meaning and promise because it is an act of submission to a higher, invisible, and spiritual being. The personification enables us to see the relative reality of the autonomous system, and not only makes its assimilation possible but also depotentiates the daemonic forces of life. When the god is not acknowledged, egomania develops, and out of this mania comes sickness.

56   Yoga takes acknowledgment of the gods as something self-evident. Its secret instruction is intended only for those whose consciousness is struggling to disentangle itself from the daemonic forces of life in order to enter into the ultimate undivided unity, the "centre of emptiness," where "dwells the god of utmost emptiness and life," as our text says.[3] "To hear such a teaching is difficult to attain in thousands of aeons." Evidently the veil of Maya cannot be lifted by a merely rational resolve; it requires a most thoroughgoing and persevering preparation consisting in the full payment of all debts to life. For as long as unconditional attachment through *cupiditas* exists, the veil is not lifted and the heights of a consciousness free of contents and free of illusion are not attained; nor can any trick nor any deceit bring this about. It is an ideal that can ultimately be realized only in death. Until then there are the real and relatively real figures of the unconscious.

B. ANIMUS AND ANIMA

57   According to our text, among the figures of the unconscious there are not only the gods but also the animus and anima. The word *hun* is translated by Wilhelm as animus. And indeed, the term "animus" seems appropriate for *hun,* the character for

[3] [*The Golden Flower,* p. 22.]

which is made up of the sign for "clouds" and that for "demon."
Thus *hun* means "cloud-demon," a higher breath-soul belonging to the *yang* principle and therefore masculine. After death,
hun rises upward and becomes *shen,* the "expanding and self-
revealing" spirit or god. "Anima," called *p'o,* and written with
the characters for "white" and "demon," that is, "white ghost,"
belongs to the lower, earthbound, bodily soul, the *yin* principle,
and is therefore feminine. After death, it sinks downward and
becomes *kuei* (demon), often explained as "the one who returns" (i.e., to earth), a revenant, a ghost. The fact that the
animus and anima part after death and go their ways independently shows that, for the Chinese consciousness, they are distinguishable psychic factors; originally they were united in "the
one effective, true human nature," but in the "house of the Creative" they are two. "The animus is in the heavenly heart." "By
day it lives in the eyes [i.e., in consciousness]; at night it houses
in the liver." It is "that which we have received from the great
emptiness, that which is identical in form with the primal beginning." The anima, on the other hand, is the "energy of the
heavy and the turbid"; it clings to the bodily, fleshly heart. Its
effects are "sensuous desires and impulses to anger." "Whoever
is sombre and moody on waking . . . is fettered to the anima." [4]

58   Many years ago, before Wilhelm acquainted me with this
text, I used the term "anima" [5] in a way quite analogous to the
Chinese definition of *p'o,* and of course entirely apart from any
metaphysical premise. To the psychologist, the anima is not a
transcendental being but something quite within the range of
experience, as the Chinese definition makes clear: affective states
are immediate experiences. Why, then, speak of the anima and
not simply of moods? The reason is that affects have an autonomous character, and therefore most people are under their
power. But affects are delimitable contents of consciousness,
parts of the personality. As such, they partake of its character
and can easily be personified—a process that still continues today, as I have shown. The personification is not an idle invention, since a person roused by affect does not show a neutral
character but a quite distinct one, entirely different from his
ordinary character. Careful investigation has shown that the

4 [*The Golden Flower,* pp. 26 and 28.]
5 Cf. *Two Essays on Analytical Psychology,* pars. 296ff.

affective character of a man has feminine traits. From this psychological fact derives the Chinese doctrine of the *p'o* soul as well as my own concept of the anima. Deeper introspection or ecstatic experience reveals the existence of a feminine figure in the unconscious, hence the feminine name: anima, psyche, *Seele.* The anima can be defined as the image or archetype or deposit of all the experiences of man with woman. As we know, the poets have often sung the anima's praises.[6] The connection of anima with ghost in the Chinese concept is of interest to parapsychologists inasmuch as mediumistic "controls" are very often of the opposite sex.

59   Although Wilhelm's translation of *hun* as "animus" seems justified to me, nonetheless I had important reasons for choosing the term "Logos" for a man's "spirit," for his clarity of consciousness and his rationality, rather than the otherwise appropriate expression "animus." Chinese philosophers are spared certain difficulties that aggravate the task of the Western psychologist. Like all mental and spiritual activity in ancient times, Chinese philosophy was exclusively a component of the masculine world. Its concepts were never understood psychologically, and therefore were never examined as to how far they also apply to the feminine psyche. But the psychologist cannot possibly ignore the existence of woman and her special psychology. For these reasons I would prefer to translate *hun* as it appears in man by "Logos." Wilhelm in his translation uses Logos for *hsing,* which can also be translated as "essence of human nature" or "creative consciousness." After death, *hun* becomes *shen,* "spirit," which is very close, in the philosophical sense, to *hsing.* Since the Chinese concepts are not logical in our sense of the word, but are intuitive ideas, their meanings can only be elicited from the ways in which they are used and from the constitution of the written characters, or from such relationships as obtain between *hun* and *shen. Hun,* then, would be the light of consciousness and reason in man, originally coming from the *logos spermatikos* of *hsing,* and returning after death through *shen* to the Tao. Used in this sense the expression "Logos" would be especially appropriate, since it includes the idea of a universal being, and thus covers the fact that man's clarity of consciousness and rationality are something universal rather than indi-

[6] Cf. *Psychological Types,* ch. V.

vidually unique. The Logos principle is nothing personal, but is in the deepest sense impersonal, and thus in sharp contrast to the anima, which is a personal demon expressing itself in thoroughly personal moods ("animosity"!).

60   In view of these psychological facts, I have reserved the term "animus" strictly for women, because, to answer a famous question, *mulier non habet animam, sed animum.* Feminine psychology exhibits an element that is the counterpart of a man's anima. Primarily, it is not of an affective nature but is a quasi-intellectual factor best described by the word "prejudice." The conscious side of woman corresponds to the emotional side of man, not to his "mind." Mind makes up the "soul," or better, the "animus" of woman, and just as the anima of a man consists of inferior relatedness, full of affect, so the animus of woman consists of inferior judgments, or better, opinions. As it is made up of a plurality of preconceived opinions, the animus is far less susceptible of personification by a single figure, but appears more often as a group or crowd. (A good example of this from parapsychology is the "Imperator" group in the case of Mrs. Piper.[7]) On a low level the animus is an inferior Logos, a caricature of the differentiated masculine mind, just as on a low level the anima is a caricature of the feminine Eros. To pursue the parallel further, we could say that just as *hun* corresponds to *hsing,* translated by Wilhelm as Logos, so the Eros of woman corresponds to *ming,* "fate" or "destiny," interpreted by Wilhelm as Eros. Eros is an interweaving; Logos is differentiating knowledge, clarifying light. Eros is relatedness, Logos is discrimination and detachment. Hence the inferior Logos of woman's animus appears as something quite unrelated, as an inaccessible prejudice, or as an opinion which, irritatingly enough, has nothing to do with the essential nature of the object.

61   I have often been accused of personifying the anima and animus as mythology does, but this accusation would be justified only if it could be proved that I concretize these concepts in a mythological manner for psychological use. I must declare once and for all that the personification is not an invention of mine,

---

[7] Cf. Hyslop, *Science and a Future Life,* pp. 113ff. [Mrs. Leonora Piper, an American psychic medium active about 1890–1910 in the U.S. and England, was studied by William James, Mrs. Henry Sidgwick, Hyslop, and others. A group of five of her psychic controls had the collective name "Imperator."—EDITORS.]

but is inherent in the nature of the phenomena. It would be unscientific to overlook the fact that the anima is a psychic, and therefore a personal, autonomous system. None of the people who make the charge against me would hesitate for a second to say, "I dreamed of Mr. X," whereas, strictly speaking, he dreamed only of a representation of Mr. X. The anima is nothing but a representation of the personal nature of the autonomous system in question. What the nature of this system is in a transcendental sense, that is, beyond the bounds of experience, we cannot know.

62   I have defined the anima as a personification of the unconscious in general, and have taken it as a bridge to the unconscious, in other words, as a function of relationship to the unconscious. There is an interesting point in our text in this connection. The text says that consciousness (that is, the personal consciousness) comes from the anima. Since the Western mind is based wholly on the standpoint of consciousness, it must define the anima in the way I have done. But the East, based as it is on the standpoint of the unconscious, sees consciousness as an effect of the anima. And there can be no doubt that consciousness does originate in the unconscious. This is something we are apt to forget, and therefore we are always attempting to identify the psyche with consciousness, or at least to represent the unconscious as a derivative or an effect of consciousness (as in the Freudian repression theory). But, for the reasons given above, it is essential that we do not detract from the reality of the unconscious, and that the figures of the unconscious be understood as real and effective factors. The person who has understood what is meant by psychic reality need have no fear that he has fallen back into primitive demonology. If the unconscious figures are not acknowledged as spontaneous agents, we become victims of a one-sided belief in the power of consciousness, leading finally to acute tension. A catastrophe is then bound to happen because, for all our consciousness, the dark powers of the psyche have been overlooked. It is not we who personify them; they have a personal nature from the very beginning. Only when this is thoroughly recognized can we think of depersonalizing them, of "subjugating the anima," as our text expresses it.

63   Here again we find an enormous difference between Buddhism and the Western attitude of mind, and again there is a

dangerous semblance of agreement. Yoga teaching rejects all fantasy products and we do the same, but the East does so for entirely different reasons. In the East there is an abundance of conceptions and teachings that give full expression to the creative fantasy; in fact, protection is needed against an excess of it. We, on the other hand, regard fantasy as worthless subjective day-dreaming. Naturally the figures of the unconscious do not appear in the form of abstractions stripped of all imaginative trappings; on the contrary, they are embedded in a web of fantasies of extraordinary variety and bewildering profusion. The East can reject these fantasies because it has long since extracted their essence and condensed it in profound teachings. But we have never even experienced these fantasies, much less extracted their quintessence. We still hav : a large stretch of experience to catch up with, and only when we have found the sense in apparent nonsense can we separate the valuable from the worthless. We can be sure that the essence we extract from our experience will be quite different from what the East offers us today. The East came to its knowledge of inner things in childlike ignorance of the external world. We, on the other hand, shall explore the psyche and its depths supported by an immense knowledge of history and science. At present our knowledge of the external world is the greatest obstacle to introspection, but the psychological need will overcome all obstructions. We are already building up a psychology, a science that gives us the key to the very things that the East discovered—and discovered only through abnormal psychic states.

5. THE DETACHMENT OF CONSCIOUSNESS FROM THE OBJECT

64 By understanding the unconscious we free ourselves from its domination. That is really also the purpose of the instructions in our text. The pupil is taught to concentrate on the light of the innermost region and, at the same time, to free himself from all outer and inner entanglements. His vital impulses are guided towards a consciousness void of content, which nevertheless permits all contents to exist. The *Hui Ming Ching*[1] says of this detachment:

A halo of light surrounds the world of the law.
We forget one another, quiet and pure, all-powerful and empty.
The emptiness is irradiated by the light of the heart of heaven.
The water of the sea is smooth and mirrors the moon in its surface.
The clouds disappear in blue space; the mountains shine clear.
Consciousness reverts to contemplation; the moon-disk rests alone.

65 This description of fulfilment depicts a psychic state that can best be characterized as a detachment of consciousness from the world and a withdrawal to a point outside it, so to speak. Thus consciousness is at the same time empty and not empty. It is no longer preoccupied with the images of things but merely contains them. The fullness of the world which hitherto pressed upon it has lost none of its richness and beauty, but it no longer dominates. The magical claim of things has ceased because the interweaving of consciousness with world has come to an end. The unconscious is not projected any more, and so the primordial *participation mystique* with things is abolished. Consciousness is no longer preoccupied with compulsive plans but dissolves in contemplative vision.

66 How did this effect come about? (We assume, of course, that the Chinese author was first of all not a liar; secondly, that he was of sound mind; and thirdly, that he was an unusually intel-

1 [*The Golden Flower* (1962 edn.), pp. 77f.]

.) To understand and explain this detachment, we
ₑₑd by a roundabout way. It is an effect that cannot be
ₓ; nothing would be more childish than to make such a
state an object of aesthetic experiment. I know this effect
ₗl from my practice; it is the therapeutic effect *par excellence,* for which I labour with my students and patients, and it
consists in the dissolution of *participation mystique.* By a stroke
of genius, Lévy-Bruhl singled out what he called *participation
mystique* as being the hallmark of the primitive mentality.[2]
What he meant by it is simply the indefinitely large remnant of
non-differentiation between subject and object, which is still so
great among primitives that it cannot fail to strike our European consciousness very forcibly. When there is no consciousness
of the difference between subject and object, an unconscious
identity prevails. The unconscious is then projected into the object, and the object is introjected into the subject, becoming part
of his psychology. Then plants and animals behave like human
beings, human beings are at the same time animals, and everything is alive with ghosts and gods. Civilized man naturally
thinks he is miles above these things. Instead of that, he is often
identified with his parents throughout his life, or with his affects
and prejudices, and shamelessly accuses others of the things he
will not see in himself. He too has a remnant of primitive unconsciousness, of non-differentiation between subject and object. Because of this, he is magically affected by all manner of
people, things, and circumstances, he is beset by disturbing influences nearly as much as the primitive and therefore needs just
as many apotropaic charms. He no longer works magic with
medicine bags, amulets, and animal sacrifices, but with tranquil-
lizers, neuroses, rationalism, cult of the will, etc.

⁶7   But if the unconscious can be recognized as a co-determining
factor along with consciousness, and if we can live in such a way
that conscious and unconscious demands are taken into account
as far as possible, then the centre of gravity of the total personality shifts its position. It is then no longer in the ego, which is
merely the centre of consciousness, but in the hypothetical point
between conscious and unconscious. This new centre might be
called the self. If the transposition is successful, it does away with
the *participation mystique* and results in a personality that

2 Lévy-Bruhl, *Primitive Mentality.*

374

suffers only in the lower storeys, as it were, but in its upper storeys is singularly detached from painful as well as from joyful happenings.

68   The production and birth of this superior personality is what is meant when our text speaks of the "holy fruit," the "diamond body," or any other kind of incorruptible body. Psychologically, these expressions symbolize an attitude that is beyond the reach of emotional entanglements and violent shocks—a consciousness detached from the world. I have reasons for believing that this attitude sets in after middle life and is a natural preparation for death. Death is psychologically as important as birth and, like it, is an integral part of life. What happens to the detached consciousness in the end is a question the psychologist cannot be expected to answer. Whatever his theoretical position he would hopelessly overstep the bounds of his scientific competence. He can only point out that the views of our text in regard to the timelessness of the detached consciousness are in harmony with the religious thought of all ages and with that of the overwhelming majority of mankind. Anyone who thought differently would be standing outside the human order and would, therefore, be suffering from a disturbed psychic equilibrium. As a doctor, I make every effort to strengthen the belief in immortality, especially with older patients when such questions come threateningly close. For, seen in correct psychological perspective, death is not an end but a goal, and life's inclination towards death begins as soon as the meridian is passed.

69   Chinese yoga philosophy is based upon this instinctive preparation for death as a goal. In analogy with the goal of the first half of life—procreation and reproduction, the means of perpetuating one's physical existence—it takes as the goal of spiritual existence the symbolic begetting and birth of a "spirit-body," or "breath-body," which ensures the continuity of detached consciousness. It is the birth of the pneumatic man, known to the European from antiquity, but which he seeks to produce by quite other symbols and magical practices, by faith and a Christian way of life. Here again we stand on a foundation quite different from that of the East. Again the text sounds as though it were not so very far from Christian ascetic morality, but nothing could be more mistaken than to assume that it actually means the same thing. Behind our text is a civilization thou-

375

sands of years old, one which is built up organically on primitive instincts and knows nothing of that brutal morality so suited to us as recently civilized Teutonic barbarians. For this reason the Chinese are without the impulse towards violent repression of the instincts that poisons our spirituality and makes it hysterically exaggerated. The man who lives with his instincts can also detach from them, and in just as natural a way as he lived with them. Any idea of heroic self-conquest would be entirely foreign to the spirit of our text, but that is what it would infallibly amount to if we followed the instructions literally.

70   We must never forget our historical antecedents. Only a little more than a thousand years ago we stumbled out of the crudest beginnings of polytheism into a highly developed Oriental religion which lifted the imaginative minds of half-savages to a height that in no way corresponded to their spiritual development. In order to keep to this height in some fashion or other, it was inevitable that the instinctual sphere should be largely repressed. Thus religious practice and morality took on a decidedly brutal, almost malignant, character. The repressed elements naturally did not develop, but went on vegetating in the unconscious, in their original barbarism. We would like to scale the heights of a philosophical religion, but in fact are incapable of it. To grow up to it is the most we can hope for. The Amfortas wound and the Faustian split in the Germanic man are still not healed; his unconscious is still loaded with contents that must first be made conscious before he can be free of them. Recently I received a letter from a former patient which describes the necessary transformation in simple but trenchant words. She writes:

Out of evil, much good has come to me. By keeping quiet, repressing nothing, remaining attentive, and by accepting reality—taking things as they are, and not as I wanted them to be—by doing all this, unusual knowledge has come to me, and unusual powers as well, such as I could never have imagined before. I always thought that when we accepted things they overpowered us in some way or other. This turns out not to be true at all, and it is only by accepting them that one can assume an attitude towards them.[3] So now I intend to play the game of life, being receptive to whatever comes to me, good and bad, sun and shadow forever alternating, and, in

[3] Dissolution of *participation mystique*.

this way, also accepting my own nature with its positive and negative sides. Thus everything becomes more alive to me. What a fool I was! How I tried to force everything to go according to the way I thought it ought to!

71   Only on the basis of such an attitude, which renounces none of the Christian values won in the course of Christian development, but which, on the contrary, tries with Christian charity and forbearance to accept even the humblest things in one's own nature, will a higher level of consciousness and culture become possible. This attitude is religious in the truest sense, and therefore therapeutic, for all religions are therapies for the sorrows and disorders of the soul. The development of the Western intellect and will has given us an almost fiendish capacity for aping such an attitude, with apparent success, despite the protests of the unconscious. But it is only a matter of time before the counterposition asserts itself all the more harshly. Aping an attitude always produces an unstable situation that can be overthrown by the unconscious at any time. A safe foundation is found only when the instinctive premises of the unconscious win the same respect as the views of the conscious mind. No one should blind himself to the fact that this necessity of giving due consideration to the unconscious runs violently counter to our Western, and in particular the Protestant, cult of consciousness. Yet, though the new always seems to be the enemy of the old, anyone with a more than superficial desire to understand cannot fail to discover that without the most serious application of the Christian values we have acquired, the new integration can never take place.

6. THE FULFILMENT

72   A growing familiarity with the spirit of the East should be taken merely as a sign that we are beginning to relate to the alien elements within ourselves. Denial of our historical foundations would be sheer folly and would be the best way to bring about another uprooting of consciousness. Only by standing firmly on our own soil can we assimilate the spirit of the East.

73   Speaking of those who do not know where the true springs of secret power lie, an ancient adept says, "Worldly people lose their roots and cling to the treetops." The spirit of the East has grown out of the yellow earth, and our spirit can, and should, grow only out of our own earth. That is why I approach these problems in a way that has often been charged with "psychologism." If "psychology" were meant, I should indeed be flattered, for my aim as a psychologist is to dismiss without mercy the metaphysical claims of all esoteric teachings. The unavowed purpose of gaining power through words, inherent in all secret doctrines, ill accords with our profound ignorance, which we should have the modesty to admit. I quite deliberately bring everything that purports to be metaphysical into the daylight of psychological understanding, and do my best to prevent people from believing in nebulous power-words. Let the convinced Christian believe, by all means, for that is the duty he has taken upon himself; but whoever is not a Christian has forfeited the charisma of faith. (Perhaps he was cursed from birth with not being able to believe, but merely to know.) Therefore, he has no right to put his faith elsewhere. One cannot grasp anything metaphysically, one only can do so psychologically. Therefore I strip things of their metaphysical wrappings in order to make them objects of psychology. In that way I can at least extract something understandable from them and avail myself of it, and I also discover psychological facts and processes that before were veiled in symbols and beyond my comprehension. In doing so I

may perhaps be following in the footsteps of the faithful, and may possibly have similar experiences; and if in the end there should be something ineffably metaphysical behind it all, it would then have the best opportunity of showing itself.

74   My admiration for the great philosophers of the East is as genuine as my attitude towards their metaphysics is irreverent.[1] I suspect them of being symbolical psychologists, to whom no greater wrong could be done than to take them literally. If it were really metaphysics that they mean, it would be useless to try to understand them. But if it is psychology, we can not only understand them but can profit greatly by them, for then the so-called "metaphysical" comes within the range of experience. If I assume that God is absolute and beyond all human experience, he leaves me cold. I do not affect him, nor does he affect me. But if I know that he is a powerful impulse of my soul, at once I must concern myself with him, for then he can become important, even unpleasantly so, and can affect me in practical ways—which sounds horribly banal, like everything else that is real.

75   The epithet "psychologism" applies only to a fool who thinks he has his soul in his pocket. There are certainly more than enough such fools, for although we know how to talk big about the "soul," the depreciation of everything psychic is a typically Western prejudice. If I make use of the concept "autonomous psychic complex," my reader immediately comes up with the ready-made prejudice that it is "nothing but a psychic complex." How can we be so sure that the soul is "nothing but"? It is as if we did not know, or else continually forgot, that everything of which we are conscious is an image, and that image *is* psyche. The same people who think that God is depreciated if he is understood as something moved in the psyche, as well as the moving force of the psyche—i.e., as an autonomous complex—can be so plagued by uncontrollable affects and neurotic states that their wills and their whole philosophy of life fail them miserably. Is that a proof of the impotence of the psyche? Should Meister Eckhart be accused of "psychologism" when he says, "God must be born in the soul again and again"? I think the accusation of "psychologism" can be levelled only at an intellect

1 The Chinese philosophers—in contrast to the dogmatists of the West—are only grateful for such an attitude, because they also are masters of their gods. [Note by Richard Wilhelm in original edn.]

379

that denies the genuine nature of the autonomous complex and seeks to explain it rationalistically as the consequence of known causes, i.e., as something secondary and unreal. This is just as arrogant as the metaphysical assertion that seeks to make a God outside the range of our experience responsible for our psychic states. Psychologism is simply the counterpart of this metaphysical presumption, and is just as childish. Therefore it seems to me far more reasonable to accord the psyche the same validity as the empirical world, and to admit that the former has just as much "reality" as the latter. As I see it, the psyche is a world in which the ego is contained. Maybe there are fishes who believe that they contain the sea. We must rid ourselves of this habitual illusion of ours if we wish to consider metaphysical assertions from the standpoint of psychology.

76   A metaphysical assertion of this kind is the idea of the "diamond body," the incorruptible breath-body which grows in the golden flower or in the "field of the square inch." [2] This body is

2 Our text is somewhat unclear as to whether by "continuation of life" a survival after death or a prolongation of physical existence is meant. Expressions such as "elixir of life" and the like are exceedingly ambiguous. In the later additions to the text it is evident that the yoga instructions were also understood in a purely physical sense. To a primitive mind, there is nothing disturbing in this odd mixture of the physical and the spiritual, because life and death are by no means the complete opposites they are for us. (Particularly interesting in this connection, apart from the ethnological material, are the communications of the English "rescue circles" with their thoroughly archaic ideas.) The same ambiguity with regard to survival after death is found in early Christianity, where immortality depends on very similar assumptions, i.e., on the idea of a breath-body as the carrier of life. (Geley's paraphysiological theory would be the latest incarnation of this ancient idea.) But since in our text there are warnings about the superstitious use of it—warnings, for example, against the making of gold—we can safely insist on the spiritual purport of the instructions without contradicting their meaning. In the states which the instructions seek to induce the physical body plays an increasingly unimportant part anyway, since it is replaced by the breath-body (hence the importance of breath control in all yoga exercises). The breath-body is not something "spiritual" in our sense of the word. It is characteristic of Western man that he has split apart the physical and the spiritual for epistemological purposes. But these opposites exist together in the psyche and psychology must recognize this fact. "Psychic" means physical *and* spiritual. The ideas in our text all deal with this "intermediate" world which seems unclear and confused because the concept of psychic reality is not yet current among us, although it expresses life as it actually is. Without soul, spirit is as dead as matter, because both are artificial abstractions; whereas man originally regarded spirit as a volatile body, and matter as not lacking in soul.

a symbol for a remarkable psychological fact which, precisely because it is objective, first appears in forms dictated by the experience of biological life—that is, as fruit, embryo, child, living
body, and so on. This fact could be best expressed by the words
"It is not I who live, it lives me." The illusion of the supremacy
of consciousness makes us say, "I live." Once this illusion is shattered by a recognition of the unconscious, the unconscious will
appear as something objective in which the ego is included.
The attitude towards the unconscious is then analogous to the
feeling of the primitive to whom the existence of a son guarantees continuation of life—a feeling that can assume grotesque
forms, as when the old Negro, angered at his son's disobedience,
cried out, "There he stands with my body, but does not even
obey me!"

77   It is, in fact, a change of feeling similar to that experienced
by a father to whom a son has been born, a change known to us
from the testimony of St. Paul: "Yet not I, but Christ liveth in
me." The symbol "Christ" as "son of man" is an analogous
psychic experience of a higher spiritual being who is invisibly
born in the individual, a pneumatic body which is to serve us as
a future dwelling, a body which, as Paul says, is put on like a
garment ("For as many of you as have been baptized into Christ
have put on Christ"). It is always a difficult thing to express, in
intellectual terms, subtle feelings that are nevertheless infinitely
important for the individual's life and well-being. It is, in a
sense, the feeling that we have been "replaced," but without the
connotation of having been "deposed." It is as if the guidance of
life had passed over to an invisible centre. Nietzsche's metaphor,
"in most loving bondage, free," would be appropriate here. Religious language is full of imagery depicting this feeling of free
dependence, of calm acceptance.

78   This remarkable experience seems to me a consequence of
the detachment of consciousness, thanks to which the subjective
"I live" becomes the objective "It lives me." This state is felt to
be higher than the previous one; it is really like a sort of release from the compulsion and impossible responsibility that are
the inevitable results of *participation mystique*. This feeling of
liberation fills Paul completely; the consciousness of being a
child of God delivers one from the bondage of the blood. It is
also a feeling of reconciliation with all that happens, for which

reason, according to the *Hui Ming Ching,* the gaze of one who has attained fulfilment turns back to the beauty of nature.

79   In the Pauline Christ symbol the supreme religious experiences of West and East confront one another: Christ the sorrow-laden hero, and the Golden Flower that blooms in the purple hall of the city of jade. What a contrast, what an unfathomable difference, what an abyss of history! A problem fit for the crowning work of a future psychologist!

80   Among the great religious problems of the present is one which has received scant attention, but which is in fact the main problem of our day: the evolution of the religious spirit. If we are to discuss it, we must emphasize the difference between East and West in their treatment of the "jewel," the central symbol. The West lays stress on the human incarnation, and even on the personality and historicity of Christ, whereas the East says: "Without beginning, without end, without past, without future." [3] The Christian subordinates himself to the superior divine person in expectation of his grace; but the Oriental knows that redemption depends on the work he does on himself. The Tao grows out of the individual. The *imitatio Christi* has this disadvantage: in the long run we worship as a divine example a man who embodied the deepest meaning of life, and then, out of sheer imitation, we forget to make real our own deepest meaning—self-realization. As a matter of fact, it is not altogether inconvenient to renounce one's own meaning. Had Jesus done so, he would probably have become a respectable carpenter and not a religious rebel to whom the same thing would naturally happen today as happened then.

81   The imitation of Christ might well be understood in a deeper sense. It could be taken as the duty to realize one's deepest conviction with the same courage and the same self-sacrifice shown by Jesus. Happily not everyone has the task of being a leader of humanity, or a great rebel; and so, after all, it might be possible for each to realize himself in his own way. This honesty might even become an ideal. Since great innovations always begin in the most unlikely places, the fact that people today are not nearly as ashamed of their nakedness as they used to be might be the beginning of a recognition of themselves as they really are. Hard upon this will follow an increasing recognition

3 *The Golden Flower* (1962 edn.), p. 77.

of many things that formerly were strictly taboo, for the reality of the earth will not forever remain veiled like the *virgines velandae* of Tertullian. Moral unmasking is but a step further in the same direction, and behold, there stands man as he is, and admits to himself that he is as he is. If he does this in a meaningless way he is just a muddled fool; but if he knows the significance of what he is doing he could belong to a higher order of man who makes real the Christ symbol, regardless of the suffering involved. It has often been observed that purely concrete taboos or magical rites in an early stage of a religion become in the next stage something psychic, or even purely spiritual symbols. An outward law becomes in the course of time an inward conviction. Thus it might easily happen to contemporary man, especially Protestants, that the person Jesus, now existing outside in the realm of history, might become the higher man within himself. Then we would have attained, in a European way, the psychological state corresponding to Eastern enlightenment.

82   All this is a step in the evolution of a higher consciousness on its way to unknown goals, and is not metaphysics as ordinarily understood. To that extent it is only "psychology," but to that extent, too, it is experienceable, understandable and—thank God—real, a reality we can do something with, a living reality full of possibilities. The fact that I am content with what can be experienced psychically, and reject the metaphysical, does not amount, as any intelligent person can see, to a gesture of scepticism or agnosticism aimed at faith and trust in higher powers, but means approximately the same as what Kant meant when he called the thing-in-itself a "merely negative borderline concept." Every statement about the transcendental is to be avoided because it is only a laughable presumption on the part of a human mind unconscious of its limitations. Therefore, when God or the Tao is named an impulse of the soul, or a psychic state, something has been said about the knowable only, but nothing about the unknowable, about which nothing can be determined.

7. CONCLUSION

83   The purpose of my commentary is to attempt to build a bridge of psychological understanding between East and West. The basis of every real understanding is man, and therefore I had to speak of human beings. This must be my excuse for having dealt only with general aspects, and for not having entered into technical details. Technical directions are valuable for those who know, for example, what a camera is, or a combustion engine, but they are useless for anyone who has no idea of such apparatus. Western man for whom I write is in an analogous position. Therefore it seemed to me important above all to emphasize the agreement between the psychic states and symbolisms of East and West. These analogies open a way to the inner chambers of the Eastern mind, a way that does not require the sacrifice of our own nature and does not confront us with the threat of being torn from our roots. Nor is it an intellectual telescope or microscope offering a view of no fundamental concern to us because it does not touch us. It is the way of suffering, seeking, and striving common to all civilized peoples; it is the tremendous experiment of becoming conscious, which nature has laid upon mankind, and which unites the most diverse cultures in a common task.

84   Western consciousness is by no means the only kind of consciousness there is; it is historically conditioned and geographically limited, and representative of only one part of mankind. The widening of our consciousness ought not to proceed at the expense of other kinds of consciousness; it should come about through the development of those elements of our psyche which are analogous to those of the alien psyche, just as the East cannot do without our technology, science, and industry. The European invasion of the East was an act of violence on a grand scale, and it has left us with the duty—*noblesse oblige*—of understanding the mind of the East. This is perhaps more necessary than we realize at present.

THE COLLECTED WORKS OF

C. G. JUNG

EDITORS: SIR HERBERT READ, MICHAEL FORDHAM, AND GER-
HARD ADLER; *EXECUTIVE EDITOR*, WILLIAM McGUIRE. *TRANS-
LATED BY* R.F.C. HULL, EXCEPT WHERE NOTED.

I N THE FOLLOWING LIST, dates of original publication are given in pa-
rentheses (of original composition, in brackets). Multiple dates indicate
revisions.

(continued)

(continued)

(*continued*)

(continued)

16. (*continued*)

The Psychology of the Transference (1946)
Appendix: The Realities of Practical Psychotherapy ([1937] added 1966)

17. THE DEVELOPMENT OF PERSONALITY (1954)
Psychic Conflicts in a Child (1910/1946)
Introduction to Wickes's "Analyses der Kinderseele" (1927/1931)
Child Development and Education (1928)
Analytical Psychology and Education: Three Lectures (1926/1946)
The Gifted Child (1943)
The Significance of the Unconscious in Individual Education (1928)
The Development of Personality (1934)
Marriage as a Psychological Relationship (1925)

18. THE SYMBOLIC LIFE (1954)
Translated by R.F.C. Hull and others
Miscellaneous writings

19. COMPLETE BIBLIOGRAPHY OF C. G. JUNG'S WRITINGS (1976; 2nd edn., 1992)

20. GENERAL INDEX TO THE COLLECTED WORKS (1979)

THE ZOFINGIA LECTURES (1983)
Supplementary Volume A to The Collected Works. Edited by William McGuire, translated by Jan van Heurck, introduction by Marie-Louise von Franz

PSYCHOLOGY OF THE UNCONSCIOUS ([1912] 1992)
A STUDY OF THE TRANSFORMATIONS AND SYMBOLISMS OF THE LIBIDO.
A CONTRIBUTION TO THE HISTORY OF THE EVOLUTION OF THOUGHT
Supplementary Volume B to the Collected Works. Translated by Beatrice M. Hinkle, introduction by William McGuire

Related publications:

THE BASIC WRITINGS OF C. G. JUNG
Selected and introduced by Violet S. de Laszlo

C. G. JUNG: LETTERS
Selected and edited by Gerhard Adler, in collaboration with Aniela Jaffé.
Translations from the German by R.F.C. Hull.
VOL. 1: 1906–1950
VOL. 2: 1951–1961

C. G. JUNG SPEAKING: Interviews and Encounters
Edited by William McGuire and R.F.C. Hull

C. G. JUNG: Word and Image
Edited by Aniela Jaffé

THE ESSENTIAL JUNG
Selected and introduced by Anthony Storr

THE GNOSTIC JUNG
Selected and introduced by Robert A. Segal

PSYCHE AND SYMBOL
Selected and introduced by Violet S. de Laszlo

Notes of C. G. Jung's Seminars:

DREAM ANALYSIS ([1928–30] 1984)
Edited by William McGuire

NIETZSCHE'S *ZARATHUSTRA* ([1934–39] 1988)
Edited by James L. Jarrett (2 vols.)

ANALYTICAL PSYCHOLOGY ([1925] 1989)
Edited by William McGuire

Jung, C. G. (Carl Gustav), 1875–1961.
[Selections. English. 1990]
  Psyche and symbol/C. G. Jung: translated by R.F.C. Hull: selected and
introduced by Violet de Laszlo. p. cm.—(Bollingen series)
  Reprint. Originally published: Garden City, N.Y.: Doubleday, 1958.
  Contents: Five chapters from Aion—The phenomenology of the spirit
in fairy tales—The psychology of the child archetype—Transformation
symbolism in the Mass—Foreword to the I ching—Two chapters from
The interpretation of nature and the psyche—Psychological commentary
on the Tibetan Book of the Dead—Commentary on The secret of the
golden flower.
  ISBN 0-691-01903-7 (alk. paper)
  1. Psychoanalysis. 2. Symbolism (Psychology) I. Hull, R.F.C. (Richard
Francis Carrington), 1913–1974. II. De Laszlo, Violet, 1900–1988. III. Title. IV. Series.
BF175.5.S95J85l3   1990   90-36021
150.19'54—dc20   CIP

352   The vision itself indicates that the main purpose of the transformation process is the spiritualization of the sacrificing priest: he is to be changed into *pneuma*. We are also told that he would "change the bodies into blood, make the eyes to see and the dead to rise again." Later in the visions he appears in glorified form, shining white like the midday sun.

353   Throughout the visions it is clear that sacrificer and sacrificed are one and the same. This idea of the unity of the *prima* and *ultima materia,* of that which redeems and that which is to be redeemed, pervades the whole of alchemy from beginning to end. "Unus est lapis, una medicina, unum vas, unum regimen, unaque dispositio" is the key formula to its enigmatic language.[24] Greek alchemy expresses the same idea in the formula ἕν τὸ πᾶν. Its symbol is the uroboros, the tail-eating serpent. In our vision it is the priest as sacrificer who devours himself as the sacrifice. This recalls the saying of St. John Chrysostom that in the Eucharist Christ drinks his own blood. By the same token, one might add, he eats his own flesh. The grisly repast in the dream of Zosimos reminds us of the orgiastic meals in the Dionysus cult, when sacrificial animals were torn to pieces and eaten. They represent Dionysus Zagreus being torn to pieces by the Titans, from whose mangled remains the νέος Διόνυσος arises.[25]

354   Zosimos tells us that the vision represents or explains the "production of the waters." [26] The visions themselves only show the transformation into *pneuma*. In the language of the alchemists, however, spirit and water are synonymous,[27] as they are

---

[24] Cf. the *Rosarium philosophorum,* in the *Artis auriferae* (1593), II, p. 206.

[25] Cf. the Cretan fragment of Euripides (Dieterich, *Eine Mithrasliturgie,* p. 105):

ἁγνὸν δὲ βίον τείνων ἐξ οὗ
Διὸς Ἰδαίου μύστης γενόμην
καὶ νυκτιπόλου Ζαγρέως βούτας
τοὺς ὠμοφάγους δαῖτας τελέσας

(living a holy life, since I have been initiated into the mysteries of the Idaean Zeus, and eaten raw the flesh of Zagreus, the night-wandering shepherd).

[26] [Cf. "The Visions of Zosimos," par. 86, III, i, 3, and—for the reference lower down to "blood"—III, v bis.]

[27] "Est et coelestis aqua sive potius divina Chymistarum . . . pneuma, ex aetheris natura et essentia rerum quinta" (There is also the celestial, or rather the divine, water of the alchemists . . . the pneuma, having the nature of the pneuma and the quintessence of things).—Hermolaus Barbarus, *Coroll. in Dioscoridem,* cited in M. Maier, *Symbola aureae mensae* (1617), p. 174.

"Spiritus autem in hac arte nihil aliud quam aquam indicari . . ." (In this art,

in the language of the early Christians, for whom water meant
the *spiritus veritatis*. In the "Book of Krates" we read: "You
make the bodies to liquefy, so that they mingle and become an
homogeneous liquid; this is then named the 'divine water.' " [28]
The passage corresponds to the Zosimos text, which says that the
priest would "change the bodies into blood." For the alchemists,
water and blood are identical. This transformation is the same
as the *solutio* or *liquefactio,* which is a synonym for the *subli-
matio,* for "water" is also "fire": "Item ignis . . . est aqua et
ignis noster est ignis et non ignis" (For fire . . . is water and
our fire is the fire that is no fire). "Aqua nostra" is said to be
"ignea" (fiery).[29]

355   The "secret fire of our philosophy" is said to be "our mystical
water," and the "permanent water" is the "fiery form of the true
water." [30] The permanent water (the ὕδωρ θεῖον of the Greeks)
also signifies "spiritualis sanguis," [31] and is identified with the
blood and water that flowed from Christ's side. Heinrich Khunrath says of this water: "So there will open for thee an healing
flood which issues from the heart of the son of the great world."
It is a water "which the son of the great world pours forth from
his body and heart, to be for us a true and natural Aqua
vitae." [32] Just as a spiritual water of grace and truth flows from
Christ's sacrifice, so the "divine water" is produced by a sacrificial act in the Zosimos vision. It is mentioned in the ancient

spirit means nothing else but water).—Theobaldus de Hoghelande, in the
Theatrum chemicum, I (1602), p. 196. Water is a "spiritus extractus," or a
"spiritus qui in ventre (corporis) occultus est et fiet aqua et corpus absque spiritu:
qui est spiritualis naturae" (spirit which is hidden in the belly [of the substance],
and water will be produced and a substance without spirit, which is of a spiritual
nature).—J. D. Mylius, *Philosophia reformata* (1622), p. 150. This quotation shows
how closely spirit and water were associated in the mind of the alchemist.
   "Sed aqua coelestis gloriosa *scil.* aes nostrum ac argentum nostrum, sericum
nostrum, totaque oratio nostra, quod est unum et idem *scil.* sapientia, quam Deus
obtulit, quibus voluit" (But the glorious celestial water, namely our copper and
our silver, our silk, and everything we talk about, is one and the same thing,
namely the Wisdom, which God has given to whomsoever he wished).—"Consilium coniugii," in the *Ars chemica* (1566), p. 120.
28 Berthelot, *La Chimie au moyen âge,* III, p. 53.
29 Mylius, pp. 121 and 123. For the blood–water–fire equation see George Ripley,
Opera omnia chemica (1649), pp. 162, 197, 295, 427.
30 Ripley, *Opera,* p. 62; *Rosarium,* p. 264.   31 Mylius, p. 42.
32 Khunrath, *Von hylealischen . . . Chaos* (1597), pp. 274f.